CERVANTES, LITERATURE, AND THE DISCOURSE OF POLITICS

What is the role of literature in the formation of the state? Anthony J. Cascardi takes up this fundamental question in *Cervantes, Literature, and the Discourse of Politics*, a comprehensive analysis of the presence of politics in *Don Quixote*. Cascardi argues that when public speech is constrained, as it was in seventeenth-century Spain, politics must be addressed indirectly, including through comedy, myth, and travellers' tales.

Cervantes, Literature, and the Discourse of Politics convincingly re-engages the ancient roots of political theory in modern literature by situating Cervantes within a long line of political thinkers. Cascardi notably connects Cervantes' political theory to Plato's, much as the writer's literary criticism has been firmly linked to Aristotle's. He also shows how Cervantes' view of literature provided a compelling alternative to the modern, scientific politics of Machiavelli and Hobbes, highlighting the potential interplay of literature and politics in an ideal state.

(Toronto Iberic)

ANTHONY J. CASCARDI is the Dean of Arts and Humanities, and Ancker Professor of Comparative Literature, Rhetoric, and Spanish at the University of California, Berkeley.

ANTHONY J. CASCARDI

Cervantes, Literature, and the Discourse of Politics

UNIVERSITY OF TORONTO PRESS
Toronto Buffalo London

©University of Toronto Press 2012
Toronto Buffalo London
www.utppublishing.com
Printed in Canada

ISBN 978-1-4426-4371-0 (cloth)
ISBN 978-1-4426-1223-5 (paper)

Library and Archives Canada Cataloguing in Publication

Cascardi, Anthony J., 1953–
Cervantes, literature, and the discourse of politics / Anthony J. Cascardi.

(Toronto Iberic)
Includes index.

ISBN 978-1-4426-4371-0 (bound). – ISBN 978-1-4426-1223-5 (pbk.)

1. Cervantes Saavedra, Miguel de, 1547–1616. Don Quixote. 2. Cervantes
Saavedra, Miguel de, 1547–1616 – Political and social views. 3. Politics and
literature – Spain – History – 17th century. I. Title. II. Series: Toronto Iberic.

PQ6353.C35 2012   863'.3   C2011-904647-4

This book has been published with the help of a subvention from the Program
for Cultural Cooperation between Spain's Ministry of Culture and United States
universities.

University of Toronto Press acknowledges the financial assistance to its publishing program of the Canada Council for the Arts and the Ontario Arts Council.

University of Toronto Press acknowledges the financial support of the Government
of Canada through the Canada Book Fund for its publishing activities.

Contents

Acknowledgments

I have incurred numerous obligations to individuals and institutions during the writing of this book and it is a pleasure to acknowledge them here. I wish to thank colleagues at various centres and departments for their generosity with invitations to present some of this work while it was in progress: at New York University to Jane Tylus of the Humanities Initiative and to Jacques Lezra of the Departments of Spanish and Comparative Literature; at Princeton University to the Department of Spanish and Portuguese for an invitation to present an Eberhard Faber Lecture, where conversations there with Marina Brownlee, Alexander Nehamas, Alban Forcione, Michael Wood, and others were especially helpful in the revision of chapters 7 and 9; at the University of Miami to Mihoko Suzuki and Anne Cruz, who were welcoming hosts and engaging interlocutors. The organizers of a special session of the annual meeting of the American Comparative Literature Association in 2008, Jess Boersma and Scott Weitraub, provided the opportunity for some of the material on indirect speech to reach an engaged and engaging audience at Harvard. David Quint was especially insightful as an interlocutor on the occasion of a visit to my Cervantes seminar at Berkeley. Quentin Skinner's astute remarks on politics and flattery in the early modern period helped me crystallize a series of insights at a time when they were just beginning to form. Daniel Boyarin's perceptive comments on Plato in the context of a rather different project helped sharpen my own sense of the connections between Cervantes and the ancient dialogic tradition. On the occasion of presentations of portions of this work informally and in graduate seminars in the departments of Spanish, Comparative Literature, and Rhetoric at Berkeley I was fortunate to have had the challenging and sympathetic attention of numerous colleagues, students, and friends.

This book was written during my term as Director of Berkeley's Townsend Center for the Humanities. I am especially indebted to the staff of that remarkable institution for having provided a level of professional support and enthusiasm for many matters outside this book, which helped make the writing of it possible.

I cite the Spanish text of *Don Quijote* according to the edition of Luis Andrés Murillo (Madrid: Castalia, 1982–7) according to volume, chapter, and page. Unless otherwise indicated, I use the English translation of the *Quijote* by Edith Grossman (New York: HarperCollins, 2003), citing page references only. Other translations, where not my own, are acknowledged in the endnotes.

CERVANTES, LITERATURE, AND THE DISCOURSE OF POLITICS

1 Introduction

Cervantes does not often figure on the list of major modern political thinkers. Only rarely is his name mentioned alongside the founders of modern political discourse – Hobbes, Locke, Montesquieu, and Rousseau, to name but a few. This may not come as a surprise. It is principally their views, not his, that have shaped our conception of what politics is, and it is likewise their way of writing, not his, that has come to set the broad standards for what political discourse might be. I turn to Cervantes and the question of politics, recognizing that he is a novelist and not a political theorist, with these facts fully in view. My aim is twofold. First, I want to offer a vision of what the discourse of politics might have amounted to had it not been dominated by the methods and concerns associated with the thinkers just mentioned. How might politics have been otherwise, and yet still fully modern? Second, I want to explore the specific ways in which *Don Quijote*, by all accounts Cervantes' most important work, is itself involved in thinking about what the polis and political discourse might be. At stake is both a new understanding of one of the pillars of modern European literature and an alternative to 'scientific' views of politics, an alternative that bears directly on how we ourselves might grasp the place of literature within the political sphere. They turn our attention to new views on one of the oldest and most persistent questions in the humanities: what is the place of literature in the (ideal) state?

'Politics' today generally refers to practical matters of public concern, especially as they are guided by pre-existing principles and beliefs. Political discourse aims to speak about the means through which collective, civic ends can be developed and pursued in light of whatever these orienting beliefs may be. These beliefs may change, but we take it for granted that one can never step outside of some set of pre-existing beliefs. At the same time, politics is understood to be a special kind of science, a branch of *sabiduría, science,* or *Wissenschaft,* that has its basis in notions about human nature, desires, values, and the workings of power. Political debates may provoke questions about competing values, but politics as we know it shies away from a consideration of 'value' except as values are constructed within some inner-worldly frame. Politics is inevitably practical, and as such, deals principally with the knowledge and techniques required to shape actions within the public world.

Such views could not always be assumed. They are in fact reflective of a specifically modern conception of politics, whose founders (especially Machiavelli and Hobbes) we can regard as having had the daring, the frankness, and in some cases the cynicism required to formulate the task of politics as a matter of rational calculation from human and worldly realities. The philosophical questions that classical political thinkers felt obliged to pursue – questions about what justice is in itself or ought to be, or about the shape of the 'ideal' state, or about the virtues of character that are required in order to rule well – began to recede from the stage with Machiavelli's prescient consideration of the requirements for rulership in 'new,' non-hereditary states, and with Hobbes's full-blown conviction that human nature could be known and defined from the laws of nature and not as an ideal. (The opening section, 'Human Nature,' in Hobbes's first major work, the *Elements of Law*, is explicit about this.)[1] These twin standpoints have come to underpin investigations into political realities and their causes and are among the key elements that led to the formation of modern politics as 'science.' This 'science' has produced alternating moods of enlightened optimism and liberal hope, and yet the scientific transformation of politics has long been understood as deeply problematic. Jürgen Habermas's critique of the 'scientific' understanding of politics, now a locus classicus on the subject, first published in 1963, formed part of well-established debates in German philosophy about the difference between ancient and modern conceptions of politics and the relations between theory and practice.[2]

Along with the displacement of political theory by the new 'science' of politics (it was 'civil science' for Hobbes, as it was for Sir Francis Bacon) came a shift in the languages deemed appropriate for political thought. To be sure, one school of scholarship, epitomized by the work of J.G.A. Pocock and Quentin Skinner, remained committed to the idea that the political arguments of even the most original thinkers emerge out of pre-existing vocabularies. But new deployments of inherited forms of language and thought came about in response to changing circumstances. In point of fact, the language of political practice that arose in conjunction with the new science of politics was the discourse of highly administered bureaucracies, and was perfected by the adepts of institutions that existed in a sometimes precarious balance of power with the interests of monarchical rule. Early modern European nations varied in the degree to which they were bureaucratically organized, but Spain was by any account one of the first quasi-rationalized political entities in Europe. This remained true in spite of the fact that certain theoretical works, such as Alonso de Castrillo's influential *Treatise on the Republic* (*Tractado de república*), adhered to Aristotle's conception of politics as the loftiest of all forms of knowledge.[3] It was for somewhat more pragmatic reasons that the first faculty of what we would call political science was proposed in Spain in the sixteenth century. In the words of Rodrigo Sánchez de Arévalo, 'good government ought to be scientific' (el buen gobierno debe ser científico).[4] The institution of the Inquisition, horrible and regressive, was also the source of tremendous administrative control.[5] Spain was what has been called a 'patrimonial bureaucracy': its privileges were for the most part inherited, but these inherited privileges were in turn administered by an intricate network of government functionaries.[6] Cervantes' grandfather, Juan de Cervantes, was himself a law licenciate, specializing in fiscal law for the Inquisition. He also served as a minor magistrate, roughly at the rank of an alderman, in a number of towns ranging from Cuenca, southeast of Madrid, to Córdoba in Andalucía.[7] Spain was also an imperial power, which is to say that it was involved in the daunting task of administering policies and laws over some very far-flung lands. The modern state such as was envisioned by the Catholic kings, required collective and coordinated procedures, as well as the ability to enforce them.[8] Politics under these conditions responded to ideological and administrative needs that were vastly different from anything that classical political theory might have imagined. A specialized law school – the Colegio de Abogados – was established in Madrid in 1595.[9] And yet these developments were hardly met with universal approval. As Don Quijote himself says disdainfully of the *letrados* who were increasingly employed in government service, 'we have seen many who command and govern the world from a chair' (330) (los hemos visto mandar y gobernar el mundo desde una silla; I, 37, p. 467). Juan Huarte de San Juan's influential *Examen de ingenios* (1575) registers a similar concern over the influence of *letrados* in the state and the decline of true virtue.

The new science of politics that emerged in early modern Europe was designed to deal with the administrative realities of a world in which Spain held considerable power and yet was constantly at war, including against neighbouring Protestant countries. At the same time, political thinking in its practical forms was increasingly oriented around empirical questions, and began to divert attention to matters of 'experience.' Indeed, seventeenth-century Spanish political theory is littered with the term *experiencia* in the secular context just as much as it is preoccupied with the question of the *república*.[10] But because this new empirical science did not firmly take hold until much later, Plato's political dialogues and Aristotle's outline of a politics based on prudential wisdom enjoyed considerable prestige. Such had already been the case for the civic humanists of the Renaissance. Valla, Erasmus, and More wrote about the constitution of the polis in ways that reflected the language of Ciceronian-republican ideals. For Erasmus, Plato's republic was modulated along Christian lines.[11] But the Aristotelian notion of 'rational persuasion' eventually came to seem like an oxymoron, even though it was precisely the element of political philosophy that Hobbes came to recognize he could not dispense with.[12] The humanist dialogue tradition, with its embrace of controversy and its free incorporation of contrasting voices, characters, and images, was consigned to a diminished role in the new, modern discourse of politics. Indeed, the modern tradition of 'political science' eventually came to acquire a distinctively anti-rhetorical and un-dialectical cast. (This is surprising given the role of rhetoric in both Machiavelli and Hobbes.) Literature, for its part, came gradually to be seen as having little direct bearing on political thought at all. The result was an odd disjuncture that has endured until the present day. The vast majority of literary critics and theorists writing now would agree that literature is political because it is immersed in the conflicts, contestations, and ideologies of the historical world. But few would argue that literature occupies any significant relationship to political ideals, or that it bears a relationship to questions of what ought to be. Part of what I hope to suggest is that the roots of these circumstances are themselves historical and that they are not mutually exclusive: the pursuit of 'ideals' may well need to proceed in the realm of history, and indeed by participation in the world of un-truth, if not in ideology itself. One need only think of *Don Quijote* in order to pinpoint the moment when literature became suspicious of literary ideals. And yet the other side of this question still remains: can literature be relevant to politics in the face of such suspicions, and if so, how? This question is implicit in the chapters that follow; central to my response is the claim that literature, and especially fiction, provides a platform for a pursuit of the truth, and with it of political ideals, within and through the realm of the manifestly false. Writing within a context that was uniquely hybrid – at once Spanish and European – Cervantes was fully aware of the fact that to think about the ideal state would have to involve thinking and writing in counter-factual terms.

This broad-brush sketch of some basic issues may help bring my specific purpose into clearer view. Taking Cervantes' *Don Quijote* as my pivotal exhibit, I hope to show that literature in the early modern age was regarded as having the potential to think both speculatively and with a critical scepticism about important political concerns of the day but also to engage the largest questions that politics might ask: What is the nature of justice, and how can it be brought to bear on the historical world? Who ought to govern in the just state, and how? What are the sources of authority that can legitimately underpin the force of law? What are the roots of political virtue? Where does the private world end and the public sphere begin? The writings of Plato and Aristotle were regarded by Cervantes' humanist predecessors as touchstones for questions such as these, even as their ancient formulations called for substantial re-articulation in light of contemporary historical circumstances. Most important, Cervantes seems clearly to have understood that political thought required engagement with literary forms of discourse. Indeed, one of my chief claims is that the great literary experiment undertaken in *Don Quijote* involved the task of finding an appropriate discourse for politics. Pre-existing theoretical discourses on the subject had gone quite far in the writings of Francisco Vitoria and Domingo de Soto; they had made a place for a politics of community and consent alongside the politics of natural law. Even the neo-scholastic philosopher Francisco Suárez, a precursor of Grotius and Pufendorf, posited clear distinctions between natural law and *ius gentium* (international law).[13] But much more remained to be done, especially where the question of literature was concerned. Cervantes' project in *Don Quijote* was to define and defend the place of literature in the polis by articulating a new structure of relationships among the most basic terms with which all political thinkers must grapple – theory and practice, contemplation and action, words and deeds. Cervantes looked to his humanist predecessors as well as to a host of contemporary genres (some literary, others not at all so) in order to craft a form of fiction that proposed a new, critical, and ironic set of relations among these terms, a form that neither accepted the distinction between 'literature' and 'politics' nor required their reconciliation.[14] In so doing, I argue, Cervantes was centrally engaged in responding to a question that one of the characters in *Don Quijote* adopts from Plato's *Republic*: what is the place of literature within the state?

To say this is hardly to suggest that Cervantes abandons the task of reflection on what politics ought to be, or that he fails to position literature in a critical relationship to politics as it exists. On the contrary, *Don Quijote* involves literature directly in reflection equally about *le politique* and about *la politique*. *Don Quijote* is a book about the constitutive disjuncture between the 'ideal' and the 'real,' but it is also, in that context, a book that confronts the need for an oblique approach to the contemporary issues that define the circumstances of the 'real.'[15] It is thus a work that recognizes the need for a far more sophisticated understanding of the relationship between theory and practice than conventional assessments tend to provide. Pure theory tends to produce a vision of an ideal but unachievable state, which may be projected onto an unspecified future or associated with a long-lost past. (Don Quixote's memorable speech to the goatherds about the mythical Golden Age provides just such an example of this kind of backward-looking myth.) But the understanding of politics as a form of science that deals skilfully with the practical matters at hand is liable to produce a vision that cannot see beyond the need to arrive at solutions for problems of immediate concern – bringing water to arid lands, reducing deficits in the national budget, defending against piracy at sea, eradicating crime. These may all have been very pressing concerns, and yet none invites talk about justice, virtue, or the way to govern where interests collide. Moreover, the blindness produced by such a limited view of politics is a blindness to the historical and ideological underpinnings of such practical problems and to their ideological roots in various collective fictions. At the very least, I think that Cervantes means for us to see that to choose between Don Quijote's inspired but irrelevant ideals and the interests of local officials and bureaucrats or national planners (e.g., the *arbitristas*) is not a satisfactory choice at all. Don Quijote is ultimately defeated by a figure, Sansón Carrasco, who was characterized by one of Spain's modern expatriate intellectuals as 'one of those jurists, children of the university of Bologna and fathers of the modern state bureaucracy, who so decisively contributed to the triumph of the monarchy vis-à-vis the power of the knightly nobility of the Middle Ages.'[16]

This conception of literature's political role placed Cervantes in a deep and sometimes contentious dialogue with the political philosophies of Plato and Aristotle, and also with the Renaissance humanists who had tried to adapt those classical views to the circumstances of the contemporary city-state. Not surprisingly, however, this crucial set of engagements has gone overlooked by many critics. Cervantes' awareness of Aristotle's literary theories, and of their reception among Renaissance humanists in

Italy and Spain, has been widely discussed, including by such well-known scholars as E.C. Riley and Alban Forcione.[17] But the question of literary theory in relation to political discourse has fallen largely outside the scope of critical debate. (Roberto González Echevarría's recent study of Cervantes and the law is one notable exception.)[18] The general neglect of the relationship between Cervantes and Plato as regards literature and politics follows from the way in which the reception of Plato has been portrayed by many literary scholars.[19] The Plato that became most familiar to many Renaissance specialists was the Plato of the *Symposium*. One of the great intellectual historians of the Renaissance, Paul Oskar Kristeller, was hardly alone in this interpretation; his essay 'Renaissance Platonism' was especially influential.[20] Insofar as the Renaissance interest in Plato was carried by Ficino's Neoplatonism, the question of politics could be avoided without too much trouble. This was true in spite of the fact that Italian scholars such as Hans Baron and Eugenio Garin saw clear links between Renaissance humanism and republican movements that contributed to the formation of modern democracy.[21] And yet there is mounting evidence that the *Republic* was of considerable importance for Renaissance thought, and that certain passages of that work, mixed with select parts of Aristotle and with classical writings on rhetoric and poetics by Horace and Cicero, were indeed central to humanist thinking about what politics might be. Ficino's 1496 *Commentaria in Platonem* was, in fact, engaged with a number of the Platonic dialogues, including the *Sophist*, that bear centrally on the question of politics. Though not often taken up by Renaissance scholars, the *Sophist* was in fact a standard resource for humanists, including discourses on questions of poetics such as Tasso's *Discorsi del poema eroico*.[22]

Moreover, literary scholars tend to overdraw philosophical interpretations of Plato as ignorant of the role of character, dialogue, and storytelling in the formation of Plato's philosophical claims. There has, in fact, been considerable discussion of these topics, not only by 'literary' philosophers such as Iris Murdoch and among classicists, but also among 'analytic' philosophers and those who specialize in the philosophy of the ancient world.[23] Charles Kahn's account of Plato as both a major literary artist and a thinker who proposed a systematic definition of philosophical goals and methods explains something of the complexity involved,[24] but does not quite get at one of the irreducible paradoxes of the *Republic*: that of a philosopher who turns to dramatic dialogue and to myth in order to give us an image of the ideal state, while also claiming that certain central kinds of literature must be excluded from the state. The irony of this situation can hardly be obscured from the perspectives that Cervantes affords, and helps clarify one role of literature in relation to politics, namely its role as a form of critique.[25] More concretely, it suggests that a corrective to the abstractions of 'theory' requires not merely a turn to the world of practice, but a self-conscious and self-consciously literary turn that refuses the neat distinction between theory and practice. In addition to the need for any theory to respond to the historical conditions of its existence, this literary turn reflects the fact that fictions play a crucial role where 'theory' recognizes the impossibility of gaining a complete and accurate view of the whole. To be sure, Cervantes presents ample evidence of characters who are absorbed in the affairs of the 'world' – seeking money or good marriages, or pursuing fame, influence, or successful careers – and who have little interest in theorizing about the unity of historical reality and conceptual thought. The division of theory and practice is of little concern to them. But Cervantes sees that simply to accept their isolated views would contribute relatively little to political thought. Moreover, when we consider the discursive space in which these fragmentary engagements with the world come together as fictions, the *Quijote* is able to transcend the limited perspectives of any of its characters without falling into the monologism that has been oddly associated with Plato. The idea of the synthesis of theory and practice is itself presented through a set of fictional characters, foremost among whom is the foolish knight himself.

My second aim complements this first set of objectives in a specifically historical way: to ask about the conditions that Cervantes confronted as a Spanish writer in the early modern age, and in so doing to ask about how these large philosophical issues were articulated within a particular historical environment, thereby to investigate the particular discursive responses they provoked. What particular set of circumstances marked Cervantes' political moment as distinct, and what bearing did these factors have on his engagement with the question of politics in *Don Quijote*? Some of these factors are well known and link Spanish circumstances to wider contexts. The beginnings of modern bureaucracy, for example, lie with the need to support standing armies, to establish taxation systems, and to organize labour on a relatively large scale. But bureaucratization in Spain was enabled by the prior existence of institutions such as the Inquisition which, as mentioned above, had highly evolved administrative arms. Likewise, the early modern state was increasingly configured as a *nation-state*, and in the case of Spain as a rather precarious nation-state which nonetheless had an empire attached. This context implied something quite different from that of the Venetian or Florentine republic or the city-based

polis that Plato, Augustine, or the humanists took as their point of reference for political thought. Politics is not just a collection of beliefs but a
network of institutions, protocols, and discourses by which practical aims
were imagined and carried out. Cervantes could see that these activities
were being organized so as to construct not merely a city-state but a 'nation,' and beyond a nation an empire. Beyond the empire, and in turn
sustaining it, was something like a 'political imaginary' to which most citizens felt obliged to adhere and into which they had been 'interpellated' as
political subjects even as they may have resisted incorporation into the
nation.[26] But Cervantes' personal experiences as a soldier in the battle of
Lepanto, as a prisoner in Algiers, as a tax collector, and as a would-be government appointee to a position in the New World (an appointment that
he never received), taught him with equal force about the political imaginary and the world of *Realpolitik*.

The Iberian Peninsula in Cervantes' day was, moreover, a mix of racial,
religious, cultural, and linguistic groups whose history of convergence and
conflicts and intermittent periods of tolerance posed enormous challenges
for thinking about the polis as an all-encompassing whole. In such heterogeneous conditions, where the nation was genuinely lacking a 'common
sense,' the prudential model of politics offered by Aristotle was strained
beyond what it could possibly bear. The practical tasks of governance had
to be thought of in conditions where much was shared within certain racial and ethnic groups but where relatively little was shared among them,
and where as a result many common elements (such as a national language
and religion) had to be imposed from above. Attempts to bind these
groups together required a combination of authoritarian power and administrative control that was hardly conducive to the pursuit of justice or
tolerance in any ideal sense. Moreover, governance had to be carried out in
an increasingly urban world and among far-flung colonies. Politics under
these conditions responded to ideological and administrative needs that
were vastly different from anything that classical political theory might
have imagined.

To consider the discourse of politics in these contexts means attending to
many things: not just to the forms of language spoken in the corridors of
power at court, to the deliberations of judges and minor officials in their
respective administrative spheres, to the pronouncements of *regidores* and
procuradores, or to the legal language of magistrates and intercessors at
work in towns and the countryside, but also to a range of philosophical
writings about governments and governance, nobility and virtue, the arts

of judgment, sovereignty, and the state, the body politic and its health, the justification of war, the nature of community, natural law, the laws among nations (*ius gentium*), and the pursuit of peace. These were all prominent among writers of various philosophical stripes in early modern Spain, ranging from scholastically trained figures like Vitoria, Suárez, and de Soto to the humanists Luis Vives, Antonio de Guevara, and Alonso de Castrillo; from those like Fadrique Furió Ceriol who produced volumes of advice for counsellors, to the anti-Machiavellians Juan de Mariana and Pedro de Rivadeneira, as well as to Juan Huarte de San Juan's influential *Examen de ingenios*, which was written with the improvement of the state clearly in mind.[27]

Moreover, the official, public structures of politics in early modern Spain placed special constraints on what could and could not be said, constraints of which Cervantes was fully aware both from his experience as the descendant of *converses* and from the suppression of Erasmian humanism, and which in turn can explain some of the literary strategies at work in his writings. To think about the ideal polis and at the same time to generate a critical response to the Spanish state required the ability to speak without saying, to adopt some 'other voice,' and to speak indirectly, so as to circumvent official constraints and to subvert the restrictions on many public forms of speech. Cervantes' engagement with politics thus reflects the need to speak about politics without always appearing to speak politically; he tends to speak obliquely, in a masked voice, and by tropes, sometimes saying too much or by hyperbole (exaggeration), and sometimes not nearly enough (by understatement). This required the strategies of the mask and of what Bakhtin called 'double discourse,' in which Cervantes was well served by the example of humanists like Erasmus, who had already explored some of the advantages to be gained by putting words of truth in the mouth of Folly. But, of course, humanism contributed much more: the emphasis on dialogue contributed to a sense of the mobility of the truth; the commitment to the vulgar languages (notwithstanding Erasmus's arguments in favour of the revival of Latin) contributed to an appreciation of the dignity of contemporary communities and their ordinary forms of self-expression; and the conscious engagement with questions of textual transmission contributed to a deep appreciation of the ethics of interpretation.[28] All of these combined to set the stage for a writer like Cervantes to adopt a set of oblique stances vis-à-vis established political structures and the official discourses that gave them support.

At the same time, Cervantes was conscious that, as a modern writer, he had arrived relatively late onto an already crowded stage. In attempting to speak about politics he was also aware of the vast accumulation of writings about matters of politics that preceded him, from Plato and Aristotle to Erasmus, Guevara, and the philosopher-jurist Vitoria. The discourse of politics in the *Quijote* is marked by Cervantes' awareness that he must deal with the question of literature's relationship to many pre-existing forms of speech. But the prior accumulation of political discourse also means that there was much to be recovered and reshaped in thinking about governments and governance, nobility and virtue, the arts of judgment, and the health of the republic. These pre-existing writings had also helped shape a political vocabulary around questions of 'ley,' 'nación,' 'soberanía,' 'patria,' 'imperio,' 'ciudad,' and, above all, of the 'república.'[29] But there were also the less obviously political language-forms of the fable and the travel report, of controversial argumentation, of the courtly conduct books and of proverbs – all of which afforded Cervantes the opportunity to explore the possibility of a political discourse embedded neither in the official institutions of politics nor in the theoretical language of classical political philosophy.

In writing the *Quijote*, Cervantes was no doubt influenced by the fact that the many chivalric texts were themselves entwined with juridical issues.[30] But in Cervantes, not surprisingly, the engagement with judicial issues results in a literary deflection of politics and yields a significant re-assertion of the discursive nature of politics itself. I say 're-assertion' because the discursive element of politics was always to some degree there, both in Plato's dialogues and in the rhetorical tradition of Cicero and the Renaissance humanists. Leonardo Bruni, Lorenzo Valla, and other civic humanists of the Renaissance had clearly marked the ontology of politics as fundamentally discursive because historical: politics exists because the ground of human experience is itself historical, and history involves the actions of the human world (*res gestae*) as well as the written account of those deeds (*historia rerum gestarum*).[31] To recognize that politics is sub-tended by a historical ontology means that it roots in creatures whose nature is to make and remake their world by means of what they say and do.[32] During the time of Charles V, questions of political community were openly discussed by the most important thinkers, including Vitoria, Suárez, and de Soto. All recognized important distinctions between natural law and the basis of international law (*ius gentium*); they also made it clear that the formation of political communities required something other than what nature could provide. Unlike the retrograde scholastic thinkers and medieval grammarians that Erasmus, Nebrija, El Brocense, and others regarded as 'barbarians,' they recognized that consent could not be deduced from nature alone, but required a specifically human form of agreement.[33] Cervantes may well invoke the idea that nature is 'God's steward' (el mayordomo de dios) both in his early pastoral novel *Galatea* and in his late romance *Persiles*,[34] but what he comes to understand about politics grows out of the realization that human beings attempt to fashion a world out of the conjuncture of words and deeds. This conjuncture never occurs in a perfect way; indeed, it seems that words and deeds are bound to be perpetually misaligned. In this, Cervantes goes beyond Vives's diagnosis of civil discord to a deeper insight into the non-convergence of deeds and words, of *res gestae* and *historia rerum gestarum*.[35] Cervantes grasps the true difficulty of politics, which cannot be reduced, as some writers might wish, simply by coming to agreement upon words.[36] The eponymous hero of *Don Quijote* remains visibly out of step with the historical world, yet he brings history itself to light by virtue of what he is *un*able to do, viz., to remake the world by what he says and tries to do. The political 'failure' of Don Quijote's project to align words and deeds is the source of a crucial insight into the nature of modern politics itself.

This much having been said, I would enter a series of cautionary remarks regarding the differences between Cervantes and some of his early modern counterparts, especially Machiavelli and Hobbes. As mentioned above, Machiavelli and Hobbes are often credited with the transformation of politics into a science. In spite of enormous differences between them, they are recognized as the progenitors of a peculiarly modern set of beliefs about the proper objects of political discourse – things such as the actions of men as they are (and not as they ought to be), the logic of power, and the strategies of successful rule. (As Bacon wrote, 'We are much beholden to Machiavel and others, that write what men do, and not what they ought to do.')[37] These figures are likewise often cited as responsible for the eclipse of classical political philosophy. The reasons are hardly mysterious. Machiavelli's conception of the political state is fundamentally non-moral; it reflects a vision of human nature in which moral qualities are not among the 'givens.' But these views about politics cannot be detached from the modes of discourse that subtend them. This includes some of the same forms of humanist rhetoric that were especially important for Cervantes. As Quentin Skinner showed in a detailed study of the rhetoric and philosophy of Hobbes, Hobbes came to recognize that he needed the very rhetoric he sought to reject in making politics a 'science.'[38] He needed it because of its crucial role in moving men to act upon whatever truths they may accept. Indeed, the writings of both Machiavelli and Hobbes – the political principles they explicate, in the particular ways they do – exemplify the fact that politics needs to *say* and not simply to *think* and *do*.

Machiavelli's texts were officially banned in Spain, but his ideas were known, and 'substitute' texts were found; indeed, Tacitus became a stand-in for Machiavellian pragmatism in a context where Machiavelli could not be invoked.[39] Hobbes is, in fact, explicit about language in politics to such a degree that he embeds it within the very essence of the political. He must do so because political institutions are built of conventions that are not in the end reducible to natural laws. Those conventions begin in language. It is true that language in turn roots in the body, but that is only its beginning. In *Leviathan* Hobbes argues that human beings are part of the natural world but are also above it. The difference between humans and all other animals is a function of the invention of language insofar as language allows human beings to overcome the limitations of the natural mind. Human beings are governed both by the laws of nature and by convention. (The section in *Human Nature* 'Names, Reasoning and Discourses of the Tongue' offers one detailed analysis of language as a naming convention that leads eventually to predication and to the combination of more complex utterances about the world.)[40] As a historical invention, language has given human beings a number of beneficial capabilities, including the ability to reason, to act as persons, and to incorporate in groups. But language has also encouraged human beings to focus on the future rather than on the present and, in thinking about the future, to become excessively concerned about their status relative to others. Language thus produces a distortion of the natural appetites, which ought to be directed to the present, in relation to circumstances that may not come to exist. These distortions are only compounded when we forsake experience for mere possibilities or fail to insist on the basic definition of terms. For Hobbes, it is not just the condition of enmity and the passion of fear (which originate in the famous hypothesis of 'the war of each against each'), but all these distortions together that produce the essential situation of politics. And yet, language also provides the potential resources to solve these problems insofar as it enables human beings to reach agreements regarding matters such as sovereignty and to persuade others to act in accordance with the laws.[41] It is thus only partially true to say that Hobbesian politics is based on a frank assessment of the strife caused by the natural passions, for insofar as the passions are human, they are always mediated by language, and language in turn has some power to resolve the conflicts they generate.

The case of Machiavelli may be more interesting still, since everything said in *The Prince* is framed as a function of the author's commitment to speak – and to speak quite frankly – about the politics of the 'real' as opposed to the ideal. That position in turn requires Machiavelli to remove the many masks that conceal the truth of things. Similarly, *The Prince* offers itself as a presentation of political wisdom framed by an adherence to political matters that have direct consequences in the world: Machiavelli aims to tell of 'la verità effetuale della cosa.' (The crucial passage occurs in chapter XV: 'mi è parso più conveniente *andare dietro alla verità della cosa*, che all'immaginazione di essa.') This means, among other things, being unafraid to speak directly about such things as the strategies for acquiring and holding power, the best uses of cruelty, and the available means for a ruler to gain prestige and remain in control. Recent translations of the crucial phrase (*la verità effetuale della cosa*), such as 'getting down to the truth' or 'considering only things that are true,' scarcely do justice to Machiavelli's emphasis on the efficacious quality of the truth in the political domain.[42] Indeed, the phrase deftly reshapes pre-existing conceptions of the (ideal) 'truth' by virtue of a bold alliance between truth and the principles of political pragmatism. Machiavelli proposes to speak not just about an abstract truth – certainly not the merely 'theoretical' truth of Plato's polis – but about the kind of truth that matters in the world (*la verità effetuale*). *The Prince* thus requires commitment to a new kind of discourse – not to the discourse of the philosophers, but to a rhetoric of examples and commentary designed to illuminate what is most effective. He puts the truth of 'things' (politics) in place of the imaginary, ideological, ideal representations of political relations. And he does so by adherence to a discursive principle that is as simple and seemingly direct as it is innovative, namely by vowing to call things by their name. To move from this principle of frankness to effective leadership Machiavelli needs only to teach the right 'skills,' which is what often becomes of 'art' in the regime of science, political or otherwise.

It has indeed been said that modernity has no remedy for Machiavellian politics.[43] Even if there were such a remedy, quixotism would certainly not be it. But Machiavelli was scarcely the first to speak or write about the truth of politics in relation to the sublunary world. To take one much earlier example, the anonymous sixth-century dialogue 'On Political Science' proposed to address the science of politics as a consequence of the mixed quality of human nature, i.e., as situated mid-way between the divine life of the pure intellect and brute, irrational, embodied nature.[44] The work is Neoplatonic in orientation and explains that political science was devised by God as a method for use by men in the condition of their temporary 'exile' on earth. Its purpose is to help human beings work towards divinization. But in practice it sees clearly that political science requires education. Not surprisingly, the same period produced a compilation of advice by the deacon Agapetus of St Sophia in Constantinople, consisting of seventy-two admonitory statements on kingly rule. This work, the *Ekthesis*, intersects directly with the 'Mirror of Princes' tradition that extends from Roman imperial times through the Hellenistic period and ultimately the Renaissance humanist tradition.[45] Although Cervantes is unlikely to have known any of the ancient texts directly, his engagement with the post-Platonic tradition of advice to rulers as a genre of political discourse is evident in the advice about how to rule that Don Quijote offers to Sancho in Part II.

Machiavelli's sceptical realism, his commitment to a demystified view of utopian politics, might appear to have been targeting quixotism *avant la letter*: 'Many have imagined republics and principalities that have never been seen or heard of,' he writes (72). But of course the reverse is rather more true: it is Cervantes who in fact carries forward a line of political critique that might not have so displeased Machiavelli, insofar as he demonstrates the ways in which Don Quijote's chivalric ideals, pertinent to an earlier age, may simply mask the realities of contemporary politics. And yet, as we will see over the course of the chapters to follow, Cervantes hardly accepts Machiavelli's solution to the problem of politics. Indeed, the *Quijote* is the perfect example of a book in which it seems nearly impossible simply to call things by their name or to speak of the singular truth of things. Moreover, the political experiment conducted on the fictional island of Barataria in Part II of the *Quijote* subjects Machiavellian politics to a series of inversions. Sancho gives a serio-comic twist to the situation that Machiavelli treats in considerable detail in *The Prince*: that of the ruler who does not inherit his dominion but who has newly acquired the territory over which he reigns, in this case the sham island Barataria.

Cervantes' relationship to contemporary politics and political ideals is complex because it draws richly from the preceding tradition, including the tradition from which *The Prince* itself derives. While *The Prince* proposes to speak about politics in a new way, it bears substantial affinities with the earlier tradition of exemplary literature, much of it of humanist orientation. As a text, *The Prince* illustrates political successes and failures by reference to a host of figures drawn from the past and the present, from Alexander the Great to the Borgias and, of special relevance in the present context, Fernando El Católico of Spain. Fernando is at once the object of Machiavelli's admiration and of his displeasure. He 'could almost be considered a new prince,' Machiavelli writes, 'because he started out as a weak monarch, but through fame and glory has become the foremost king of Christendom ... [He] has always plotted and carried out great feats that have captured the imagination of his people and kept their eyes on the outcome' (102–3). Furthermore, Machiavelli's broad-ranging engagement with examples reflects some of the ambivalence that he seems to have developed toward humanistic, literary pursuits during the period of his exile in the Tuscan countryside after the fall of the Florentine republic in 1512. Machiavelli's aspirations as a writer were, in fact, literary as much as they were political; and yet, as Victoria Kahn and Albert Ascoli have pointed out in connection with his response to Ariosto's *Orlando Furioso*, Machiavelli approached the matter of poetry with considerable ambivalence: Machiavelli wished he had been included in Tasso's list of poets, and while in exile the study of letters certainly did provide spiritual sanctuary from what they characterize as 'the squalor of a life of enforced *otium*,'[46] but he seems ultimately to have concluded that to be included among the ranks of the poets meant being excluded from contemporary politics.

Cervantes reached strikingly different conclusions. The *Quijote* does far more than illuminate the ideological gaps between a utopian vision of politics and the political circumstances of the world at hand. He does 'more' than illuminate that gap because he insistently probes the ways in which it might be filled, only to discover that it is bound to remain in place. The kindred issue of political theory in relation to political practice is never far away. Indeed, there is something at the very heart of 'quixotism' that suggests the essential disjuncture between a theoretical 'ideal' and the practical world. As mentioned above, the world of 'practice' can be elucidated in terms of the assemblage of factors that came together in early modern Spain. As for 'theory,' my view is that Cervantes sets a conjuncture of contemporary discourses about the health of the 'republic' against a series of philosophical views whose deepest roots lie in Plato's *Republic*, where their relationship to the discourse of literature is brought front-and-centre into focus. Neo-Aristotelian concerns about fiction and reality, verisimilitude, and the allowable uses of the marvellous are early modern additions to a set of questions that took the problem of literature in its relationship to politics as the crucial matter.

Seen this way, we can recognize that Cervantes recuperates a more complex understanding of the relationship between literature (or 'poetry,' broadly understood) and politics than most conventional interpretations of the *Republic* allow. Whereas those interpretations regard Plato as the enemy of the poets because of what is said about mimesis in *Republic*, Books III and X, Cervantes reflects back on a view of Plato as an ironic and philosophical poet, who regards literature (and especially the dialogue form) as essentially political. Concomitantly, he understands that there may be far more at stake in neo-Aristotelian concerns about verisimilitude and the marvellous than the moral or aesthetic need to restrict the imagination. If literature can, in fact, free itself from the fact-world of practice without embarking on unbridled flights of fancy, then it might also serve for thinking about politics in ways that pure theory cannot. In this, literature can offer some of what Plato might have hoped to find in writing about an ideal state even while recognizing that the ideal was nothing that could be achieved in human terms.

2 What the Canon Said

It seems to me that those books they call 'novels of chivalry' are harmful to the state.[1]

The Canon of Toledo, *Don Quijote*, I, 47

In chapter 47 of *Don Quijote*, Part I, one of Cervantes' best informed and most articulate characters makes an explicit reference to the problem of literature and politics. The character is the Canon of Toldeo, a literary theorist in thin disguise, and the remark is offered by way of preface to his extended critique of the romances of chivalry. The books of chivalry, he suggests in a political judgment, are 'harmful to the state' (perjudiciales en la república). The statement is characteristic of much of what we find in Cervantes in that it is at once completely direct and utterly oblique: seemingly direct in its claims and in its judgments, and nearly so in its allusion to one of the central questions of Plato's *Republic*, but oblique because it never makes entirely clear just what the political danger of these books might be. Things are hardly resolved when the Canon tries to give a further explanation of what he means. If the remark is a clue as to how Cervantes formulates the relationship between literature and politics, then it is a highly puzzling clue indeed. The comment raises a large and important question without fully answering it; moreover, it embeds that question in a context that seems to deflect and diffuse its explicit point. Don Quijote may be an aberrant character, even someone who lives outside the law, but the books he has read hardly seem to represent a threat to the foundation of the state. Not unlike Plato (though to very different ends) Cervantes seems to work obliquely even where his characters appear to be direct.

It is not altogether clear whether the additional questions to which this particular comment of the Canon of Toledo leads – questions concerning truth and history, verisimilitude and unity, pleasure and the imagination – are genuinely connected to his worries about the health of the 'republic' or not. Are the objections raised in Books III and X of Plato's *Republic* genuinely relevant here, or is the Canon's allusion to the *Republic* nothing more than a literate feint? The *Republic* addresses the question of literature because Plato thought it important to say some things about how the citizens of the state and its guardians ought to be educated and formed, about which books ('poetry' in the broad, original sense) ought to be allowed into the republic and which ones kept out. Among Cervantes' more immediate predecessors, Erasmus gave detailed consideration to what the 'Christian Prince' ought and ought not to read. The romances in particular, Erasmus says in *The Education of the Christian Prince*, might encourage 'tyrannical' behaviour. 'It will take very little to incite a naturally wild and violent boy to tyranny if, without being equipped with an antidote, he reads about Achilles or Alexander the Great or Xerxes or Julius Caesar. But today we see a great many people enjoying the stories of Arthur and Lancelot and other legends of that sort, which are not only tyrannical but also utterly illiterate, foolish, and on the level of old wives' tales, so that it would be more advisable to put one's time into reading the comedies or the myths of the poets than into that sort of drivel.'[2]

Erasmus was doubtlessly a conduit for Plato's ideas, if Cervantes did not learn them from Plato's texts directly.[3] But why are the books of chivalry regarded by the Canon as 'harmful to the state' and how might we then understand the broader issue of literature's relationship to politics? The evasiveness with which Cervantes approaches these questions might itself be a key to the fact that he regards the relationship between literature and politics as oblique. But, unlike a number of critics who have regarded the Canon as a more or less reliable spokesperson for Cervantes' own literary-critical views, I take the Canon as one of a number of voices that Cervantes deploys throughout the text, sometimes in order to test the limits of contrasting views, including ones to which he himself might stand opposed; the text as a whole acts like a refractive sound-chamber for any individual assertion that is spoken within it.[4] This does not mean discounting the seriousness of the Canon's remarks, and still less does it mean disconnecting his views about literature and the 'republic' from some of the fundamental political questions raised by the *Quijote*. But it does imply attending to the particular forms of indirection by which Cervantes pursues these matters and, beyond that, understanding that the Canon's views are incorporated within, and surpassed by, a literary work in which the question of politics is engaged both through 'explicit' statements as well as tacitly and in forms of discourse that are not ostensibly 'about' politics at all. We should not forget that in one of his other references to 'la república' – this one in the Prologue to the *Novelas ejemplares* – Cervantes said that his role as a writer was to put a billiards table in the middle of the town square ('Mi intento ha sido poner en la plaza de nuestra república una mesa de trucos').[5] Indeed, we need to be especially alert to the ways in which Cervantes crosses serious and playful forms of discourse. His reflection on literature and politics has a serious purpose, to which a form of playfulness is essential.

An outline of the context in which the Canon speaks may be helpful before proceeding further. The remark about the harmful political effects of the books of chivalry is offered just at the moment when Don Quijote has been placed in an ox-cart cage and is being led forcibly back home under the impression that he has been seized by phantoms and is suffering from the effects of some unprecedented enchantment. Indeed, the idea of an 'unprecedented enchantment' seems to be the only way in which he can align this humiliating adventure with the purposes of his noble project. 'I have read many extremely serious histories of knights errant, but never have I read, or seen, or heard of enchanted knights being carried in this fashion at the pace promised by these sluggish and dilatory animals ... Perhaps in these our modern times, however, chivalry and enchantments follow in a path different from the one they followed in ancient times' (405–6) (Muchas y muy graves historias he yo leído de caballeros andantes; pero jamás he leído, ni visto, ni oído, que a los caballeros encantados los lleven desta manera y con el espacio que prometen estos perezosos animals ... Pero quizá la caballería y los encantados destos nuestros tiempos deben de seguir de otro camino que siguieron los antiguos; I, 47, p. 557). Around him are the local Priest and the Barber, some mule drivers, as well as the characters who first made their appearances in the intercalated stories that are introduced while Don Quijote was in the Sierra Morena – Fernando, Luscinda, Cardenio, and Dorotea (with Dorotea here playing the role of the Princess Micomicona).

When the Canon looks at Don Quijote and observes that the books of chivalry are 'perjudiciales en la república' he means to suggest, Socrates-like, that they are harmful to the citizens of the state, and therefore harmful to the state as a whole. Given the paternal and Christian-pastoral inclinations of the Canon, the reasonable assumption is that those who govern the state are duty-bound to look after the well-being of its citizens. His charge brings with it an echo of the pronouncements made at the

Council of Trent, where an entire session was devoted to the role of the bishops in limiting the spread of 'suspected and pernicious' books, especially in the city of Rome ('Whereas ... the number of suspected and pernicious books, wherein an impure doctrine is Contained, and is disseminated far and wide, has in these days increased beyond measure ... It hath been thought good, that Fathers specially chosen for this inquiry, should carefully consider what ought to be done in the matter of censures and of books, and also in due time report thereon to this holy Synod; to the end that It may more easily separate the various and strange doctrines, as cockle from the wheat of Christian truth').[6]

In the Canon's view, the health of the republic depends on the spiritual health of the individuals who comprise it. Although he does not himself have the vocabulary to explain it, the notion of the 'spiritual' at work behind his thoughts encompasses the realms we would describe as the 'psychological' and the 'moral.' The Canon is clear that politics requires a view toward issues of public moral health, even if that means restraining the figure who emphatically defends the principles of civic justice. I will have more to say below about the way in which the Canon attempts to link morality and politics by means of literary theory; for now I simply note that his impulse to bind the two together draws on an ancient idea, especially important in the *Republic*, that the polis can be understood as the psyche writ large. The soul, for Plato, is reflected in the polis, and viceversa; finding the good for the city means finding what is good for the soul, and likewise, cultivating the souls best suited to lead it.[7] This is to say that the Canon's censure of the books of chivalry needs to be situated squarely within the context of debates, going back to Plato, about which works an educated citizenry ought to read, about the place of various kinds of literature (e.g., tragedy, epic, and lyric poetry) within the state, and about the relative merits of many different kinds of discourse – literary, philosophical, mythical, moral, and historical, to name a few.

As is typical of much of what is said in *Don Quijote*, the Canon's remarks are resonant across many different spectrums. Among these the moral and medical associations of what he says have a direct bearing on the political implications of his remarks. As for the moral dimension, the need to fortify the bonds between morality and politics was a pressing concern in a context where these two spheres of life were increasingly understood as separate, as governed by different rules, and as institutionally distinct. Machiavelli's *Prince* offered what was essentially an apology for this state of affairs. But in the context of a Spain that was largely anti-Machiavellian, the overarching political agendas of a newly formed nation, a growing empire seemed to demand the support of a moral regime. In-deed, what is remarkable in the Canon's comments is the idea that the theory and practice of literature might help bind politics and morality more tightly together. It is a lofty and ambitious goal that attempts to work both at the level of a national literary 'policy' and on the microlevel of individual readers and books. It should neither be discounted for what it aspires to achieve nor taken as a reflection of Cervantes' views.

The question of the health of the republic draws as well on a range of contemporary thinkers who deploy medical language in order to establish parallels between the health of the individual and the health of the state. Concerns over the spiritual health of readers were prominent in the writings of Alfonso de Madrigal (especially in *De optima politia* [*The Ideal Government*]), Miguel Sabuco, Juan Huarte de San Juan, Gallego de la Serna, and Antonio de Guevara.[8] Indeed, the explicit purpose of Huarte's *Examen de ingenios* was to improve the republic by proposing a rational understanding of the benefits and disadvantages of different psychological types (*ingenios*). As he says at the beginning of the book, he is interested in the health of the social body figured as the *república*.[9] These ideas held sway in part because of an underlying set of beliefs that good governance brings good health to the republic. A signal formulation of this crucial point was offered by Alonso de Castrillo in the *Tractado de república*, about which I will have more to say below: 'there is nothing clearer in the world than good government for the health of the republic.'[10]

But there is also a dimension to the Canon's remarks that resonates with a contemporary set of affairs involving the enforcement of laws, the procedures of punishment, the restraint of individual liberties, and the official censure of books in early seventeenth-century Spain. Such questions would have been quite apparent to the characters who stand as witnesses to Don Quijote in the ox-cart cage, and equally clear to readers of Cervantes' book. Recall that when the Canon begins to speak, Don Quijote has just narrowly escaped being taken prisoner for having contravened a royal decree by having liberated the galley slaves in chapter 22. One of the mule drivers he meets carries an official warrant for his arrest, and in chapter 45 the muleteer carefully compares the warrant's description to the figure he sees before him ('among the warrants he was carrying for the detention of certain delinquents, he had one for Don Quixote, whom the Holy Brotherhood had ordered arrested, because he had freed the galley slaves. When the officer remembered this, he wanted to certify that the description of Don Quixote in the warrant was correct, and after pulling a parchment from the bottom of his shirt, he found what he was looking for and began to read it slowly, because he was not a very good reader, and at each word he read he raised his eyes to look at Don Quixote, comparing the description in the warrant with Don Quixote's face, and he discovered that there was no question but that this was the person described in the warrant' [396]) (entre algunos mandamientos que traía para prender a algunos delincuents, traía uno contra don Quijote, a quien la Santa Hermandad había mandado prender, por la libertad que dió a los galeotes. Imaginando, pues, esto, quiso certificarse si las señas que de don Quijote traía venían bien, y sacando del seno un pergamino, topó con el que buscaba, y poniéndose a leer de espacio, porque no era buen lector, a cada palabra que leía ponía los ojos en don Quijote, y iba cotejando las señas del mandamiento con el rostro de don Quijote, y halló que sin duda era el que el mandamiento rezaba; I, 45, p. 546).[11] Don Quijote's version of 'justice,' seemingly indiscriminate and anachronistic and applied for no 'good reason' other than that it corresponds to what he has read in the books of chivalry, sets itself up in clear opposition to any organized institutional set of legal or juridical principles of the kind that might legitimize the use of force. It would naturally butt up against the 'absolute' authority of the state, which purports to act systematically even while in disregard of concerns that it may be arbitrary and harsh.

At the same time, Don Quijote's ox-cart imprisonment echoes other instances of captivity and punishment in the novel, each of which radiates with a series of further political associations: the story of Zoraida and the Captive (I, 37, 40–1), the Barber's story of the *locos* in Seville who are kept inside cages (II, 1), and of course Don Quijote's pathetically courageous encounter with the caged lions who are being brought from Orán to the court (II, 17). Any sort of imprisonment was, of course, serious business, and the Captive's tale includes some graphic descriptions of the cruelties of state-rendered justice, telling in quasi-autobiographical fashion of the merciless treatment of Christian prisoners who were forced to row on the Turkish galleys. It is true that the Holy Brotherhood may have been somewhat less threatening in its practices, but this body was nonetheless capable of making threats of severe punishment and of acting upon them. Sancho is certainly afraid of them. In Part I, chapter 23, Sancho nervously warns that the Holy Brotherhood is apt to have little patience with Don Quijote's knight-errantry,[12] and in Part II, chapter 41, he recalls the name of a small town in La Mancha, Peralvillo, where the Santa Hermandad was known to have carried out some of its executions. The hastiness of the punishments meted out by the Santa Hermandad was of proverbial fame; as one well-known proverb said, 'Peralvillo justice: try the man after he's hanged.'[13]

From its origins in 1476 with the consolidation of numerous individual brotherhood 'associations,' the Holy Brotherhood was empowered to apprehend common criminals as a way to ensure local peace and secure the authority of the central monarch. But the group first appears in the *Quijote* in the context of the comic chaos that follows after Don Quijote's burlesque misadventure with Maritornes at the inn. Maritornes may be vulgar, even grotesque, and Don Quijote may be ridiculous in his approach to her as a Petrarchan-styled lover, but to think that the Santa Hermandad would be called upon to put an end to Don Quijote's madness is nearly absurd. The matter has further implications for the way in which we regard the Canon of Toldeo's remarks made in the face of Don Quijote in the ox-cart cage. Both episodes deal with potentially grave concerns about official power obliquely and with comic intent. Indeed, the circumstances surrounding the Canon's speech in Part I rightly lead us to wonder whether his remarks are to be taken seriously at all; at the very least, they lead us to consider the role of that seriousness within a context that seems to swing widely between the comic and the grave. But to reiterate a point raised above, what may surprise most of all is that the Canon of Toldeo seems convinced that an approach to political matters ought to involve a *literary* critique. He avoids the most immediate and practical political questions that are quite obviously at play in the episode – questions about the legitimacy and scope of the authority of the Santa Hermandad, about the legality of Don Quijote's 'random' act of justice in liberating the galley slaves, about the blind consistency of official forms of power, and about the effects of Inquistorial authority – in order to pursue a series of theoretical questions about literature and its effects. He turns to the relatively bookish questions of verisimilitude, of the demand for formal unity, and of Horace's injunction for poetry to instruct as well as please. What do these matters have to do with politics?

In what follows here, I want to probe the possibility that the Canon's 'theoretical' considerations in fact stand at the centre of a crucial set of concerns about the political role of literature, and that while he may be misguided in his approach, his allusion to Plato's fundamental question is far more than just a feint. Indeed, the entire novel could be read as an exploration of Plato's concern in the very different historical circumstances of the early modern age. That said, we must also understand that the Canon has also lost touch with some of Plato's original concerns. No Platonist, the Canon reflects the increasingly common desire to base politics on a view of truth that responds to regulative Aristotelian ideals that are all but deaf to the speculative powers of fiction – i.e., its ability to conceive of worlds that do not exist. This is not surprising given the Canon's background and cultural location. After all, what could be more 'reasonable' than to try to ground something as nebulous and intangible as a moral-political 'state' on a relatively concrete, realist conception of the truth, and to envision those forms of fiction that might be best suited to it? But in so doing, the Canon also recapitulates a shift away from the indirect, literary approach to questions of politics characteristic of the *Republic* to the more systematic kind of theorizing developed by Aristotle and expounded by some Renaissance literary theorists writing under his influence. To be sure, the Canon's view of the truth is not as flat-footed as that expressed by some other characters in the novel, many of whom scarcely engage in reflective thinking, theorizing, or fictionalizing at all. Sancho, the Humanist Cousin, and the Priest, to mention but a few, are all adherents, in various ways, to an unproblematized view about the world of 'facts.' The Cousin, for example, hopes that his fact-filled books will be 'very beneficial and no less diverting for the nation' (599) (de gran provecho y no menos entretenimiento para la república; II, 22, p. 205). Sancho shares some of his curiosity and his hopes. But when we come to consider Sancho's brief display of wisdom on the fictional island of Barataria we will see that politics requires something other than what *either* theoretical reflection *or* an attention to a world of facts can provide. Indeed, the point is that politics involves the search for a form of life that must lie in between the guidance of theory and the knowledge of facts.

The political implications of the Canon's views about literature reach well beyond what he explicitly says. At the same time, the substance of what he says is inseparable from the terms in which his views are framed. His appeal to verisimilitude as the standard for truth echoes a set of well-known ideas, drawn mainly from neo-Aristotelian literary texts that are appended to his Platonic questions about literature and politics. These are offered as an answer to the central concern that these Platonic questions generate, viz., what kind of literature can serve the highest political ends? Just as Cervantes invariably invokes, refashions, and prismatically refracts a host of other preformulated views throughout the novel, so too the Canon voices a series of neo-Aristotelian ideas to which have been added bits of Horace, Cicero, and Quintilian, as well as notions drawn from their Italian and Spanish humanist heirs. Thus, in addition to recapitulating an ancient shift from Plato to Aristotle in matters of literature and theory, the Canon's speech also reflects the kind of decontextualized assemblage of disparate theoretical views that was characteristic of Renaissance thinking about matters of literature, politics, and ethics. Moreover, the heterogeneous nature of the Canon's speech also raises the question of whether, and how, we are to think about politics in the context of a discursive whole that seems to be prismatic in its form. It is a problem that runs throughout the novel and is indeed constitutive of it. Cervantes works by reassembling fragments of pre-existing discursive frames, often as acts of literary resistance or critique, but this opens the more difficult question of how the discourse of politics is to be conceived if not as a discourse about the whole, of which the polis is itself an image. This is also to say that the Canon's literary theorizing remits us to an encounter with questions for which Plato's *Republic* is perhaps the most crucial point of reference. In the *Republic*, we come to learn that speaking of one thing requires speaking about the whole, even if digressively and by the indirect means of dialogue, image, and myth. This is above all the case with respect to the polis, which is regarded as an epitome of the whole. This is not because Plato understands the polis itself to be the whole in any concrete way, but rather because he understands the polis to be a finite *figure* for the whole. Since the 'whole' is potentially infinite, while discourse is finite, the required form of political discourse is one that allows us to speak about the whole while recognizing our own necessarily partial views.

Unlike some of his early modern counterparts, Cervantes seems to have understood this matter, if not as a philosophical fact then certainly in an intuitive and literary fashion. Cervantes inherits the Platonic insight that it is imperative to speak about the whole as the hypothetical unity of theory and praxis (in other terms of words and deeds) just as he understands the need to renounce speech claiming to be complete on the grounds that such discourse is likely to be infused with authoritarian ideas, ideas whose force is to assert themselves, pre-emptively, in place of the whole – in more modern political terms, as speaking *for* all others. As I will explain in further detail below, Cervantes' literary practice – speaking the truth and denying it, speaking the truth under the guise of various partial and imperfect voices, through the veils and the masks of fiction – was one of the lasting developments of his encounter with humanism, both in its Christian-Erasmist versions and in its more secular-civic varieties. Certain modes of humanist discourse, intertwined with the deft and agile use of rhetoric, provided Cervantes with strategies for speaking the truth under the conditions of political constraint.[14] And while various forms of constraint are characteristic of virtually every culture, they were arguably more severe in seventeenth-century Spain than elsewhere in Europe because of the factors mentioned above – the status of *conversos* and the suspicion of Erasmian humanism. In this conjuncture of contexts, Cervantes derived the means, through fiction, by which to construct the possibilities for a form of free speech that also reflects on its own constraints. Constraint can become strategic opportunity.

The Canon's talk of the 'republic' should also give us a clue that a particular, historically inflected approach to politics looms large in Cervantes' thoughts. The term 'republic' was prominent in contemporary theoretical discussions of the state, especially among humanists, even if talk of the *estado* (especially in the sense of 'razón de estado' in the tradition of Giovanni Botero's *Discorsi sopra la ragion di stato* of 1589), of the *imperio*, and eventually of the *nación*, were more common in official contexts. The *república* figures importantly in the opening of Antonio de Guevara's *Relox de príncipes* and especially in what Guevara writes about the importance of justice and the qualities of the ideal judge.[15] Guevara's views were likewise of central importance in the debates about which books should (and should not) be read. There was, moreover, something high-sounding and learned about the term *república*. It conjures up the city-state of Florence, the ideal republic of Venice, and above all the ancient republic of Rome.[16] In addition to the obvious reference to Plato's *Republic* it is reminiscent of the language that Renaissance humanists favoured in their discussions of politics and that underlay their interest in what was then the only surviving book of Cicero's emulation of Plato, the 'Somnium Scipionis.'[17]

Not surprisingly, perhaps, some of these writings took the notion of the 'republic' (*res publica*) as a way to sharpen the claim that the polis was grounded in society and in community, i.e., to reinforce the idea that it was the equivalent of a 'commonwealth.'[18] There is a communitarian political orientation even in the writings of Vitoria, who regards human beings as fundamentally social and therefore civil animals. Vitoria follows Aristotle in regarding human beings as social animals, who form communities in order to satisfy basic needs; but, as with de Soto's arguments about the difference between natural law and the *ius gentium*, 'only political community permits mutual communication and aid, and therefore appears as superior to any other form of association.'[19] At the same time, Vitoria thought of a 'republic' as necessarily plural, so much so that his fundamental conception of the republic makes essential reference to other republics.[20] But it is not only Vitoria. There was a remarkable flexibility shared by other Salamanca thinkers in this orbit, Domingo de Soto among them. He was a close colleague of Vitoria's, and Charles V's confessor, and his writings are important for the clear distinctions they make between natural law and the law nations (*ius gentium*). The latter depends upon communities of agreement and consent, understood specifically as human capacities, and not upon anything that may be deduced from nature alone.[21] As for the question of differences among human communities, and the allied question of plurality that Vitoria raises, I will discuss in chapter 7 how the political reality of early modern Spain increasingly became one that struggled with such matters at the practical level. The conjuncture of diverse communities in Cervantes' Spain placed obstacles in the way both of humanistic efforts to think in communitarian terms and of official attempts to imagine Spain as a unified nation.

However, perhaps most important of all for what Cervantes thinks of in relation to the *república* was the book mentioned above, written in the wake of the Comuneros revolt, by a Trinitarian friar, the *Tractado de república con otras hystorias y antigüedades* (Burgos, 1521) of Alonso de Castrillo. Though seldom mentioned in connection with the *Quijote*, this is a work that Cervantes seems very likely to have known. For Castrillo, the idea of the *república* was built on the Aristotelian notion of the *politia*, which is how the Greek term for the polis had previously been rendered into Spanish by Alonso Fernández de Madrigal ('El Tostado') in 1529.[22] Castrillo conceives of the *república* as a form of political association established on the basis of community and communication, 'an order according to which citizens must come together to form a city ... This order will be constituted either by the citizens placing over themselves a single individual to govern forever, or by alternating for equal periods of time, or when the most virtuous or powerful succeed in gaining advantage over the rest.'[23] Writing in the wake of the Comuneros uprising, and citing St Augustine as an authority, Castrillo regards the city and the home as the primordial forms of all political association.[24]

Now, the Canon's remarks in chapter 47 are not the first time that we hear talk of the 'republic' in *Don Quijote*, nor is it the last.[25] The narrator invokes the term very early on in the novel, when he explains that Don Quijote's purpose as a knight errant was to earn fame for himself and to be of service to 'his republic' ('it seemed reasonable and necessary to him, both for the sake of his honor and as a service to the nation [*república*], to become a knight errant' [21]) (le pareció conveniente y necesario, así para el aumento de su honra como para el servicio de su república, hacerse caballero andante; I, 1, pp. 74–5). Don Quijote's desire for fame is pervasive in the early chapters of Part I, as he looks forward to the dawning of a new 'golden age' that will redeem the present and restore the *siglo de oro* that he describes in chapter 11 ('Fortunate the time and blessed the age when my famous deeds will come to light, worthy of being carved in bronze, sculpted in marble, and painted on tablets as a remembrance in the future' [25]) (Dichosa edad y siglo dichoso aquel adonde saldrán a luz las famosas hazañas mías, dignas de entallarse en bronces, esculpirse en mármoles, y pintarse en tablas para memoria en el futuro; I, 2, pp. 80–1). Insofar as Don Quijote thinks that the achievement of fame is the basis for the formation, or reformation, of the state, his heroic project involves a reorientation in political thought. In fashioning himself as a hero, Don Quijote seems convinced that the reformed republic will be realized by his singular deeds; the fame he hopes to win by heroic action is the precondition for his restorative political ideals. The discursive form of this particular kind of political imagination involves a form of prolepsis, because in attempting to think about the founding of the state, Don Quijote regards himself as already in the service of political ideals. But it is more complicated than simple prolepsis, since what Don Quijote attempts is not the originary act of founding, or forming, a state, but rather reforming it. He claims to be able to undertake this task because he is both a heroic individual and because, thanks to his books, he claims to remember what it means to honour true nobility.

There were, of course, numerous antecedents for thinking about the founding of politics on memory and fame, ranging from classical antiquity to the sixteenth century. Fame originates in deeds worthy of being remembered, and the city is often conceived as a place where those memories can endure. Indeed, the oldest forms of civic consciousness were inseparable from the need to monumentalize and preserve the memory of those individuals who had done great deeds. And yet, not so many decades before Cervantes, the anonymous text of the Spanish novella El Abencerraje laments that such examples have been discounted in Spain because they are so common. It is said that Rodrigo de Narváez 'performed deeds of great valour, and particularly in the battle of Antequera his deeds were worthy of being remembered forever, especially since this Spain of ours has so little by the way of valour, being so natural and ordinary ... [and] not like those Romans and Greeks where, when someone risked his life, they made him immortal in their writings and raised him to the heavens.' [26] Notwithstanding the political anxieties at work here, or perhaps because of them, the very prospect of creating a lasting political state by the actions of a heroic individual becomes especially fraught when the Canon of Toldeo claims that the very kinds of books that Don Quijote reads, the books that model and mirror his heroic desires, are in fact harmful to the state ('perjudiciales en la república').

These worries suggest a literary crisis that in turn masks a crisis of political faith. If we are to believe the Canon, then either Don Quijote cannot achieve the kind of literary fame he would hope to attain and still find a place in the state, or there must be some other relationship between literature and politics than whatever is reputed to follow from the suppression of these 'harmful' books. This question is one that Cervantes very much hopes to address in the very book we are reading, which is deeply engaged with the problems of politics and writing, theory and practice, on the threshold of a post-heroic age. My overarching suggestion is that Cervantes deals with this set of questions by establishing a prismatic literary space, within which all the established discourses of politics can be refracted through a critical lens. This space is unequal to the one that the Canon envisions, but it is hardly inconsistent with the literary and critical practices of Cervantes' humanist predecessors, and ultimately with the discursive orientation of Plato's own *Republic*.

Following his talk of the health of the 'republic,' the Canon presents a series of views that seem to express a reasonable set of ideas about literature – all too reasonable, one might be tempted to say. While his underlying questions derive from Plato, his responses as indicated above are a compilation of Renaissance commonplaces – educated and high-sounding commonplaces, whose roots reach back to Aristotle and Horace, but commonplaces just the same. As a host of modern critics including E.C. Riley and Alban Forcione have pointed out, many of the topics that concern the Canon – especially the question of verisimilitude and the limits of the marvellous – had their proximate origins in the raging *romanzo* polemic in sixteenth-century Italy, where battle lines were drawn over questions about whether or not the romances were to be censured for failing to adhere to the principles of verisimilitude.[27] The views at play in these debates, drawn initially from Aristotle's *Poetics* and from Horace's 'Ars Poetica,' were in turn adapted to conditions in which the romance and the modern verse epic, rather than tragedy or the ancient epic, were the imaginative forces to contended with, and where historical writing had increasingly come to claim a privileged access to the 'truth' on the basis of its purported faithfulness to the facts or the presentation of authorial experience.[28] Luis Vives's *De ratione dicendi* provided one important bridge between these classical ideas and the Spanish humanist tradition.[29] But the allusions to Aristotle, Horace, and their Renaissance commentators and heirs in the *Quijote* further reflect the self-conscious way in which Cervantes both absorbs and distances himself from a series of widely circulated, pre-articulated views. Such views about literature were, moreover, most often meant for some other genre – for tragedy, the epic, or the romance – but hardly for the new generic prism that was begun with the *Quijote*. Just as Cervantes both incorporates and deflects a host of literary genres throughout the novel, so too he deals prismatically with literary theory on topics that would have been familiar to his more educated readers.

In a broad survey of literary theory in the Renaissance, Bernard Weinberg described the process by which European writers before Cervantes tended to compile their theoretical views from sometimes divergent classical sources. The process suggests a fundamental disorientation and levelling among theoretical predecessors as much as it implies a synthesis of the classics: 'for those who use this method all statements in all texts are of an equal value. Since each one is in a sense torn from its context, it loses its status as a first principle, or as an intermediate statement, or as the final conclusion of a long process of deductive reasoning. The structure of a given document disappears ... It becomes possible, for example, to wrest a single statement from the *Republic* of Plato and discuss it in comparison with a single statement taken from Aristotle's *Politics*, paying no attention to the fact that the two treatises have different points of departure, proceed by a different method of argumentation, produce different conclusions.'[30] Weinberg was quite right in saying this. But his analysis raises a further set of questions about whether Renaissance writers were able to imagine literature, or politics, as providing the basis for views that could in turn be integrated into any sort of coherent whole. Examples of this further problem abound. Matteo San Martino's *Osservationi grammaticali e poetiche della lingua italiana* (1555), for instance, begins with Aristotle, proceeds with Cicero, moves on to Horace, and concludes with a final statement where, as Weinberg himself says, 'All are lumped together in the most helter-skelter fashion' (Weinberg, *A History*, 1:139). There are commentaries on Aristotle that present the *Poetics* as improvements on or refinements of Plato (Maggi and Lombardi, for instance, in *In Aristotelis librum de poetica communes explanationes*, 1550; or Castelvetro's *Chiose intorno al libro del Comune di Platone*, which was redacted after his famous commentary on Aristotle's *Poetics*).[31]

Moreover, the Canon's remark about the role of literature in the 'republic,' and his subsequent critique of the romances of chivalry are fashioned out of words and ideas that had already been predigested by Spanish theorists. Writing in 1580 in a book published in Alaclá de Henares (the *Arte poética en romance castellano*), Miguel Sánchez de Lima had levelled a political critique of the romances of chivalry in terms that anticipate the

Canon's remarks in *Don Quijote*. By way of a defence of poetry against charges that it is the product of madness, Sánchez de Lima identifies books of chivalry as dangerous to the 'Christian republic' for their 'lies and vanities' (mentiras y vanidades), while he nonetheless defends 'poetry' in the more general sense: 'What more shall I say about Poetry? Except that it is as beneficial to the Christian Republic as the books of chivalry are harmful, for they serve no other purpose but to corrupt the souls of young men and women ... For from some of them there is nothing good at all to be gained for the soul, but only lies and vanities.'[32]

But the mixing of sources we see reflected in the Canon's speech was not only evidence of confusion. It was also the basis of a liberating modern experience. Cervantes, for his part, seems to have found a response to possible anxieties about the incoherence of such views by deploying literature as a critical tool for deflecting aspirations for a reconstruction of their coherence. He was aware of having inherited a set of precepts that seemed to belie any hope for a totality of discourse and thought; rather than pursue the search for any final synthesis, he understood that it was more important for political reasons to impede any such attempts. This was especially so given the fact that official government bodies were busy declaring which kinds of books were harmful to the state.

Defending poetry against Plato's apparent attacks was no easy task. The important 1595 work by Alonso López Pinciano, the *Philosophía antigua poética*, devotes considerable effort to a clarification of Plato's stance regarding the expulsion of the poets from the ideal republic. His first argument, voiced through one of the characters in the dialogue, is that Plato meant to censure certain kinds of poetry, not the poets themselves. On the contrary: Plato's critique places poetry on a par with medicine and politics and other important arts (curing, hunting, seafaring, governing, and other 'imitative arts'), but none of which proves sufficiently systematic or reliable:

> Their intention ... in that first place in the third book of the *Republic*, is not to condemn poetry, but rather the poets ... In the second place, in the *Epinomis*, I do admit that poetry itself is censured, but one has to break through this husk and get into the heart of what's inside, where one notes that Plato's purpose in that dialogue was to arrive at true wisdom, which he denies can be in the majority of the arts including the most important ones; and having said that true wisdom does not reside in the arts of healing, hunting, ruling and governing, and navigating, or in any of the imitative arts, he says that it lies in Politics. And he gives a reason: because the other arts do not proceed

by scientific and evidentiary means but are based on conjecture. Which is to say that, if Plato speaks ill of poetry there it is also true that he disparages Medicine and Politics and all the rest, which not only are not bad but rather are extremely dignified and very important.[33]

Prompted by the sight of Don Quijote in the ox-cart cage, the Canon's project of bringing aesthetic 'discipline' to literature is better seen as his attempt at a response to a fundamental political concern that he is himself unable fully to address: how to bring lawful order to the state, given the 'literary' threats against it. The Canon is a political thinker *manqué*. His neo-Aristotelian principles can scarcely approach the most important political issues at stake, but instead consign readers to a diet of relatively dull and compliant texts as a way of ensuring health and order in the state. His view is that imaginative literature can at best serve to display an author's intellectual talents, that it can offer opportunities for a capacious mind to show its excellence ('the opportunity for display that [the books of chivalry] offered a good mind,' 413) (el sujeto que ofrecían [los libros de caballerías] para que el buen entendimiento pudiese mostrarse en ellos; I, 47, p. 566), but that it can only bridge the gap between the way things are and the way they ought to be in the most flat-footed way, viz., by offering a reasonable likeness or semblance of the world. The literary ideal that supports the Canon's political interests is likewise 'aesthetic' only in the most limited sense of the term:

> Fictional tales must engage the minds of those who read them, and by restraining exaggeration and moderating impossibility they enthrall the spirit and thereby astonish, captivate, delight, and entertain, allowing wonder and awe and joy to move together at the same pace; none of these things can be accomplished by fleeing verisimilitude and mimesis. (412)

> Hanse de casar las fábulas mentirosas con el entendimiento de las que las leyeren, escribiéndose de suerte que, facilitando los imposibles, allanando las grandezas, suspendiendo los ánimos, admiren, suspendan, alborecen y entretengan, de modo que anden a un mismo paso la admiración y la alegría juntas; y todas estas cosas no podrá hacer el que huyere de la verosimilitud y de la imitación. (I, 47, p. 565)

Most important, perhaps, the Canon's engagement with the neo-Aristotelian understanding of verisimilitude grants literature very limited licence to speculate or hypothesize. Indeed, the hypothesizing function of literature, so prized in other accounts of its abilities in antiquity and the Middle Ages, including among figures such as Boethius, is virtually absent from the Canon's account.[34] Its adherence to Aristotle's association of literature with the realm of the 'probable' as opposed to the historical 'possible' constrains the notion of the 'probable' by conceiving of it in relation to the world that exists, not the world that ought to be. This is how it attempts to answer Plato's concerns about the political dangers of poetry. The result is a double distortion, hardly uncommon among Renaissance writers, of Aristotle's views about literature and of Plato's views about poetry and politics.

What became formulated in Aristotle's concern for verisimilitude, in fact, originated in Plato's understanding of the relationship between true and false images. This concern is articulated both in the *Republic* as well as in one of Plato's more challenging dialogues, the *Sophist*, which was the subject of a detailed commentary by Ficino in 1496.[35] The point of the *Sophist* on the matter of images is this: the difference between 'true' images and 'false' ones corresponds to the difference between icons and phantasms. The practice of making true images or icons (also known as the practice of eikastics) yields images that preserve the 'just proportions' of their originals. The idea of any other kind of resemblance, and certainly of 'verisimilitude' in a neo-Aristotelian sense that would connote resemblance to probable facts, formed no part of Plato's thinking. This is, in part, because the Platonic notion of an 'original' is not something that can be located within the empirical world. On the contrary, the only true 'originals' are the ideas, and originals can only be made by a god. The highest possibility available to all other beings is to intuit the ideas and to fashion images that stand in a relationship of just proportion to them.[36] 'Verisimilitude' makes little sense in such a context.

The difference between icons and phantasms is precisely the point on which Tasso invokes the *Sophist* (235b–6c) in Book II of his *Discorsi del poema eroico*. Fracastoro's dialogue between Andrea Navagero and Giambatttista della Torre, *Navagero; or, A Dialogue on the Art of Poetry (Navagerius sive de Poetica Dialogus)* likewise owes its conception of imitation and deception to this distinction.[37] Moreover, the example of the *Quijote* itself goes to show that the Aristotelian notion of 'verisimilitude' as understood by so many thinkers of the Renaissance was neither a reliable governing principle for fiction nor a way to enable fiction to help us consider the way things might be. In a commentary on the first of these two points, Vicente Lloréns pointed out the asymmetries between the Captive's story in Part I of the *Quijote* and the episode of Ricote and Ana Félix in Part II – that historical events and historically impossible events give rise to equally fantastic conclusions (to wit: the Captive's return to Spain with Zoraida, and Ana Félix's rescue from execution by order of the viceroy of Cataluña). In his words, 'Cervantes had reiterated throughout his works that idea that verisimilitude was not sufficient to draw a dividing line between fable and history. Reality – of which his own life stood as proof – could be as lacking in verisimilitude as anything invented.'[38] The episode with Ana Félix, the beautiful *morisca*, is historically impossible. The Captive's return to Spain with Zoraida is improbable but historically possible. Something like it in fact happened to Cervantes. By contrast, what happens with Ricote and Ana Félix is less improbable from a novelistic standpoint, but historically impossible in that a viceroy of Cataluña could not protect an expelled *morisco* who had returned to Spain under cover.[39] Precisely because the world of the historical 'real' may well be stranger than the world of 'fiction,' the notion of verisimilitude in such instances is better seen as challenged by the truth rather than as a way to regulate fictional attempts simply to exceed it. But this is also to say that the demand for verisimilitude was guided by assumptions about what things 'fiction' and 'politics,' 'theory' and 'practice,' ought to be. The Canon is naive in believing that he has a 'theory' about fiction, and not that his literary policies may have themselves been drawn from politically aligned ideas about the real. What the Canon says about verisimilitude must accordingly be regarded as a set of statements about literature that mask the complications engendered by his own political commitments. They seem scarcely to reflect the sophistication of Cervantes' literary practice. Verisimilitude is a way of masking the double bind that defines the quixotic structure, i.e., that there is a perpetual non-convergence of the 'real' and the 'ideal.' It masks that double bind by restraining the one thing that makes such a structure livable, i.e., the very thing the Canon objects to as an absence of verisimilitude – fantasy.

Moreover, the Canon is hardly a reliable or consistent critic even within the framework of his own assemblage of views. He is perfectly able to contradict himself, and in fact admits to having a fondness for the very books of chivalry he censures. He is, in other words, susceptible to the very fantasies he would deny in the name of 'verisimilitude.' Those fantasies bring him something that is otherwise lacking in his existence. While he describes his attraction to the books of chivalry in terms of self-censure ('moved by a false and idle pleasure') (llevado de un ocioso y falso gusto, is the phrase), he nonetheless indicates that he has himself tried to write a romance of chivalry, albeit one that would adhere to all the 'rules.'[40] Critics have customarily taken the Canon's reference to an 'ideal' romance as an indication of Cervantes' own ambition to write a 'purified' form of romance that resulted in his *Trabajos de Persiles y Sigismunda*. But there is little evidence that Cervantes had conceived the *Persiles* by 1605, and still less that the work was underway. The Canon's words echo again with Plato's objection to any works that cultivate 'childish and vulgar passions' (*Republic*, X, 608a).[41] Additionally, the Canon's reliance on the principle of verisimilitude, his invocation of the principles of good aesthetic form, and his suggestion that there are both good pleasures and bad ones, provide the grounds for a perfectly 'reasonable' defence of literature within the framework of a certain conception of the 'healthy' state, but they imply norms that he cannot himself fully respect. His own fantasies get in the way of his literary politics.

Clearly, the Canon's attempt to guard the state against the 'unhealthy' influences of literature is inadequate as a general formulation of the relationship between literature and politics, much less as a form of political theory. His own allusions to politics are, if anything, overdetermined. One pregnant lexical choice that the Canon makes is his use of the term 'perjudiciales.' The word – likewise presaged in Sánchez de Lima's *Arte poética en romance castellano* – adds a prosecutorial inflection to the Canon's remarks. Books of chivalry are judged in a way that suggests the procedures of Inquisitorial prosecution, the rendering of official censures, and the pronouncement of punitive sanctions. Indeed, the term was prominent in Pedro de Rivadeneira's 1595 anti-Machiavellian tract on politics and governance, the *Tratado del príncipe cristiano* (written 'for the just purpose of combating such harmful opinions').[42] As is often remarked, the Canon's commentary in chapter 47 continues the work of the Priest and the Barber in their 'scrutiny' of Don Quijote's library in chapter 5, in which the books deemed most harmful were ordered to be burned. Approximately fifty years before Part I of the *Quijote* appeared, in 1558, an order (an official 'Pragmática') was issued by the Cortes at Valladolid requiring that, under penalty of death, all books printed in Spain, as well as all books imported into the country, be licensed by the Consejo de Castilla. The first Spanish Index of Prohibited Books appeared in 1559. As part of a lengthy process of review and scrutiny, several copies of any approved book had to be submitted to an official censor in order to ensure compliance with official laws.[43] Some of the criteria invoked in the 'scrutiny' of Don Quijote's books in chapter 5 of Part I resonate with the lists of the Quiroga *Index* of 1583 and 1584, behind which were Mariana and other Counter-Reformation ideologues.[44] When the Canon speaks again in chapter 47 the context once more suggests a mock-Inquisitorial prosecution, which pits a 'political' version of the truth against the power of imaginative literature over the passions. While this is not a 'public' trial like the one we see in chapter 5, and while no books are ordered burned this time, we are nonetheless meant to recognize the Canon as the kind of learned cleric who might have been responsible for rendering official judgments about which books were to be entered onto the Inquisition's lists and which ones spared.[45]

The Canon is one of the voices of authority that Cervantes inserts throughout the *Quijote*; the choices he makes about which books to endorse and which ones to censure confirm that role. In a string of examples that begins with the Old Testament's Book of Judges,[46] he offers examples of books that can provide virtuous models of heroism – virtuous both literarily and morally, one is led to presume. He then proceeds to mention hallowed examples from classical antiquity, and finally moves on to consider a detailed list of writings from virtually every region of Spain. This section of the Canon's discourse culminates in a brilliant rhetorical flourish, the aim of which is to effect a powerful and authoritative telescoping of present and past.

> If, following your natural inclination, you still wish to read books about great chivalric deeds, read Judges in Holy Scripture, and there you will find magnificent truths and deeds both remarkable and real. Lusitania had a Viriato, Rome had a Caesar, Carthage a Hannibal, Greece an Alexander, Castilla Count Fernán González, Valencia a Cid, Andalucía a Gonzalo Fernández, Extremadura a Diego García de Peredes, Jerez a Garcí Pérez de Bargas, Toledo a Garcilaso, Sevilla a Don Manuel de León. Reading about their valorous deeds can entertain, instruct, delight, and astonish the highest minds. (424)

> Si todavía, llevado de su natural inclinación, quisiere leer libros de hazañas y de caballerías, lea en la Sagrada Escritura el de los Jueces. Un Viriato tuvo Lusitania; un César, Roma; un Aníbal, Cartago; un Alejandro, Grecia; un conde Fernán González, Castilla; un Cid, Valencia; un Gonzalo Fernández, Andalucía; un Diego García de Paredes, Estremadura; un Garcí Pérez de Vargas, Jerez; un Garcilaso, Toledo; un don Manuel de León, Sevilla; cuya lección de sus valerosos hechos puede entretener, enseñar, deleitar y admirar a los más altos ingenios que los leyeren. (I, 49, pp. 578–9)

His speech binds the power and authority of heroes drawn from canonical texts – the Bible above all – to the relatively recent heroes of Spain.

The reference to Judges in the passage above is in all likelihood meant as an allusion to the prodigious feats of Samson, which had become the stuff of popular legend.[47] But all the other figures mentioned by the Canon, however mythical in stature, are historical. And yet Cervantes shows just how hard critics like the Canon had to work in order to provide legitimizing principles for the contemporary state based on models from the past. Given his own preference for books of chivalry, it is with some regret and a sense of resignation that the Canon begins his discourse on the subject of disciplined reading: 'Come, come, Señor Don Quijote, take pity on yourself! Return to the bosom of good sense, and learn to use the considerable intelligence that heaven was pleased to give you, and devote your intellectual talents to another kind of reading that redounds to the benefit of your conscience and the increase of your honor!' (424) (¡Ea, señor don Quijote, duélase de sí mismo, y redúzgase al gremio de la discreción, y sepa usar de la mucha que el cielo fue servido de darle, empleando el felicísimo talento de su ingenio en otra letura que redunde en aprovechamiento de su conciencia y aumento de su honra! I, 49, p. 578).

At this level of engagement, there was no need to make the case that literature was political. On the contrary, Cervantes crafts the Canon's discourse against a historical backdrop in which literature was very clearly and officially politicized in the sense that it was subject to state authority and control. Indeed, one of Cervantes' greatest challenges was to find a way for literature to speak the truth in spite of such constraints. The discourses of the Canon and the Priest, which touch on literature and truth, must themselves be read as products of the will to speak under oppressive conditions, rather than as explicit expressions of Cervantes' beliefs. And yet, the ostensible goal of the Canon and the Priest – to make literature safe for politics – is one that the *Quijote* transforms well beyond what these characters say, in part because much of what they say cannot be taken at face value.

This last point is made abundantly clear when the Priest attempts to follow up the Canon's remarks with a critique of the popular theatre, the *comedia*. In taking up the Canon's lead, the Priest offers an analysis of the *comedia* in which he proposes that there ought to be a state-appointed censor to determine which works should be represented and which ones not. 'All these difficulties, and many others I will not mention, would cease if there were at court an intelligent and judicious person who would examine each play before it was performed, not only those produced in the capital, but also those put on anywhere in Spain, and without his approval, stamp, and signature no magistrate anywhere would permit a play to be performed' (418) (Todos estos inconvenienetes cesarían, y aun otros muchos más que no digo, con que hubiese en la Corte una persona inteligente y discreta que examinase todas las comedias antes que se representasen; no sólo aquellas que se hiciesen en la Corte, sino todas las que se quisiesen representar en España; sin la cual aprobación, sello y firma ninguna justicia en su lugar dejase representar comedia alguna; I, 48, p. 572). Plato resounds in what he says, but at the same time the Priest's remarks touch all too directly on the contemporary question of official censorship and can easily be interpreted as yet another not-so-sly allusion to Inquisitorial practices. One imagines that the Inquisition censors must have read quite literally, and either did not recognize or could not acknowledge the cutting irony in the Priest's remarks. But certainly they could not have missed the thrust of the Niece's observation in II, 6: 'Your grace should remember that everything you say about knights errant is invention and lies, and each of their histories, if it isn't burned, deserves to wear a sanbenito or some other sign that it has been recognized as the infamous ruin of virtuous customs' (493) (Advierta vuestra merced que todo eso que dice de los caballeros andantes es fábula y mentira, y sus historias, ya que no las quemasen, merecían que a cada una se le echase un sambenito, o alguna señal en que fuese conocida por infame y por gastadora de las buenas costumbres; II, 6, p. 81). That said, there were also advocates including the likes of Luis Vives, who tarried with the idea of censorship in a serious way. His writings on education conclude with this concession: 'In those matters in which men may become better or worse by reading books, it is expedient that there should be certain public magistrates for the examination of books. These must be men conspicuous and well-trained amongst the whole people, for their judgment, learning and integrity.'[48]

As I will discuss further in chapter 9, these matters have a direct bearing on what it meant for Cervantes to write under conditions of constraint. Here I want to pursue the suggestion that the discussion between the Canon and the Priest also echoes with the moment in Plato's *Republic* where Socrates proposes to censor certain forms of epic and tragic poetry because of the harmful effects they have on their audiences. References to Plato's views on this subject were not unusual in commentaries on the Inquisition's practices. One document from the period on this topic, falsely attributed to Fray Jerónimo Zurita ('Acerca de la prohibición de obras literarias por el Santo Oficio') (On the Prohibition of Literary Works by the Holy Inquisition), explains that while some books in both Latin and Spanish might be morally harmful in the habits they encourage ('works that damage customs'; los libros que dañan las costumbres), Plato's *Republic* was nonetheless at fault in its exclusion of the poets.[49] In some of what poets do – in their ability to promote the serious consideration of weighty matters, for instance – poets ought to be regarded as necessary as medical doctors. As for the *Republic* itself, one prong of the argument is that tragedies encourage an unheroic, feminine disposition, that they reduce men to tears and ought therefore to be excluded from the ideal state, which needs to cultivate heroes ('in our private griefs we pride ourselves on ... our ability to bear them in silence like men, and we regard the behaviour we see on the stage as womanish,' *Republic*, 605e). Ironically, Cervantes' Priest is collaborating with Don Quijote in echoing Plato's interest in ensuring the cultivation of heroes to ground the state. And yet the Priest has forgotten the irony that is central to the formulation of Plato's views – including the irony by which Plato allowed himself to draw liberally on 'literary' resources (dialogue, myth, character, settings) while articulating a political critique of literature. Plato – here a precursor of the Canon of Toledo – had himself been the author of several literary works. The 'recantation' by which Plato rejects tragedy and censors the poets thus calls for more careful handling than is customary. We should note that some of the views ascribed to 'Plato,' which border on the ridiculous, are placed in the mouth of characters who can hardly be taken as reliable spokespersons for Plato's own ideas.

The Canon's speech reflects greater learning and refinement than the Priest's, but is scarcely any more aware of the need for irony. On the contrary, the Canon's expectation is that literature should be a plausible mirror of the truth itself, and that if it cannot be grounded in the literal truth as a representation of the real – to which there are plenty of adherents in the novel, beginning with the first narrator and culminating in the Humanist Cousin – then it ought to adhere to something like the representation of or a semblance of the real (verisimilitude). I would repeat that he attempts to answer Plato's critique of poetry with a theory of truth based on Aristotle's *Poetics*. His move is significant in a number of ways, among them because it exemplifies the particular kind of rhetorical deflection that occurs throughout the novel when characters attempt to render intangible matters concrete.[50] The Canon's notion of 'verisimilitude' engages in a similar process of substitution, writ large: in response to a question about the political role of literature, he invokes Aristotle's notion of verisimilitude, understood as a 'plausible semblance of the real'; this idea substitutes for the far more complex and less tangible version of literary truth that would be required to answer the platonic critique of poetry spoken by

Socrates, viz., that poetry deals in phantasmatics rather than eikastics,[51] and excites the passions beyond what reason can control. The theory of verisimilitude is itself a grand distortion of Plato's views about the relationship between image and truth, for the 'real' to which verisimilitude holds fiction accountable is, for Plato, only a realm of appearances.

Not surprisingly, however, an interest in verisimilitude re-emerged just when imaginative literature was impelled to compete with empiricist forms of historical discourse. The Canon appears to be one of the more moderately tempered figures in the *Quijote*. He brings an empirically oriented interpretation of literature to bear on Socrates' charge that poetry was less than true and could create an imbalance in the psyche by placing the passions ahead of cool reason. This same line of reasoning comes into play in Part II when, amid howls of laughter from the Duke and the Duchess, the Countess Trifaldi observes that some poems are so powerfully moving that their authors ought to be exiled from the state, just as Plato had ordered:

> 'The song seemed like pearls to me, and his voice like honey, and after that, I mean from that time on, seeing the harm that came to me because of these and other verses like them, I believed that from virtuous and harmonious republics poets must be banished, as Plato advised, at least the lascivious ones, because they write verses that are not like those of the Marquis of Mantua, which entertain children and women and make them weep, but are sharp, like tender thorns that pierce your soul and, like bolts of lightning, wound you there without tearing your clothes … And so I say, my lords and ladies, that these versifiers very rightly ought to be banished to lizard-infested islands.' (708–9)

> 'Parecióme la trova de perlas, y su voz de almíbar, y después acá, digo, desde entonces, viendo el mal en que caí por estos y otros semejantes versos, he considerado que de las buenas y concertadas repúblicas se habían de desterrar los poetas, como aconsejaba Platón, a lo menos, los lascivos, porque escriben unas coplas, no como las del marqués de Mantua, que entretienen y hacen llorar los niños y a las mujeres, sino unas agudezas que, a modo de blandas espinas, os atraviesan el alma, y como rayos os hieren en ella, dejando sano el vestido … Y así, digo, señores míos, que los tales trovadores con justo título los debían desterrar a las islas de los Lagartos.'[52] (II, 38, pp. 333–4)

As has often been observed, Renaissance interpreters of Aristotle were less interested in his account of tragedy as such and rather more interested in seeing the *Poetics* as a source for the kinds of normative guidelines that could be used to regulate contemporary literary practice. Indeed, Aristotle's Renaissance interpreters found norms even on topics, such as the unity of place, where Aristotle had prescribed none. As for the Canon's concern about literature and politics, his goal is not to rule literature out of bounds of the ideal state – he is, after all, a literary man himself – but to insure the health of the state and to limit the spread of Don Quijote's 'madness' by requiring that literature adhere to a version of the truth as faithfulness to plausible facts. This is his legitimation strategy for literature, and it is part of the larger political hope that the right kind of literature, literature that would respect a particular understanding of its relationship to the truth, can in turn provide a moral foundation for the state. He was scarcely alone in doing so. The Renaissance attempt to 'redeem' poetry from Plato's charges against it goes back at least to Francesco Patrizi's late fifteenth-century work *De institutione republicae*. But implicit in this view is the conviction that a state requires something like agreement on a world of 'facts' against which the claims of all forms of discourse can be tested, and to which a national 'literary policy' might refer.[53]

In sum, the Canon begins with a concern about the health of the 'republic' and the role of literature within it, and concludes by assigning literature a relatively circumscribed place within the discourse of politics, in part by accepting a narrow conception of the truth. The Canon's bargain is this: we can make literature 'safe' for the state if we constrain fantasy, if we restrict truth-claims to the realm of the plausible, if we limit its ability to touch the soul, and if we demand that it adhere to the principles of 'good form.' The *Quijote* has almost none of these qualities. As Cervantes notes in II, 44, the first Part of the work was itself judged disorganized and digressive by readers who were interested in a more unified plot. And, immediately following the Canon's discourse, Don Quijote offers what is by any measure one of the most outrageously fantastic stories of the entire first Part, the tale of the Knight of the Lake. Its fantastical qualities are hardly sui generis. It is rich with allusions to the *Libro del Caballero Zifar* and to Boccaccio, though without ever mentioning either one. The Canon's resounding approval of Don Quijote's story of the Knight of the Lake is, moreover, an occasion that exposes his own bias, as a pleasure-seeking reader, in favour of the books that his literary policies would censure.

> Books that are imprinted with a royal license and with the approval of those officials to whom they are submitted, and read to widespread delight, and celebrated great and small, poor and rich, educated and ignorant, lowborn

and gentry, in short, by all kinds of persons of every rank and station: can they possibly be a lie, especially when they bear so close a resemblance to the truth and tell us about the father, the mother, the nation, the family, the age, the birthplace, and the great deeds, point by point and day by day, of the knight, or knights, in question? Be quiet, your grace, and do not say such blasphemies, and believe me when I tell you what you, as an intelligent man, must do in this matter, which is to read these books, and then you will see the pleasure you derive from them.

If you do not agree, then tell me: is there any greater joy than seeing, before our very eyes, you might say, a lake of boiling pitch, and in it, swimming and writhing about, there are many snakes, serpents, lizards, and many other kinds of fierce and fearsome creatures, and from the middle of the lake there comes a extremely sad voice, saying 'Thou, O knight, whosoever thou mayest be, who looketh upon this fearful lake, if thou wishest to grasp the treasure hidden beneath these ebon waters, display the valor of thy mighty heart and throw thyself into the midst of its black and burning liquid, for if thou wilt not, thou canst not be worthy of gazing upon the wondrous marvels contained and enclosed within the seven castles of the seven enchantresses which lieth beneath this blackness. (428)

Los libros que están impresos con licencia de los reyes y con aprobación de aquellos a quien se remitieron, y que con gusto general son leídos y celebrados de los grandes y de los chicos, de los pobres y de los ricos, de los letrados e ignorantes, de los plebeyos y caballeros, finalmente, de todo género de personas, de cualquier estado y condición que sean, ¿habían de ser mentira?; y más llevando tanta apariencia de verdad, pues nos cuentan el padre, la madre, la patria, los parientes, la edad, el lugar y las hazañas, punto por punto y día por día, que el tal caballero hizo, o caballeros hicieron. Calle vuestra merced, no diga tal blasfemia (y créame que le aconsejo en esto lo que debe de hacer como discreto), sino léalos, y verá el gusto que recibe de su leyenda. Si no, dígame: ¿hay mayor contento que ver, como si dijésemos: aquí ahora se muestra delante de nosotros un gran lago de pez hirviendo a borbollones, y que andan nadando y cruzando por él muchas serpientes, culebras y lagartos, y otros muchos géneros de animales feroces y espantables, y que del medio del lago sale una voz tristísima que dice: 'Tú, caballero, quienquiera que seas, que el temeroso lago estás mirando, si quieres alcanzar el bien que debajo destas negras aguas se encubre, muestra el valor de tu fuerte pecho y arrójate en mitad de su negro y encendido licor; porque si así no lo haces, no serás digno de ver las altas maravillas que en sí encierran y contienen los siete castillos de las siete fadas que debajo desta negregura yacen? (I, 50, p. 584)

Don Quijote's vivid tale of the Knight of the Lake is suspended adroitly in the realm of the hypothetical; the 'as if' of the narrative frame creates the discursive mask that allows the fiction to go forward (as it does for several pages). Given this condition of suspended discursive articulation, the narrative induces the Canon into a state of wonder that allows him to entertain the paradoxical pleasures and insights provided by the consideration of an otherwise impossible world. Moreover, the Canon's approval of Don Quijote's fantastic narrative betrays his own investment in the very kinds of stories he says are 'harmful' to the state.

The Canon's response is principally one of wonder (*admiratio*). Securely grounded in the rhetorical tradition, *admiratio* was widely recognized as one of the ways in which an orator could sustain the persuasive power of discourse. And yet Don Quijote is not ostensibly engaged in persuasion in his account of the Knight of the Lake at all. Rather, his 'amazing' account of the Knight of the Lake was conceived as a demonstration of the fact that pleasure may itself be a guide to truth. As he asks in the passage above, can books that meet with the approval of so many readers be full of lies? ('¿habían de ser mentira?'). But what, then, is the place of pleasure in the state?

In spite of his own powerful enjoyment of Don Quijote's tale, the Canon's 'official' view is that pleasure is one of the most personal and potentially unruly responses to literature. This, he argues, is the reason it is of grave danger to the state. But his formulation of the issue presents us with yet another *mélange* of ideas drawn from the somewhat confused reading of Horace, Plato, and Aristotle that was not uncommon in the Renaissance. His initial conception is Horatian insofar as it ascribes a moral and pedagogical function to literature. As the Canon says of the popular books, they are 'meant only to delight and not to teach, unlike moral tales, which delight and teach at the same time' (412) (atienden solamente a deleitar, y no a enseñar: al contrario de lo que hacen las fábulas apólogas, que deleitan y enseñan juntamente; I, 47, p. 564). At the same time, his Platonic inclinations lead him to seek a higher ideal for the association of aesthetic form and virtue. There is, he says, a 'true pleasure' that can be found in adherence to ideals of beauty as demonstrated through the formal qualities of harmony and proportion. This 'true pleasure' is a pleasure of the soul that, according to Platonic and Neoplatonic accounts, makes its first appeal to the eye as the most direct conduit to the soul. But this Platonic idea is in turn confused with an Aristotelian notion, drawn principally from *De anima*, that whatever can be known in human terms must necessarily involve the imagination (*fantasia*): 'delight conceived in the soul must arise from the beauty and harmony it sees or contemplates in the things that the eyes or the imagination place before it, and nothing that possesses ugliness and disorder can please us,' 412) (el deleite que en el alma se concibe ha de ser de la hermosura y concordancia que vee o contempla en las cosas que la vista o la imaginación le ponen delante; y toda cosa que tiene en sí fealdad y descompostura no nos puede causar contento alguno; I, 47, pp. 564–5). The soul sees not just literally but through an imaginative eye as well.

The Canon nonetheless understands that pleasure is political because it is associated with the opinion of the masses, who needed either to be acknowledged or controlled for the economic power of the choices they make. There seems little doubt that the Canon's reference to the 'confused judgment of the presumptuous mob' (415) (el confuso juicio del desvanecido vulgo; I, 48, p. 568) is to be understood as a response to the emergence of this new class of literary consumers in early modern Spain and their tastes.[54] While any mention of the general public, the *vulgo*, was bound to conjure up the ordinary theatergoers who made the Lopean *comedia* so successful, and of which Cervantes was notoriously jealous, we do well to recall that the Canon's speech was written several years before Lope published his defence of this practice in the *Arte nuevo de hacer comedias* (1609). Moreover, when the Canon condemns the 'presumptuous mob' (desvanecido vulgo) and when the Priest subsequently describes the *comedias* as responding to the tastes of the *vulgo*, they also echo Socrates' objection to the way in which poets appeal to the demands of the 'ignorant multitude' (*Republic*, 602b). These are among some of the oldest demophobic ideas in the Western tradition, in which the suspicious pleasures and the uneducated opinions of the masses are often related.[55] Plato himself recognizes that poetry has long had a reputation as having been produced by 'the crowd of heads that knows too much' in *Republic*, 607c. The Priest's idea of a state censor would go a long way toward controlling the *vulgo*, but Cervantes fully recognizes that it is yet another transposition of views about pleasure and politics that root in the *Republic*. The Canon's censor would promote only those forms of literature that would allow for the beneficial use of leisure time (in contrast, say, to the idleness of the reader to whom *Don Quijote* is addressed); he envisions literature as providing 'virtuous entertainment, not only to the idle but to those who are most occupied' (418) (para honesto pasatiempo, no solamente de los ociosos, sino de los más ocupados; I, 48, p. 572).[56] And yet the Priest's extreme reaction also blurs the distinction between the 'desocupado lector' (idle reader) and the alert, attentive, initiated reader whose intelligence is required in order to interpret it. In his ideal world, all readers would be consigned to the relatively bland delights of 'honest recreation' (honesto pasatiempo).

All of what the Canon says about literature, the 'republic,' and the principle of verisimilitude exposes us to threads of a much larger and more intricate set of questions about literature and politics. His reasoning is not foreign to the arguments that Hobbes later makes in *Leviathan* against taking what amount to 'absurd speeches' 'upon credit ... from deceived Philosophers, and deceived, or deceiving Schoolmen.'[57] Hobbes recommends not relying on books for anything at all, remarking that 'they that trusting onley to the authority of books, follow the blind blindly' (*Leviathan*, I, ch. 5, p. 117). As for the Canon's role as a 'reliable spokesman' for Cervantes' views, the case seems clear: the Canon's attempt to guard the state against the 'unhealthy' influence of certain books is scarcely adequate as a formulation of Cervantes' engagement of the relationship between literature and politics, much less as the basis of a political theory. As we will see in chapters to follow, the limitations of the Canon's critical powers are brought strikingly to light in reference to the episode on Clavileño and Don Quijote's descent into the Cave of Montesinos. The question in these episodes is not to determine whether imagined things can be aligned with the laws of nature or with conditions of reasonable probability, but rather to show that there may be something more at stake politically in imaginative literature than standards of verisimilitude can discern. The desire to regulate these sham fantasies suggests an adherence to the real that serves, in the end, to ignore the force of the imagination in the formation of political communities – those that exist now and those that might be created. (I will discuss the special allure of the real, in connection with Cervantes' response to imagined communities, in chapter 7 below.) But to explore those questions further we need a wider analytical frame, one that can encompass both the explicitly 'political' parts of the book, such as Don Quijote's advice to Sancho on governance and Sancho's own experiences as governor of the sham 'island' called Barataria, and those parts of the book that are not explicitly political at all, but which nonetheless have to do with such things as community, society, the economy, history, and practice. The major speeches and interpolated narratives that engage these topics are Cervantes' way of carrying forward a tradition of literary-political discourse that descends just as much from the genres of fable and myth as from treatises on literature or political tracts. In proceeding, we must attend both to what Cervantes says throughout the course of the book as well as to the things that he chooses for political reasons to say indirectly or not at all.[58]

3 Views from Nowhere

Of all the discussions of politics that are taken up in *Don Quijote* the most intriguing of all may be one in which the reader never knows exactly what is said. At the very beginning of Part II, when Don Quijote is safely back at home recuperating, the narrator explains that he converses at length with the Priest and the Barber about matters of political theory and practice. Their conversations seem to span a wide range of topics, from broad-gauged political theory to the discussion of contemporary national problems and speculation about how present-day Spain might be transformed into an ideal republic. Their discussions revolve around what the narrator calls questions of government and of 'razón de estado,' which is sometimes translated as 'matters of state' but which has the force of describing the 'interests of the state' as informed by contemporary ideas about 'reason of state.' The phrase was drawn from the title of Giovanni Botero's 1589 work, and was closely aligned with matters of practical politics; for conservative Spanish writers such as Rivadeneira it clearly suggests the worrisome abandonment of political ideals in favour of a more calculating and pragmatic political science.[1] And yet the term that was associated with Plato and Cicero – 'la república' – and with more noble, humanist ideas about politics is never far away in what Cervantes writes. Indeed, the three interlocutors in this off-stage dialogue are said to generate a wholly new image of 'la república' in the course of their conversations. They are reformist thinkers:

> in the course of their conversation they began to discuss what is called reason of state and ways of governing, correcting this abuse and condemning that one, reforming one custom and eliminating another, each one of the three becoming a new legislator, a modern Lycurgus, a latter-day Solon, and they

so transformed the nation that it seemed as if they had placed it in the forge and taken out a new one, and Don Quijote spoke with so much intelligence regarding all the subjects they touched upon that his two examiners thought there was no doubt that he was completely well and his sanity restored. (459–60)

en el discurso de su plática vinieron a tratar en esto que llaman razón de estado y modos de gobierno, enmendando este abuso y condenando aquel, reformando una costumbre y desterrando otra, haciéndose cada uno de los tres un nuevo legislador, un Licurgo moderno, o un Solón flamante; y de tal manera renovaron la república, que no pareció sino que la habían puesto en una fragua, y sacado otra que la pusieron; y habló don Quijote con tanta discreción en todas las materias que se tocaron, que los dos esaminadores creyeron indubitablemente que estaba del todo bueno y en su entero juicio. (II, I, p. 42)

Given its position at the very opening of Part II, this passage reminds us that the quixotic project to restore knight-errantry is, in fact, the comic transposition of an underlying political project that has both theoretical and practical dimensions. Indeed, Cervantes repeats the reference from this passage to the legendary Lacedaemonian legislator Lycurgus much later, in chapter 50 of Part II, when the Duke's *mayordomo* praises Sancho for the wisdom of his judgments on Barataria: 'In my opinion Lycurgus himself, who gave his laws to the Lacedaemonians, could not have made a better judgment than the one the great Panza has given' (792) (Tengo para mí que el mismo Licurgo, que dio leyes a los lacedemonios, no pudiera dar mejor sentencia que el gran Panza ha dado; II, 51, p. 427).[2] Indeed, it is during the course of his governance of the sham 'island' Barataria that Sancho comes to resemble just the kind of 'new legislator' (nuevo legislador) that the narrator refers to in the passage cited above.

As for the allusion to the 'new republic,' it is altogether possible that Cervantes also had the influential *Diálogo de Lactancio y el arcediano* (*Dialogue between Lactancio and the Archdeacon*) of Alonso de Valdés in mind.[3] It is, of course, impossible to trace these lines definitively, and there was no shortage of ideas about political reform throughout the sixteenth and seventeenth centuries,[4] but Valdés was important. His concern was with the possibility of establishing radically 'new' political arrangements, including those that might best be imagined as restoring the mythical Golden Age. His underlying hope was that a radically reformed republic would give rise to a generation of new men, thus realizing an ethical vision that has roots in St Paul's exhortation to 'put on the new man created according to God in justice of holiness and truth' in the epistle to the Ephesians (induite novum hominem qui secundum Deum creatus est in iustitia et sanctitate).[5] But Don Quijote is himself already a version of the *hombre nuevo* – albeit shaped according to models from the past – who has completely refashioned himself according to noble ideals. The real trouble is that he has no new world to accompany him.[6] On the contrary, the contemporary world seems to be in a state of decline. As we shall see, this is one reason why the subject of the Golden Age comes to serve as an imaginary blueprint for his thinking about the possibility of a radically reformed political state. It is, of course, the outline of an impossible world, and yet it serves to establish a hypothetical standpoint from which to survey and critique the deficient social relations that any truly reformed republic would have to correct. It is, moreover, one of the first instances in which we come to understand that something politically quite important lies concealed underneath the cloak of Don Quijote's madness.

The figure we hear about at the opening of Part II, who discourses fluently about politics, is presented as remarkably cogent in what he says about matters having to do with the state ('habló don Quijote con tanta discreción'). He scarcely resembles the enthusiastic character we see at the beginning of Part I, who reads avidly in fiction but who is so disengaged from the public world that he forgets even to tend to his own estate. And yet the mental equilibrium that permits Don Quijote to converse wisely about politics with the Priest and the Barber seems be relatively short-lived. He does not remain 'normalized' for very long. As soon as the Barber decides to test Don Quijote's mental stability by mentioning rumours of a possible attack by the Turks, Don Quijote is catapulted into his quixotic 'madness.' (The allusion to a threat against national security is yet another element from the opening chapter of Part II that is repeated later on, when Sancho learns that his 'island,' Barataria, has come under attack by unidentified enemies.) Don Quijote's response to the Barber is to recommend a coordinated response of all the knights errant in Spain. This makes a mockery of his potential for any real engagement with practical politics; indeed, it places his political proposals on a par with the most far-fetched solutions proposed by the contemporary *arbitristas*, to whom he here makes direct allusion: 'Well [my scheme] ... is neither impossible nor absurd, but is, rather, the easiest, most just, most practical, and shrewdest that has ever occurred to any planner' (460–1) (Pues el [advertimiento] mío … ni es imposible ni disparatado, sino el más facil, el más justo y el más mañero y breve que puede caber en pensamiento de arbitrante alguno; II, 1, p. 43). He goes on to outline his plan for national defence in detailed terms:

> What else can His Majesty do but command by public proclamation that on a specific day all the knights errant wandering through Spain are to gather at court, and even if no more than half a dozen were to come, there might be one among them who could, by himself, destroy all the power of the Turk … Is it by any chance surprising for a single knight errant to vanquish an army of two hundred thousand men, as if all of them had but one throat or were made of sugar candy? Tell me, then: how many histories are filled with such marvels? (461)

> ¿Hay más sino mandar su Majestad por público pregón que se junten en la corte para un día señalado todos los caballeros que vagan por España, que aunque no viniesen sino media docena, tal podría venir entre ellos, que solo bastase a destruir toda la potestad del Turco? … ¿Es cosa nueva deshacer un solo caballero andante un ejército de docientos mil hombres, como si todos juntos tuvieran una sola garganta, o fueran hechos de alfenique? Si no díganme: ¿cuántas historias están llenas destas maravillas? (II, 1, p. 44)

The allusion to 'el Turco' serves to remind the reader that questions of politics in the *Quijote* are, in fact, inseparable from questions of contemporary history, and that the period between the fall of Granada in 1492 and the official expulsions of the *moriscos* in the years leading up to 1609 involved a number of internal political crises of which Cervantes was well aware. Any engagement with the question of politics in Cervantes' Spain is likewise inseparable from the complex social and religious problems that arose following the expulsion of the Jews in 1492. The episodes of the Captive and Zoraida in Part I and of Ricote and Ana Félix in Part II are among the most obvious examples of Cervantes' engagement with those issues and, as mentioned in chapter 1 above, in ways that contravene the principles of verisimilitude set forth by the Canon of Toledo.

But everything we hear from Don Quijote about politics, contemporary or otherwise, theoretical or practical, sane or deluded, in both Part I and Part II, must be understood as spoken under the aegis of a peculiar kind of madness. His mythical speech on the Golden Age is one such example. This does not mean that his words are to be discounted as insane. But we do need to bear in mind that the 'madman' offers us indirect and oblique sources of insight, and not the articulation of anything to be taken in a straightforward or conventional way, either as political theory or as commentary on contemporary events. Moreover, *Don Quijote* as a novel presents itself as a discursive space in which anything spoken seriously is refracted in a comic prism; likewise, it is a space where things that appear entirely comic invariably have serious implications. To cloak wisdom under the veils of fiction and folly was hardly anything new. It was a practice that Cervantes had inherited from his humanist predecessors Erasmus and More, who likewise thought it necessary to place the words of wisdom in unlikely places, including in the mouths of fools. What the reader requires in all such cases are the tools by which to interpret 'foolish' political wisdom. Some of those tools are historical, as I will discuss in connection with the project of nation-building in chapter 7, but some are interpretive and theoretical, and therefore undemonstrable by historical examples alone. To see Don Quijote as the last man who accepts the idealism of the past and hopes to revive it requires a particular historical insight, to be sure; but to recognize that he is not simply a fool, and that the world has become full of greater fools than he, requires a form of intelligence that history itself may not provide. We need to see that he offers not mere folly but something transcendentally comic.

Several of Don Quijote's longer speeches in Part I offer just this form of insight. They are clearly moments in which the 'madman' has something wise to say. Indeed, nearly all of Don Quijote's extended speeches in Part I – the discourse on the mythic Golden Age and the disquisition on Arms and Letters above all – provide a framing for political questions that aspire to some general level of insight. And yet they stop short of articulating a political theory in any conventional sense and have no intention of addressing practical political matters at all. (The same is true of the episode on Clavileño in Part II, although there it is the question of vision, rather than of speech, that is at stake, as far as the possibility of 'theory' is concerned.)[7] And yet the speeches in Part I do not conform to any of the contemporary debates about political principles. They do not, for instance, consider the differences between monarchies and republics, or whether Christian legal principles should apply to indigenous populations in newly discovered lands, or whether a just war can be waged against religious enemies. They draw instead on the discourse of myth and on the procedures of rhetorical argumentation as ways of exploring questions that were thought to lie at the foundation of all politics. They are reflective of ancient considerations of what is the best life – whether political or otherwise: whether a life of philosophical contemplation or a life of action; whether a life lived self-sufficiently and autonomously, or a life lived in association with others (and if so, in what arrangement); whether a life devoted to pleasure, or a life that strives to insulate itself against accidents, misfortune, and the experience of loss. They, in turn, lead to questions about who should govern in the state, and about how one ought to prepare for such a role. And they are questions about the qualities necessary for acting justly in instances of practical concern. In the process of reflection on such classical political questions, Cervantes also explores a series of more substantive issues that are necessary for an understanding of political life – issues concerning hierarchy and community, the distribution of goods and property, and the prospects for implementing political reform guided by a sense of what the polis ought to be. The speeches in Part I can thus be understood as preparation for some of the more explicitly political situations we see in various episodes in Part II. Equally, the political episodes of Part II serve to test some of the more 'abstract' considerations broached in Part I so as to bring politics back down to earth. As I will explain in a later chapter, once Sancho leaves the governorship of Barataria, this process of testing gives way to an inquiry into the limits of politics overall.

Arching over these considerations lies a set of questions about the relationship between discourse and politics. But instead of asking directly about the limits of fiction and about what kind of literature ought to be allowed in the state, as the Canon does, the issue raised by the speech on the Golden Age has to do with the relationship between myth and truth. What would be the reasons for thinking that a speech built around a mythical idea could be associated with politics at all? A preliminary answer is that the speech Don Quijote makes to the goatherds is supremely rhetorical in nature and that Cervantes was keenly aware of the inseparability of rhetoric and politics. In sustaining the association between rhetoric and good governance Cervantes hewed closely to the example of the civic humanists of the Italian Renaissance, and before them of Cicero, who recognized that rhetoric was essential for forging the link between theoretical intelligence and practical wisdom: 'There is to my mind no more excellent thing than the power, by means of oratory, to get hold on [sic] assemblies of men, win their good will, direct their inclinations wherever the speaker wishes, or divert them from whatever he wishes. In every free nation, and most of all in communities which have attained the enjoyment of peace and tranquility, this one art has always flourished above the rest and ever reigned supreme ... The wise control of the complete orator is that which chiefly upholds not only his own dignity but the safety of countless individuals and of the entire state.'[8] We can surmise that Cervantes was well trained in rhetoric. Don Quijote's deft use of argumentation *in utramque partem* in the discourse on Arms and Letters makes this clear, as does his emphatic use of vivid description (*enargeia*) in his description of the flocks of sheep in I, 18.[9] When Don Quijote speaks about Dulcinea to the Duke in II, 32, his rhetorical powers are compared to those of Cicero and Demosthenes; throughout the book he demonstrates an ability to speak copiously on virtually any topic of his choosing. Even the topic of the 'defence of the realm' alluded to above reflects a rhetorical lineage, in this case deriving from Aristotle's *Rhetoric*, where the section on deliberation (I. 3) elaborates at length on this very subject.

But rhetoric is not a matter of mere technical verbal skill. Don Quijote himself speaks of the need to bind compelling speech together with action. Humanists took these to be the coequal elements of a civic ideal. Vives, for one, argued that they stood together at the root of all societies: 'All human societies are linked together and kept within their bounds by two things in particular,' Vives wrote, 'justice and speech, and if either one is missing, it would be difficult for any group or any society, whether public or private, to endure for very long.'[10] Thus it is not surprising to find that beyond their rhetorical nature – and recognizing that they are, in the end, addressed to quite meagre audiences – Don Quijote's speeches take up matters that are basic to any general consideration of politics; they suggest themselves as alternative versions of what political theorizing might be.

The speech on the Golden Age – the first of Don Quijote's two long speeches in Part I – is crucial in this regard. It outlines the imaginary, which in this case is also to say *impossible*, conditions from which to consider the political world as it is against the light of a world without politics at all. It offers a mythical vision of a perfect world, a fiction, which in turn brings into focus the questions around which contemporary politics is formed. It offers a view of social relations from a standpoint that would seem to render politics as we know it irrelevant. Conditions such as the inequality of power and wealth, the scarcity of material goods, the interest in private property, etc., are all absent from the Golden Age. More to the point, the Golden Age defines itself as the condition of their absence. Indeed, Don Quijote's speech takes up a series of issues that are not so much political as prepolitical. It proposes a vision of the world from outside the historical conditions that make politics necessary. The speech is not only the re-articulation of a myth, or, as has also been argued, the projection of a utopian vision that serves as a counter-image to society as it stands,[11] but the construction in language of an impossible, imaginary stance from which a vision of political society might in turn be articulated. Unlike the discourse of *The Prince*, in which Machiavelli proposes to tell the truth about politics directly, and from a ground-level stance, here we have a view as if from nowhere. The idea of a Golden Age offers something very much like a myth, which in its serious forms could be regarded as offering a non-scientific but nonetheless truthful account of things we might not otherwise be able to comprehend.[12] In spite of the fact that it is placed in the mouth of a fool, it is a myth that aims at the truth because it proposes to imagine the 'in-principle' conditions from which to see politics and see it as it ought to be. It does so by systematically negating the world as it is. The speech on the Golden Age is thus the counterpart to the vision of the wholly 'transformed republic' that Don Quijote mentions to the Priest and the Barber in the conversation that is described in chapter 1 of Part II. But, as I will discuss below, the problem of relating this mythical form of political imagination to the requirements of practice, which are indeed historical and need to reflect the world as it is, even in its imperfections, remains woefully unsolved. It leaves out the thought that 'theory' might itself need to be informed by practical matters.

And yet, there is more than a local purpose to Don Quijote's engagement with the discourse about the Golden Age, and it has to do with the relationship between myth and the political questions that run throughout the *Quijote*. The discourse of myth provides Don Quijote with a way of speaking 'generally' while not speaking wholly in the abstract. As a myth, the vision of the Golden Age stands in relation to theory as a kind of story that carries a potent conceptual force, but which cannot be bound historically. (There is, in fact, an important parallel to Don Quijote's speech in Plato's *Statesman*, where Plato draws quite consciously on myth in attempting to arrive at a 'complete description' of the ideal statesman.)[13] As Hans Blumenberg noted, the Greek understanding of what it meant to tell a myth (*mythos mythesthai*) meant telling a story that is not dated and not datable 'so that it cannot be localized in any chronicle, but a story that compensates for this lack by being "significant" in itself.'[14] Myths have what Blumenberg described as an iconic consistency; they provide a way of anchoring explanations of things that might otherwise go without any explanation at all. They have what might be described as the explanatory power of a speculative history that can serve as an alternative to philosophical accounts.

Indeed, part of what Cervantes shows is that the idea of a stark contrast between *mythos* and *logos* is overdrawn. Indeed, when Plato himself speaks of myth in the *Protagoras* it is in the context of an account that could take either a narrative or an analytical form.[15] In that dialogue, Protagoras asks whether he should frame his views about how virtue may be taught 'in the form of a story or as a reasoned argument.' The listeners on hand respond that he should simply choose 'whichever form he pleased.'[16] Does this mean that they are not able to see a difference between the two, or that there is no difference to be seen? In the end, Protagoras offers both: first a story that incorporates the myths of Prometheus and Epimetheus, and then an argument about the teachability of the virtues.

As I will discuss in connection with the episode on Clavileño, the discourse of myth is not quite the same as the discourse of theory, even if they may serve related purposes. Indeed, their discursive differences amount to more than what Protagoras might admit. Theory is non-narrative, and myth does not pretend to offer the kind of analytical perspective that underpins theory. Nor are the discourses of narrative and analysis the same thing in terms of their wider ambitions. As I will discuss in a later chapter, what came to be regarded as *theoria* separated itself from the richly endowed, story-like explanations of myth in the hope of establishing a vision that could be systematic and general. Theory seems intent on reducing the 'surplus of meaning' that seems part and parcel of myths, which tend to say more than they may consciously know.[17] While the conventional wisdom is that myth was superseded by theory, it would be overhasty to conclude that Cervantes has Don Quijote take up the topic of the Golden Age in order to demonstrate how a naive and 'false' way of viewing the world had been eclipsed by something with better access to the truth. Quite the contrary. It would seem that the self-conscious use of myth such as we find in the discourse on the Golden Age can provide an opportunity to reflect on the purpose that theory might serve, including its relation to practice.

The fundamental distinctions between *mythos*, *theoria*, and along with these *historia*, are reflected in what Renaissance thinkers took to be the basic differences between Plato and Aristotle, both in terms of the way they write and in terms of what they teach. In the case of Plato, the language of myth is crucial to the reflective insight that to acquire true knowledge often involves a real or imaginary journey, to far-off places or to other times. Plato regards myth as an indispensable complement to theoretical activity – indispensable because theory cannot in itself provide a complete account of the whole. Aristotle's abandonment of the language of myth in favour of analytical discourse was, by contrast, consistent with his abandonment of Plato's dramatic and literary philosophical procedures and, in turn, with his far greater confidence in the ability of *theoria* to grasp the truth. His works present themselves as complete and consistent accounts of whatever body of material might be under consideration. Aristotle's account of *theoria* was, moreover, considerably more technical than Plato's, and his practice considerably more systematic.

And yet there was a remarkable desire among many Renaissance writers to recuperate Aristotle for the tradition of *rhetorical* thinking, especially through the use of invention and by reliance on the topics in the process of argumentation. The rhetorical uses of Aristotle included the *Nicomachean Ethics* and the *Politics* as much as the *Rhetoric*, and stood in sharp contrast to the scholastic appropriations of Aristotelian metaphysics. As Ernesto Grassi noted, the Renaissance rehabilitation of Aristotle had to overcome a long history in which rhetoric and poetry were regarded as disconnected from knowledge of the fundamental nature of things.[18] (The medieval tradition had tended to regard rhetoric as non-scientific, and offered Aristotle as an authority in the matter. Duns Scotus, for instance, said that he would give no account of grammar and rhetoric because 'they do not appear to have to do with the nature of things, but rather with the law of the human voice, which according to the view of Aristotle and his followers deal not with nature but with the habits of speech, or with particular objects and persons, which is far removed from the nature of things.')[19]

The larger backdrop against which Cervantes redirects our attention to myth was also one in which politics was coming under increasing pressure to conceive of itself as a science, to adhere to new, experience-based standards of truth, and so to jettison the discourse of myth in favour of the development of more reliable and systematic languages for itself. As already noted, these efforts culminated elsewhere in Europe, most notably in the work of Hobbes, who was among the first to treat politics as a science. But some of the groundwork for these developments, which required a careful analysis of truths about human nature and attention to experience, had been laid by some of Cervantes' contemporaries. In *El consejo y consejeros del príncipe*, for instance, Fadrique Furió Ceriol insists on the importance of experience as a complement to theoretical learning. While Furió Ceriol may be no Machiavelli, he nonetheless contributed to the formation of a new discursive position with respect to the things that matter most for politics: not only the polis as it might be but, of equal importance, attention to experience as it is.

Don Quijote's speech on the Golden Age is prompted by the mere accident of a few acorns. But this is a highly pregnant, literary, and historical 'accident,' not just a material prompt. It signals the thematic adjacency between the myth of the Golden Age and the literary topos of the pastoral world.[20] As has often been said, the pastoral vision tends to flourish as the product of urban societies; its idyllic landscapes and its languorous swains draw attention to the fact that the polis is in fact formed around effortful work and is associated with organized city life. Indeed, the theoretical conception of the polis was seen since at least Plato to depend upon the organized differentiation of labour. Moreover, Cervantes plainly understood the pastoral as a mask, and he knew enough from his predecessors in this genre that the world of literary shepherds and shepherdesses was hardly a place of untroubled human happiness. As the episode of Grisóstomo's funeral procession (I, 12–14) makes perfectly clear, and as Cervantes' repeated invocations of Garcilaso's mournful poetry suggest, the pastoral landscape was often tinged with human loss.

At the same time, the topos of the Golden Age is closely linked to the contradictory idea of a mythical history of mankind, in which the deficiencies of the present age are set in contrast to the imagined perfections of an 'original' moment outside of historical time. The literary sources of Don Quijote's vision of the Golden Age, long well-known, support these associations. They include contemporary Spanish writings (Juan de Mal Lara's *Filosofía vulgar*, Antonio de Guevara's *Relox de príncipes* and *Menosprecio de corte y alabanza de aldea*) as well as classical texts, among which count Seneca's *Moral Epistles*, Cicero's *On Invention*, Hesiod's *Works and Days*, and of course Ovid's *Metamorphoses* (I, 89–112), which was popular enough to have been translated into Spanish twice in the late 1500s (by Pedro Sánchez de Viana in 1589 and again by Jorge de Bustamante in 1595). The following sections of Ovid's text, an anchor for the Renaissance tradition, stand at the core of Don Quijote's speech:

> In the beginning was the Golden Age, when men of their own accord, without threat of punishment, without laws, maintained good faith and did what was right. There were no penalties to be afraid of, no bronze tablets were erected, carrying threats of legal action, no crown of wrong-doers, anxious for mercy, trembled before the face of the judge; indeed, there were no judges, men lived securely without them. Never yet had any pine tree, cut down from its home in the mountains, been launched on ocean's wave, to visit foreign lands: men knew only their own shores ... The peoples of the world, untroubled by any fears, enjoyed a leisurely and peaceful existence, and had

no use for soldiers. The earth itself, without compulsion, untouched by the hoe, unfurrowed by any share, produced all things spontaneously, and men were content with the foods that grew without cultivation ... It was a season of everlasting spring, when peaceful zephyrs, with their warm breath, caressed the flowers that sprang up without having been planted.[21]

Some of what is impressive about Cervantes' use of his many varied sources is his incorporation of very minor details, such as the acorns, which are explicitly mentioned both in Hesiod and in the *Metamorphoses* (I, 106). Ovidian inspirations notwithstanding, Don Quijote's recourse to the discourse of myth does not entirely drive out history. It seems that nothing in the *Quijote* ever can or does. When, for instance, Don Quijote takes the abundance of the oak as an example of liberal generosity – a form of natural *liberalidad* – Cervantes is also responding to the sixteenth-century practice of selling off great stands of oak trees that had formerly been held as communal property. As Noël Salomon noted, the practice was eventually opposed by the Spanish Cortes.[22]

The myth of the Golden Age belongs to a special subclass of myths: it is a species of origin myth in that it gives an account of how things were at the very beginning, at a time before time. Cervantes' interest in origin myths makes a very pointed reappearance in the chapters of Part II that precede Sancho's ascent to the governorship of Barataria, and I will have more to say about them in the context of Don Quijote's and Sancho's discussions with the Humanist Cousin.[23] As with many origin myths, the discourse on the Golden Age can either explain the way things are or can conceal ideological ends by masking the conflicts of power and interest that shape present possibilities. It can serve speculative, quasi-theoretical ends by proposing to explain the beginnings of things that nobody has ever pretended to witness – as a hypothesis – or it can conceal whatever ulterior motives may be at work in such accounts. With myth no less than with any other type of fable, or any discourse built of images, those explanations are valid only insofar as one recognizes that the meaning of myth is never literally true. But myth offers a grounding insight into the truth, and the discourse on the Golden Age is an early instance in which Cervantes recognizes that fiction is a discursive condition of the truth.

As a 'mythic' construction, Don Quijote's vision of the Golden Age is unusual in that it is built principally by a process of subtraction. It is fashioned by removing every problematical relationship and every controversial force from the world. It is akin to the construction of a 'theoretical' stance by means of the systematic negation of the very conditions that shape the polis in the realm of practice. The analytical perspective it offers is achieved by a process of speculative negation ('what if we were to take away selfishness, private property, the need for work, etc.'). It is 'speculative' not so much because it is the product of an intellectual musing but because it aims at the construction of a world from a hypothetical stance. This is one of the forms in which Cervantes asks Plato's question about what the just city ought to include and, just as in Plato, it turns out that the most 'appealing' city may not be the most just. In fact, the most appealing city may well turn out to be what Plato characterizes as a city fit for pigs (*Republic*, 372d). Moreover, the myth of the Golden Age proves inadequate as a political ideal because it negates the world for more than just 'theoretical' reasons. Indeed, Cervantes seems to have some sympathy for Cicero's view that there could be nothing more baneful than the equal distribution of property.[24] It is, rather, an ideal that depends upon the negation of the wide range of endeavours that are associated with practice. For this reason, Cervantes repeatedly corrects and revises the myth of the Golden Age over the course of subsequent chapters. Indeed, Don Quijote's vision of the Golden Age will be tested numerous times throughout the novel, and its negation of existing conditions will in turn be negated by examples drawn from the lives of various fictional characters who cannot fit themselves within the Arcadian world that seems to be its closest counterpart.

In Part I, for instance, the discourse on the Golden Age is implicitly tested and tried as various characters attempt to orient their lives around the pastoral dream. One of the most striking of these is Marcela, whose radical assertion of autonomy also represents a refusal of the basic condition of politics, i.e., community with others. Not surprisingly, the myth of Narcissus plays a significant role in Cervantes' account of Marcela.[25] But so, too, the scene at Camacho's wedding in Part II (ch. 20) represents an instantiation of the Golden Age among the nascent bourgeoisie, where Sancho gazes upon gargantuan culinary delights – a steer on a roasting spit, innumerable hares and plenty of chickens, 'infinite' gamebirds, a wall built entirely of cheeses, and more than sixty wineskins filled to nearly bursting – for which no labour or effort on his part are required:

> The first thing that appeared before Sancho's eyes was an entire steer on a roasting spit made of an entire elm; and in the fire where it was to roast, a fair-size mountain of wood was burning, and six pots that were placed around the fire were not made in the common mold of other pots, because these were six huge cauldrons, each one large enough to hold the contents of an entire slaughterhouse: they contained and enclosed entire sheep, which sank out of

view as if they were doves; the hares without their skins and the chickens without their feathers that were hanging from the trees, waiting to be buried in the cauldrons, were without number; the various fowl and game hanging from the trees to cool in the breeze were infinite.

Sancho counted more than sixty wineskins, each one holding more than two *arrobas*, and all of them filled, as was subsequently proven, with excellent wines; there were also mounds of snowy white loaves of bread, heaped up like piles of wheat on the threshing floor; cheeses, crisscrossed like bricks, formed a wall; and two kettles of oil larger than a dyer's vats were used to fry rounds of dough, which were then removed with two strong paddles and plunged into another kettle filled with honey that stood nearby ...

Twelve small, tender suckling pigs were sewn into the belly of the steer to give it flavor and make it tender. The various spices seemed to have been bought not by the pound but by the *arroba*, and all of them were clearly visible in a large chest. (584–5)

Lo primero que se le ofreció a la vista de Sancho fue, espetado en un asador de un olmo entero, un entero novillo; y en el fuego donde se había de asar ardía un mediano monte de leña, y seis ollas que alrededor de la hoguera estaban no se habían hecho en la común turquesa de las demás ollas, porque eran seis medias tinajas, que cada una cabía un rastro de carne: así embebían y encerraban en sí carneros enteros, sin echarse de ver, como si fueran palominos; las liebres ya sin pellejo y las gallinas sin pluma que estaban colgadas por los árboles para sepultarlas en las ollas no tenían número; los pájaros y caza de diversos géneros eran infinitos, colgados de los árboles para que el aire los enfriase.

Contó Sancho más de sesenta zaques de más de a dos arrobas cada uno, y todos llenos, según después pareció, de generosos vinos; así había rimeros de pan blanquísimo, como los suele haber de montones de trigo en las eras; los quesos, puestos como ladrillos enrejados, formaban una muralla, y dos calderas de aceite, mayores que las de un tinte, servían de freír cosas de masa, que con dos valientes palas las sacaban fritas y las zabullían en otra caldera de preparada miel que allí junto estaba ...

En el dilatado vientre del novillo estaban doce tiernos y pequeños lechones, que, cosidos por encima, servían de darle sabor y enternecerle. Las especias de diversas suertes no parecía haberlas comprado por libras, sino por arrobas, y todas estaban de manifiesto en una grande arca. (II, 20, pp. 187–8)

It has been suggested that this Cockaigne-like scene in fact helps lead Sancho to believe in the possibility of a 'people's utopia' when he comes to be given the governorship of Barataria.[26] But the abundance at Camacho's wedding is hardly just natural. It is hyperbolic, if not in fact unnatural. It is copious in excess. Cervantes may have been aware of Cicero's esteem of agriculture as the most desirable form of free labour (as Cicero says of profit-making activities in *De officiis*, 'none is better, more fruitful, more enjoyable, more worthy of a man than agriculture'),[27] but Camacho enjoys the fruits of the earth because he has the money to buy whatever he wants.[28]

The social vision implicit in the myth of the Golden Age will be further tested by the political fiction of Barataria, where Sancho is asked to rule amidst luxury while deprived of enjoyment, and not merely to rule but also to defend his island 'realm.' As far as Don Quijote is concerned, however, the principal attraction of the Golden Age lies in everything that it does not include. He does not understand his speech as a form of political discourse, but rather takes it as a dream-like vision of history. In this, Cervantes no doubt has something to suggest about the propensity to regard certain forms of theory as if they were dreams. And yet, Don Quijote's attraction to this vision allows Cervantes the opportunity to explore the preconditions of politics, free from prior assumptions, and exempt from the pre-existing conditions that impinge on the historical world. Indeed, the vision of the Golden Age is akin to what later political philosophers would come to call the 'state of nature.' The 'state of nature' can incorporate wholly 'natural' republics, such as the community of the bees that Don Quijote glancingly mentions in chapter 11, perhaps with Alonso de Castrillo again in mind: 'In the fissures of rocks and in the hollows of trees diligent and clever bees established their colonies, freely offering to any hand the fertile fruit of their sweet labor' (p. 76) (En las quiebras de las peñas y en lo hueco de los árboles formaban su república las solícitas abejas, ofreciendo a cualquiera mano, sin interés alguno, la fertile cosecha de su dulcísimo trabajo; I, 11, pp. 155–6).[29] Castrillo in fact offers a gloss on Virgil that highlights the intelligence and orderliness of the hierarchy of the bees, suggesting that it is a model for the relations between rulers and citizens.[30] The topic was, in fact, an ancient one made famous by Aristotle, and later noted by Hobbes in tracing the beginnings of civil government.[31]

But even with the bees Don Quijote characterizes the state of nature in terms of the vices it lacks. The bees, for instance, exemplify a form of generosity that is enabled by their lack of interest ('the clever bees established their colonies, freely offering to any hand the fertile harvest of their sweet labor' [76]) (formaban su república las solícitas y discretas abejas, ofreciendo a cualquiera mano, sin interés alguno, la fértil cosecha de su dulcísimo trabajo; I, 11, p. 155). The state of nature is imagined as free from possessions and, by extension, free from the language of possessiveness ('those who lived in that time did not know the two words *thine* and *mine*' [76]) (los que en ella vivían ignoraban estas dos palabras de tuyo y mío; I, 11, p. 155). Hobbes later echoes such ideas in a modern register in the first part of the *Elements of Law* in saying that 'every man hath by nature right to all things,' and that it is a situation in which *meum* and *tuum* have 'no place.'[32] (Hobbes's perspective is particularly modern insofar as this is for him equally a matter of the *names* 'mine' and 'thine.') The *Leviathan*'s image of the state of nature is, however, not nearly so positive:

> In such condition, there is no place for industry; because the fruit thereof is uncertain: and consequently no culture of the earth; no navigation, nor use of the commodities that may be imported by sea; no commodious building; no instruments of moving, and removing such things as require much force; no knowledge of the face of the earth; no account of time; no arts; no letters; no society; and which is worst of all, continual fear, and danger of violent death; and the life of man, solitary, poor, nasty, brutish, and short.[33]

By contrast, the Golden Age is marked by the absence of fraud, deceit, and malice (*Don Quijote*, I, 11, p. 156), by the freedom from the imposition of arbitrary laws ('la ley del encaje'), and by the social harmony that these absences allow ('all was peace, friendship, and harmony'; todo era paz, amistad, concordia). Likewise, the underpinnings of social harmony lie in the absence of labour and of everything that labour is imagined to entail. Echoing a passage in the *Republic* (414–15), Plato's *Statesman* describes the time when men lived under the mythical government of Kronos as the moment when all were implicitly brothers because they were children of the earth. The Stranger speaks to Socarates,

> As for your enquiry concerning the age when all good things come without · man's labor, the answer is that this also most certainly belongs to the former era, not to the present one. In that era ... savagery was nowhere to be found nor preying of creature on creature, nor did war rage nor any strife whatsoever ... there were no political constitutions and no taking of wives and begetting of children. For all men arose up anew into life out of the earth ... They had fruits without stint from trees and bushes; these needed no cultivation but sprang up of themselves out of the ground without man's toil. For the most part they disported themselves in the open needing neither clothing nor couch, for the seasons were blended evenly so as to work them no hurt, and the grass which sprang up out of the earth made a soft bed for them. This is the story, Socrates, of the life of men under the government of Kronos. (271c–2b)

Politics is necessary, according to the *Statesman*, because men now live under the government of Zeus.

The notion of a universal brotherhood among all men as 'children of the earth' provides one set of supports for the idea of a 'naturalized' political union, specifically for the idea of a *nation*. In Don Quijote's rather more tendentious language, the earth is mother, not father, and labour is imagined as sexual violation; tools, a human invention, serve this unfortunate end: 'the heavy curve of the plowshare had not yet dared to open or violate the merciful womb of our first mother, for she, without being forced, offered up, everywhere across her broad and fertile bosom, whatever would satisfy, sustain, and delight the children who then possessed her' (76–7) (aún no se había atrevido la pesada reja del corvo arado a abrir ni visitar las entrañas piadosas de nuestra primera madre, que ella, sin ser forzada, ofrecía, por todas las partes de su fértil y espacioso seno, lo que pudiese hartar, sustentar y deleitar los hijos que entonces la poseían; I, 11, p. 156). But in railing against work as a sign of the degraded historical condition of mankind, Don Quijote also loses sight of one of the fundamental humanist principles of civic life: that politics begins equally in *words* and in *work*.[34] Politics continuously grapples with the ways to bridge these, just as it struggles to find a bridge between theory and practice. But the hub of the quixotic problematic lies in the repeated discovery of the non-convergence of these terms. Don Quijote is guided by 'words' (i.e., books) that cannot provide him with the basis of meaningful work in the world; in speaking about the Golden Age he fantasizes an originary moment when no work was required, and likewise demonizes the fall from this prepolitical state.

Don Quijote nonetheless imagines the 'state of nature' as one in which basic needs are well satisfied. Desires scarcely exist, and so hardly need to be appeased: 'no one, for his daily sustenance, needed to do more than lift his hand and pluck it from the sturdy oaks that so liberally invited him to share their sweet and flavorsome fruit' (76) (anadie le era necesario para alcanzar su ordinario sustento tomar otro trabajo que alzar la mano y alcanzarle de las robustas encinas, que liberalmente les estaban convidando con su dulce y sazonado fruto; I, 11, p. 155). Moreover, because Nature is imagined as being 'naturally' generous, no moral imperative is required to be *liberal* (generous) toward others. *Liberalidad* is a social virtue described in the *Nicomachean Ethics*. 'The liberal man, like other virtuous men, will give for the sake of the noble, and rightly; for he will give to the right people, the right amounts, and at the right time, with all the other qualifications that accompany right giving; and that too with pleasure or without pain.'[35] Not surprisingly, then, one of the challenges Cervantes sees is to imagine what 'liberality' might mean outside the state of nature. It is a theme that appears at various moments in the book (e.g., in the episode of Camacho's wedding, and in Don Quijote's visit to the home of the Caballero del Verde Gabán) where Cervantes asks specifically about the relationship between *liberalidad* as a virtue and the flaunting of wealth.[36]

Don Quijote introduces the speech on the Golden Age with a pronouncement about chivalry that at first seems quite contrary to his customary insistence on the importance of categorical distinctions. Inviting Sancho to sit down beside him and eat acorns, he says of chivalry, as St Paul said of love, that it is the great equalizer: 'one may say of knight errantry what is said of love: it makes all things equal' (75) (de la caballería andante se puede decir lo mesmo que del amor se dice: que todas las cosas iguala; I, 11, p. 154). This brief allusion to equality – which is not the secular egalitarianism of the eighteenth century, but something closer to the moral equality imagined by the Christian humanists – is nonetheless inseparable from Don Quijote's naturalized understanding of the hierarchies that must remain as part of social life: 'I want you to sit here at my side and in the company of these good people, and be the same as I, who am your natural lord and master; eat from my plate and drink where I drink' (75) (quiero que aquí a mi lado y en compañía desta buena gente te sientes, y que seas una mesma cosa conmigo, que soy tu amo y natural señor; que comas en mi plato y bebas por donde yo bebiere; I, 11, p. 154). And yet, the communitarian hope and promise of these words, reflected in the potent image of a shared meal, will return at many subsequent points of the novel, as Cervantes tries, through his characters, to imagine the conditions for unconstrained social relations even as he tries to un-imagine the relations that impede their realization. As I will discuss in a later chapter, the formation we have come to call 'nationalism' is precisely one of those constraints; not insignificantly, the great wave of European nationalism has been linked specifically to the language of possessiveness of the kind Don Quijote decries in this speech.[37]

As far as Sancho is concerned, however, it might well seem that independence may be preferable to the perils of a life shared with Don Quijote. Moreover, Sancho knows all too well that in any social situation he is likely either to be cast in a subordinate role or, as on Barataria, asked to accept greater responsibilities than he is willing or able to bear. Sancho will again come to entertain fantasies of independence after he has experienced the burdens of governance and has relinquished his role as governor of Barataria. But when seated beside Don Quijote and the goatherds in Part I, his understanding of what it means to share a meal with his master is based on a logic of need, not desire or an ideal;[38] in other words, it is based on the fantasy of a need so basic (and of a satisfaction so complete) that it would seem to be exempt from desire, because ontologically prior to it: 'I can tell your grace that as long as I have something good to eat, I'll eat it just as well or better standing and all alone as sitting at the height of an emperor … what I eat, even if it's bread and onions, tastes much better to me in my corner without fancy or respectful manners, than a turkey would at other tables where I have to chew slowly, not drink too much, wipe my mouth, not sneeze or cough if I feel like it, or do other things that come with solitude and freedom' (76–7) (sé decir a vuesa merced que como yo tuviese bien de comer, tan bien y mejor me lo comería en pie a mis solas como sentado a par de un emperador. Y aun, si va a decir verdad, mucho mejor me sabe lo que como en mi rincón con melindres ni respetos, aunque sea pan y cebolla, que los gallipavos de otras mesas donde me sea forzoso mascar despacio, beber poco, limpiarme a menudo, no estornudar ni toser si me viene gana, ni hacer otras cosas que la soledad y libertad traen consigo; I, 11, 154).[39]

The mythical, prepolitical moment of the Golden Age articulated by Don Quijote, and Sancho's fantasy of pure need, stand as bookends for the social and political explorations that occupy Cervantes throughout most of the book. The shepherds who listen to Don Quijote in chapter 11 of Part I inhabit a world that the knight's rapturous, mythical discourse obscures. Convention requires it thus. They understand nothing of what Don Quijote has at stake in his invitation to Sancho to share some acorns with him. Still less are they aware of the topical adjacency between the myth of the Golden Age and the set of pastoral tropes that their own presence invokes. Indeed, here they are scarcely conscious of themselves as literary creatures, much less as counter-conventional figures set within an artificial literary world. It is only much later in the novel, after Sancho has relinquished his rule on Barataria, that we see the pastoral at the opposite extreme of conventionality, having fully absorbed its literary self-consciousness and thus having become decoupled from the fundamental political questions Cervantes associates with it in Part I. The 'false arcadia' (fingida arcadia) of II, 58, for example, is imagined as a playground for the idle rich, who have appropriated the pastoral strictly for their own pleasure and entertainment. Even for Don Quijote and Sancho the myth of arcadia seems to support an increasingly fantasmatic set of desires as the novel develops. As Part II advances, myth comes to hypothesize very little.

Especially after Don Quijote's defeat by the Knight of the White Moon, the pastoral genre is increasingly marked as a purely artificial trope, not as a vehicle for social imagining or as the support for a political critique. It is the vehicle by which Don Quijote and Sancho and a few others attempt to fortify the powers of their waning imaginations. While the pastoral continues to serve as a means to evoke the question of poetic power, and while the force of Garcilaso's poetry remains quite tangible ('Oh, harder than marble!' ¡oh más endurecida que marmol!), the social and political issues associated with it and with the Golden Age as a space for political theorizing are by and large gone by the time we reach the end of Part II.

Don Quijote nonetheless has his own account of the waning of the Golden Age. He maps the shift from the mythical Golden Age to the present 'Age of Iron' as if it were in fact a function of history. But the question raised by the waning of the Golden Age is not a question about history; rather it is a question about the relationship between history and myth. Cervantes was clearly sceptical about myth, but he was equally sceptical about the discourses of historical 'fact' that replaced it, and could see that these allowed little room for the theoretical work that myth helped carry out. While he may have regarded myth as having been 'undone' by history (rather than by science) he nonetheless saw that the idea of a passage from myth to history was impossible for logical reasons alone. If the Golden Age was indeed perfect, then nothing within it could have disturbed its peace; and if there was nothing to disturb its ideal peace, then the origins of history and the roots of practical politics are not just unexplained but unexplainable. One cannot travel from the mythical Golden Age to the present age by means of history – and certainly not by the kind of history that Don Quijote imagines. Not surprisingly, given his keen awareness of the need to frame conceptual limit-cases in mythical terms, Plato offers a mythical account of how this transition might occur in the *Statesman*.[40] Much closer to Cervantes, Antonio de Guevara offered a similar account in which the mythical core is transposed to a story about good and evil:

> In that first age and golden time everyone lived in peace. Each person took care of his own lands, planted his olive trees, picked his fruit, cared for his vines, reaped his wheat for bread and raised his children; and because they were sustained solely by their own labour they lived without prejudice. Oh, human evil! Oh, treacherous and evil world, which never allows things to remain the same ... two thousand years had gone by since we knew what the world was, and God allowing it to happen and humans finding a way, plows were transformed into weapons, oxen into horses, spurs into lances ... and

finally the very sweat that was for the cultivation of his estate was transformed into blood, to the detriment of his republics.[41]

By contrast, Don Quijote attempts to construct a historical genealogy of decline in order to explain a moral shift. Indeed, he invokes 'history' not just in order to explain the course of decline itself but, in turn, to explain himself – i.e., to explain why he, the knight who appears to be a historical anomaly, is in fact a historical necessity. The knight errant who is supremely out of step with the world, must exist *because* of the changes that history has brought about: 'As time passed and wickedness spread ... the order of knights errant was instituted: to defend maidens, protect widows, and come to the aid of orphans and those in need. This is the order to which I belong' (77) (Andando más los tiempos y creciendo más la malicia, se instituyó la orden de los caballeros andantes, para defender las doncellas, amparar las viudas y socorrer a los huérfanos y a los menesterosos. Desta orden soy yo; I, 11, p. 157). This is about as clear a self-accounting as any that he gives throughout the book, and it underwrites his 'quixotic' political project: to remedy the injustices of the present by reviving the 'Golden Age.' As he says to Sancho while they listen to the frightening sounds of the fulling mills, 'Know that I was born, by the will of heaven, in our iron age, to revive the one of gold, or the Golden Age, as it is called. I am he for whom are reserved dangers, great deeds, valiant feats' (142) (Has de saber que yo nací, por querer del cielo, en esta nuestra edad de hierro, para resucitar en ella la de oro, o la dorada, como suele llamarse. Yo soy aquel para quien están guardados los peligros, las grandes hazañas, los valerosos hechos; I, 20, p. 238).

The reference to the 'age of iron' is straight out of Ovid, though doubtless also mediated by a host of other texts, including Book II of Macrobius's fourth-century 'Commentary' on the 'Somnium Scipionis' and Castrillo's *Tractado de republica*. The follow-through comes in II, 1: 'I only devote myself to making the world understand its error in not restoring that happpiest of times when the order of knight errantry was in flower. But our decadent age does not deserve to enjoy the good that was enjoyed in the days when knights errant took it as their responsibility to bear on their own shoulders the defense of kingdoms, the protection of damsels, the safeguarding of orphans and wards, the punishment of the proud, and the rewarding of the humble' (464–5) (Solo me fatigo por dar a entender al mundo en el error en que está en no renovar en sí el felicísimo tiempo donde campeaba la orden de la andante caballería. Pero no es merecedora la depravada edad nuestra de gozar tanto bien como el que gozaron las edades donde los andantes caballeros tomaban a su cargo y echaron sobre sus espaldas la defensa de los reinos, el amparo de las doncellas, el socorro de los huérfanos y pupilos, el castigo de los soberbios y el premio de los humildes; II, 1, p. 48). Just as for Castrillo, this mythical view of history serves to explain Spain's increasingly conflictive circumstances, 'a Spain torn apart in its very entrails by the violence of civil wars and popular revolts,' as one commentator aptly said.[42]

It is worth recalling that the speech on the Golden Age begins with a phrase that repeats the terms in which Don Quijote had expressed his desire for fame at the very beginning of Part I.[43] 'Fortunate the age and fortunate the times called golden by the ancients' (76) (Dichosa edad y siglos dichosos aquellos a quien los antiguos pusieron nombre de dorados; I, 11, p. 155). The 'historical' account he offers, which is later expanded in the discourse on Arms and Letters, culminates in its vision of the eclipse of the heroic project of knight-errantry and the rise of 'courtier knights.' The topic of the two kinds of knighthood is invoked with some frequency throughout the book, and goes to show that Don Quijote's imaginary mapping of the passage from myth to history does indeed bear some connection to contemporary circumstances. It reflects a critical view of the idle nobility. But against what set of alternatives, one might well ask, did such a critique carry any force in Cervantes' mind? Certainly not against the mythic construction of a Golden Age or the revival of chivalry. Why might Don Quijote have entertained the fantasy of a world without possessions, or money, or the interests they reflect? The fact of the matter is that such a world is scarcely consistent with Don Quijote's own chivalric ideals.

In Part I, Don Quijote repeatedly denies that he needs money at all, citing its absence in the books of chivalry by which he guides his conduct.[44] One of Cervantes' likely sixteenth-century antecedents on this point was Castrillo, who points out that the ancient heroes (the Romans, to be precise) did not succeed in conquering the world because of the power of their wealth but rather were able to conquer wealthy peoples by their virtue: 'The Romans did not buy the world with their wealth, but with their virtue conquered the wealthy.'[45] Don Quijote lives principally in a world of symbolic values, where honour is paramount and where public recognition is key. The principles of exchange value are wholly alien to him; he regards an interest in luxuries with scorn, as appropriate for what we would call 'carpet knights,' whose very existence is taken as symptomatic of history's moral decline: 'Most knights today would rather rustle in damasks, brocades, and the other rich fabrics of their clothes than creak in chain mail; no longer do knights sleep in the fields, subject to the rigors of heaven ... Now sloth triumphs over diligence, idleness over work, vice over virtue, arrogance over valor, and theory over the practice of arms, which lived and shone only in the Golden Age and in the time of the knights errant' (465) (Los más de los caballeros que agora se usan, antes los crujen los damascos, los brocados y otras ricas telas de que se visten, que la malla con que se arman; ya no hay caballero que duerma en los campos, sujeto al rigor del cielo ... Agora ya triunfa la pereza de la diligencia, la ociosidad del trabajo, el vicio de la virtud, la arrogancia de la valentía, y la teórica de la práctica de las armas, que solo vivieron y resplandecieron en las edades del oro y en los andantes caballeros; II, 1, p. 48).

Don Quijote's lament over the defeat of practice by theory in matters of chivalry resonates deeply with the views expressed in his speech on Arms and Letters in Part I. But it is principally in the characters of the Duke and the Duchess that we see the kind of decadence that Don Quijote associates with the nobility of the robe rather than the sword. The Duke and Duchess live on a large and luxurious estate, in a world of damask and brocade. There is, of course, a historical significance to Cervantes' critique of aristocratic decadence, but that critique opens out onto larger issues that are at play since at least the discourse on the Golden Age in Part I. Their life of luxury calls to mind the vulgar pursuits that many humanists opposed. 'The Character and Studies Befitting a Free-Born Youth,' by Pier Paolo Vergerio, for example, argued that 'luxuries weaken the human mind and body, but toil strengthens and hardens them.'[46] Such views are, in turn, indebted to Aristotle's critique of the 'banausic' individual, i.e., the type who spends in excess and cultivates entertainments and luxuries that contribute nothing to virtue.[47] Insofar as such an individual is held captive by these pleasures, he is opposed to the truly free individual who is fit to rule. The Aristotelian stance on this topic inspired a great variety of later humanist writings, including educational treatises that deal with the need to strengthen character by the avoidance of luxury.

But if the question is indeed the just city, and the qualities of the just ruler, then we need to be careful not to overestimate the value of the simple life. Indeed, the 'golden age' resembles one of the very types of city Plato described in the Republic as unacceptable alternatives to the just city. In its initial characterization it would seem ideally simple and virtuous, and certainly not unhappy. '[Our citizens] will produce corn, wine, clothes, and shoes, and will build themselves houses. In the summer they will for the most part work unclothed and unshod, in the winter they will be clothed and shod suitably. For food they will prepare wheat-meal or barley-meal for baking or kneading. They will serve splendid cakes and loaves on rushes or fresh leaves, and will sit down to feast with their children on couches of myrtle and bryony; and afterwards they will drink wine and pray to the gods with garlands on their heads, and enjoy each other's company. And fear of poverty and war will make them keep the numbers of their families within their means.'[48] Nonetheless, Plato's Glaucon protests that this primitive society remains uncivilized. There is certainly no room for philosophy in it. It is, he says, rather like 'founding a community of pigs' (Republic, 372a). Cicero takes up this line of thinking when he describes the 'Golden Age' not as a 'state of nature' but as uncivilized and crude: 'There was a time in which men roamed over the fields like wild animals, lived from the food that grew wild, and acted according to the powers of the body rather than the mind. They had neither divine religion nor human duties. No one paid attention to lawful marriages; no one viewed children as their own ... In this way, through ignorance and error, the passions of the soul – a blind and aimless ruler – misused the powers of the body – a dangerous servant.'[49]

One of the ironies about the Golden Age seems to be this: that with the elimination of the difference between 'mine' and 'thine' all other differences are in danger of being erased as well. The result leads not to an ideal state but to potential chaos. A society without some degree of individuation or any order risks degenerating into a world bereft also of the virtuous principles of differentiation that characterize a civilized state. Plato himself proposed the division of labour as fundamental to the ideal polis. (Huarte de San Juan explicitly takes Plato's idea as the operating principle for his analysis of the different types of ingenio and their role in the state.) The tasks of all inhabitants would be distributed so that each could pursue the endeavours to which he is best suited. In the background of Plato's account stands the idea that the state must cultivate a specific class of guardians, who can be called on for the purposes of protection and defence:

> Soldiering is not so easy a job that a man can be a soldier at the same time as he is a farmer or shoemaker or follows some other trade; why you can't even become a competent draughts or dice player if you don't practice seriously from childhood, but only do it in your spare time. Does a man become competent as an infantryman, or in any other branch of military service, the moment he picks up a shield or any of the other tools of the soldier's trade? ... The business of defence, just because it is the most important of all, requires a correspondingly complete freedom from other affairs and a correspondingly high degree of skill and practice. (Republic, 374)

In speaking insistently about the need for defence Don Quijote imagines himself as a successor of one of these guardians.

It is quite true that money becomes of far greater concern to Don Quijote in Part II of the novel and that his waning chivalric ambitions can be aligned with his acknowledgment of the role of money in the world. While Cervantes certainly shares Plato's view of the deficiencies of the 'luxurious city' and embraces Aristotle's critique of excess, it would be far too simple to regard money itself as the source of decline in the *Quijote*, whether in ethical or in socio-political terms. The association of money and decline would seem, rather, to correspond to a quixotic set of ideas whose foundations are themselves mostly in myth. Moreover, Cervantes incorporates one memorable story that seems to go to great lengths to say just the opposite, i.e., that social struggles ultimately revolve around intangible things, and that the desire for recognition, distinction, and symbolic value abound in circumstances where there is in the end no 'thing' to be possessed at all.

The story in question is the tale of the braying aldermen in chapters 25 and 27 of Part II. It serves as a complement to Don Quijote's discourse on the Golden Age insofar as it tells a story of interpolitical rivalry instigated by the unexplained theft of an ass that belonged to the *regidor* of one of the towns ('[a councilman] lost a donkey through the deceitful efforts of one of his servant girls, but it's a long story' [620]) (por industria y engaño de una muchacha criada suya, y esto es largo de contar, le faltó un asno; II, 25, p. 228). In fact, the story is about the 'double' loss of an ass: the stolen beast is first found (minus saddle and reins) but then escapes back to the mountains again, before the aldermen attempt to lure it back home with their braying.

Without wishing to repeat the story in its entirety, the outlines of it are important to recall, for in its fable-like way it involves a return to issues that resemble those broached in the speech on the Golden Age. If the speech on the Golden Age presents the quixotic version of an origin myth, the fable of the stolen ass presents the myth of the theft of origins, or of origins grounded in theft. It suggests that the social and political orders are not arranged around material goods, or needs and their satisfaction, but on desire, whose ultimate object seems always lost; it suggests also that the gap between the 'civilized' polis and the world of nature (in this case, the wild mountains to which the missing ass returns) is both greater than anyone might imagine and too great to be crossed. But it also suggests that there remains something 'of nature' in the 'civilized' polis.

In terms of genres, the episode shifts us from the framework of myth, which was Don Quijote's way of thinking through 'foundational' questions in Part I, to the discourse of fable and folklore. It is a 'traditional' story, of a kind characteristic of oral traditions, that is repeated in all its details ('Everybody who knows the truth of the matter tells the story with the same details, and in the same manner that I'm telling it now' [621]) (Con estas circunstancias todas, y de la misma manera que yo lo voy contando, lo cuentan todos aquellos que están enterados de la verdad de la cosa; II, 25, p. 231). The naivety of the story's folkloric background helps veil the sophistication and depth of the points it makes. Indeed, the story of the stolen ass is not unlike an origin myth in that it tells of how a group of people acquires their political identity and name: though the town itself goes unnamed, the people call themselves 'los del rebuzno' (the braying people). The name is an example of one of the many metonymic substitutions that run throughout the story, all of which serve in place of the tangible 'thing' that the townspeople want to recover. The name 'the braying people' derives from an attribute of something that is unexplainably absent and irrecoverably lost – an ass that has been stolen for reasons that are buried in some other, unrecounted story. Indeed, the efforts to establish and protect the civic identity of the town involve a series of attempts first to locate and then to find a substitute for the lost object of desire: by the braying of the alderman (*regidores*) who try to locate the missing ass by imitating the noises it makes, and then by the efforts of the 'rival' town that attempts to do the same. The braying aldermen at first ridiculously mistake the noises of each other for the sounds of the missing ass ('between you and a jackass there's no difference at all as far as braying is concerned, because never in my life have I seen or heard anything more lifelike' [621]) (de vos a un asno, compadre, no hay alguna diferencia, en cuanto toca al rebuznar, porque en mi vida he visto ni oído cosa más propia; II, 25, pp. 231–2). But the braying catches on, and eventually becomes established as a principle of social order that is strong enough to hold in place interpolitical rivalry: 'The natives of a town are known by their braying, just as blacks are known and differentiated from whites; and this unfortunate mockery has gone so far that often the mocked, holding weapons in their hands and marching in formation, have come out to do battle with the mockers, and no one and nothing, neither fear nor shame, can stop it' (623) (Son conocidos los naturales del pueblo del rebuzno como son conocidos y diferenciados los negros de los blancos; y ha llegado a tanto la desgracia desta burla, que muchas veces han salido contra los burladores los burlados a darse la batalla, sin poderlo remediar rey ni roque, ni temor ni vergüenza; II, 25, p. 233).

As the meaning of braying noise shifts, the sense of its purpose becomes obscured. The *rebuzno* is a lure for the ass, a symbol of social and political identity, and finally an insult. But this is also to say that the noise plays a key role in a field of second-order political relations that imagine themselves as having fundamental importance (as, for example, in protecting the security of the town against rivals). Not surprisingly, Sancho is the one to remark at the transformation of something as naive and 'natural' as braying into a form of conflict: 'It's foolish to lose your temper just because you hear somebody bray,' says Sancho:

> I remember when I was a boy, I used to bray whenever I felt like it, and nobody held me back, and I did it so well and so perfectly that when I brayed all the donkeys in the village brayed, but that didn't stop me from being my parents' son, and they were very honorable people, and even though this talent of mine was envied by more than a few of the conceited boys in my village, I didn't care at all … And then he held his nose and began to bray so enthusiastically that all the nearby valleys resonated with the sound. But one of the men who was near him, thinking he was mocking them, raised a long pole that he had in his hand and hit him so hard with it that he knocked Sancho Panza to the ground. (641)

> Es necedad correrse por sólo oír un rebuzno, que yo me acuerdo, cuando muchacho, que rebuznaba cada y cuanto se me antojaba, sin que nadie me fuese a la mano, y con tanta gracia y propiedad, que en rebuznando yo, rebznaban todos los asnos del pueblo, y no por eso dejaba de ser hijo de mis padres, que eran honradísimos; aunque por esta habilidad era invidiado de más de cuatro de los estirados de mi pueblo, no se me daba dos ardites … Y luego, puesta la mano en las narices, comenzó a rebuznar tan reciamente, que todos los cercanos valles retumbaron. Pero uno de los que estaban junto a él, creyendo que hacía burla dellos, alzó un varapalo que en la mano tenía, y dióle tal golpe con él, que, sin ser poderoso a otra cosa, dio con Sancho Panza en el suelo. (II, 27, p. 255)

Sancho renaturalizes the noise, moves it out of the arena of the human considered as *zoon poilitikon* back into the realm of *zoon* pure and simple.[50]

The story is a fable-like tale that says something significant not only about the political interest in identifying (and recovering) an important 'thing' (a possession or a good), but also about naturalist theories of society and about the political role of origin myths. The story presents its own version of an origin myth, in form of a tale about the way in which political cohesion may be forged precisely where the original 'thing' is lost. The central figures in the episode, the alderman, are clearly *political* figures; they are charged with maintaining the laws and with matters of local rule, and yet they find themselves drawn to search for an elusive political ground. Indeed, the tale suggests that political theory goes astray in thinking that the problems of any polis can be solved, or the foundations of any state set firmly in place, by locating its originating source. As with the myth of the Golden Age, Cervantes seems to have recognized that justice may well require the re-education of something as fluid as a desire for the return to origins, rather than the location of origins or the satisfaction of needs.

4 Controversies

In the whole kingdom of the activities of man, speech holds in its possession a mighty strength.

Luis Vives[1]

The speech to the goatherds on the topic of the Golden Age represents one of Cervantes' first explorations of the mythical basis of political theory and is a significant rhetorical accomplishment in its own right. The speech exhibits the mastery of an impressive range of classical and Renaissance literary tropes and texts, but this rhetorical tour de force also demonstrates Cervantes' engagement with a particular species of origin myth as a way of opening a space for a critique of society and the state. The speech stands as an example, at a relatively early stage in the book, of Cervantes' 'literary' investigation of the foundations of political thought. Within that framework, Don Quijote's address to the goatherds serves two contradictory ends. One is to debunk the power of myth as a 'mere' fantasy that cannot possibly say anything meaningful about the world (the Golden Age has nothing to do with anything real, including for the meagre goatherds who listen to it); the other is to offer an alternative to political theory in the form of a vision that derives its force from the essence of fantasy, i.e., from its ability to negate one world and hypothesize another. Indeed, Cervantes' engagement with myth as a set of 'false beliefs' serves in turn to empower a form of discourse whose basis lies in an idea (in this case, the idea of a 'Golden Age') that is not just lacking in verisimilitude, but impossible. The power of this kind of discourse in relation to the world of the 'real' is further demonstrated in subsequent episodes, as various characters come to reveal just how much they are driven by impossible imaginings about who they are or what they aspire to be.

But the displacement of fantasy as a simple dream-world on the order of the Golden Age (or in the form of Don Quijote's idealized world of knight-errantry) by a conjuncture of contemporary historical events involves more than the deflation of myth, first because Don Quijote has a way to explain that very process within the framework of the myths he invokes (as the transition from the Golden Age to the present 'age of iron'), and second because the force of fantasy over history proves itself to be quite powerful in relation to many other episodes within the novel (e.g., in the episode of Marcela and Grisóstomo, in the 'Tale of Foolish Curiosity,' or in relation to the expulsion of the *moriscos* in the episodes involving Ricote and Ana Félix in Part II). Fantasy is driven by desire, which may well have the power to destroy those who are propelled by it, but it cannot be eliminated. Thus it is within the scope of fantasy, rather than outside it, to imagine a reconciled world, one in which competing desires can be aligned in some harmonious way. It is likewise within the scope of fantasy – a fantasy of political reason, to be specific – to imagine the elimination of the passions that are thought harmful to the state, such as Plato has Socrates propose in the critique of tragedy in the *Republic*. Similarly, Cervantes' Canon of Toledo has ideas about which literary works would fit into *his* ideal republic; his attempt to rule fantasies out of bounds are in turn based on an idea of what the 'ideal republic' might be. In both instances, what counts as a rational vision of the ideal polis is communicated through the language of image and myth or as a fiction, and not in 'rational' terms.

To speak of politics in terms of myth, and by extension of fiction, is to recognize the fact that there is no simple line dividing ideas produced in 'theory' from those directed toward 'practice.' More than this, fiction has the power to upset the differences between theory and practice just as it upsets the desire to see the two reconciled. While the idea of a distinction between 'theory' and 'practice' is deeply rooted, it should be said at the outset that there is no discourse in the *Quijote* that is purely theoretical or purely practical. Beyond this, Cervantes seems aware that the idea of constructing a bridge between theory and practice with the aim of unifying them is itself the product of a particular fantasy – the fantasy of a complete and non-contradictory *speech*. Cervantes will turn to a related issue in the episode of Clavileño, where he raises the question of a complete and non-contradictory *vision*. But the point remains the same: a vision of the whole (of the whole earth, of the world, in the case of the flight on Clavileño) is possible only insofar as the characters subject themselves to a fiction about vision when they can, in fact, see almost nothing. This gently parodies

Luis Vives's claim that the historian ought to write like a supernatural witness who sees from a distance and possesses a knowledge of the hidden meaning of events.[2] When Sancho subsequently takes up his governorship of Barataria, we find what would seem to be an attempt to derive a political practice from a set of theoretical insights. But Barataria is itself a fiction created by the Duke and the Duchess, something they have fabricated to match the fantasies that Sancho has acquired from Don Quijote. So too with discourse: the speech on the Golden Age is possible only because a pre-existing set of fictions enables Don Quijote to imagine the rustic goatherds as the shepherds of an arcadian world.

The second of Don Quijote's major speeches in Part I, the discourse on Arms and Letters in chapter 37, takes up the question of theory in relation to practice from a highly formalized rhetorical standpoint. Its framework is that of a discourse organized around two conflicting sides of a single issue: the techniques of rhetorical *controversia* and argumentation *in utramque partem* (on both sides of a question) lie at its heart. The question of which is the better path in life, arms or letters, stands as a proxy for the dispute over the relative merits of theory and practice, as it does for a set of classical philosophical questions about the relationship between the active life and the life of contemplation. But because theory and practice seem unable to meet, it offers an opportunity for reflection on the dislocation between words and deeds that lies at the core of Don Quijote's situation, taking in train a set of adjacent questions about the relationship between speech and work and about the potential isolation of history from the realm of ideals. All these questions are set within the context of a shift from the heroic world of Don Quijote's imagination to the aristocratic values and administrative politics of early modern Spain. Indeed, part of what Don Quijote offers is a response to the eclipse of heroic values by revitalizing a form of rhetoric that makes the case for the value of heroic action (*armas*) over an approach to the world that would rely on books (*letras*).

The speech in itself is virtuosic and parodic. The 'fantasy' that underpins it is that a single individual might bind learning and action seamlessly together in a complete and virtuous life. That ideal reverberates throughout the *Quijote*, in part because it was etched in the literary imagination by the example of the soldier-poet Garcilaso de la Vega, whose resonant third eclogue spoke of the equally noble callings of the sword and the pen ('tomando, ora la espada, ora la pluma') (wielding now the pen, now the sword).[3] Other moments in the novel suggest that the unity of *armas* and *letras* is either a fantasy or absurd. When Sancho Panza is about to be appointed governor of Barataria, for instance, the Duke reminds him that he will need to dress 'partly as a scholar and partly as a captain.' What would this look like? It is difficult to imagine, above all in the case of Sancho, in spite of the Duke's insistence on the idea: 'Clothes must suit the position or profession that one follows,' says the Duke, 'for it would not be correct for a jurist to dress like a soldier, or a soldier like a priest ... On the ínsula I'm giving you, arms are as necessary as letters and letters as necessary as arms' (729) (Los trajes se han de acomodar con el oficio o digidad que se profesa, que no sería bien que un jurisperito si vistiese como soldado, ni un soldado como un sacerdote. Vos, Sancho, iréis vestido parte de letrado y parte de capitán, porque en la ínsula que os doy tanto son menester las armas como las letras, y las letras como las armas; II, 42, p. 356). In Part II, Don Quijote emerges from the distresses brought on by the impostures at Camacho's wedding so successfully that, in the narrator's account, he is taken as 'a Cid in arms and a Cicero in eloquence' (597) (por un Cid en las armas y por un Cicerón en la elocuencia; II, 22, p. 203). This is hyperbolic, not to say impossible.[4]

Indeed, the *combinatoria oppositorum* that this ideal would suggest is at least as improbable as the fantasies that would have been rejected by narrow-minded neo-Aristotelian critics for failing to meet the standards of verisimilitude. It produces results at least as strange as the 'reconciliation' of perspectives around the object that seems to be both a barber's basin and a helmet (the *baciyelmo*). I will turn to the issues raised by the case of the *baciyelmo* toward the conclusion of this chapter, but first I hope to explain how the formal structure of Don Quijote's speech on Arms and Letters, not only its subject matter, helps sustain the fantasy of a Janus-like view of a single question. In Cervantes' hands, the deconstruction of such a fantasy happens because of the pressures that come to bear upon it from the literary sources that feed it: from the swerves and distortions produced by Don Quijote's prior, fiction-based commitment to *armas,* from the instabilities embedded within the humanist tradition of deliberation about the relative merits of arms and letters, and finally, after the speech has concluded, from the Captain's story of the improbable events of his own life as a soldier.

Cervantes' way of addressing the non-convergence of theory and practice lies in the circumstances of the speech itself – in the fact that it is delivered, over dinner, in the context of a mock-symposium, and to a silent audience, by a character who seems blind to the fact that he is not at all well suited to consider both sides of the question at all. As the narrator

duly notes when Don Quijote is about to speak, the speech is directly related to the discourse on the Golden Age ('They ate very happily, even
more so when Don Quixote stopped eating, moved by a spirit similar to
the one that had moved him to speak at length when he ate with the goatherds' [328]) (cenaron con mucho contento, y acrecentóseles más viendo
que, dejando de comer Don Quijote, movido de otro semejante espíritu
que el que le movió a hablar antes como cuando cenó con los cabreros; I,
37, p. 464).[5] Not unlike the speech to the goatherds, or the Canon's remarks about the books of chivalry, for that matter, the speech on Arms
and Letters reads like a heterogeneous compilation of contemporary and
ancient sources. Part of what Cervantes does in all these speeches is to re-
voice his antecedents, subjecting each of them to the echoes and influence
of the others. This results in a dislocation of sources, to be sure, but that
displacement purposefully goes further, to destroy the possibility that any
of this material might be refashioned into an integrated whole. Rather,
these speeches bear resemblance to the form that Bakhtin described as a
subgenre of menippean satire, the diatribe.[6] The 'diatribe' is not a harangue, but rather a speech that is internally dialogic, one that is structured, as Bakhtin explains, in the form of a conversation with an absent
interlocutor, or simply with oneself.[7] In strict terms, the speech on Arms
and Letters is indeed a monologue, but it is meant to be internally dialogic
by arguing both sides of a question before a silent audience.

More specifically, the discourse on Arms and Letters marries the diatribe with the humanist rhetorical tradition of *controversia*, whose links to
the menippea can be traced through Lucian and Erasmus, who was himself
the author of the well-known *Diatribe*. In that tradition, orators were
trained to make arguments on both sides of any given question (arguing *in
utramque partem*), exposing each of a set of opposed views to the pressures of the other, in the hope of capturing the many-sided qualities associated with a complex and dynamic conception of the truth. Pérez de
Oliva's *Diálogo de la dignidad del hombre* draws on a similar strategy,
whose roots lie in the tradition of legal disputation and debate.[8] But, as we
shall see in the case of Don Quijote's speech, dialogic argumentation could
also result in a dizzying set of reversals and inversions, leading ultimately
to the possibility of confusion and civil strife that political thinkers such as
Hobbes thought important to guard against.

These are disconcerting thoughts, in part because it is often assumed
that humanist rhetoric lay at the heart of a reformist ethical vision of how
the polis ought to be shaped and ruled as a community of discourse: not
by adherence to pre-established ideas, but by an active and open process

of dialectical inquiry. The practice of argumentation *in utramque partem* represented an effort to model the world of politics in ways that neither arguments about 'first principles' nor a Machiavellian pragmatics of political power were able to envision. In a way that we might be tempted to construe as 'liberal,' in part because of its emphasis on tolerance, the discursive space of civic humanism was conceived as an ethical space committed to the discovery of the truth through open dialogue. In this conception, the ideal polis was modelled on the process associated with argumentation, not on an idea. This, in turn, established a set of discursive practices whose value for politics was institutionalized through rhetorical education. As I will explain in concluding, it was this very tradition that Hobbes found deeply problematic, in spite of his own rhetorical training.

The Renaissance rhetorical tradition took it as axiomatic that political speech required more than persuasion and recognized that dialectic was integral to all forms of *inventio*, including the analysis of many sides of any given question. But the notion that rhetoric could serve dialectic had been established since Aristotle. It was, in fact, one way in which Aristotle attempted to salvage something of the idea of open inquiry implicit in Plato's dialogues while freeing rhetoric from the charge that it was open to abuse by anyone who might wish to speak on any given topic, even without genuine knowledge of the truth. Cicero explicitly credits Aristotle with having codified the practice of controversial speech ('Aristotle trained young men ... so that they might be able to uphold either side of the question in copious and elegant language').[9] But it was Cicero's own *De oratore*, more than Aristotle, that served Renaissance humanists for guidance about what an orator must do: 'We must state our case; afterwards define the dispute; then *establish our own allegations; subsequently disprove those of the other side; and in our preparation expand and reinforce all that was in our favour, while we weakened and demolished whatever went to support our opponents.*'[10] Indeed, humanists recognized that one of Cicero's essential aims was to establish *controversia* as part of a comprehensive methodology for rhetorical training in a way that would serve politics. Erasmus was among Cicero's foremost heirs. His text on the art of letter-writing (*De Conscribendis Epistolis*), for instance, suggests the value of 'for and against learning' on a host of questions:

Which life is superior, the active life which the Greeks call practical, or the contemplative, which they call theoretical? Is celibacy better, or wedlock? Does art or natural ability contribute more to speaking? Is the modern kind of theology superior to the older one? Is military service or the study of literature more useful for the acquiring of reputation? Is jurisprudence or the study of medicine more profitable for the securing of wealth? ... Who was the better general, Hannibal or Scipio? Was Plato a more outstanding philosopher than Aristotle? Which poet was more learned, Virgil or Hesiod? Who was more remarkable for his eloquence, Demosthenes or Cicero?[11]

Before considering what becomes of 'controversial' argument in Cervantes' hands, it is worth underscoring that this form of rhetoric was not meant to be 'theoretical' or 'scientific' in any conventional sense. On the contrary, the underlying rhetorical practice to which Don Quijote's 'inquiry' into the question of arms vs. letters makes reference was designed to resist the formation of a unified set of views (*doxa*) about the way things are or ought to be. It was conceived as one way to overcome theory's apparent inability to reflect on the many facets of the practical world. Its discursive force is driven by the conviction that 'theory' was likely to yield a univocal view of things, that any view stated generally and in the abstract might foreclose the process of challenging and testing alternative positions, and that any such 'theory' would be detrimental to politics. Thus it is of tremendous importance when a thinker like Hobbes comes to challenge *controversia*, suggesting that the encouragement of contradiction is not a model for politics at all, but an invitation to civil war. For Hobbes, *controversia* is terrifyingly close to contradiction, and on that subject he clearly follows Aristotle's logic: 'Both parts of a contradiction cannot possibly be true,' he writes, 'and therefore to enjoyne the beliefe of them, is an argument of ignorance.'[12]

Concerns about the dangers of *controversia* were hardly new with Hobbes, in part because many forms of controversializing had been developed since antiquity. Reaction to *controversia* was at least as old as reactions to the pre-Socratic philosophers, who by some accounts were the first to cultivate the discursive principle of opposing views. Protagoras in particular had composed two books of 'Antilogies,' and Diogenes Laertius's *Lives* helped establish his reputation as the first to have recognized that truth is not one-sided, but that on every issue there are two opposing arguments.[13] The views attributed to Protagoras were well known in the Renaissance, initially through a minor comment in Aristotle's *Metaphysics*, then more substantially through Ficino's translation and summary of Plato's *Protagoras*. In Plato's dialogue, it is Socrates who attempts to restrain Protagoras's tendency to proliferate opposing views by arguing that 'each thing has one contrary and no more.'[14] Aristotle took an even more rigorous view of the matter. He saw the essence of deliberation not just as involving two sides of an issue, or as a matter of finding a way to choose between one course of action and another, but as investigating whether things are true or false; dialectical argumentation is designed to address questions 'that admit of being or not being the case' (*Rhetoric*, I. 4, p. 84). It was not until Cicero that the model of *controversial* argumentation be- . came a highly valued practice once again. No one before him is known to have translated Plato into Latin, and the text he chose to translate was in fact the *Protagoras*.[15] In a crucial passage near the beginning of *De oratore*, for instance, Cicero insists that the orator 'must argue every question on both sides, and bring out on every topic whatever points can be deemed plausible.'[16] As noted above, it was Cicero who served as a model for the Renaissance ideal of rhetoric as a form of political philosophy among humanists such as Coluccio Salutati, Leonardo Bruni, and Lorenzo Valla.

But in Erasmus, the effort to argue both sides of any question becomes nearly hyperbolic. In *De conscribendis epistolis*, for instance, Erasmus writes that 'the students' skill in invention will be improved if they practise recantations, arguing against what they have just proposed; what you have previously lauded to the skies, you dash down to the depths with violent denunciation; or first advocate something, then urge its avoidance.'[17] This passage suggests one of the enduring worries about deliberative oratory, of concern to all those interested in defending the philosophical powers of *controversial* argumentation: that argumentation *in utramque partem* might spin out of control, never reaching the fundamental questions underlying politics. This worry went to the heart of concerns about the uses of rhetoric in the service of truth-seeking. What guarantees were there that argumentation *in utramque partem* could arrive at an understanding of the true nature of anything – of virtue, or justice, or the good, for example? Additional concerns revolved around the risks of under-controversializing the complexities of any given question.[18] As I will discuss in connection with the *baciyelmo*, any approach to argument that could imagine opposition as only two-sided, as restricted to a choice between *this* and *that*, was bound to seem limited. But so too were there fears that the proliferation of alternatives ad infinitum might never reach the heart of things, or would end, as Hobbes worried, in civil strife. Ethical worries were allied to these concerns. Indeed, one of Plato's central complaints about rhetoric – equal in force to anything he says about poetry – was that the rhetorician could craft an argument on virtually any topic out of just about anything.[19]

In the course of his address on Arms and Letters Don Quijote makes explicit reference to the tradition of *controversia* and of the need to consider matters 'according to the arguments that each side may advance' (según son las razones que cada uno por su parte alega; I, 38, p. 469; translation mine). The speech is framed in terms of a lawyerly exploration of the best way to defend the *república*: 'Among [the arguments] is the claim that without letters arms could not be sustained, because war also has laws to which it is subject, and laws are subsumed under what are called letters and lettered men. The reply of arms to this is that laws cannot be sustained without arms, because with arms nations are defended' (331) (dicen las letras que sin ellas no se pueden sustentar las armas, porque la guerra también tiene sus leyes y está sujeta a ellas, y que las leyes caen debajo de lo que son letras y letrados. A esto responden las armas que las leyes no se podrían sustentar sin ellas, porque con las armas se defienden las repúblicas; I, 38, p. 469). At the same time, the speech goes directly to matters of ethics and takes up alternative and opposing conceptions of the good. The disputational 'question' at stake in it coincides with some of the central questions of Plato's *Republic* and of Aristotle's *Nicomachean Ethics*: what is the best life for man? This is perhaps the most basic of all the questions of practical reasoning, hence of politics. And yet Don Quijote narrows it down to two possibilities. The choice between arms and letters represents his highly compressed version of the fundamental contrast that Plato and Aristotle drew between the active and contemplative forms of life.

Some of these questions reappear in Part II, initially in a context where Don Quijote takes up the more practical matter of how best to make one's fortune in the world and to gain honour. In addressing his niece and his housekeeper near the very beginning of Part II, Don Quijote echoes one of the examples offered in Erasmus's *De conscribendis*[20] and again presents two alternatives. 'There are two roads, my dears, which men can take to become rich and honored: one is that of letters, the other that of arms. I have more arms than letters, and my inclination is toward arms, for I was born under the influence of the planet Mars' (495) (Dos caminos hay, hijas, por donde pueden ir los hombres a llegar a ser ricos y honrados: el uno es el de las letras; otro, el de las armas. Yo tengo más armas que letras, y nací, según me inclino a las armas, debajo de la influencia del planeta Marte; II, 6, pp. 83–4). Then, just after his descent into the Cave of Montesinos, in chapter 24, Don Quijote once again argues for the value of *armas* against the ideal of *letras* as practised by the courtly nobility. In this case, however, speaking to a page, he demonstrates the inadequacy of his own ability to argue coherently in favour of *armas* even while he admits to being enticed by their glitter and glory: 'There is nothing on earth more honorable or beneficial than serving God, first of all, and then your king and natural lord, especially in the practice of arms, by means of which one achieves, if not more wealth, at least more honor than through letters, as I have said so often; although letters have founded more estates than arms, those who pursue arms have I do not know precisely what kind of advantage over those who pursue letters, but I do know what kind of splendor places them above all others' (618) (No hay otra cosa en la tierra más honrada ni de más provecho que servir a Dios, primeramente, y luego, a su rey y señor natural, especialmente en el ejecicio de las armas, por las cuales se alcanzan, si no más riquezas, a lo menos, más honra que por las letras, como yo tengo dicho muchas veces; que puesto que han fundado más mayorazgos las letras que las armas, todavía llevan un no sé qué los de las armas a los de las letras, con un sí sé qué de esplendor que se halla en ellos, que los avenjata a todos; II, 24, p. 228).

For Don Quijote to consider whether the best life is the life of military service, committed to arms and the defence of the polis, or the life of the student, devoted to books and committed to the discipline of the mind, is also to draw on a long history of many such discussions in the aftermath of Plato's and Aristotle's seminal texts. Pier Paolo Vergerio took up Plato's side in his essay, 'Character and Studies Befitting a Free-Born Youth': 'States would be far more blessed,' he wrote, 'if philosophers ruled or if their rulers happened to be philosophers.'[21] Don Quijote, the knight errant, has precious little sympathy for the idea that philosophers should rule, regardless of whether that idea was attributed to Plato or to Aristotle's endorsements of the contemplative life. Even his advice to Sancho in advance of Sancho's experimental governance on Barataria is relatively practical. Indeed, the discourse on Arms and Letters presents an occasion in which Don Quijote only appears to consider the two alternatives openly. Its entanglements are the effect of a predisposition to the course of *armas*, set within the context of a humanist need to balance arms with letters, or practice with learning. Those entanglements are magnified in Don Quijote's speech, which introduces a new level of instability into whatever genuine ethical issues might be at stake in it. The ethical problem that the speech considers – how best to live – involves a series of theoretical reflections on what is, in the end, a matter of practice. But insofar as practice is fundamentally political, it naturally suggests a concern for matters of justice and the law, and ultimately an endorsement of peace as the highest good ('peace, which is the greatest good that men can desire in this life' [329]; la paz, que es el mayor bien que los hombres pueden desear en esta vida; I, 37, p. 466). Each of the two possible pathways in life that Don Quijote considers, the life of a soldier and the life of a student, is weighed in this light. Nonetheless, the potential confusion created by the back-and-forth reasoning of the speech makes a conclusion nearly impossible to reach. When controversial disputation moves out of the realm of the hypothetical schoolroom exercise, prudence is required to draw conclusions and move toward action. The speech on Arms and Letters is not only symptomatic of the absence of prudence, hence of a speech that remains within the realm of the hypothetical, but of an instance in which the conclusions drawn can at best support Don Quijote's fictional project.

By its own example – i.e., insofar as it is a discursive construction deeply conscious of the antecedent rhetorical tradition – the speech clearly demonstrates the virtues of 'letters.' But just as in Castiglione's influential *Book of the Courtier*, which had been translated into Spanish by Juan Boscán, the commitment to letters is meant as no disservice to arms, and potentially as the source of their greater glory. 'You all know how mistaken the French are in thinking that letters are detrimental to arms,' says the Count; 'it is true glory that is entrusted to the sacred treasury of letters, as all may understand except those unhappy ones who have never tasted them' (I, 43, p. 69).[22] Speaking directly of 'las letras humanas' Don Quijote explains that their true purpose is political, and that their aim is to ensure justice and lawfulness ('to maintain distributive justice, and give each man what is his, and make certain that good laws are obeyed. A purpose, certainly, that is generous and high and worthy of great praise' [329]; poner en su punto la justicia distributiva y dar a cada uno lo que es suyo, entender y hacer que las buenas leyes se guarden. Fin, por cierto, generoso y alto y digno de grande alabanza; I, 37, p. 466). But this is hardly a stable position. Don Quijote, the erstwhile knight, presents an impressively learned argument that to pursue 'arms' is likewise to pursue peace, though by a logic that seems counterintuitive. As Don Quijote explains, 'This peace is the true purpose of war, and saying arms is the same thing as saying war. Accepting it as true that the purpose of war is peace, which is greater than the purpose of letters' (329) (Esta paz es el verdadero fin de la guerra; que lo mesmo es decir armas que guerra. Propuesta, pues, esta verdad, que el fin de la guerra es la paz, y que en esto hace venjata al fin de las letras; I, 37, p. 466). Moreover, anything Don Quijote might say about the choice between arms and letters is under the influence of his fixed ideas about the virtues and glories of the soldier's life, and by extension of the life of action rather than of reading or contemplation. Don Quijote is hardly lacking for humanist precedents in the view that the *vita activa* is the one best suited to politics; none other than Leonardo Bruni argued specifically so.[23] But that precedent is also a literary one, just as Don Quijote's commitment to *armas* is the product of his books.

Indeed, we do well to recall that Don Quijote's enthusiasm for knight-errantry as an embodiment of the *vita activa* had emerged from the singularly inactive Alonso Quijano's over-commitment to reading. The 'desocupado lector' (idle reader) to whom the *Quijote* is directed is perhaps an even more extreme example of aversion to activity. As a consequence, there is a strange complexity in Don Quijote's speech, and in Cervantes' text in general, that sets it apart even from many humanist statements on this topic. As noted above, Don Quijote's speech turns out to be anything but a fair and open-ended inquiry into the relative merits of the two professions. On the one hand it is a tangled and over-controversialized speech, and internally duplicates the procedures of pro and contra argument on both sides of each question. And on the other hand it seems not even-handed enough. It scarcely resembles the humanist attempt to locate a middle way between opposing views by imagining an ethical synthesis of divergent ways of life. Numerous examples suggest that such an ideal was itself surprisingly difficult to hold in place; the humanist idea of a 'middle ground' seems inevitably to separate into alternating positions. Vergerio, for instance, writes that 'as soon as age will permit them to use their limbs, [they] ought to accustom themselves to arms; and they should be charged with learning their first letters as soon as they can form words. Immediately thereafter they should get a foretaste of the activities and studies they will pursue throughout life, and practice their rudiments. Both of these activities they can easily pursue by turns.'[24] Alternation of this sort is not synthetic. By contrast, Don Quijote's argument is weighted toward one side. His vehement defence of knight-errantry is interlaced with a critique of the life of the student, to which any humanist would have been an adherent.

While the underlying form of Don Quijote's discourse might suggest an alliance between the forms of rhetorical *controversia* and the process of dialectical inquiry, that alliance is undone by Don Quijote's commitment to a fiction that he wholly believes. To be sure, Don Quijote does stop to acknowledge the merits and difficulties of the student's life. He duly notes how the trials and tribulations of a life devoted to study are evident in the student's proverbial poverty. But he goes on to say that the student's suffering can scarcely compare with the hardships endured by the soldier, who routinely risks his life in the course of battle. Moreover, Don Quijote insinuates that the student's relatively minor sufferings can only yield the dubious kinds of official honours that are sought after by venal *letrados*:

'It is easier to reward two thousand lettered men than thirty thousand soldiers, because the first are rewarded by positions that of necessity must be given to those in their profession ... But let us leave this aside, for it is a labyrinth difficult to leave' (331) (Es más facil premiar a dos mil letrados que a treinta mil soldados, porque a aquellos se premian con darles oficios que por fuerza se han de dar a los de su profesión ... Pero dejemos esto aparte, que es laberinto de muy dificultosa salida; I, 38, p. 469).

The comment goes to the heart of the political questions of what it means not just to live well but to govern well, of who is capable of doing so, and of what preparation a virtuous ruler ought to have: 'To become distinguished in letters costs time, sleepless nights, hunger, nakedness, headaches, bouts of indigestion, and other things of this sort, some of which I have already mentioned,' he says, 'but to become a good soldier requires everything required of a student, but to so much higher a degree that there can be no comparison, because at every step the soldier risks losing his life' (332) (Alcanzar alguno a ser eminente en letras le cuesta tiempo, vigilas, hambre, desnudez, vaguidos de cabeza, indigestiones de estómago, y otras cosas a éstas adherentes, que, en parte, ya las tengo referidas; mas llegar uno por sus términos a ser buen soldado le cuesta todo lo que el estudiante, en tanto mayor grado, que no tiene comparación, porque a cada paso está a pique de perder la vida; I, 38, pp. 469–70). These issues are later brought to a head in Don Quijote's advice preceding Sancho's governorship of Barataria. (I will discuss those episodes in chapter 6 below.) Here, Don Quijote echoes Plato's argument that the business of defending the state is more difficult than most other tasks, and requires specialized skills: 'Soldiering is not so easy a job that a man can be a soldier at the same time as he is a farmer or shoemaker or follows some other profession ... Does a man become competent as an infantryman, or in any other branch of military service, the moment he picks up a shield or any of the other tools of the soldier's trade?' (*Republic*, 374c–d). Given, moreover, the historical context in which the task of governing was increasingly being placed in the hands of lawyers and government functionaries, it hardly seems surprising that Don Quijote would resolve the question of arms vs. letters the way he does. The soldier, he argues, is a more genuine servant of the law than any lawyer; perhaps better phrased, the soldier acts in defence of the principle of lawfulness itself: 'With arms nations are defended, kingdoms maintained, cities defended, rods made secure, seas cleared of pirates; in short, if not for arms, nations, kingdoms, monarchies, cities, roads, and sea lanes would be subject to the hardship and confusion that war brings for as long as it lasts' (332) (con las armas se defienden las repúblicas, se conservan los reinos, se guardan las ciudades, se aseguran los caminos, se despejan los mares de corsarios, y, finalmente, si por ellas no fuese, las repúblicas, los reinos, las monarquías, las ciudades, los caminos de mar y tierra estarían sujetos al rigor y la confusión que trae consigo la guerra el tiempo que dura y tiene licencia de usar de sus privilegios y sus fuerzas; I, 38, p. 469).

The speech on Arms and Letters may thus well be conceived as if it were a dialectical inquiry into the 'difficult question' of the merits of two competing ways of life; and Don Quijote may well, in fact, portray this as an unresolved question ('materia que hasta ahora está por averiguar,' I, 38, p. 469). But, as we have already begun to see, Don Quijote is not really open to persuasion at all. His own commitments are made emphatic and clear as soon as he begins. He takes the occasion of the speech as an opportunity to defend the virtues of knight-errantry and to inveigh against the study of *letras* as a relatively ineffective and ignoble pursuit. Indeed, the significance of the speech depends ultimately on the way in which the procedures of *in utramque partem* argumentation are set within a discursive framework that is subject to the exorbitant and unbalanced rhetoric of a character who may only appear to be speaking reasonably. When Don Quijote speaks 'rationally' (i.e., logically), he does so nearly to excess. The two-sided argument of the speech, in fact, makes a series of spiralling swerves that transform it into something of a self-cancelling artefact. Moreover, its very form seems to work at cross-purposes to the ethical principles informing it. Don Quijote's defence of arms is justified by the claim that peace is the goal of any just war and the highest good,[25] but this defence is presented in a discursive form that was itself regarded as a form of combat, even by its chief pacifist advocate, Erasmus. Erasmus may well have declared the pursuit of peace and concord to be the very 'sum and substance' of his religion, but some of his rhetorical theories were clearly committed to the value of *controversia* as a form of verbal combat.[26] The simile was not new; Plato in fact compared dialectic to a 'battle' in *Republic*, 534c. But there is an irony in the cultivation of verbal combat among pacifist humanists that Cervantes cannot have missed.

Beyond this, the partisan views in favour of soldiering that Don Quijote injects into the dialectical framework of this speech are all eventually reframed in the context of the novel's much larger discursive space, where they come to appear as excessive, and not merely as evidence of rhetorical prowess or impressive examples of *copia*.[27] The discourse on Arms and Letters is set in the context of a symposium of sorts, but a mock symposium

– a humble banquet served up at a long table by Juan Paolmeque to the guests who have assembled at the inn. Indeed, Don Quijote's address to the characters seated at the table around him resembles a number of the longer speeches inserted in Plato's dialogues, not the least relevant of which is Protagoras's discourse – a 'long and magnificent display of eloquence,' as is said in the dialogue that bears his name – on the subject of education and the virtues (*Protagoras*, 328d). But, unlike Plato's dialogue, and rather more like what we find in Castiglione, the attendees at Don Quijote's 'symposium' are a group of characters who have been excerpted from one set of fictional contexts and inserted into another: 'They all sat at a long refectory table, for there were no round or square ones in the inn, and they gave the principal seat at the head of the table to Don Quixote, although he had tried to refuse it, and then he wanted Señora Micomicona at his side, for he was her protector. Then came Luscinda and Zoraida, and facing them Don Fernando and Cardenio, and then the captive and the other gentlemen, and on the ladies' side the priest and the barber. And in this manner they ate very happily' (328) (Sentáronse todos a una larga mesa como de tinelo, porque no la había ni redonda ni cuadrada en la venta, y dieron la cabecera y principal asiento, puesto que él lo rehusaba, a don Quijote, el cual quiso que estuviese a su lado la señora Micomicona, pues él era su aguardador. Luego se sentaron Luscinda y Zoraida, y frontero dellas don Fernando y Cardenio, y luego el cautivo y los demás caballeros, y al lado de las señoras, el cura el el barbero. Y así, cenaron con mucho content; I, 37, p. 464). Just after Don Quijote finishes the speech, the narrator remarks that everyone at the table, except Sancho (whom he notes was occasionally distracted), sat listening in rapt attention to Don Quijote's wise remarks.

Cervantes brings the doubly fictional status of the banquet guests into relief by having Don Quijote refer to them (and to himself) according to the identities by which they appear in his imagination, even while he recognizes that they do not appear as such to anyone else: 'Who in this world, coming through the door of this castle and seeing us as we appear now, would judge and believe that we are who we are? Who would believe that this lady at my side is the great queen we all know she is, and that I am the Knight of the Sorrowful Face whose name is on the lips of fame?' (328) (¿cuál de los vivientes habrá en el mundo que ahora por la puerta deste castillo entrara, y de la suerte que estamos nos viere, que juzgue y crea que nosotros somos quien somos? ¿Quién podrá decir que esta señora que está a mi lado es la gran reina que todos sabemos, y que soy yo aquel Caballero de la Triste Figura que anda por ahí en boca de la fama? I, 37, p. 465). In such instances, acknowledgment of the non-truth of the fiction is precisely what allows it to persist as a fantasy relatively impervious to the force of the real. It has already incorporated the force of the real inside it. Given this context, Don Quijote's defence of arms is bound to seem at once mad and lucid, or lucid and mad. 'In this manner, and with these rational arguments, Don Quixote continued his discourse, and no one listening to him at that moment could think of him as a madman; rather, since most were gentlemen engaged in the practice of arms, they were very pleased to listen' (329) (De tal manera y por tan buenos términos iba prosiguiendo en su plática Don Quijote que, por entonces, *ninguno de los que escuchándole estaban le tuviese por loco*; antes; *como todos los más eran caballeros*, a quien son anejas las armas, le escuchaban de muy buena gana; I, 37, p. 466, emphasis added). At the conclusion of the speech, one of the more educated members of the group, the Priest, goes out of his way to voice his approval of Don Quijote's views:

> Don Quixote gave this long discourse while the others were eating, and he forgot to bring a single mouthful of food to his lips, although Sancho Panza told him several times that he should eat and that later there would be time to say all he wanted to say. Those who listened to him were overwhelmed again with pity at seeing that a man who apparently was intelligent and rational in all other matters could lose those faculties completely when it was a question of his accursed and bedeviled chivalry. *The priest said that he was correct in everything he had said in favor of arms, and that he, though lettered and a graduate of the university, was of the same opinion.* (333; emphasis mine)

> Todo este largo preámbulo dijo Don Quijote en tanto que los demás cenaban, olvidándose de llevar bocado a la boca, puesto que algunas veces le había dicho Sancho Panza que cenase; que después habría lugar para decir todo lo que quisiese. En los que escuchado le habían sobrevino nueva lástima ver que hombre que, al parerer, tenía buen entendimiento y buen discurso en todas las cosas que trataba, le hubiese perdido tan rematadamente en tratándole de su negra y pizmienta caballería. *El cura le dijo que tenía mucha razón en todo cuanto había dicho en favor de las armas, y que él, aunque letrado y guardado, estaba de su mesmo parecer.* (I, 38, p. 471; emphasis mine)

But here we are again reminded that Cervantes sets rhetorical argumentation *in utramque partem* within a literary context where characters seem consistently to adopt stances contrary to their declared interests, or to invert the positions with which they are otherwise associated. In so doing,

Cervantes casts light on a world where language never seems to travel in a straight line and in which the activities of 'saying' and 'doing' seem bound forever to diverge.

The context of the *in utramque partem* speech on Arms and Letters rightly leads one to ask whether politics be conceived as a matter of structuring a framework for rational debate, where different opinions or 'points of view' can confront one another before an ideal judge, or whether it needs to be more open or more restricted. Clearly, neither the Priest nor anyone else at the table can be considered as anything other than an internal voice in the polyphonic conversation of the scene. And yet with the Priest's remarks, just as with the Canon's views of the romances of chivalry in chapters 47 and 48, and so many others throughout the book, this is an occasion when characters are unable to resist expressing judgments about various forms of discourse, pronouncing speeches or texts good and well-formed, or otherwise. Moreover, there seems to be an irrepressible temptation to judgment, not to say an element of coercion, deeply embedded within the dialogue tradition itself.[28] In the context of the *Quijote*, characters seem incessantly to be evaluating what is said, marking speeches as intelligent and learned, or too long or disorganized. (I will discuss this question at greater length in the concluding chapter; the speech on the Golden Age, for instance, is described as a 'lengthy harangue.')[29] While the dialogue form is potentially liberating and restorative, and while *controversia* may well embody an ideal of discursive freedom, it brings with it its own set of formal constraints.

It is clear from remarks in *Don Quijote*, Part II, that some readers of the first Part would have preferred a less 'disorganized' text. Specifically, the objections addressed in Part II, chapter 3, are directed to the semblance of disorder created by the insertion of the interpolated 'Tale of Foolish Curiosity.'[30] But the more important point is that Cervantes positions Don Quijote's 'controversial' speech within a highly fluid fictional setting, where the notion of two-sided argumentation seems if anything to underestimate the complexities confronted by characters whose lives are virtually inseparable from the fictional moulds in which they are formed: Marcela and Grisóstomo in relation to the pastoral, Ginés de Pasamonte in relation to the picaresque, Anselmo and Lotario in relation to the Italian novella, Zoraida in relation to the Moorish novel, and so on. Indeed, the more complex context of the speech on Arms and Letters derives from the fact that its rhetorical ideals are eventually submitted to the far more powerful set of critical reflections that fiction allows: the Canon of Toledo as learned on literary matters; the Humanist Cousin in Part II as an epitome of the desire for encyclopedic knowledge; Sansón Carrasco as a university graduate, who masquerades as a knight errant and challenges Don Quijote to equal combat. As noted above, the Priest's commendation of Don Quijote's speech is followed by the story of the returned captive, Captain Viedma, who in fact has lived and now narrates one of the two alternatives presented for consideration as part of Don Quijote's speech. Beginning in I, 39, the Captain recounts the story of his own life from the moment when his father asked each of his sons to choose one path in life.[31] What are the options? Two of the possibilities he presents are, predictably, *armas* and *letras*: 'I would like, and it is my desire, that one of you should pursue letters, another commerce, and the third should serve the king in war' (335) (querría, y es mi voluntad, que uno de vosotros siguiese las letras, el otro la mercancía, y el otro sirviese al rey en la Guerra; I, 39, p. 474).

I will have more to say about the captive's story in chapter 8 below. My point here is that Cervantes seems to turn from the rhetorical refraction of opposites, within the space of a set of hypothetical alternatives, to an engagement with narrative forms that would seem to propel these questions toward the world of the real. And yet, those forms are themselves based upon narrative frames in which history is never immune to the pressures of fantasy. Set thus against the backdrop of the Captive's tale, Don Quijote's version of *controversia* may well seem to be insufficiently *controversial*, even reductive. The Captive is a fictional character whose story appears to be grounded in a history that Cervantes himself had lived; that history is retold as a narrative romance involving his relations with the beautiful *mora* Zoraida. By contrast, Don Quijote is unaware of the fact that as a character he is himself born from a marriage of mixed ambitions, some literary and others military, the child of Cervantes' own attempt to reconcile the two poles of his own career as a solder and a writer.[32]

The ideal of a reconciliation of opposites speaks to the much discussed subject of the eclipse of controversial argumentation during the later stages of the Renaissance. Commentators on the history of humanism and rhetoric often characterize the decline of *controversia* as a cultural loss greater than the loss of a mere rhetorical technique or a method of argumentation insofar as it suggests the loss of tolerance, a weakening of the bond between *ratio* and *oratio*, and the loss of an appreciation of the power of language to challenge the concentration of authority in a single, monological voice.[33] By comparison, the univocal forms of speech characteristic of early modern philosophy, including the epistemology of Descartes and the politics of

Hobbes, reflect a turning away from controversial argumentation, which came to be viewed as confused and conflictive. But the shift was hardly categorical or abrupt. Thomas Sloane, for one, has described a process by which the discursive practice of *controversia* was gradually displaced because of rising confidence in the accessibility of the truth through forms, including certain discursive forms, as the preferred instruments of 'modern' knowledge and understanding. But the disappearance of *controversia*, Sloane suggests, was also generated through innovations in *dispositio* (the arrangement of arguments in a speech); these in turn fuelled a vigorous, ultimately non-humanist desire to organize the elements of speech and thought in fixed rather than fluid ways.[34]

A related concern bears upon the question of 'perspectivism' in the *Quijote*. Contrary to most interpretations, which regard Cervantean perspectivism as a way in which language attempts to embrace the many-sided richness of the world, it seems that certain forms of perspectivism might in fact reduce the world to a set of simple either/or propositions: either windmills or giants, a castle or an inn, a barber's basin or a helmet, all according to some pre-established frame of reference. In the *Quijote*, the attempted resolution of such frozen oppositions around the linguistic 'invention' of the *baciyelmo* would seem to offer a way out of these impasses by proposing an alternative, both/and structure (the basin-helmet). And yet this hypothetical solution to the problem of perspectivism is itself unstable, and can help shed light on some of the reasons why the principles of *controversia* might themselves have come under pressure. Recall briefly the circumstances surrounding the *baciyelmo*. Don Quijote sees this as the fabled helmet of Mambrino, while the other characters, including some 'experts' (among them a barber), accept it as an ordinary shaving basin. There are opposing views about the matter, but in this case the contradictory views are brought together in the creation of a new linguistic entity, the basin-helmet (*baciyelmo*). Is this the resolution of opposing views by a stroke of verbal genius, the comic *inversion* of a Solomonic decision to divide things in two? Perhaps, but the truth is that the *baciyelmo* produces an even more intensified *coincidentia oppositorum*. It creates an impossible entity – or an entity that is possible only in language – out of a dichotomous set of views. Indeed, the *baciyelmo* might well be regarded as the kind of fiction that could not conform to prevailing standards of verisimilitude. While proposing to image the harmonization of opposites, it corresponds to nothing real.

Hobbes had something important to say about a very similar issue: 'Though men may put together words of contradictory signification, as

Spirit, and *Incorporeall*,' he wrote, 'yet they can never have the imagination of any thing answering to them.'[35] The *baciyelmo* is by contrast an emblem of unresolved conflicts, and indeed of the intensification of controversies within the rhetorical tradition. Not surprisingly, this was just the kind of thinking that the new science of politics hoped to remedy. Hobbes was schooled in the rhetorical tradition, and yet it seems to have been his exposure to the possibilities of *controversia* that convinced him of the need to resist the proliferation of contradictory positions. As Rosalie Colie underscored, the cultivation of paradox in the Renaissance had grown to 'epidemic' proportions.[36] Hobbes reacted against it and sought the means to reduce the political conflicts he saw as implicit in it. In fact, he argues that it is precisely because language, as a feature of human invention, allows for contradiction that politics requires a fundamental commitment against *controversia*.[37]

If, as Hobbes explains in *The Elements of Law*, we are led into confusion by something as simple as ordinary equivocation – using the word 'faith' to mean things as different as religious belief and keeping a promise, for example – then philosophy must proceed by establishing clear definitions. 'Definition' according to Hobbes is designed to remove equivocation, and so to alleviate 'that multitude of distinctions, which are used by such as think they may learn philosophy by disputation.'[38] Definitions stand at the beginning of discursive reasoning, serving as the rough equivalent of axioms. As Hobbes says, there is no disputing whether definitions are to be admitted to or not: they are, in fact, prior to names, 'for in teaching philosophy the first beginning is from definitions; and all progression in the same, till we come to the knowledge of the thing compounded' (*De corpore politico*, VI, 15, p. 207). Hobbes's confidence in the power of definitions and in their importance for politics reflects a refusal of prudential reasoning founded on dialectical argumentation, and likewise a turning away from the flexibility of rhetorical discourse, as necessary in order to establish the non-controversial truths that are produced in language: 'Seeing then that *truth* consisteth in the right ordering of names in our affirmations, a man that seeketh precise *truth*, had need to remember what every name he uses stands for; and to place it accordingly; or else he will find himself entangled in words, as a bird in lime-twiggs; the more he struggles the more belimed' (*Leviathan*, ch. 4, 105).

But the matter of deciding between contraries, or eliminating them, is something that continued to concern Hobbes, precisely because he recognized that contradictions do not derive from the human inheritance of nature. Truth is a feature of language, not of things (see *Leviathan*, ch. 4).

There are, to be sure, differences that can be traced to differing natural endowments, divergent inclinations, and conflicting passions. But politics arises out of the relatively late developments of 'second nature,' in language. Well beyond the world of the senses and the natural passions, there arises the political need to curtail the controversies that originate in language. Even if some things can be established as naturally true, in a singular sense, it is especially important for political reasons to recognize that while contradiction is endemic to language, contradictory things cannot both at the same time be true. For Hobbes, civil strife is bound to emerge from contradiction just as it is from the 'elementary' sources of discord – from competition, lack of trust, and the quest for fame and glory. But language is as much a source of the problem as it is the route to a solution. Indeed, one view of language as stated in the *Leviathan* rests on a conviction that language can capture 'the similitude of the thoughts and passions of one man to the thoughts and passions of another.'[39] This is because names allow us to have conceptions of things not just in their particularity, where individuals may well differ, but in their common generality as well. And that in turn may relieve us of contradictions: 'We captivate our Understanding and Reason when we forbear contradiction; when we speak as (by lawful Authority) we are commanded; and when we live accordingly' (*Leviathan*, ch. 32, p. 110).

Translated politically, the need to resolve opposing views stems from a conviction that the principles of non-contradiction and the availability of general names provide the only feasible underpinning for a commonwealth that inevitably has to be built upon 'second nature' – built, that is, on a foundation of words. Indeed, Hobbes guards carefully against the dangers of contradiction in all the circumstances involving rhetorical orations (*Leviathan*, ch. 30, pp. 392–3). 'To consider the contrariety of mens opinions, and Manners in generall, It is they say, impossible to entertain a constant Civill Amity with all those, with whom the Businesse of the world constrains us to convene' (*Leviathan*, 'Review and Conclusion,' pp. 717–18). Hobbes held a particularly dark view of what that 'business' involved: 'nothing else but a perpetuall contention for Honor, Riches, and Authority.' Not surprisingly, he requires a legislator, who, like a God, knows all these passions but experiences none of them. But the sovereign does not need to act as a prudential judge, nor to decide which voices from the many that may be brought forth can and will be heard. This is because the Hobbesian theory of politics creates the legitimacy of the sovereign out of a hypothetical compact formed by the members of the polis to invest all power in him.

I have dealt with Hobbesian theory both because it can provide some crucial points of contrast with the rhetoric of *controversia* in the *Quijote* and also to help draw out the political implications and limits of *in utramque partem* argumentation and of linguistic invention in Cervantes' novel. With Hobbes's example in mind, we can recognize the significance of the fact that while there are many arguments in Cervantes' text, and many judges, including those among the characters who listen to Don Quijote's speech, there is nobody who occupies the position of the sovereign. In this, the *Quijote* is much more like Plato's dialogues than a philosophico-political treatise. The idea of a synthesis of points of view can only, in fact, be associated with a position that is perforce external to the text. Some have ascribed that position to God, others to the kind of reader (though hardly the 'idle reader') that the text implies.[40] Cervantes himself is silent on the point. It would in any case be equally wrong to conclude that the speech on Arms and Letters positions controversial argumentation as the pathway from the realm of theory to the realities of political practice. On the contrary, the speech seems to reduplicate the divisions between theory and practice on each side of the arguments it pursues. Moreover, the speech seems to suggest that the process of weighing alternative views cannot so much as begin without drawing on a pre-existing set of discursive frames whose viability in the present is sustained by a set of fictional ideas. Politics may well depend on language, if language may indeed be part of 'second nature,' but language is not merely words; it is discourse, which carries with it the inheritance of the past and of pre-existing systems of belief.

5 The Practice of Theory

Cervantes' engagement with the procedures of controversial argumentation in Don Quijote's discourse on Arms and Letters suggests that one of the animating aspirations of politics – the idea of constructing a discursive bridge between the separate domains of theory and practice – may be impossible to achieve. The alternating views of the theoretical and the practical paths lead to a set of alternatives that seem 'undecidable.' Better said, perhaps, it is decidable, but only insofar as some pre-existing fiction allows it (in Don Quijote's case, this is the fiction about the knight errant's orientation to arms). But this fiction cannot mask the fact that theory and practice are co-implicated in one another. To say that the choice between them, because of their ongoing involvements with one another, is impossible is hardly to suggest that Cervantes is not interested in pursuing the roots of their entanglements. On the contrary, he seems intent on probing this very set of issues. In so doing, it is his own adherence to the discourse of fiction that allows Cervantes to avoid the risks that accompany each one: in the case of theory, believing that one has produced a complete and coherent account of the polis as a whole; and in the case of practice, believing that theory is nothing more than a distraction, whose concerns are abstract, idealistic, or otherwise irrelevant to matters presently at hand.

Holding aside for the moment Don Quijote's advice to Sancho about governing and Sancho's governorship on Barataria – which certainly count among the most important political experiments in the book – Cervantes seems scarcely to imagine a fictional episode that does not have some set of implications for the ways we think about these issues. Whether the topic at hand involves his characters in matters of history, the economy, questions of marriage, the family, or the law; or whether involving fathers and their sons and daughters, merchants and soldiers, lovers and husbands or wives, or suitors who confront questions about love while under the influ-ence of various forms of family authority and state power, Cervantes al-ways seems to be bringing some question about politics, either theoretical or practical, into view. He was deeply engaged in thinking about the per-vasiveness of the political, about where it begins and ends, and about its discursive formation in relation to the powers of fiction to expose various forms of prejudice and illusion through mechanisms that are themselves clearly 'made up.'

Such concerns pervade both parts of the novel. But it is nonetheless true, and worth reiterating, that as we move from Part I to Part II the mat-ter of politics is brought into the foreground in increasingly explicit ways. This is but one dimension of the more general logic of thematic and struc-tural mirroring that links the two parts. Consider, for example, the way in which the story of the Captive and Zoraida (Part I) is echoed in the his-torically contextualized episode of Ricote and Ana Félix (Part II), or the way that the character Roque Guinart (Part II) echoes Ginés de Pasamon-te (Part I) within the context of contemporary Catalan politics. When Ginés de Pasamonte does reappear, it is to present a puppet show that calls to mind the persistent military threat posed by the Turks. But at the same time the episodes of Part II tend to be considerably more theatrical than their counterparts in Part I. Indeed, the episodes of Maese Pedro's puppet show, the journey on Clavileño, Sancho's experience on the 'island' of Barataria, and nearly all the other doings at the ducal palace, involve staged events. Cervantes clearly has something to say in Part II about the rela-tionship between politics and theatre, where self-consciousness, or the lack thereof, becomes an issue of crucial importance.[1]

Given the fact that virtually all of Cervantes' engagements with politics take place through the fictional means of character, plot, dialogue, image, theatre, and the like, what, if anything, can be said about his relationship to theoretical thought in the political domain? Is there in fact a language of political theory in the *Quijote* that can be identified as a distinct form of discourse, one that might articulate general principles and rules for politics in a way that other forms of speech might not provide? What are the roots of political 'theory' as Cervantes engages them?

The received view of 'theory,' of course, is that it is not just one way of speaking among others, and certainly not anything 'made up,' but involves speaking of the truth in its most general sense. The sense of privilege as-sociated with theory derives from its claims to see things from a stand-point that is detached from the give-and-take of the practical world, to reflect on questions of practice, and finally to craft a discourse corresponding to these insights. Indeed, the idea of theory implies a way of seeing as much as a way of speaking. It implies a way of seeing that proposes to look beyond the world of appearances and the flux of history to essences, and that dreams of gazing on the world from a place where it can be viewed as a complete and coherent whole. What we regard as theory involves a kind of seeing that has long been associated with Plato's metaphysics of the forms. In spite of the fact that none of the Platonic dialogues, including the *Republic*, is an example of 'theoretical' discourse in any modern sense, Plato's thinking was nonetheless associated with a set of ideas that proved to be central in grounding subsequent Western notions about what 'theory' might be: a discursive articulation of the rational vision of metaphysical truths and, ideally, an articulation of those truths as a whole.

The story of how Plato's metaphysics became associated with a kind of discourse to which the Platonic dialogues are themselves inimical is important to notice, since Cervantes seems to have been directly engaged in thinking about the distortions produced by theory-like discourse when it comes to politics. It is a concern that goes back at least to Aristotle's reinterpretation of Plato's ideas in such a way that 'theory' was transformed from a public and civic form of vision into a detached, private way of viewing things, one that did not in itself require a direct connection to practical matters.[2] The *Nicomachean Ethics* insists upon distinguishing the different kinds of reasoning that apply to different domains of knowledge, separating theory from practice. This is integral to Aristotle's defence of practical reasoning in the fields of ethics and politics, but serves as well to isolate and reify 'theory.' It is by contrast Cervantes' sympathy for the humanist project of philosophical reform that sets him far closer to Plato's interest in the dialogic exposition of various 'civic' forms of theory and, through figures like Lucian, to an understanding of the roots of theoretical activity in practice. Indeed, the episodes in the *Quijote* that deal most directly with the issue of 'theoretical' knowledge resonate with crucial moments in the *Republic* in such a way as to draw us back to Plato's own understanding of the relationship between the practical roots of theory and the formation of the state. In Plato, the Allegory of the Cave, with its crucial moments of visual deception, of ascent into the light, and of subsequent return to the realm of the shadows, plays a crucial role in addressing questions about education, and likewise in thinking about the kind of wisdom that is required in order to govern well. But we should not pass too quickly over the fact that the Allegory of the Cave is, after all, an allegory, an associative view constructed of images, and not a theory or a metaphysical account of the necessary and sufficient conditions for truth-statements. In more technical terms, Plato's Allegory of the Cave is 'a protreptic discourse that urges the reader to embrace the life of philosophical *theoria*.'[3] The situation is similar in the *Phaedo*, where Plato draws on myth and on the writings of ancient geographers such as Herodotus to talk about things that are seen from the 'ends of the earth.' The *Phaedo* offers an idea about ultimate things by conjuring up visions of a world on the outer edge of the one we know. This vision in turn allows Plato to speculate about things we could not know by any empirical means, including the nature of perfection and the life of the soul after death.[4]

In Cervantes, a similar engagement with 'theory' involves a vision of things from some equally extreme perspectives – from the depths of the Cave of Montesinos and from the imaginary perspective of the heavens in the episode on Clavileño, the wooden horse. Together with Maese Pedro's puppet show, these episodes provide some of the crucial experiences in which Don Quijote and Sancho must be tested before Sancho is given the chance to govern. The episodes of descent and ascent offer contrasting perspectives from which the characters attempt to see things as they 'truly are': in the form of Don Quijote's dream vision from 'below' in the Cave of Montesinos, and from the imaginary perspective of the heavens 'above' in their mock voyage on Clavileño. In the Cave Don Quijote sees visions of some of the figures of the archaic chivalric past. The question he raises is whether these visions are true or false. Likewise, the voyage on Clavileño offers the characters a perspective from which they might see the earth and all human life as it truly is, hence, in which they may become free to act wisely within the political arena. To gaze upon the world from the heights of the heavens is a humbling experience that was long thought capable of freeing the soul from social and civic constraints.[5]

These episodes are resonant with references to a broad set of textual and historical antecedents, through which the question of the 'true vision' necessary for politics (the vision of 'theory') is enriched by engagement with deeply rooted myths that tell of the hero's journeys of descent and ascent. The 'theorist' and the hero share at least this much by way of common genealogy. Prominent among these antecedents are Virgil's account of Aeneas's passage through the underworld (*Aeneid*, VI), Ariosto's description of Astolfo's descent into hell and subsequent flight to the heavens on a hippogriff (*Orlando Furioso*, 33, 34), and Lucian's *Icaromenippus*. I will have more to say about these antecedents in connection with the particular role of origin myths in the political imagination. Questions of origins aside, Cervantes seems to have been deeply interested in Plato's way of thinking literarily and through images about what is required in order to see things from the perspective that wise governance requires. These connections between Plato and Cervantes are not merely associative. They can be explained through Cervantes' intellectual involvement in the humanist tradition and its attempt at a philosophical reform of inherited scholastic views. Indeed, it was the humanist rereading of Plato on the question of philosophy and politics that allowed Cervantes to grasp a very different set of possibilities in the Platonic dialogues than the ones that had been handed down through Aristotle and the Neoplatonists.

The crucial episodes in Part II of *Don Quijote* at issue here all acknowledge the desire to seek deeper or higher planes of insight as the basis for political rule, but they also subject the desire for pure knowledge to a series of critiques associated with the power of myth as a potential source of insight and with an appreciation of the practical origins of what we have come to regard as 'theory' in the abstract.[6] They reengage the pre-Aristotelian roots of theoretical activity, which lie not in a conceptual framework of 'ideas' but in a set of practices associated with travels and travel narratives, with reports about festivals in far-off places, with stories of rituals observed in foreign lands, and with underlying mythical forms in which transformation is framed in terms of a journey. Recent scholarship has, in fact, pointed out that the genealogy of 'theory' among Aristotle's predecessors lay in the civic practice wherein an individual, the so-called *theoros*, would travel abroad for the purpose of witnessing spectacles, rituals, and other events, generally in order to report back to the city.[7] Stories about the *theoros* were consistent with the tales of wandering sages in ancient Greece and with mythical accounts of journeys to the underworld and to the heavens; but the travels of the *theoros* came to have a distinctively political profile within this broad panorama. As Andrea Nightingale explains, 'In many cases, the *theoros* was sent by his city as an official ambassador: this civic *theoros* journeyed to an oracular center or festival, viewed the events and spectacles there, and returned home with an official eyewitness report ... the practice of *theoria* encompassed the entire journey, including the detachment from home, the spectating, and the final reentry. But at its center was the act of seeing, generally focused on a sacred object or spectacle ... This sacralized mode of spectating was a central element of traditional *theoria*, and offered a powerful model for the philosophic notion of 'seeing' divine truths' (*Spectacles of Truth*, 3–4).

It is often said, following Socrates in the *Theatetus*, that philosophy begins in wonder, but it might be still more accurate to say that theory begins with reflection on the kind of astonishment that is genealogically related to the traditions of travel and spectatorship. What Plato added to this paradigm in adapting it to the conditions of reflective thought is consistent with archaic, mythopoetic ideas about the trials of the hero and the life-changing power of travels to places of origin or to strange and distant lands. This in turn becomes a founding 'fable' for philosophy, with the corresponding emphasis on vision and report.[8] Nightingale explains that in the *Republic*, Plato divides the 'journey' of *theoria* into the three phases found in traditional theoretical practice: 'In the first, the philosopher departs from the human and terrestrial world and goes in search of the Forms; having detached himself from society, he enters into a state of *aporia* and *atopia*. In the second, the philosopher reaches the metaphysical "region" of reality and engages in the contemplation of the Forms. Paradoxically, the precondition for this metaphysical "vision" is a blindness to the human and terrestrial world … Finally, in the third phase, the philosophic *theoros* "returns" to the city' (*Spectacles of Truth*, 97). But the *theoros* returns home transformed. His wonderment at the things he has seen in far-away places produces an enlightened scepticism, a detachment, a critical distance from worldly interests. The civic *theoros* is, moreover, compelled to give an account of what he has seen and learned, and in this way to translate his 'theoretical' wisdom into practical activities that might benefit the polis. But upon return he may nonetheless seem like a stranger in his own land.

The related figure of the 'theory-navigator' was not uncommon in the Renaissance,[9] but the most plausible and direct connection between Cervantes and the archaic roots of *theoria* in these practices was the *Relox de príncipes* of Antonio de Guevara, which offers an extended account of what amounts to the activity of the *theoros*, in a chapter entitled 'Phetonio y las leyes de los Lacedemonios.' The direct connection between *theoria* and politics in Guevara was hardly lost on Cervantes. 'Phetonio' is an apocryphal figure whom Guevara claims to have derived from the writings of Diogenes Laertius (*Lives of the Philosophers*) and Plato (*Republic*). He is described as a philosopher who was sent by the Thebans to Sparta in order to observe their customs and to learn about their famous laws.[10] Guevara's account preserves the underlying sense that *theoria* involves the cycle of a journey: a departure, an encounter with strange, mysterious, or unintelligible things (with an *aporia* in the original sense of the term), and finally a return to the city from which the *theoros* had departed, though in a more enlightened state. What Phetonio brings back from Sparta is based on detailed philosophical observation about how the Spartans maintained public order, reporting that he had observed their ways in great detail over the course of a year.[11] Furthermore, he notes that as a philosopher he is required not simply to observe what is done but to understand why.[12] But what Phetonio presents by way of his 'report' is not a summary of the Spartan laws; upon return from his theoretical journey he deposits a gallows, whips, manacles, and the like, in the public square: 'I do not bring you their written laws,' he says, 'but rather I bring the instruments by which they keep their laws.'[13] The 'telling' implicit in the reporting function of theory here leads to 'showing.'

Guevara recognizes and helps transmit an understanding of the roots of *theoria* that had been lost in the Aristotelian tradition. But he was not alone. In Fadrique Furió Ceriol's book of advice for counselors (*El consejo y consejeros del príncipe*, 1559), it becomes crucially important for the advisor to the prince not just to travel, but to do so with a mixture of curiosity and prudence: 'This voyage must be curious and prudent, not careless or foolish, as is often the case with lazy men and vagabonds ... A sure and certain way to tell the character of a man is to see if he has benefitted from his travels or not ... Look at what he says about the places he has visited, and if he condemns foreign lands wholesale and praises his own in a similar way, then you know such a person is driven by his passions or is careless or does not pay attention or is foolish or crazy; for such a soul there is no distinguishing between things hence no way to make choices, and without choosing there can be no prudence, and where prudence is lacking everything else is.'[14]

These insights needed to be recovered in part because Aristotle had dropped the idea that *theoria* ought to involve a round-trip voyage and public report. For Aristotle, the role of the *theoros* was to contemplate a spectacle for the sake of the spectacle itself, as he says in the fragmentary *Protrepticus*.[15] He was likewise convinced of the non-productive nature of theoric activity, which he associated with a life of detached contemplation. Aristotle was thus responsible for the shift in the view of 'theory' from its origins as a practice of spectatorship and report to a type of intellectual vision dissociated from praxis. It was, for example, Aristotle's perspective that Covarrubias represented when he glossed the term *teórico* in the 1611 *Tesoro de la lengua castellana, o española* as a Greek word 'meaning speculation, meditation, and contemplation, from the term θεωρείν, *animo contemplari*.'[16]

But 'theory' in the Aristotelian sense is neither by use nor by inheritance a Cervantine term. Nor was the Aristotelian sense of the term prevalent among the sources on which Cervantes might have relied. Long before Cervantes' time, the Greek term *theoria* had been supplanted in most Latin and Romance contexts by *scientia; scientia* came in turn to refer to a range of specific knowledge domains.[17] In Cervantes, *ciencia* was invoked in contexts ranging from astrology to warfare.[18] *Ciencia* was moreover regarded as a crucial ingredient in philosophy itself. When Cervantes' talking dogs, Cipión and Berganza, discuss the meaning of 'philosophy' in 'El Coloquio de los perros,' Berganza points to the kinship of *ciencia* and *sofía*:

> BERGANZA: Tell me, if you know, what philosophy is. Though I use the word, I don't know what it means. I only know it's supposed to be good.
> CIPIÓN: Here it is in a nutshell – the expression has two Greek roots, *philos* and *Sophia*. *Philos* means love, and *Sophia* means science, so that philosophy means 'love of science,' and a philosopher, 'a lover of science.

> BERGANZA: Qué quiere decir filosofía ¿que, aunque yo la nombro, no sé lo que es? sólo me doy a entender que es cosa buena.
> CIPIÓN: Con brevedad te la diré. Este nombre se compone de dos nombres griegos, que son *filos* y *sofía*; *filos* quiere decir amor, y *sofía*, la ciencia; así que *filosofía* significa 'amor de la ciencia', y *filósofo*, 'amador de la ciencia.'[19]

But not all forms of *ciencia* were regarded as equal. Questions were constantly being raised among writers and intellectuals about which forms of *ciencia* were to be counted as valid and which ones not, as well as about which form was the highest. Was poetry a *ciencia*? Don Quijote certainly defends it as such in his conversation with the Caballero del Verde Gabán in II, 18. Was politics indeed, as Aristotle had said, the highest form of knowledge? And if so, on what foundations did it rest? What kind of insight could limit the overweening forms of pride that tended to attach themselves to claims of *ciencia*?

The humanist engagement with questions of political and social 'theory' often took the form of narrative fictions, sometimes of utopian fictions written under the pretext of the exotic travel report. In More's *Utopia*, for instance, Raphael Hythlodaeus is introduced as having returned from travels to foreign lands to give 'a copious account of unknown nations and countries' where he had gone 'as a traveler, or rather a philosopher.'[20] The premise of Montaigne's essay 'Des Cannibales' is that it is instigated by the report of a friend who had lived for some ten or twelve years in Brazil. Though the report proposes to surpass both Lycurgus and Plato, it none-theless echos what Plato is said to have learned from Solon about the lost kingdom of Atlantis, 'telling how he learned from the priests of the city of Saïs in Egypt that in days of old, before the Flood, there was a great island named Atlantis.'[21] The upshot is a utopian social construct that coincides with the 'negativity' of the Golden Age, in which there is no clothing, nor any words to denote falsehood, treachery, dissimulation, or avarice. Though it is a later text, Campanella's *City of the Sun* (1623) presents a cap-tain's account of what he has seen in his far-off travels, first to Taprobane and then to the City of the Sun.

Taprobane was, in fact, the ancient name for Ceylon and corresponds to the Greek designation for an island that was deemed to lie at the eastern limit of the known world, thought to be a dwelling place of sirens. The island had in fact appeared on sixteenth-century maps, and 'Taprobana' serves the Condesa Trifaldi in II, 38, as one the points of orientation in her description of the imaginary kingdom of Candaya.[22] (Camões also men-tions it in the very first stanza of the *Lusíadas* and later describes it as fra-grant with exotic cinnamon groves.)[23] Don Quijote invokes Taprobana, with a few letters transposed, as 'Trapobana,' a place ruled by the imagi-nary Alifanfarón (I, 18). In all these instances, the insights culled by the traveller to strange lands are offered in the form of a narrative account rather than as what we have come to regard as 'theoretical' discourse. The-ory roots in the practice of travel and in the genre of the travel report. Where no actual travel was involved, fiction stands in.

The movement from ancient *theoria* to the humanist use of travel reports and travel fictions as an occasion for political thinking would almost cer-tainly have been impossible without the immense interest in exotic locales sparked by the early modern voyages of exploration and conquest. Spurred on by any number of wholly practical interests – in exotic spices, in pre-cious metals, and in the conquest and conversion of non-Christians – the ancient roots of 'theory' joined forces with early modern interests in narra-tives about unprecedented journeys to wondrous lands. Indeed, Cervantes' great, late, Byzantine romance, the *Trabajos de Persiles y Sigismunda*, would have been inconceivable without the geographic and anthropologi-cal writings of Olaus Magnus. As for travel reports from the Mediterranean world, the widely read text ascribed to Andrés Laguna, the *Viaje de Turquía*, was a mixture of travel observations and character transforma-tion.[24] Laguna's interest in daily life in Greece and Turkey is clearly seen in what would in a genealogical sense be called 'theoretical' terms – i.e., by an observer who stands outside the Turkish context and who uses it as a way to measure life at home in Spain. It is one of many texts that link the popular genre of travel writing to reflection on the way things might be imagined in some exotic 'other' world.

This is also to say that the roots of 'theory' branch out into a variety of contemporary literary genres with which Cervantes was quite familiar. The original purpose of the theoric journey was to travel in order to see and then to consider and report on what is true and what is not. This was especially the case with voyages to extreme locations. When Pedro Mártir de Anglería writes about Columbus's voyages in his *Décadas de orbe novo* (1511), for instance, he begins by recounting the admiral's hope to discover 'islas limítrofes' for the West.[25] (The discovery and command over islands is, in turn, a matter that informs Sancho's governorship on the fictional 'ínsula' of Barataria.) Building on all these traditions, fictional travel reports provided early modern thinkers with the opportunity for a kind of speculation that was at least as broadly framed in its political aims as the practice of ancient *theoria* was.

But herein lies one of the most important questions about the relationship between stories of marvellous things seen in foreign lands and the development of political thought as a 'theoretical' enterprise. How might the marvellous visions of romance and exotic travel reports provide the basis for thinking truthfully about the nature of politics? Which perspectives, which forms of reflection, and which kinds of discourse (narrative or otherwise) could best cultivate the kind of wisdom that would benefit the polis as a whole and the ruler in particular? Which accounts were to be regarded as false or as unreliable sources of wisdom? How might one to distil any guidance about matters of political practice from stories about strange worlds? To ask these questions is to reframe some of the concerns voiced by the Canon of Toledo in Part I, while recognizing that mere verisimilitude is hardly the issue: what, if anything, is the speculative relationship between the 'fantasies' of romance literature involving exotic travel and ideas about governance in the state?

The debate between the Canon and Don Quijote has often been regarded as anticipating the discussion of Don Quijote's descent into the Cave of Montesinos in Part II with Sancho and the Humanist Cousin.[26] But neither the Cousin nor Sancho is any more insightful an arbiter of such matters than the Canon. Sancho is naive and the Cousin is portrayed as a fact-hungry pedant who distorts the sense of history in asking about Don Quijote's descent into the Cave. His forebears would have included the early encyclopedists and polymaths who were long known for their attempts to make the learning of the ancients in natural science more widely accessible. Lucian already parodies their efforts in the *True History*, where the protagonist sets off on a voyage 'out of a certain intellectual restlessness, a passion for novelty, a curiosity about the limits of the ocean and the peoples who might dwell beyond it,' and returns with the preposterous account of a 'true history' that, in its very preface, explicitly denies any claims to truth.[27]

'Visions': In the Cave and in the Celestial Spheres

This is the background against which we can consider Don Quijote's dream-vision in the Cave of Montesinos, the 'wonders' he witnesses while watching Maese Pedro's puppet show, and the fantastic flight with Sancho on the magical horse, Clavileño. (The episode of the braying aldermen, which offers its own pointed commentary on politics in fable-like form, is interpolated among these adventures.) The two episodes of descent and ascent incorporate visions of astonishing things; they are punctuated by an episode in which a legendary scene is seemingly brought to life on the stage by Maese Pedro, a criminal turned puppeteer. Two of these episodes involve imaginary journeys, and all of them involve some kind of narrative account or report that proposes to interpret what is seen. Indeed, the specific reason why Don Quijote is shown the marvels in the Cave of Montesinos is so that he can report on what he saw: Montesinos leads Don Quijote through the cave so that he can return and tell the world about what lies therein ('para que des noticia al mundo de lo que encierra y cubre la profunda cueva por donde has entrado'; I, 23, p. 212).[28] In Maese Pedro's puppet show it is a young assistant, concealed behind the stage, who narrates the drama that the puppets enact. And in the episode of Clavileño there is a running narration that is provided by the members of the ducal court; following these is Sancho's own account of the episode to the Duchess.

Equally important is the fact that all these narrative reports are subjected to critical assessment by some very sceptical listeners, whose efforts, in turn, reveal a set of mistaken ideas about how such visionary experiences ought to be understood. Some of these listeners regard the stories they hear as susceptible to empirical proof of one kind or another. A certain degree of scepticism is certainly warranted. But when taken together these episodes offer a set of inquiries into the relationship between truth, history, and politics that is principally about the kind of vision that wisdom requires and not about factual truth or the limits of fantasy. How can we ever arrive at insights into the unseen by means of observation?

And how can we assess the truth-value of things that are impossible to see by the physical sense of sight? The question is similar to the one Glaucon asks in *Republic*, VII, about the dialectical journey and its culmination in the vision of the Forms, to which Socrates replies that the journey should not be taken for literal truth at all ('whether it really is true or not, this is not worth affirming, but that it looks something like this I do affirm,' 533a). The issue for Cervantes has likewise to do with the non-empirical nature of the most important truths, which must nonetheless be presented either discursively or imagistically, which is to say by means of *mythoi* or images (icons). Moreover, it is only when these questions have fully been considered that the problem of governance can be posed in a meaningful way. Don Quijote's political advice to Sancho, and Sancho's governorship on the fictional island of Barataria are, in a sense, only possible after the hero has probed the things hidden inside Montesinos's Cave and has then looked down on the earth with his squire from the heavenly heights, for both episodes involve a fundamental shift in perspective through a 'theoretical' journey that promises to help the two see clearly.

As a way of reinforcing the claim that the issues at play in these episodes are not about empirical truths and physical sight, but about vision and 'theory,' consider the fact that in the episode of the Cave of Montesinos the reader always knows that Don Quijote is asleep and dreaming. But Don Quijote does not know this, at least not right away. Don Quijote believes that he is in the presence of the legendary figures who have populated the great archive of his imagination – Montesinos, the hero Durandarte who had been killed at Roncevaux, and Baldovinos. Indeed, he dreams of an especially warm welcome from Montesinos, who says that he has been long waiting for Don Quijote to visit: 'For many long years, O valiant knight Don Quixote of La Mancha, we who dwell in this enchanted solitude have waited to see thee, so that thou couldst inform the world of what lies contained and hidden in the deep cave which thou hast entered, called the Cave of Montesinos: a feat reserved only for thy invincible heart and wondrous courage. Come thou with me, illustrious knight, for I wish to show thee the marvels hidden within this transparent castle, of which I am warden and perpetual chief guardian, for I am the same Montesinos after whom the cave is named' (605–6) (Luengos tiempos ha, valeroso caballero don Quijote de la Mancha, que los que estamos en estas soledades encantados esperamos verte, para que des noticia al mundo de lo que encierra y cubre la profunda cueva por donde has entrado, llamada la cueva de Montesinos: hazaña sólo guardada para ser acometida de tu invencible corazón y de tu ánimo estupendo. Ven conmigo, señor clarísimo, que te quiero mostrar las maravillas que este transparente alcázar solapa, de quien yo soy alcaide y guarda mayor perpetua, porque soy el mismo Montesinos, de quien la cueva toma nombre; II, 23, p. 212). Upon emergence from the cave Don Quijote affirms that what he reports was truly seen and heard, and in ways that draw him toward the realm of empirical proof ('what I have recounted I saw with my own eyes and touched with my own hands' [611]) (lo que he contado lo vi por mis propios ojos y lo toqué con mis mismas manos; II, 23, p. 220). Indeed, the phrase makes a direct allusion to the Gospel of John (20:25–9), and to doubting Thomas's demand for ocular proof of the central article of Christian faith ('Except I shall see in his hands the print of the nails, and put my finger into the print of the nails, and thrust my hand into his side, I will not believe').[29]

Nonetheless, Don Quijote himself begins to doubt what he saw in the cave. The cave was, after all, dimly lit, just as in Plato. At one point he even asks Maese Pedro's prophesying monkey whether his visions were dreams or not. But the monkey is in the employ of a trickster and a criminal posing as a gypsy puppeteer is as good a clue as any to the fact that asking about the truth of Don Quijote's visions is asking the wrong question, and certainly asking it of implausible informants. The episode with the prognosticating monkey is both a parody of superstition and a response to misguided confidence in the powers of human reason. (Cf. Vives, in De tradendis disciplinis, who writes: 'Man has received from God a great gift, viz., a mind, and the power of inquiring into things; with which power he can behold not only the present, but also cast his gaze over the past and the future.')[30]

Not surprisingly, however, what Don Quijote sees in this subterranean world resonates with the things that he has read in the chivalric romances. The journey into the cave is, among other things, a journey back to his own literary and mythical origins. The most immediate 'source' for the episode is, in fact, in a published book contained in Don Quijote's library, a sequel to the Amadís entitled Las sergas de Esplandián.[31] This textual resonance also underscores the fact that Don Quijote has not, in fact, journeyed anywhere exotic at all, except in his reading and in his mind. (The episode of the Cave of Montesinos also marks the point where Don Quijote's interests become dominated by private concerns rather than by his commitment to civic ideals. His desire to transform Dulcinea back into the woman of his dreams becomes a personal concern rather than a civic quest.) Don Quijote appears to know all about Montesinos, but what he does not seem to know in any conscious way is that he is cast as a mock theoros in an epic dream that resonates with the Aeneid and the Orlando

Furioso, and specifically with the descents of Aeneas and Astolfo into the underworld. At the same time, the description of the Cave of Montesinos resonates deeply with Virgil's account of the cave known in Greek as Avernus, 'a deep cave … yawning wide and vast, shingly, and sheltered by dark lake and woodland gloom, over which no flying creatures could safely wing their way; such a vapour from those black jaws poured into the over-arching heaven' (*Aeneid*, VI, 237–41). Cervantes makes it a point to pursue these Virgilian connections in the episode of Maese Pedro's puppet show, when his narrator offers a direct citation of the opening of book 3 of the *Aeneid*, taken directly from a Spanish translation made in 1555 by Gregorio Hernández de Velasco.[32] The engagement with Virgil no doubt reflects Cervantes' awareness of the fact that Aeneas's mission involves the (re)founding of a city. As for the resonances with the *Furioso*, we should not forget that Ariosto's Astolfo enters hell through the mouth of a cave and that Astolfo's descent directly anticipates his flight up into the heavenly spheres on the magical horse (*Orlando Furioso*, 33–4).

The descent into the Cave of Montesinos is a theoric voyage that is also a *nostos*, a journey home, to the heart of the heroic past, an adventure down to see the hidden secrets of the underworld; for Don Quijote it represents a voyage to origins. Insofar as it may be a source of wisdom, it also stands in line with the philosophical journey of descent or *katabasis* that marks the beginning of the *Republic*, as Socrates and Glaucon head down (*katabên*) toward Piraeus.[33] But the wisdom of the Cave of Montesinos turns, in part, on the fact that this is the first time it is suggested to Don Quijote that the figures from the chivalric past are not merely past, or part of a store of exemplary historical figures, but dead. Don Quijote is unable to resurrect them. And while Maese Pedro offers a puppet version of the chivalric legends that fully draws Don Quijote in, it becomes clear that if he is to imagine a basis for action in the world it must be in accordance with some other paradigm; the heroic dream is no longer relevant in the way he would imagine. The episode of the Cave of Montesinos is thus the beginning of a turn in the novel, a moment when Don Quijote undergoes a death-like sleep and transformation. It promises to yield insights into the secrets of things hidden deeply in the past, some since the very foundation of the world. And yet the experience in the cave leaves Don Quijote filled with doubt about the true existence of the great heroes.[34]

Given these facts, what perspective might a mythical vision given in a dream have to offer on the truth, and what bearing might this truth have on Don Quijote's mission in the world? Macrobius's fourth-century *Commentary on Scipio's Dream* was one well-known text that offered a broad view of such matters.[35] Of the five types of dreams, three were deemed sources of the truth: oracular dreams, in which some revered figure reveals what will or will not transpire; prophetic dreams, in which a prediction about the future does indeed come true; and 'enigmatic' dreams, which require an interpretation in order to be understood, since they conceal their true meaning 'with strange shapes and veils.'[36] Don Quijote is desperate to identify his dream visions as true; it is to this end that he consults Maese Pedro's prophesying monkey. The reason for his hope is clear: to find confirmation that the figures from the chivalric romances do exist, and to discover that Montesinos would entrust their secrets to him, would reinforce Don Quijote's purpose in the world. The matter haunts Don Quijote, in part because he believes that he can only complete his mission in the world if he can discern these visions to be real. That task is itself part of the epic quest, inherited from the *Aeneid* (VI), where Virgil's narrator describes the two gates through which the underworld figures may pass up into the light; the gates separate the true shades from the false ones. One gate is said to be made of horn, and to give the true spirits passage up into the light; the other is described as 'gleaming with the sheen of polished ivory,' and in turn sends false visions to the world above.[37] But Don Quijote's interlocutors – Sancho and the Humanist Cousin – have their own, post-mythical notions about how to assess the truth of what he claims to have seen in the Cave. Their questions have little to do with the significance of stories of descent, with the truths revealed by dreams, or with the transformative journey of the *theoros*; on the contrary, they demonstrate a distortion of the larger purpose of the theoric journey and a misguided sense of what Don Quijote's imaginary encounter with his historical origins might mean. Sancho and the Cousin ask for informational details. They inquire whether the underworld figures eat and sleep, and how they meet their bodily needs. Indeed, the two display less fascination than curiosity about Don Quijote's report. The Humanist Cousin is especially interested in incorporating information from Don Quijote's account into a work he has in progress, a supplement to Polydore Vergil's book on discoveries and inventions, *De inventoribus rerum* (1499). This kind of miscellany was quite popular in the sixteenth century, as witnessed by texts such as Pedro Mexía's eclectic *Silva de varia lección* (Seville, 1540). The Cousin is especially interested in Don Quijote's account of the cave because he wants to find out about such things as the legendary transformations of the Guadiana River and the lagoons of the Ruidera, topics which are again laden with mythological overtones and Ovidian connections that the Cousin redirects in empirical fashion. But he is equally interested in observations about the origins of playing cards, and other such trivia.[38] Indeed, every question the two ask of Don Quijote seems to echo some chapter of *De inventoribus*, including 'Who first invented truces and treaties,' 'Who first planted grape vines,' and 'Who first built houses of mud or brick.'

Much has been written about the Cousin's misplaced interest in Don Quijote's dream vision. His educated curiosity about what Don Quijote saw in the cave is scarcely better placed than Sancho's interest in trivial and mundane questions about who was the first person ever to scratch his head, or who the first gymnast was. But the larger point of all this has to do with Cervantes' engagement with stories about origins, of which Polydore's work was one distorted reflection. Polydore's aim in creating this record of inventions was 'to see that no one is cheated of his glory since discovery is being first ... [and] to show those who want to imitate whom they ought to follow.'[39] He proceeds with his account by reference to the stockpile of information accumulated in the great books of the past – in the writings of Pliny, Herodotus, Aristotle, Plutarch, and Cicero, among many others. The concerns of the Humanist Cousin are of special note because he has dedicated himself to a project of 'demystification' in commitment to the truth. He has already completed a *Spanish Ovid* (*El Ovidio español*) which consists of a burlesque version of Ovid's *Metamorphoses*; he regards this work as especially useful for political life. Moreover, he is concerned about questions of origins: he is searching for the true (which for him means the non-mythical) roots of human and natural things. He describes the book as 'a new and rare invention, because in it, in a parodic imitation of Ovid, I describe who La Giralda of Sevilla was, and the Angel of the Magdalena, and the Vecinguerra Drainpipe in Córdoba, who built the Bulls of Guisando, and the Sierra Morena, and the fountains of Leganitos and Lavapiés, in Madrid, not forgetting the fountains of El Piojo and El Caño Dorado, and the fountain of la Priora, and each has its allegories, metaphors, and transformations that delight, astonish, and instruct, all at the same time' (600) (de invención nueva y rara; porque en él, imitando a Ovidio a lo burlesco, pinto quién fue la Giralda de Sevilla y el Ángel de la Madalena, quién el Caño de Vecinguerra, de Córdoba, quiénes los Toros de Guisando, la Sierra Morena, las fuentes de Leganitos y Lavapiés, en Madrid, no olvidándome de la del Piojo, de la del Caño Dorado y de la Priora; y esto, con sus alegorías, metáforas y translaciones, de modo que alegran, suspenden y enseñan a un mismo punto; II, 22, p. 206).

The Cousin's inquiry may well represent an attempt to substitute verifiable 'facts' for unreliable myths and idle speculation, and so to bring the truth 'down to earth.' In place of the theoretical insight that travel and transformation might provide, the Cousin is constructing a compendium of curiosities, a kind of *Wunderkammer* in prose that has little or no civic purpose. By contrast, the writings of Polydore Vergil included a political history (the *Historia Anglia*, modelled in part on the *Etymologies* of Isidore of Seville) in which the task of discovering origins was clearly directed toward political ends. His goal in that book was to show how the search for remote and inaccessible origins could be converted into a modern political project, a project about possible new foundations.[40] His fictional descendant in Cervantes, the Cousin, is engaged not just in an abuse of 'theory' but also in a distortion of the role of *historia* in political life.

Cervantes was no doubt aware of arguments endorsing the theoretical importance of history, including those that saw history principally as a source of universalizing truths. Consider Luis Cabrera de Córdoba, who wrote in *On History: How to Understand and Write It* (*De historia: para entenderla y escribirla*, 1611) that 'the person who carefully attends to ancient histories and takes heed of what they teach, has a light by which to see future things, since in one respect the world is all the same.'[41] But even for him the purpose of writing is to be found in its pragmatic aim to serve the public good ('el fin de la historia es la utilidad pública,' 35). In order to meet any of these demands, history must involve something much more than the recording of observed events. As Giuseppe Mazzotta remarked in relation to this episode, Cervantes recognizes that '*historia* is not just a fabric of natural observations, as the humanist [Cousin] believes. It is also, like Alberti's view of painting, a visionary text interwoven with legends, heraldry, chivalric memories, and archaic narratives … As [Don Quixote] digs into the burial ground of history and its sediments, his memory is the oracle telling him, through the sage Merlin, that he himself will revive the ancient cult of chivalry. He has, thus, learned that the value of mythic origins lies in their power to determine the plot of history and its future forms' (*Cosmopoiesis*, 90).

More accurate, though, might be to say that Cervantes attempts to distinguish between different types of truth. He maintains these distinctions even while he recognizes that the role of myth is to provide an understanding of things that are in themselves inaccessible to human sight. As we have already glimpsed, questions of origins are among the most important of truly inaccessible things. When the Humanist Cousin and Sancho speak about the Cousin's project, Sancho suggests that the name 'Adam' can serve as an answer to questions about origins, and the Cousin accepts it as such: 'Tell me, Señor,' he says to the Cousin, 'because you know everything, who was the first man to scratch his head? To my mind it must have been our father Adam' (600) (Sabráme decir ... pues todo lo sabe, quién fue el primero que se rascó en la cabeza, que yo para mí tengo que debió de ser nuestro padre Adán? II, 22, pp. 206–7). 'Yes, it must have been,' responded the cousin, 'because Adam undoubtedly had a head and hair, and this being the case, and Adam being the first man in the world, at some hour he must have scratched his head' (600) ('Sí sería' respondió el primo, 'porque Adán no hay duda que tuvo cabeza y cabellos, y siendo esto así, y siendo el primer hombre del mundo, alguna vez se rascaría'; II, 22, pp. 207). Then when he asks who was the first tumbler in the world, Sancho Panza answers that 'the first acrobat in the world was Lucifer, when he was tossed or thrown out of heaven and went tumbling down into the pit' (601) (fue Lúcifer, cuando le echaron o arrojaron del cielo, que vino volteando hasta los abismos; II, 22, p. 207). Don Quijote rejects this idea not because it seems preposterous but because it is inconsistent with Sancho's character: 'That question and answer are not yours, Sancho; you heard someone else say them' (601) (Esa respuesta no es tuya, Sancho: a alguno la has oído decir; II, 22, p. 207.) He fails to see that myths are traditional, i.e., that they come with an authority that is prior to the individual who may transmit them. But it is also a mistaken appropriation of myths to believe that they can give us information about matters of fact. It would be better to think that names like 'Adam' and 'Lucifer' can demonstrate that myths – which for Cervantes include dreams and sacred scriptures – can help to anchor truths that are otherwise inaccessible. Hence the interest that such questions hold for all foundational projects, including the founding of new states.

What Don Quijote makes of these visions is, in the end, no better suited to the exigencies of the political world than what the Cousin has to say. He attempts to support the authority of origins by appealing to a relatively wide range of texts. The books of chivalry can scarcely be distinguished from sacred scriptures in this regard. Well before the dialogue with the Humanist Cousin, Don Quijote responds to a question from the Barber about whether Amadís was a giant by citing the Bible; the allusion is to the book of Genesis (6:1–4). This is how Don Quijote endorses the veracity of the books he has read: 'Holy Scripture, which cannot deviate an iota from the truth, shows us that [giants existed] by telling us the history of that huge Philistine Goliath, whose stature was seven and a half cubits, which is inordinately tall' (467) (La Sagrada Escritura, que no puede faltar un átomo en la verdad, nos muestra que los hubo [gigantes] contándonos la historia de aquel filisteazo Golías, que tenía siete codos y medio de altura; II, 1, p. 50). The earlier dialogue with the Barber resembles the conversation between Don Quijote and the Humanist Cousin for its references to erudite and 'scientific' books and for the allusion to a dubious *Cosmografía* by the archbishop Turpin, widely known as the author of a mendacious history of Charlemagne. Here Don Quijote refers to a specific *arbitrio* he has in mind, which is to say to a remedy for the social, economic, and political problems of contemporary Spain, and above all for an economically viable 'defensa del reino': 'All these [Amadís, Palmerín, don Belianís, Reinaldos, Perión and all the others he mentions in the first chapter of Part II] ... were knights errant, the light and glory of chivalry. They, or knights like them, are the ones I would like for my scheme; if they were part of it, His Majesty would be well served and save a good deal of money, and the Turk would be left tearing his beard; therefore I do not wish to remain in my house' (my translation) (Todos estos [Amadís, Palmerín, don Belianís, Reinaldos, Perión, etc.] ... fueron caballeros andantes, luz y gloria de la caballería. Déstos, o tales como éstos, quisiera o que fueran los de mi arbitrio; que a serlo, su Majestad se hallará bien servido y ahorrará de mucho gasto, y el Turco se quedará pelando las barbas, y, con esto, no quisiera yo quedar en mi casa; II, 1, p. 49).[42] While Don Quijote does indeed spring into action in order to defend the Christian puppets Melisendra and Gaiferos from the enemy forces during Maese Pedro's show, the point of the episode is to show that his flawed vision depends on a distortion of the difference between original and copy. The episode is a perversion of the theoretical journey in two regards: first, in that Don Quijote in fact travels nowhere, and second in that the 'spectacle' he witnesses is not a source of wonders but a sham. These experiences lead him to take a secondary role when Sancho receives his promised 'island' to govern.

Images True and False

The voyage of Don Quijote and Sancho on Clavileño is widely recognized as the successor to the episode in the Cave of Montesinos. In addition to their mythical interconnections, both have a bearing on questions of perspective and the nature of 'theoretical' vision. As Cervantes approaches the episode of Sancho's governorship on Barataria we come to see more and more clearly that the question of 'theoretical' vision in fact has implications for politics. But in between the 'theoretical' episodes of descent and ascent are several other incidents, including the story of the *rebuznos*, the adventure on the enchanted boat, the entrance into the ducal palace where the 'flight' on Clavileño is eventually staged, and Maese Pedro's puppet show. Of these intervening episodes, the puppet show is of particular importance for the matter of theory and its roots in spectatorship. It speaks directly to the question of vision, here in relation to the subject of true and false images. While the reader understands that the show is small and rudimentary, the puppet theatre is presented as yet another world of wonders. It is a theatrical spectacle described as exhibiting countless *novedades*. 'Let's go see the puppet show of our good master Pedro, for I believe it must hold some surprises.' 'What do you mean, some! ...' responded Master Pedro. 'Sixty thousand are contained in this show of mine; I tell your grace, Senor Don Quixote, that it is one of the most specuacular things in the world today' (628) ('Vámonos a ver el retablo del buen Maese Pedro, que para mí tengo que debe tener alguna novedad.' '¿Cómo alguna?' respondió maese Pedro. 'Sesenta mil encierra en sí este mi retablo; dígole a vuesa merced, mi señor don Quijote, que es una de las cosas más de ver que hoy tiene el mundo'; II, 25, p. 239).

Maese Pedro's puppets enact a story derived from a mixture of Carolingian and Arthurian ballads – much in the way that Don Quijote mixes his sources – which in turn gives Cervantes the opportunity to make one of his many veiled references to contemporary preoccupations with the Turks. Maese Pedro's show makes the very common association of Sansueña (Sansoigne, Sajonia) with Zaragoza, and of the tower of Sansueña with sumptuous Qasr Aljafariya (the Aljafería Palace), built in the second half of the eleventh century for the Banu Hud dynasty. Don Quijote's concern is for the safety of the captive Melisendra and for Gaiferos, the hero who has come to rescue her from the unwelcome advances of one of her captors. As the two exit the tower and are pursued by enemy forces, Don Quijote leaps into action, destroying puppets and puppet-stage alike. Maese Pedro's complaint following his 'defeat' by Don Quijote involves a strange and subtle inversion of roles, in which Maese Pedro aligns himself with Rodrigo, the ancient king of Spain, who was once a commander of great forces but who now controls nothing.

As already noted, Don Quijote's behaviour in the episode may be taken as an all too obvious example of what Plato meant in warning about the consequences of theatrical 'imitation' in *Republic* III and X. But if we consider Maese Pedro's identity more closely, and not just Don Quijote's enthusiastic response to the puppet show, the episode becomes considerably more complex. We know that Maese Pedro is, in fact, the same character as Ginés de Pasamonte, one of the galley slaves Don Quijote had freed in Part I. But he had effectively been stripped of any official certification of his civic identity by the terms of the punishment that originally sent him to the galleys. This is the point of Cervantes' reference to his being sent to the galleys as a form of 'civil death' in Part I ('va [a las galeras] por diez años … que es como muerte civil'; I, 22, p. 271).[43] We also know from Part I that he is also the author of an unfinished autobiography, which is to say of a work of literary self-invention. When Ginés then returns in Part II, he is disguised as a gypsy and comes riding Sancho's missing donkey.[44] Following Don Quijote's descent into the cave, the narrator takes pains to explain how Ginés has transformed himself into an itinerant puppeteer. The description moves from the question of his identity as the rogue thief who 'fixes' some of the flaws in the narrative of Part I, to his status as an outlaw and a fugitive, and finally to his diguise as gypsy-puppeteer: 'This Ginés de Pasamonte, whom Don Quixote called Ginesillo de Parapilla, was the man who stole Sancho Panza's donkey … This Ginés, fearful of being captured by the officers of the law who were looking for him so that he could be punished for his infinite deceptions and crimes, so numerous and of such a nature that he himself wrote a long book recounting them, decided to cross into the kingdom of Aragón, cover his left eye, and take up the trade of puppet master, for this and sleight of hand were things he knew extremely well' (637) (Este Ginés de Pasamonte, a quien don Quijote llamaba Ginésillo de Parapilla, fue el que hurtó a Sancho Panza el rucio … Este Ginés, pues, temeroso de no ser hallado de la justicia, que le buscaba para castigarle de sus infinitas bellaquerías y delitos, que fueron tantos y tales que él mismo compuso un gran volumen contándolos, determinó pasarse al reino de Aragón y cubrirse el ojo izquierdo, acomodándose al oficio de titerero; que esto y el jugar de manos lo sabía hacer por estremo; II, 27, pp. 249–50).

There is more to be said. We already know from Part I that Ginés cannot see quite straight ('al mirar metía el un ojo en el otro un poco'; I, 2, p. 270).[45] The mention of the eyepatch in the description cited above resonates with this detail and has oddly important implications for someone who has taken up the business of making staged presentations for others to watch. The fact of his distorted vision is of further relevance for a range of questions about who in fact he is. Ginés is many things: a pícaro, a gypsy, a puppeteer, a convict on the loose, an author, and the owner of a trick monkey purchased from some liberated Christian captives who had been returned from North Africa. But he is also a charlatan and mountebank, which is to say, a kind of shape-shifter whose changing identity allows him to mirror and distort the look of things, including himself. His kinship with Pedro de Urdemalas of Cervantes' *comedia* by that name is unmistakable. So seen, the issue at stake in his puppet show is not only a critique of the theatre as a kind of spectacle that may incite unruly passions among the audience, but the possibility of distinguishing between those who create true appearances and those who make false semblances.

Not unlike the shape-shifting Pedro de Urdemalas, Ginés is by virtue of his background the creator of a set of potentially false and deceiving appearances. He is, in turn, set within a narrative where various other kinds of shape-shifting seem to be a frequent occurrence, as a gentleman becomes a knight in armour, an inn becomes a castle, and duennas grow beards. But Master Pedro's deepest ties are with the figure of the sophist. One wonders how Don Quijote might conceive of deriving anything true from what he presents. Indeed, the terms in which Ginés is described draw liberally on the text of Plato's *Sophist*, which had been discussed by Pico della Mirandola in 'De ente et uno' ('Of Being and Unity') and was the subject of a detailed commentary by Ficino among his commentaries on Plato.[46] Plato's dialogue revolves around the effort to distinguish between the sophist (who is also the rhetorician) and the philosopher; along with the statesman, these figures are central to Plato's effort to identify the ideal ruler. Like the sophist, Maese Pedro is 'one of the genus of conjurors' or wonder-workers (235b). He is a shape-shifter who works principally through language by distorting its perspectives.[47] For Plato, the sophist is also a criminal (239c), a ventriloquist (252c), an enchanter, and imitator (235a).[48] He practises the arts of lying and enchantment (241b). In technical terms, he is a maker of phantasms – which is to say of false images – in speeches (239c–d). For all these reasons, the sophist is especially difficult to discern; anyone in search of him will discover that he is hard to pin down and likely to wiggle away (231c). While it is true that the philosopher cannot easily be seen clearly either, this is, in Plato's view, for a very different reason: the philosopher is a god-like figure, bathed in bright light, whereas the sophist resembles a 'fugitive into the darkling of "that which is not"' (254a). Insofar as the sophist lays claim to a political skill (Plato calls his skill a political *technē* in the *Protagoras*, 319a), he is also the counter-image of the philosopher and, by extension, an inverted image of the philosopher-king.

Don Quijote is not in any conventional way a 'philosopher,' but neither is he a sophist. In respect of his foolish wisdom one might well see him as an amalgam of philosopher and sophist. He epitomizes by inversion the position of *docta ignorantia:* he is the wise fool. And yet Ginés is also one of the many figures in Part II who present themselves as inverted images – better said, perhaps, as partial images – of just this same figure. Among them are the Don Quijote's challenger, the Caballero de la Blanca Luna (who is in reality Sansón Carrasco, a university graduate), the Catalan outlaw Roque Guinart, who seems to have had considerably more success with the project of social justice than Don Quijote, and Maese Pedro himself, whose claim to fame resonates with the terms in which Don Quijote decribes himself.[49] His crimes, like Don Quijote's heroic deeds, are said to be greater than those of all other outlaws combined 'He alone had committed more crimes than all the rest combined, and was so daring and such a great villain that even though he was bound in this way, they still did not feel secure about him and were afraid he was about to escape' (168) (tenía aquel solo más delitos que todos los otros juntos, y que era tan atrevido y tan grande bellaco, que, aunque le llevaban de aquella manera, no iban seguros dél, sino que temían que se les había de huir; I, 22, p. 270). The result of these inverted identities is the creation of a world in which Don Quijote is asked to look upon inverted copies of himself, in spite of the fact that he is himself already a 'copy' whose existence is only tenuously linked to the originals he imitates.

What has all this to do with politics? The answer becomes increasingly clear as Cervantes approaches the episode of Sancho's governorship on Barataria. The critical point in relation to the puppet show is that the requirements of spectatorship, from which theory originates, include the ability to distinguish between what is true and what is false in the realm of images. Just as in his dream, the puppet show presents Don Quijote with images whose 'originals' either never existed or have been lost for good. The heroes that he reads about in books, or thinks he sees in the Cave of Montesinos, or imagines having come to life on the stage, are in fact locked forever in the imaginary past; they return only as phantasms, and no force of dream or theatrical imitation can revive them for him in any other way. Looking forward, we understand that Sancho's experience as governor of Barataria likewise takes place in a simulacral world, albeit one that pretends to make reference to the present rather than the past.

Clavileño

Given the suggestion that Maese Pedro is a kind of sophist, or at any rate a maker of false imitations, we can glean that the engagement with 'theory' in the *Quijote* intersects with experiences of spectatorship that may be true and reliable, or deceptive and false. On one level all the major 'spectatorial' episodes preceding Sancho's governorship, and the governorship itself, are clearly staged as false 'imitations,' as encounters with phantasms rather than as with icons. There is no visit with Montesinos, but only a dream; Gaiferos and Melisendra are not in flight, they are only characters in a puppet show; and likewise there is no voyage on Clavileño, but only an elaborate mechanical hoax that leads Don Quijote and Sancho to believe that they have travelled up into the heavens and look down upon the earth. And finally there is no island for Sancho to govern, but only a grand theatrical pretence.

And yet on another level these spectacular visions are all potential sources of truth, and indeed of a kind of truth that has implications for an understanding of what politics requires and ought to be. For example, the dream-like vision in the Cave of Montesinos, and the dialogue with Sancho and the Cousin about what Don Quijote says transpired there, lead to the recognition that no search for the fundamental principles of action or belief can yield an encounter with origins, historical or otherwise. All claims to transmit the authority of origins directly are in some important regards false, even while the myths by which they are explained may well be true. (As Machiavelli was fully aware, the challenge of modern politics begins when it is necessary to legitimize power that does not derive, by heredity, from origins. Politics is thus for Machiavelli a domain where myth, as a discourse about origins, does not apply.)

In the case of the puppet show, the perils of precipitous action in what seem to be compelling circumstances suggest that the fears and ambitions that ruled the old chivalric world must be set aside; they must be recognized as mere repetitions and reenactments in modern times, where wisdom requires an awareness of the fact that politics is rather like theatre. Indeed, one of the central points of all these episodes of spectatorship is a reinforcement of the Ciceronian and Tacitean insights that all political action is performance in a theatrical world. These episodes thus have a double face. They point to insights that may be gained by witnessing unfamiliar spectacles or by viewing the existing world from a fundamentally different point of view. But, especially when it comes to Barataria, they also address the need for self-awareness in the face of circumstances that are constructed and controlled by actors whose powers are concealed behind the scenes, so as to deprive the spectators of the awareness that they are, in fact, witnessing representations.

The journey on Clavileño stands to transform the perspectives of knight and squire from a point of view that is 'above' and 'beyond' the things of the ordinary world. One of the crucial implications of the episode is that this distance will give Don Quijote and Sancho access to a well-proportioned view of worldly things. But matters are hardly this simple, in part because this 'perspective' is a fiction created by powerful political characters, the Duke and the Duchess. A distanced and detached perspective on the world would seem to suit a person hoping to discharge the duties of political leadership, but the journey on Clavileño makes an offer of truth that is contingent upon an elaborate, theatrical falsehood. Indeed, the entire episode unfolds under the sign of the prankish lies of the Dukes.

There are, to be sure, a series of mythical associations that the journey on Clavileño calls to mind. One of the Dukes' retinue, the Dueña Dolorida, identifies Clavileño by reference to a line of renowned horses: Pegasus, Brilladoro, Frontino, Boötes, Peritoa, and Orelia, among others (II, 40, p. 341). Clavileño is compared to these mythical horses as well as to the horse involved in the most famous betrayal of all classical antiquity, the Trojan horse (II, 41, p. 348). After they mount the wooden effigy, Don Quijote and Sancho cover their eyes (or rather, the Duke and Duchess see to it that their eyes are covered, as befits the perpetrators of the deceit) and the two 'take flight' on Clavileño. What they see in their imaginations matches the Ptolemaic view of the cosmos, which is hardly insignificant given the raging controversies over the new sciences of Galileo and Copernicus. But they do not limit themselves to 'scientific' observations about what they see. Sancho offers a thought that goes to the heart of the difficulty of a prudential and perspectival vision of reality. He tells how he took a peek from under the blindfold and saw that the earth was the size of a mustard seed and that human beings were the size of hazelnuts: 'Since I have some dab of curiosity in me and want to know what it is that people try to stop me and keep me from knowing, very carefully, without anybody seeing me, right at my nose I pushed aside just a little bit of the handkerchief that was covering my eyes, and I looked down at the earth, and it seemed to me that it was no larger than a mustard seed, and the men walking on it not much bigger than hazelnuts, so you can see how high we must have been flying then' (my translation) (Yo, que tengo no sé qué briznas de curioso y de desear saber lo que se ne estorba e impide, bonitamente y sin que nadie lo viese, por junto a las narices aparté tanto cuanto el pañizuelo que me tapaba los ojos, y por allí miré hacia la tierra, y parecióme que toda ella no era mayor que un grano de mostaza, y los hombres que andaban sobre ella, poco mayores que avellanas; porque se vea cuán altos debíamos de ir entonces; II, 41, p. 353).

In *Cosmopolis*, Giuseppe Mazzotta suggested that the journey on Clavileño serves to correct human pride. This correction involves something rather more weighty than what even the ideal courtier needs to know by way of the need to limit self-flattery. It was in fact a familiar epic motif.

To cite one contemporary example, the *Lusíadas* contains a very similar vision of the earth as seen from the heavens, and likewise draws conclusions about human ambition. (In Camões's poem, the earth is the 'hostel' for a humanity that is characterized as 'too ambitious to be content / With the afflictions of solid land' and so has 'launched out on the restless oceans.')[50] The adventure on Clavileño shows that pride is rooted in a distorted and exaggerated perspective of things. It has the figural form of a hyperbole.[51] In its extreme forms, pride leads mortals to adopt perspectives that ought to belong to the gods. Because of this distortion, pride cultivates a desire to take on more than one can accomplish. Such is the force of the association between the Clavileño episode and the myth of Phaeton, to which the duennas make a direct allusion when cautioning Sancho not to lose his balance: 'Hold on, valiant Sancho, you're slipping! Be careful you don't fall, because your fall will be worse than that of the daring boy who wanted to drive the chariot of his father, the Sun!' (722) (¡Tente, valeroso Sancho, que te bamboleas! ¡Mira no cayas; que será peor tu caída que la del atrevido mozo que quiso regir el carro del Sol, su padre! II, 41, p. 349). The passage accurately reflects Ovid's characterization of Phaeton as 'full of confidence in himself' (*Metamorphoses*, II, 103–41), and it resonates as well with Lucian's satire *Icaromenippus: An Aerial Expedition* in which the character Menippus brashly challenges established power and inverts accepted values: 'A very short survey of life had convinced me of the absurdity and meanness and insecurity that pervade all human objects, such as wealth, office, power. I was filled with contempt for them, realized that to care for them was to lose all chance of what deserved care, and determined to grovel no more, but to fix my gaze upon the great All.'[52]

But the presiding moral force behind the Clavileño episode as a whole derives from the *Somnium Scipionis*, no doubt via Macrobius's much-read 'Commentary' on it. Originally the concluding book of Cicero's *De re-publica* (the rest of which remained lost until 1820), the point of the *Somnium Scipionis* was to suggest that a virtuous ruler must temper pride, which demonstrates itself as the overestimation of fame. A celestial perspective, from which the earth appears to be small, provides one of the best ways to accomplish the necessary reduction. The theme of the smallness of the earth when seen from the perspective of the heavens is the very centrepiece of Scipio's dream. 'I kept turning my eyes back to earth,' says Scipio; to which Africanus replies:

> I notice you are still gazing at the home and habitation of men. If it seems small to you (as indeed it is) make sure to keep your mind on these higher

regions and to think little of the human scene down there. For what fame can you achieve, what glory worth pursuing, that consists mainly of men's talk? … That entire land mass which you occupy has been made narrow from north to south and broader from east to west. It is like a small island surrounded by the sea which on earth you call the Atlantic, the Great Sea, or the Ocean. Yet observe how small it is in spite of its imposing name. Has your fame been able to find its way from these civilized and familiar lands to the far side of the Caucasus …? And even those who talk about us now – how long will they continue to do so?[53]

Macrobius's commentary on this passage draws a succinct conclusion from a wealth of geographical speculation about the shape of the earth and the distribution of land masses: '[Cicero's] reason for emphasizing the earth's minuteness was that worthy men might realize that the quest for fame should be considered unimportant since it could not be great in so small a sphere.'[54] Not surprisingly, Machiavelli inverts this wisdom in advising that 'men often deceive themselves in the belief that they will conquer pride with humility.'[55]

The more conventional, moral perspective on humility could nonetheless be in tension with the humanist conviction in the power of reason to confer dignity on human beings. Fernán Pérez de Oliva's 'Dialogue on the Dignity of Man' is deeply invested in the idea that reason is the source of human dignity; it is but one of many texts that echo the *Somnium Scipionis* in pointing out that the inhabited earth is in fact small in size, and that the human beings who dwell upon it are far less well naturally endowed than many of the animals: 'We circle the earth, measure the oceans, ascend up to the sky, and see its grandeur, count its movements, and do not stop until we reach God, who is not hidden from us. There is nothing that remains concealed, nothing removed from us, nothing left in darkness, where human understanding is available.'[56] (Not surprisingly, Pérez de Oliva was also the author of a treatise on the new cosmography, the *Cosmographia nova*.)

Reason (*entendimiento*) was not exactly the same thing as learning. There was little doubt among humanists that the study of books and an immersion in *letras* were key resources in the project of moral education. But the views just cited cast a somewhat different light on the ambition at work behind certain kinds of learning. As for the episode on Clavileño, it begins not as an adventure involving *letras* at all, but as an adventure of *armas*. Don Quijote's hope is to free the duennas from the curse that has disfigured their appearances by travelling to Candaya in order to defeat the evil Malambruno. And yet the episode is one that ultimately involves the bounds of what may be known by *letras* and the purposes for which learning is designed. Like Scipio's dream, the flight on Clavileño provides the opportunity to adopt a perspective that shows the limits of arrogance and pride in relation to all human pursuits. Just as in Macrobius, the observations on the smallness of the earth form the context for Don Quijote's later advice about the virtues necessary for civic life: prudence, temperance, courage, and justice.

It is not surprising that Don Quijote would be an ally in this project, but it may seem odd to find him endorsing the virtues of humility. He is so often arrogant and bold in what he says and in what he attempts to do. The humility he advises is meant for Sancho, and especially for Sancho's benefit as the future governor of Barataria. Among his first advice to Sancho in II, 42, there is an allusion to Aesop's cautionary fable of the frog who tried to inflate himself to the size of an ox. Moreover, Don Quijote's understanding of 'humility' is aligned with status and lineage and not with perspective or insight. He means to tell Sancho that he can and ought to be virtuous in spite of his humble origins. He urges Sancho to 'take pride in the humbleness of your lineage, and do not disdain to say that you come from peasants' (730) (Haz gala, Sancho, de la humildad de tu linaje, y no te desprecies de decir que vienes de labradores; II, 42, p. 358). But Don Quijote is hardly consistent in his advice. The further promise that he makes to Sancho is that he will win eternal fame by governing well: 'If you follow these precepts and rules, Sancho, your days will be long, your fame eternal, your rewards overflowing' (732) (Si estos preceptos y estas reglas sigues, Sancho, serán luengos tus días, tu fama será eterna, tus premios colmados; II, 42, pp. 359–60). Perhaps there is also an echo here of Machiavelli's *Discourses on Livy*, I, 2, referring to what Lycurgus accomplished as a lawmaker in Sparta in creating a state that lasted for more than 800 years, 'resulting in the highest praise for him and in tranquility for that city.'[57] That said, Machiavelli had ideas about how an individual might rise above humble beginnings by means of fraud ('That One Moves from Humble to Great Fortune More Often through Fraud than through Force,' *Discourses*, II, 13, pp. 185–7). His chosen example is drawn from Xenophon's *Life of Cyrus*, a text to which the *Quijote* urges us to return: 'No other conclusion can be drawn from his action except that a leader who wishes to undertake great enterprises must learn how to deceive' (*Discourses*, II, 13, p. 185).

It is true that in their conversation the Duchess tries to correct Sancho's perspective by reminding him that a vision of the earth as the size of a mustard seed is inconsistent with the vision of men the size of hazelnuts.

Since a hazelnut is much larger than a mustard seed, such a vision must be false, or at best incoherent. Indeed, the Duchess tries further to amend Sancho's perspective by instructing him that what he takes as a complete and total view of reality is not in fact such: 'From just one side you can't see all of whatever you may be looking at' (726) (Por un ladito no se vee [*sic*] el todo de lo que se mira; II, 41, p. 353). The Duchess is, in one very important sense, right: there is no perspective from which anyone can grasp the world as a whole. But she nonetheless leaves the artificial and incomplete context of Sancho's vision – the fact that it is a staged affair – intact for him to believe. Sancho, for his part, adopts Don Quijote's familiar theory of enchantments in order to explain what he believes he saw: 'I don't know about those lookings,' he tells the Duchess. 'All I know is that it would be nice if your ladyship would understand that since we were flying by enchantments by enchantment I could see all the earth and all the men no matter how I looked at them' (726) ('Yo no sé nada de esas miradas,' replicó Sancho, 'sólo sé que será bien que vuestra señoría entienda que, pues volábamos por encantamento, por encantamento podía yo ver toda la tierra y todos los hombres por doquiera que los mirara'; II, 41, p. 353). Save Don Quijote, who experiences the episode with questions about the Cave of Montesinos still on his mind, it is completely clear to everyone except Sancho that the things he claims he saw from Clavileño could not have been true in and of themselves. Sancho collaborates in his own deception, which blinds him to the fact that from this fictitious horse he could not have seen the earth or human beings in the way he describes. And yet the episode provides Sancho with a potentially transformative insight that has the potential to influence his political ambitions. Just before the Duke grants him his 'island' to govern, Sancho explains: 'After I came down from the sky, and after I looked at the earth from that great height and saw how small it was, the burning desire I had to be a governor cooled a little; where's the greatness in ruling a mustard seed, or the dignity or pride in governing half a dozen men the size of hazel nuts?' (728) (Después que bajé del cielo, y después que desde su alta cumbre miré la tierra y la vi tan pequeña, se templó en parte en mí la gana que tenía tan grande de ser gobernador; porque, ¿qué grandeza es mandar en un grano de mostaza, o que dignidad o imperio el gobernar a media docena de hombres tamaño como avellanas que, a mi parecer, no había más en toda la tierra? II, 42, p. 355).

Set within the context of a deceptive contrivance, the episode on Clavileño may well be the purest example of a 'theoretical' voyage in the novel. It raises the question about whether a radical change of perspective, of the kind that would be afforded by a voyage above the earth, might provide an opportunity to see things with a clarity that is not available from any standpoint on the earth. The hope that informs the episode is that a shift in perspective might yield a truthful vision of the way things really are, that it might allow things to be seen free of distortion, in their accurate likeness and their just proportion. But, as noted above, Don Quijote and Sancho are blindfolded during the episode, and so cannot 'see' anything in any literal sense at all. Moreover, there is no ultimate truth in these fictional heavens that would be visible by means of physical sight anyway. Indeed, Cervantes uses the episode in order to stress the notion of the non-empirical nature of certain sources of insight, including those that might benefit the polis. If what the characters learn through this faux theoretical voyage is in fact true, this is because the journey must be interpreted in a figural sense, much as one would interpret a myth. The 'report' about wonders seen in travel to extreme locations initially associated with the 'theoretical' voyage of antiquity has here migrated to the world of fiction. Fiction is aligned with dreams and fanciful flights and may act as a surrogate for the theoretical journey. But the ultimately earthbound Sancho does not fully grasp the fact that his insights originate in a set of made-up circumstances, and that the Dukes themselves remain in control of the context of his beliefs.

Demonstrating the limits of theory, the journey on Clavileño is nevertheless necessary preparation for the political experiment of Sancho's rule on Barataria. It is not only a theoretical voyage but a kind of trial that Sancho must endure before acceding to the governorship of the island. (Sancho must, for instance, try to conquer his fears, and Don Quijote notes that Sancho's fear in this episode is comparable to the great terror he felt in the episode of the fulling mills.)[58] Furthermore, the discovery that there may be no perspective from which one can see things clearly and in their entirety, and that every perspective is partial and potentially contradictory of others, is one of the ways in which Cervantes adapts the principles of *docta ignorantia* to political matters. One of the principal insights of Cusanus's *De docta ignorantia* lies in the two-part recognition: first, that we may never be able to find a 'fixed point' within an infinite universe from which to observe things in a secure fashion and, second, that awareness of this inescapable limitation is one of the keys to wisdom. 'If someone did not know that a body of water was flowing and did not see the shore while he was on a ship in the middle of the water, how would he recognize that the ship was being moved?'[59] The very same question begs to be asked, modified so as to suit the circumstances, in relation to the episode on Clavileño. How could Sancho and Don Quijote possibly know that they were not, in fact, moving anywhere at all on the wooden horse? In Cervantes' case, the deception has a very clear and proximate cause in the machinations of the Duke and the Duchess, which is also to say, in the often invisible forms of power exercised by those who are able to control political and social circumstances. I will return to the question of political power and influence in chapter 7 below. But before doing so I turn to Sancho's experiences as governor of Barataria, and to Don Quijote's advice to his Squire. In the episode of Sancho's governorship, Cervantes countenances the possibility of a reorientation of political ideals that brings the insights gained during the imaginary flight on Clavileño 'down to earth.' But as we also shall see, the experiment on Barataria is but a preamble to politics, an example *a contrario* that provides an occasion for further reflection on the relationship between politics and non-political forms of life.

6 Politics Brought down to Earth

Following the 'theoretically' suggestive adventures into the depths of the Cave of Montesinos and up into the celestial spheres on Clavileño, Cervantes turns toward questions of politics within the realm of terrestrial practice. How might the wisdom that Sancho has gained on Clavileño help him during his tour of duty as governor of his coveted 'island'? And how might Don Quijote's experiences in the Cave and on the magical horse help him advise Sancho about how best to rule? We move from adventures that revolve around the *vita contemplativa* to a consideration of politics within the framework of the *vita activa*. That ancient distinction was hardly an unfamiliar one among humanists. In *Utopia*, for instance, Thomas More described the difference between theoretical reason and practical wisdom as the difference between one kind of philosophy 'that makes everything to be alike fitting at all times' and another that 'is more pliable, that knows its proper scene, accommodates itself to it, and teaches a man with propriety and decency to act that part which has fallen to his share.'[1] But *Utopia* as a book and 'utopia' as a non-place are something else: they are fictions that allow for reflection on the very gap that the division between 'theory' and 'practice' seems to create.

That More's particular form of fiction and Sancho's Barataria involve imaginary places is not insignificant. For, at some level, all politics involves the governance of territories and the rule over their inhabitants. The polis may be an idea, but politics involves actions that are carried out within the boundaries of a given place by means of policies, laws, judicial decisions, and the like. (As I will discuss in the next chapter, the early modern idea of political 'place' was increasingly conceived as a nation.)[2] The premise that governing ought to be associated with the rule over a territory is something that Sancho certainly believes, in part because it allows Don Quijote's promise of an island to be mapped onto the historical realities that had been unfolding since the 'discovery' of the New World. In approaching his governorship on Barataria, Sancho has come a long way from the time in Part I when he thought of his 'tierra' in purely local terms ('I left my home place and my children and my wife to come to serve your grace, thinking I would be better off, not worse' [my translation]; Yo salí de mi tierra y dejé hijos y mujer por venir a servir a vuestra merced, creyendo valer más y no menos; I, 20, p. 239).[3]

Sancho regards the idea of being appointed the governor of an island-realm as the fulfilment of a rich and happy fantasy; it is a fantasy that he has acquired as if by contagion from Don Quijote, who in turn acquired it from a mix of sources in history and the romances of chivalry. And yet the 'island' is a fictional realm created as a large-scale prank. It is, in fact, a village on the Dukes' estate, not a territory or a state in any true political sense. Nor it is just fictional in an innocent way; it is an elaborate sham in which some of the villagers participate, and about which its 'governor' remains utterly deceived and ultimately disappointed as regards the privileges of a ruler in relation to the demands placed upon him. Its status as a false utopia is underscored by the Duke's presentation of it as perfectly symmetrical ('an island, right and true, round and well-proportioned' [728]) (un ínsula hecha y derecha, redonda y bien proporcionada; II, 42, p. 355) and, moreover, as a place of great natural abundance, 'exceedingly fertile and bountiful, where, if you know how to manage things, with the riches of the earth you can approach the riches of the sky' (728) (sobremanera fértil y abundosa, donde si vos os sabéis dar maña podéis con las riquezas de la tierra granjear las del cielo; II, 42, pp. 355–6). Its abundance recalls the display of plenty that Sancho had seen and enjoyed in the episode of Camacho's wedding.[4] But Barataria is clearly a false paradise set in the midst of a courtly world. Quite contrary to what the Duke suggests, Sancho's principal 'reward' for his good work as governor is, in fact, nothing material at all; it is an increase in self-knowledge. In this, however, Sancho satisfies an ancient philosophical demand ('know thyself') in exactly the form it had been presented to him by Don Quijote: 'You must look at who you are and make an effort to know yourself, which is the most difficult knowledge one can imagine' (730) (Has de poner los ojos en quien eres, procurando conocerte a ti mismo, que es el más difícil conocimiento que puede imaginarse; II, 42, p. 357). One consequence of the episode on Barataria is that Sancho comes to learn by experience something he had recognized intuitively as true at the very beginning of his political career: 'They can dress me ... however they want; no matter what clothes I wear I'll still be Sancho Panza' (729) (De cualquier manera que vaya vestido seré Sancho Panza; II, 42, p. 356).[5] The remaining question is whether and how a fiction as false as Barataria can provide access to the truth.

Remarkably, Sancho's 'island' is the only place in the novel where we observe anything like governance in action. Elsewhere in the *Quijote* the practical workings of politics are relegated mostly to the background, or are referenced principally by means of insinuation. This 'backgrounding' is, in fact, a significant feature of Cervantes' approach. For example, we see the consequences and effects that political power has for Ginés de Pasamonte and the other galley slaves in Part I, but we do not see into the heart of the law, nor witness any legal reasoning or process of official judgment. The galley slaves are described as 'people forced by the king' (gente forzada del rey) but, just as in Velásquez's *Las Meninas*, the king never comes directly into view. Cervantes is here playing on the double meaning of *forzada*, and as part of this oblique approach to questions of politics and power Don Quijote finds it quite preposterous that the king might 'force' (violate) anyone at all: 'What do you mean, forced?' asked Don Quixote. Is it possible that the king forces anyone?' (163) ('¿Cómo gente forzada?' preguntó don Quijote. '¿Es posible que el rey haga fuerza a ninguna gente?' I, 22, p. 265). The seemingly offhand remark gestures toward the natural-law philosophy of thinkers like Francisco Suárez, according to which all men were born free and could not by nature claim to dominate others rightfully.[6] To take another case, we see the well-intentioned lawlessness of the Catalan bandit Roque Guinart in Part II, but we do not see the workings of a legal system, either affirmatively or otherwise. Likewise, we see the fear that is instilled by the Holy Brotherhood in episodes mentioned above, but we see nothing of the state apparatus that sanctions and enables their activities.

This oblique approach to power allows Cervantes to explore the porous boundaries between the 'political' domain and other spheres of life. As I will discuss further in subsequent chapters, Cervantes does so in order to probe two interrelated facts: first, as had been suggested by writers from Aristotle and Cicero to Vitoria, that political relations are constituted out of elements that are not inherently political – the relations of the family, civil society, ethics, the economy, religion, and so forth; and second, that once a political domain is formally established, as a state, politics has the ability to insinuate itself back into virtually every sphere of life, including the 'prepolitical' domains out of which it was ostensibly formed. Especially in the context of an absolutist state, the formal constitution of the political sphere tends to render all relations political. (One fantasy of such societies is that all such relations were political to begin with.) This is to say that the domains of domestic life, religion, ethics, etc., become reabsorbed into the political sphere, and that various official policies and state laws in turn came to regulate such things as who can marry and who cannot, who can inherit property and who cannot and, as in the case of Ricote and his daughter, Ana Félix, who can remain within the nation-state and who must leave.

This having been said, there is nonetheless a general division of labour between the two parts of the novel as regards the way in which Cervantes addresses the question of politics and its 'others.' Many of the episodes of Part I, and especially the intercalated stories, tend to concentrate on the 'constitutive elements' of politics – i.e., on the various institutions and forms of association out of which formal politics seems to be built. Many episodes in Part II, by contrast, tend to show how an officially constituted political state finds ways to insinuate itself into virtually all spheres of life, including the family, civil society, the economy, and so forth. This division between the two Parts is nonetheless hardly rigid, and because the novel is cumulative in its effect and recursive in its structure, the episodes of Part II also impel us to 'read back' over the episodes of Part I and to recognize that the forms of association sometimes imagined as constituting the 'elements' of politics are themselves shot through with the very same relations of power, fantasy, and sometimes of force, that characterize formal politics. The contextual reasons are both historical and ideological – historical in the sense that an enlarged and more powerful state did, in fact, come to extend its reach to civil matters, including family relations, and private life; and ideological to the extent that the state portrays itself as having arisen naturally out of various pre-political forms of association.

But, to reiterate the larger point, Cervantes approaches few if any of these questions in a direct way. Quite the contrary, Cervantes is consistently indirect and oblique in his engagements with these issues. The reasons are numerous. Prominent among them is the fact that many of the 'official' workings of politics were themselves hidden from view. In addition to the public politics – royal decrees (*pragmáticas*), the decisions of the Courts, the edicts of judges, and the official pronouncements of various ministers and councils – there were countless decisions of low-level bureaucrats and administrators, unofficial alliances of state offices and religious groups, and all manner of quasi-official policies relating to matters of gender, religion, and race. One of the great legal questions of the time was, in fact, whether laws had to be promulgated in order for them to have force. Vitoria takes this up explicitly in his lectures on Thomas Aquinas's

Summa ('On Law').[7] Indeed, it is the ubiquitous but often concealed form of political power that helps account for Cervantes' need to speak indirectly and obliquely about politics. Consequently, Cervantes is often dealing with questions of politics even where he is treating matters that are not explicitly 'themed' as political. As we have already seen, many of the forms of discourse that are pressed into service in the course of his attempts to explore questions about what politics is and what it ought to be – the discourses of myth and fables, of dialogues, travel reports, and so on – are not inherently 'political' at all.

When Cervantes finally comes to stage the scenes of Sancho's governorship on Barataria, and when Don Quijote counsels him about how best to rule, we might well be cautious in thinking that at last we have arrived at an explicit statement of Cervantes' political ideas. We should nonetheless be careful not to take Don Quijote's advice to Sancho or Sancho's actions as governor as direct expressions of Cervantes' stance – just as the Canon of Toldeo turns out not to be a wholly reliable source of Cervantes' literary theory. All these voices are certainly at play in some serious way, but the novel is constructed so as to give the lie to the very idea of a single 'reliable source.' This applies to politics as much as to everything else. The overarching question is how this unreliability may be a source of truth. In the case of political matters, this means that even where we seem to be offered a direct exposition of views about political praxis – e.g., how Sancho should govern, questions of justice, judgment, the virtues, and civil defence – we remain within a discourse that is oblique and indirect, in a field of positions that may be self-cancelling, and in the presence of bona fide statements that are nonetheless framed as fictions. In the case at hand, where Sancho is given an island to govern, laws to make, and judicial cases to decide, the most reasonable thing may well be to assume that Cervantes is, in the end, thinking about something other than, or in addition to, questions of politics. In other words, these chapters address a number of factors that are hidden from ordinary conceptions of politics. At work behind Don Quijote's advice to Sancho and Sancho's attempt to rule, and largely invisible to them both, is a fraudulent fiction constructed by a pair of wealthy aristocrats who construct a world in which they can control the very conditions under which questions of justice and virtue are considered. The issue is that of politics in relation to a set of false frames. Is there a fundamental difference between fraudulent fictions and those that are accurate images of the truth? Can something of importance for politics emerge from fictions that are false?

To confront these questions suggests that the idea of a movement from the theoretically suggestive episodes on Clavileño and in the Cave of Montesinos to the world of political practice on Barataria island is significantly more complex than what can be captured by the idea of the practical implementation of theoretical insights. The notion of a shift from the theoretical heights (or the historical depths) to the mid-world of practice is, in fact, a shift between forms of fiction. Fiction has different forms. Throughout the novel, the quixotic fiction generates fantasies beyond the books that inspire it and that the Canon of Toledo rejects; Sancho's fantasy of the governorship of an island is one of its products. But this fantasy goes further in that it is seemingly made real. That process of 'making real' underscores the degraded interests of the Duke and the Duchess. Moreover, Cervantes seems to be suggesting that the debasement of fiction parallels a debasement of ideals; specifically, it is indicative of the state of practical politics in a world where the nobility has lost sight of its genuine role – has lost sight of the fact that true nobility entails virtue – a role that ought to rest on the ability to tell the difference between true fictions (icons) and false ones (phantasms). No less than the flight on Clavileño, the episode on Barataria is an instance in which a close-knit alliance of status and wealth allows for a control of fantasy-production; that control enables elaborate *burlas* aimed, lamentably, at deceiving two characters who are hardly in need of assistance in this regard.[8]

The apparently explicit, political episodes of Sancho's governorship and Don Quijote's advice must accordingly be read on two levels. One level does, indeed, require an earnest consideration of Don Quijote's maxims and of Sancho's efforts to govern his island in a manner that is consistent with the principles of virtue. How is one best to rule, and who is best suited for the task? How should the ideal ruler behave? How best to make laws? How to judge difficult cases? What training is required to do such things well? Can the art of governance be learned at all? As many critics have noted, Cervantes' engagement with such questions can be traced to sources in the abundant literature of practical advice for princes and kings. Marcel Bataillon described Don Quijote's advice to Sancho as a 'manual of practical wisdom.'[9] At the same time, Don Quijote's advice introduces a new, more pragmatic way of speaking about such things as behaviour, tact, virtue, and respect. The plainness of Don Quijote's speech and his surprising affinity for political society reflects his new role as counsellor to the governor-elect. As the advice books would often explain, the counsellor to the prince or king must himself be a person of true virtue. Not surprisingly,

Don Quijote argues that he would be ashamed if Sancho were not to succeed in his new role ('If you govern badly the fault will be yours and mine the shame' [736]); Si mal gobernares, tuya será la culpa, y mía la vergüenza; II, 43, p. 365). The prospect of success in governing is something that Don Quijote presents in terms of the promise of eternal fame and social gain: 'If you follow these precepts and rules, Sancho, your days will be long, your fame well-earned, your rewards overflowing, your joy indescribable; you will marry your children as you wish, they and your grandchildren will have titles, you will live in peace and harmony with all people' (732) (Si estos preceptos y estas reglas sigues, Sancho, serán luengos tus días, tu fama será eterna, tus premios colmados, tu felicidad indecible, casarás tus hijos como quisieres, títulos tendrán ellos y tus nietos, vivirás en paz y beneplático de las gentes; II, 42, pp. 359–60).[10]

The discourses of princely advice and of practical wisdom are framed by an elaborate fiction that is concealed from the very characters who attempt to approach politics in earnest. Indeed, any analysis of Don Quijote's advice and of Sancho's judgments as governor requires an acknowledgment of the fact that the two are the unwitting pawns of a pair of aristocrats, whose personal power and wealth undermine whatever virtuous ends might be pursued by the Knight and his Squire. Within this fiction, what counts as 'political discourse' is constructed so as to include an education into the kind of behaviour appropriate for participation in political society. Don Quijote freely advises Sancho about how he ought to dress and eat, how he ought to speak, what he ought to wear, etc. 'Political society' may of course refer to many things, and in its largest sense would include all the elements of association that might comprise the polis. But in this particular instance 'political society' means aristocratic society. Given Don Quixote's affinity for the chivalric past, Cervantes presents the aristocratic face of politics as an exaggerated moment in the sweeping historical arc across which warriors were gradually 'civilized,' their combative instincts tamed, and their behaviour transformed into patterns that were better suited to more highly organized and administered contexts. In becoming Sancho's counsellor, Don Quijote himself undergoes this transformation in a way that is consistent with a reformed, humanist conception of the virtues.

This historical process was described by Norbert Elias in a path-breaking analysis of the changing relationships between power and civility in the late Middle Ages and early modern world. Elias described a sweeping historical process that can help explain some of the irony involved in the fact that Don Quijote, a partisan of knight-errantry, comes to offer advice to

Sancho about how to behave in a courtly world. The invention of manners, the 'civilizing' of the warrior impulses, and the bringing of myriad forms of relatively violent behaviour under control were enabling factors behind the formation of social and political institutions in which the coordination of efforts became increasingly complex and in which the chains of interdependence became less direct. Crucial to all this was the courtly transformation of the warrior class. In the course of such a process, the risk of violence was reduced by means of a proto-Hobbesian monopolization of force by 'civil society':

> In the earlier sphere, where violence is an unavoidable and everyday event, and where the individual's chains of dependence are relatively short, because he largely subsists directly from the produce of his own land, a strong and continuous moderation of drives and affects is neither necessary, possible nor useful. The life of the warriors themselves ... is threatened continually and directly by acts of physical violence; thus, measured against life in more pacified zones, it oscillates between extremes. Compared to this other society, it permits the warrior extraordinary freedom in living out his feelings and passions, it allows savage joys, the uninhibited satisfaction of pleasure from women, or of hatred in destroying and tormenting anything hostile. But at the same time it threatens the warrior, if he is defeated, with an extraordinary degree of exposure to the violence and the passions of others, and with radical subjugation, such extreme forms of physical torment as are later, when physical torture has become the monopoly of a central authority, hardly to be found in normal life. With this monopolization, the physical threat to the individual is slowly depersonalized. It no longer depends quite so directly on momentary affects; it is gradually subjected to increasingly strict rules and laws; and finally, within certain limits and with certain fluctuations, the physical threat when laws are infringed is made less severe.[11]

We can easily align this account with the contrast between Don Quijote's impulsively violent behaviour in Part I and the tempered advice to Sancho in Part II that seems as if it were a blend of Erasmus and Castiglione. But what this account does not explain is the incorporation of relatively 'disciplined' forms of violence and humiliation within the aristocratic world, as when Don Quijote is mauled by cats, or when his beard is lathered with soap. These things seem to happen not for any underlying political reason but rather as a demonstration of the fact that certain forms of incivility were, in fact, preserved as part of civilized society. Moreover, Elias's account of the sociogenesis of the court does not ask about the role of fiction in its configuration; it overlooks the fact that various kinds of fiction helped sustain the semblance of a 'total world,' one that seemed to have the power to subsume or eliminate external perspectives and alternative beliefs. As I hope to suggest, Cervantes probes this very question in the episodes of Sancho's rule over the island. His engagement with fiction – which here leads to a critique of fictions that lack any self-critical dimension – yields a vision of politics that contests the values of a degraded courtly world.

The notion of a clear or simple contrast between theory and practice is thus complicated by the fact that both involve something – fiction – that is neither theoretical nor practical. For even a reoriented and reformed understanding of the role of theory in relation to the realm of practice, one that would bring both politics and theory back down to earth, has difficulty remaining on an even keel in contexts that are not transparent to the actors involved. It would thus be more accurate to say that we move from episodes about theory and its limits to episodes that show the limits imposed on practical politics by the artificial contexts in which all 'real-world' matters of politics, 'practice' (*strictu sensu* included) are embedded. We might be led to believe that Cervantes' explorations of the varieties of political discourse culminate in the practical experiment on Barataria, but even the name 'Barataria' suggests that the experiment is a sham, a cheap fraud, and so not to be taken at face value:

> The successful and amusing conclusion of the adventure of the Dolorous One so pleased the duke and duchess that they decided to move forward with their deceptions, seeing that they had a very accommodating individual who would accept them as true; and so, having devised their scheme and instructed their servants and vassals as to how they ought to behave toward Sancho in his governorship of the promised ínsula, the next day, which was the one following the flight of Clavileño, the duke told Sancho to prepare and ready himself to leave and be a governor, since his ínsulanos were waiting for him as if for the showers of May. (727–8)

> Con el felice y gracioso suceso de la aventura de la Dolorida, quedaron tan contentos los duques, que determinaron pasar con las burlas adelante, viendo el acomodado sujeto que tenían para que se tuviesen por veras; y así habiendo dado la traza y órdenes que sus criados y sus vasallos habían de guardar con Sancho en el gobierno de la ínsula prometida, otro día, que fue el que sucedió al vuelo de Clavileño, dijo el duque a Sancho que se adeliñase y compusiese

para ir a ser gobernador, que ya sus insulanos le estaban esperando como el
agua de mayo. (II, 42, p. 355)

And yet, Sancho's rule on Barataria and the preparation for it present yet
another set of instances in which things that are truly important lie concealed in what would appear to be a mere *burla*. Additionally, the experiment on Barataria complicates Machiavelli's division of principalities
between those that are inherited and those that are won by force, since
Barataria is a realm that Sancho has neither inherited nor acquired by conquest or annexation. The results are clearly mixed. Sancho fares relatively
well as a judge in response to ordinary cases of fraud and deceit, but he is
hardly a match for the higher-level deceptions that the Duke and Duchess
have staged.

Thus, rather than move us in a seamless fashion from the realm of theory
toward the world of practice, these episodes magnify the over-simplifica-
tion inherent in the very idea of such a progression. To be able to bridge the
gap between theory and practice requires something other than the 'quixotic' idea of implementing the principles of justice in a finite and resistant
world. This is not only because the world is indeed finite and resistant but
because it is shaped and crafted according to the designs of sometimes deceitful human beings, who direct various forms of power toward those
ends. If things were otherwise, then some of the most pressing matters of
political concern, in early modern Spain or anywhere, might easily be resolved simply by following the advice of economists and planners. We can
certainly appreciate the need to bring politics down to earth. As Plato's
Socrates pointed out, the philosopher who falls into a ditch while contemplating the stars or who, having left the cave of ordinary life, cannot find his
way around, is a ridiculous and useless figure.[12] In Spain, the most serious
advisors to the crown that included important economists of the presti-
gious Salamanca school, the *arbitristas*, were well aware of what needed to
be done.[13] At the same time, they were scarcely about to point out the fictional basis of much of what was transpiring in the Spanish state. Cervantes
clearly saw that the problems of politics could not so simply be addressed.
Especially when the concealed powers of the Duke and the Duchess as
masters of a political fiction are taken into account, it becomes clear that
something other than 'theory' or 'practice' needs to be factored into politics. Politics, it seems, involves a fictional turn that can make the forces at
work within the world of practice seem invisible by transforming what is
clearly 'false' into the invisible preconditions of the 'true.'

This places the wisdom gained on Clavileño and in the Cave of Montesinos in a very different light: humility leads to wisdom only insofar as it is a revelation of the ultimately contingent and provisional nature of a political world that is always susceptible to the power of controlling fictions. Neither the things that any character says or does in relation to the public world, nor the things he believes about himself, are free from these constraints. The contingency of politics explains its susceptibility to the deceptive exercise of power. (A figure like Machiavelli argues that some degree of deception is inevitable in the exercise of political power.) In other words: the voyage on Clavileño yields the insight that the truth of any set of experiences is perspectivally shaped and so can always be reframed. And yet it would seem to be the structural ambition of certain political formations to conceal this truth; in particular, it was of interest to the political aristocracy in Spain to do just this in order to conceal one particular truth about status: that those who occupy the highest station may well be bereft of virtue. Cervantes thus directs the moral interest in humility toward an engagement with the fictional conditions that make virtue and status appear to be aligned, where in fact they are often at odds.

Sancho is a key figure in the discovery of these facts, even while he is initially an unwitting victim of the Dukes' political prank. We know that Sancho's eagerness to gain the territorial rewards of adventure has been tempered by his experience on Clavileño and that his political dreams have been humbled and brought 'down to earth.' But at the same time he recognizes the need for a revaluation of all earthly values by reference to a perspective that neither he nor anyone else can possibly inhabit. As he explains to the Duke, in a tone that seems partly an example of his genuine humility and partly adopted as a strategy to ingratiate, 'If your lordship would be kind enough to give me just a tiny part of the sky, something no bigger than half a league, I'd be happier to take that than the best ínsula in the world' (728) (si vuestra señoría fuese servido de darme una tantica parte del cielo, aunque no fuese más de media legua, la tomaría de mejor gana que la mayor ínsula del mundo; II, 42, p. 355). The remark requires the Duke to concede the limitations of his own powers, albeit in a tone of aristocratic deference that seems disingenuous, if not downright condescending: 'Look, Sancho my friend ... I can't give anybody a part of the sky, even one no bigger than my nail; those favors and dispensations are reserved for God alone. What I can give you, I do, which is an ínsula (translation mine) (Mirad, amigo Sancho ... yo no puedo dar parte del cielo a nadie, aunque no sea mayor que una uña; que a solo Dios están reservadas esas mercedes y gracias. Lo que puedo dar os doy, que es una ínsula; II, 42, p. 355). By contrast, Don Quijote's reversal of perspective leads to a scepticism about 'theory' and the *ciencia* of government and to a bona fide articulation of the principles of public and private virtue. He is quick to dismiss the value of any 'science' of government and proposes instead – in good Aristotelian fashion – that good governance depends upon personal character qualities rather than on anything that can be known as a *ciencia*, in the abstract. Qualities of character are revealed through what one says and does rather than by what one may know: 'Simply because of the last words you have said I judge you worthy of being the governor of a thousand ínsulas: you have a good nature, and without that no learning is worthwhile; commend yourself to God and try not to wander from your first purpose' (373) (Por solas estas últimas razones que has dicho, juzgo que mereces ser gobernador de mil ínsulas: buen natural tienes, sin el cual no hay ciencia que valga; encomiéndate a Dios, y procura no errar en la primera intención; II, 43, p. 365).

What Sancho has, in fact, just said in these 'últimas razones' to Don Quijote – the 'theory' that serves in Don Quijote's mind to prove Sancho's worth – reflects a profound and critical deflation of the aristocratic presumption that virtue is aligned with social status:

> just plain Sancho will get by on bread and onions as well as the governor does on partridges and capons; besides, everyone's equal when they sleep, the great and the small, the poor and the rich; and if your grace thinks about it, you'll see that it was you alone who gave me the idea of governing, because I don't know any more about the governorships of ínsulas than a vulture; if you think the devil will carry me off because I'm a governor, I'd rather go to heaven as Sancho than to hell as a governor. (373)

> así me sustentaré Sancho a secas con pan y cebolla, como gobernador con perdices y capones; y más, que mientras se duerme, todos son iguales, los grandes y los menores, los pobres y los ricos; y si vuestra merced mira en ello, verá que solo vuestra merced me ha puesto en esto de gobernar; que yo no sé más de gobiernos de ínsulas que un buitre; y si se imagina que por ser gobernador me ha de llevar el diablo, más me quiero ir al cielo que gobernador al infierno. (II, 43, p. 365)

Such arguments were charged with the historical force of a process by which the social markers of honour and rank had become increasingly detached from any necessary connection to the virtues, and were associated instead with the categories of social class, where privilege attaches principally to wealth.

If Cervantes outlines an ethical frame in which virtue might indeed be valued over rank, this is in part so as to point up what has been called the problem of 'status inconsistency' among the nobility, i.e., the discrepancy between social rank and nobility of character.[14] There were, of course, many earlier attempts to identify the problem of 'status inconsistency.' Among the precursors of *Don Quijote*, the *Lazarillo de Tormes* was among the most important. The *Lazarillo* openly acknowledges the kind of 'status inconsistency' that revolves around the corruption of the nobility; its argument is that they have not earned success at all: 'I'd also like people who are proud of being high born to realize how little this really means, as Fortune has smiled on them, and how much more worthy are those who have endured misfortune but have triumphed by dint of hard work and determination' (porque consideren los que heredaron nobles estados cuán poco se les debe, pues Fortuna fue con ellos parcial, y cuánto más hicieron los que, siéndoles contraria, con fuerza y maña remando, salieron a buen puerto).[15] Cervantes, by contrast, understands that there is something potentially more resistant than 'fortune' to be dealt with in confronting status inconsistency, and this is the deeply embedded, systemic, and ultimately ideological means by which those who occupy a 'high station' in life are able to produce the justifications that occlude this discrepancy: that while many good and noble individuals may claim that they are engaged in the pursuit of virtue, nothing could be farther from the truth. In fact, when Sancho is finally appointed governor of Barataria Don Quijote goes out of his way to remark that this reward seems unreasonable and unjust. He makes it a point to say that Sancho has by sheer luck been granted a reward for which he has not worked at all: 'You, before it is time and contrary to the law of reasonable discourse, find yourself rewarded with all your desires. Others bribe, importune, solicit, and are early risers, plead, persist, and do not achieve what they long for, and another comes along and without knowing how or why finds himself with the office and position that many others strove for; and here the saying certainly applies and is appropriate: aspirations are ruled by good and bad fortune' (729) (Tú, antes de tiempo, contra la ley del razonable discurso, te vees premiado de tus deseos. Otros cohechan, importunan, solicitan, madrugan, ruegan, porfían, y no alcanzan lo que pretenden; y llega otro, y sin saber cómo ni cómo no, se halla con el cargo y oficio que otros muchos pretendieron; y aquí entra y encaja bien el decir que hay buena y mala fortuna en las pretensions; II, 42, p. 357).[16] These words aptly describe the problem of status inconsistency, albeit in the inverted form that is produced under the influence of the ducal fiction. Not surprisingly, then, Don Quijote will devote a significant portion of his efforts as political counsellor to making recommendations about how Sancho might bring his external appearance and behaviour in line with courtly expectations.

That Sancho should want an island is hardly unexpected within the framework of the *Quijote*. Don Quijote had, after all, promised him one as early as chapter 7 of Part I. This promise was overdetermined, to say the least, given Don Quijote's imitation of his literary antecedents. If Gandalín, the legendary squire of Amadís, was made a count and given to rule over Insula Firme, then why should Sancho not be similarly rewarded?[17] Moreover, the literature of travel and conquest had for a century been filled with reports of fabulously happy islands scattered across the seas. The geographer Olaus Magnus no doubt had a hand in the prevalence of these accounts,[18] as did the Italian humanist Giovanni Botero's *Relaciones universales del mundo*, which had just been translated into Spanish.[19] In Part I of the *Persiles* a group of characters including Auristela, Transila, Ricla, and Constanza arrive on an island that has all the markings of a utopic space, ruled by the classical virtues. (It is, in fact, what Machiavelli decribes as a non-hereditary state.)

> Heaven gave me as my homeland one of the islands near that of Hibernia; it's so large it's called a 'kingdom,' though one not inherited or passed down by succession from father to son. Its inhabitants choose as their ruler whomever they think best, always striving to insure he's the best and most virtuous man to be found in the kingdom. Without the intervention of pleadings and negotiations, and without being wooed by promises or bribes, the king emerges from the common consensus and takes up the scepter of absolute command, which lasts as long as he lives or until his virtue diminishes. Because of this, those who aren't kings try to be virtuous in order to become one, while those already kings strive to be even more virtuous so they won't be obliged to stop ruling. Thanks to this, soaring ambition's wings are clipped, greed is grounded, and although hypocrisy is everywhere at work, in the long run its mask falls off and it fails to win the prize. As a result the people live in peace, justice triumphs and mercy gleams, and the petitions of the poor are handled with dispatch while those of the rich are not dispatched one bit better because of their wealth. The scale of justice is not tipped by bribes nor by the flesh and blood of kinship, and all business dealings proceed reasonably according to the rules. Finally, it's a kingdom where everyone lives free from the threat of insolence and where each person enjoys what is his.

Una de las islas que están junto a la de Ibernia me dio el cielo por patria; es tan grande que toma nombre de reino, el cual no se hereda ni viene por sucesión de padre a hijo: sus moradores le eligen a su beneplácito, procurando siempre que sea el más virtuoso y mejor hombre que en él se hallara; y sin intervenir de por medio ruegos o negociaciones, y sin que los soliciten promesas ni dádivas, de común consentimiento de todos sale el rey y toma el cetro absoluto del mando, el cual le dura mientras le dura la vida o mientras no se empeora en ella. Y, con esto, los que no son reyes procuran ser virtuosos para serlo, y los que los son, pugnan serlo más, para no dejar de ser reyes. Con esto se cortan las alas a la ambición, se atierra la codicia, y, aunque la hipocresía suele andar lista, a largo andar se le cae la máscara y queda sin el alcanzado premio; con esto los pueblos viven quietos, campea la justicia y resplandece la misericordia, despáchanse con brevedad los memoriales de los pobres, y los que dan los ricos, no por serlo son mejor despachados; no agobian la vara de la justicia las dádivas, ni la carne y sangre de los parentescos; todas las negociaciones guardan sus puntos y andan en sus quicios; finalmente, reino es donde se vive sin temor de los insolentes y donde cada uno goza lo que es suyo.[20]

To return to Barataria: ultimately it is the Duchess who disingenuously appropriates both Don Quijote's promise of an island and Sancho's dreams of reward. Speaking on behalf of her husband, the Duchess proposes to honour Don Quijote's promise to Sancho in the name of a continuity of *caballeros andantes* and courtly knights, i.e., as a fictional 'refutation' of the historical process that had separated these two varieties of knightly nobility. Additionally, she falsely commits the Duke as an ally against all the worldly interests that might conspire to deprive Sancho of his just reward. The deference she demonstrates toward Sancho by addressing him in the third person borders on condescension:

Our good Sancho already knows that what a knight has promised he attempts to fulfill, even if it costs him his life. The duke, my lord and husband, though not a knight errant, is still a knight, and so he will keep his word regarding the promised ínsula, despite the world's envy and malice. Sancho should be of good heart, for when he least expects it he will find himself seated on the throne of his ínsula and his estate, and he will hold his governorship in his hand and not trade it for another of three-pile brocade. My charge to him is that he attend to how he governs his vassals, knowing that all of them are loyal and wellborn. (680)

Ya sabe el buen Sancho que lo que una vez promete un caballero procura cumplirlo, aunque le cueste la vida. El duque, mi señor y marido, aunque no es de los andantes, no por eso deja de ser caballero, y así, cumplirá la palabra de la prometida ínsula, a pesar de la invidia y de la malicia del mundo. Esté Sancho de buen ánimo, que cuando menos lo piense se verá sentado en la silla de su ínsula y en la de su estado, y empuñará su gobierno, que con otro de brocado de tres altos lo deseche. Lo que yo le encargo es que mire cómo gobierna sus vasallos, advirtiendo que todos son leales y bien nacidos. (II, 33, p. 300)

These complications place a set of important truths within a manifestly false and disingenuous frame. The narrative of Sancho's governorship is founded on a set of optimistic and progressive premises that deserve attention: first, that while he may not know anything about governing to begin with, he can learn; and second, that while he may not be of noble birth, he may nonetheless prove himself to be virtuous. The Duchess herself indulges Sancho's ideas, no matter how implausible they might be: 'In this business of governing it's all a matter of starting, and it may be that after two weeks of being a governor I'll be licking my lips over the work and know more about it than working in the fields, which is what I've grown up doing.' 'You're right, Sancho,' said the duchess, 'because nobody is born knowing, and bishops are made from men, not stones' (680) ('En esto de los gobiernos todo es comenzar, y podría ser que a quince días de gobernador me comiese las manos tras el oficio y supiese más dél que de la labor del campo, en que me he criado.' 'Vos tenéis razón razón, Sancho,' dijo la duquesa, 'que nadie nace enseñado, y de los hombres se hacen los obispos, que no de las piedras' (II, 33, p. 300). But we are in the realm of the 'as-if.' If such ideas were indeed true – true in the world and not just true of ideas about the world – Sancho would be a superb (and implausible) example of the *novus homo*, one ancient paradigm for which was Cicero, who was famous as the first in his family to be appointed to the Roman senate.[21] He would also exemplify one of the fictions sustained by the courtesy books: that the manners and style reflected at court can be acquired, in principle by anyone, and that a transformation in behaviour may lead to a transformation in character. This is the corollary of an underlying Erasmian idea, summed up in the phrase 'monachatus non est pietas' (the habit does not make the monk). But the truth is that the Dukes understand that the possibility of such a transformation is at best a fiction, for Sancho or for anyone else in their courtly realm; in fact, they work so as to ensure that it will not take place. The 'truth' of what the Duchess says, in a cheap and easy echo of Erasmus, about the humble origins of high ranking officials ('de los hombres se hacen los obispos') can be spoken only under the veil of a fiction that runs contrary to the fact that she and her husband are wholly in control of the very conditions under which Sancho comes to power and attempts to rule. As William Childers observed in relation to Spain's 'internal colonialism,' indeed, the episode masks a situation in which a large and significant class of Spanish peasants had been falsely led to recognize their capacity for self-governance, since it was the nobility who maintained control over them by manipulating their self-understanding and sustaining the illusion of their inclusion in national politics.[22] The question is whether Sancho can in these circumstances acquire any kind of knowledge consistent with authentic virtue.

That all these considerations are embedded within the ducal fiction creates something more complex than a simple masking of social truths by means of widely accepted falsehoods. As noted above, the unmasking of shared falsehoods in the name of social critique was the established work of a variety of texts, especially of picaresque fiction, including the *Lazarillo de Tormes*.[23] But beyond what we see in the picaresque, the circumstances at the ducal court in the *Quijote* create something much closer to the kinds of relations that are ideologically conditioned: these are situations in which otherwise evident falsehoods enable and sustain belief in something that comes to be accepted as true by creating the invisible conditions for its possibility. Don Quijote's surprise that the king might 'force' anyone, pursued through the double entendre referred to above, signals a similar functioning of ideology as a concealed fiction. As the wordplay helps reveal, such situations depend upon the co-existence of two mutually supportive 'truths,' each of which is independently false. The pact between Don Quijote and Sancho to accept each other's beliefs in the Cave of Montesinos and the voyage on Clavileño points to just this structure of mutual supports.

Cervantes thus presents a complex set of relations in which principles that one might well wish to accept as 'true' (e.g., Don Quijote's advice to Sancho about how to rule virtuously) are framed by circumstances that are patently false (the fiction of Sancho's governorship over the island of Barataria). The 'truth' about the nature of virtue, as articulated in Don Quijote's first offering of advice to Sancho, as well as by some of Sancho's prudent decisions as judge, may indeed represent a significant reorientation in political theory according to a reformed understanding of the nature of virtue. But the fact remains that the articulation of the humanistic principles of virtue as espoused by Don Quijote and enacted by Sancho in his rustic way is occasioned by conditions that are set in place by the Dukes, who falsely create and control the semblance of a complete and coherent world. In fact, this is a nearly 'ideal' world, one in which an unlettered but nonetheless virtuous peasant ultimately comes to occupy the highest office in the land. Moreover, it is the characters' attachment to a belief in the possibility of acting virtuously that allows the ducal fiction to go unchallenged by them. To say that the Dukes' elaborate fiction of a world occasions Don Quijote's bona fide advice to Sancho is in one respect simply to indicate that there would be no opportunity for Don Quijote to counsel Sancho at all were it not for their machinations. But this is also to say that the Dukes have not just appropriated Don Quijote's promise to Sancho; they have appropriated the quixotic 'idea' itself.

Don Quijote, Counsellor

Embedded within the ducal fiction that frames these ideas and sets them into play are thus a series of episodes that engage them as if true: Don Quijote's 'advice' to Sancho (which roots in the question of the public and private virtues) and Sancho's deployment of his role as civil judge and guardian of the state. Sancho has already served as a kind of ambassador, whose assignment has been to deliver letters to and from Don Quijote and his beloved Dulcinea. But now that Sancho prepares to step out of his ambassadorial role and rule, we can see that Don Quijote's advice on governing (II, 42–3) acts as a kind of discursive counterweight to the speech on the Golden Age and the discourse on Arms and Letters of Part I. Don Quixote is, of course, never short of opinions when it comes to advising Sancho about all kinds of things, but it may be surprising that he has so much to say when Sancho is about to take up the governorship of the island-kingdom that the Duke and the Duchess have arranged for him. Indeed, the episode places Don Quijote in an odd situation, since the island has not been won by any heroic means at all. On the contrary, Sancho has gotten it on the cheap, as its very name suggests ('it was called Barataria ... because he had been given the governorship at so little cost' [474]) (se llamaba la ínsula Barataria ... por el barato con que se le había dado el gobierno; II, 45, p. 375).[24]

As if not fully aware of the political theatre of which he is a part, Don Quijote offers his advice to Sancho on matters of governance in straightforward terms. And we, who witness that theatre knowing its limitations, nonetheless attend to what Don Quijote has to say. Always the accomplished rhetorician, Don Quijote proceeds to speak in the language of the

Renaissance humanists. His advice to Sancho harkens back to a time when questions of politics were articulated in relation to an underlying account of the virtues of character. His overarching idea is that the business of governing is not a question to be answered in the abstract, but neither does it follow from a legalistic orientation to specific matters of policy or praxis. Rather, Don Quijote's advice to Sancho suggests that governing requires a special kind of intelligence, a form of 'practical wisdom' (*phronēsis*) that can best be described in terms of the qualities of character of the ruler.

Cervantes may well have been aware that this humanist orientation roots in Aristotle's ethical ideas about practical wisdom. And he was certainly aware that ideas about practical reason were tied up with a particular kind of literature, specifically, with the *doctrinales de príncipes* and more generally with the literature of advice to rulers and their counsellors that extends back to Cato's *Dicta*,[25] to Plato's *Statesman*, and to the *Paraenesis* of the Greek rhetorician Isocrates. Don Quijote's advice to Sancho about how to govern draws on a long and hallowed line of texts advising princes and those who educate them. Previous commentators on this tradition have identified 'sources' for Don Quijote's advice that also include Xenophon's *Education of Cyrus* (the *Cyropaedia*), which had just recently been rediscovered, and which was cited approvingly by Castiglione in *The Courtier* and by Machiavelli in *The Prince*.[26] Numerous references in the *Quijote* to the fabled Lacedemonian legislator Lycurgus suggest that Cervantes was especially aware of Xenophon as the author of the 'Constitution of the Lacedemonians.'

The contemporary forms of this genre include various 'mirrors' and 'dials' for princes such as Francisco de Monzón's *Libro primero del espejo del príncipe christiano* (which was dedicated to Philip II) and Antonio de Guevara's *Relox de príncipes*,[27] manuals of princely education, both 'Christian' and otherwise (including Felipe de la Torre's *Institución de un rey christiano* and Pedro de Rivadeneira's *Tratado del príncipe cristiano*), handbooks, *vade mecums*, books offering practical political advice along the lines of the *Instrucción política y práctica judicial* by Cervantes' contemporary, Alonso de Villadiego,[28] as well as books of advice for counsellors to the prince along the lines of Fadrique Furió Ceriol's *Consejo y consejeros de príncipes* and Guevara's own *Aviso de privados o despertador de cortesanos*. Machiavelli's *Prince* must also be seen as belonging to this broad line of texts even though it speaks to the prince who would rule effectively rather than virtuously.

This rich and varied array of predecessor texts provides the broader context for the humanist *regimine principum*, with which the pre-Barataria episodes of advice are deeply engaged.[29] The cornerstone of that line of writing was Erasmus's *Enchiridion militis christiani* (*Education of a Christian Prince*)[30] written in 1516 and dedicated to Prince Charles, the future Emperor Charles V. Indeed, Don Quijote's remarks read like a compendium of advice extracted from the *Enchiridion*, mixed with passages of the *Adagia* and the *Apothegms*. The advice about humility and the avoidance of flattery, the remarks about the prince as an embodiment of the law, and the comments on the avoidance of war and about the virtue of clemency, are all thoroughly Erasmian in character. As distilled in Don Quijote's advice, these precepts revolve around two interlocking principles: that good governance begins in self-governance, and that the political virtues are consistent with the ideals of Christian humanism. This represents a turn from Don Quijote's allegiance to chivalric ideals, and in fact this first round of advice to Sancho is punctuated by a great nod of approval from the narrator ('Who could have heard this speech of Don Quixote and not taken him for a very wise and well-intentioned person?' [732]); (¿Quién oyera el pasado razonamiento de don Quijote que no le tuviera por persona muy cuerda y mejor intencionada? II, 43, p. 360). The ideal ruler should fear God, curb human pride, and practise piety; he should bend the bar of justice, if at all, in the direction of compassion and clemency. He should recognize that mercy is worth more than justice itself.[31] Rather than act as principles from which any particular action can be calculated, these maxims revolve around the central belief that public and private forms of virtue must be fashioned from the same cloth.

And yet there is a still more personal set of considerations that Don Quijote introduces when advising Sancho, considerations that centre on behaviour and manners, and that register the protocols and the status preoccupations of courtly life rather than humanist ideals about the virtues. They reflect the fact that the public comportment of the self was paramount in the courtly world, and particularly so where there might be wide status gaps, such as between Sancho's humble origins and the refined context of the ducal court. The second part of Don Quijote's advice, in fact, refers almost entirely to manners. Don Quijote advises Sancho to keep his nails trimmed, to avoid eating garlic and onions (thinking that his foul breath might belie his rustic background), to speak slowly and without interjecting too many proverbs, not to chew on both sides of his mouth or to belch in public, to avoid slouching when in the saddle, to drink and sleep in moderation, and so on. The instruction in table manners may well derive from Lucas Gracián Dantisco's 1593 Spanish translation of Giovanni della Casa's *Galateo*, in which an older man gives similar advice to his nephew. But there are broader connections to Erasmus, whose widely read work of 1530, *De civilitate* (*On Manners*), offered advice about everything from how to behave at banquets to how to brush your teeth.[32] There is an enormous gap in status between Sancho and the aristocrats, and these recommendations are meant to disguise that gap by correcting those habits, as if to suggest that the precondition for governing in such a world is to behave in ways that will be acceptable at court.

Given the courtly context, Don Quijote's advice to Sancho calls for an amplification of what we understand by 'discourse' in the context of politics. Especially in the courtly world, where nearly all forms of behaviour could be read as signs, the literature of advice to princes and rulers was of a piece with writings about how to succeed socially. In one of the texts anchoring this tradition, *The Courtier*, Castiglione is committed to the courtly idea that excellence must be demonstrated in refined and cultivated contexts, not only in the heroic world of action. The dialogues in *The Courtier* explore a series of ideas about courtly comportment and can certainly be seen as informing Don Quijote's advice to Sancho. After all, the second set of Don Quijote's recommendations takes full account of the fact that Sancho is a peasant who needs to refashion himself in order to fit into a refined world. The advice offered to Castiglione's ideal courtier, which originates in Plutarch and was refracted through Thomas More, might well serve Sancho: to guard against flattery, even if it is true,[33] to dress modestly, to avoid affectation in speech, to exercise good taste, and to recognize that the world is rife with 'status inconsistency,' as when Castiglione's Pallavicino adduces the example of those of noble birth who are ridden with vices and those who are humble exercising true virtue, about all of which he says, by way of alibi, that Fortune is the cause.[34] The interlocutors of *The Courtier* consider these and many other questions in the context of a play-like dialogue that has a serious intent. The book takes the form of an extended moral and social inquiry cloaked as a fictional dialogue whose basis lies in a commitment to the serious results of various forms of 'play,' including verbal play. In *Don Quijote*, by contrast, the Duke and the Duchess sponsor an exaggerated and distorted sense of 'play,' one that is bereft of moral purpose and that turns malicious: *serio ludere* in their hands becomes *ludere* with intent to sting. The courtier's pleasant pastimes, as well as the music, the poetry, the dancing, and all the other ingenious games referred to in *The Courtier* (I), yield to a series of mean-spirited pranks.[35]

Governor Sancho

We are led to believe that Don Quijote's advice succeeds in influencing Sancho's behaviour as governor. Sancho does listen carefully to Don Quijote's advice and, as the narrator says, 'He attempted to commit his advice to memory, like a man who intended to follow it and use it to bring the gestation of his governorship to a successful delivery' (732) (Procuraba conservar en la memoria sus consejos, como quien pensaba guardarlos y salir por ellos a buen parto de la preñaz de su gobierno; II, 43, p. 360). Moreover, Sancho writes to Don Quijote that he has followed his instructions on such specific things as the inspection of hazelnut vendors.[36] But we do not know, nor is the narrator able to say, whether any of the cases presented to Sancho is genuine or stage-managed. Whatever prudence Sancho exhibits as judge seems to be the result of his instincts and inclinations. His is the wisdom of the honest and astute peasant, and runs contrary to the budding interest in 'scientific' forms of governing. Most of the cases presented to him have their basis in legends and folklore, and call for an instinctive form of wisdom, not for complex legal expertise or specialized judicial training. In this fictional world Sancho appears to have the wisdom of 'a great governor' and the judicial acumen to rival the legendary legislator of the Spartans, Lycurgus (II, 51).

We can view Sancho's instinctively sound judgments as a counterweight to the comparatively thin schoolbook learning of the new class of lawyers and university-trained magistrates. The cases he decides are instances of fraud or deception that need above all a relatively sharp wit and an independent will. They are explorations of the relationship between fiction and the social order rather than opportunities for the subtle interpretation of legal principles. As Luis Murillo suggested, each one of the cases in question involves an instance of a fraud masked as a form of truth, just as Barataria is a fraud masked as true on a much larger scale.[37] Sancho is fortunate enough to find that his peasant wisdom is able to cut through these layers of deception and to unmask the fraudulent claims presented to him. But the additional point is that the forms of deceit that underlie politics at the highest levels may be equally present among ordinary citizens. Not all of the inhabitants of Barataria are aware that Sancho is merely a fictional ruler, which means that the deceivers among them may be genuinely deceptive, not merely the unwitting pawns of the Duke and the Duchess.

In responding to the cases presented to him, Sancho nonetheless relies on what one proverb dubs the 'juicio de buen varón,' which is to say, the informal principles of the upstanding citizen or 'good man' who places common sense above legal strategies. As a kind of *villano honrado*, Sancho resembles the noble villager who was put on stage in plays like Lope de Vega's *Fuenteovejuna* and *El villano en su rincón*. He receives the plaintiffs with virtually no bureaucratic interference and administers justice swiftly. In the first of the cases that Sancho is asked to consider, a tailor has responded to a deceitful client with what he in turn regards as a form of 'just fraud.' The tailor is ordered to forfeit the money and the client the cloth; the hats the tailor has made are ordered sent to the inmates of a jail; the suggestion may be that the prisoners in jail are probably deceitful enough to deserve them.[38] Next come two old men, the one who has lent some money to the other and demands its repayment, and the other who claims that he has already paid it back. As an astute observer of human behaviour, Sancho notices that the defendant gave a valuable cane to the plaintiff just while swearing that he did not have any money; Sancho fathoms that the missing money may well lie concealed in the defendant's cane, and orders it broken apart, upon which the gold coins come falling out.[39] Last in this first string of plaintiffs comes a woman who alleges that a local rancher has violated her. Sancho orders the rancher to try taking a sack of coins away from the woman, knowing that she is likely to defend her money with great zeal. Sancho's point is that if she had been as committed to defending her body as she is to guarding the money she might not have lost her virginity.[40] The result of these judgments and of the ones to follow in II, 47 and 49 is that while Sancho's common-sense wisdom is indeed validated, the fiction of Barataria seems legitimized as the occasion for virtuous rule.

Sancho is likewise intent on diminishing the extravagant claims of characters who avail themselves of various forms of disguise in order to escape difficult conditions. He prefers plain-dealing in all its aspects over any sort of fiction. This comes to light especially in the case with the young woman who is brought to him, dressed in her brother's clothes and clearly in distress, as he makes his rounds of the island in II, 49. The brother-sister pair seems to resemble some of the cross-dressed figures of Part I, but here the cross-dressing also raises questions of parent-child relations, not just of sibling identity. Initially, the woman presents herself as the daughter of Pedro Pérez Mazorca; but Pedro Pérez is known not to have had any daughters at all and, upon questioning, the woman readily admits that she is in fact the daughter of Diego de la Llana, 'a distinguished gentleman, and very rich' (779) (hidalgo principal y rico; II, 49, p. 411). She explains that she had, in fact, exchanged clothes with her brother in order to escape confinement in her father's house, where she had lived in isolation. (The episode may have been written with Antonio de Guevara's *Relox de príncipes* again in mind; one of Guevara's examples, in fact, concerns one of the very legislators to whom Sancho is favourably compared, Lycurgus.)[41] Sancho's response to the woman's complaint is that she has emotionalized her plight beyond its true gravity: 'Certainly, Señores, this has been a childish prank, and to tell about this foolishness and daring, there was no need for so many long tears and sighs; just saying, "We're so-and-so and such-and-such, and we left our father's house in disguise to enjoy ourselves, just out of curiosity, for no other reason," would have been the end of the story without all that sobbing and weeping and carrying on,' p. 781) (Por cierto, señores, que ésta ha sido una gran rapacería, y para contar esta necedad y atrevimiento no eran menester tantas largas, ni tantas lágrimas y suspiros; que con decir: 'Somos fulano y fulana, que nos salimos a espaciar de casa de nuestros padres con esta invención, sólo por curiosidad, sin otro designio alguno,' se acabara el cuento, y no gemidicos, y lloramicos, y darle; II, 49, p. 414).

More challenging in the end are the tests of stamina to which Sancho is put. A sumptuous banquet is prepared, but the state 'doctor' assigned to look after him forbids him to eat much of anything. The moment affords Cervantes an occasion to poke fun at another class of university graduates. The doctor is called Pedro Recio de Mal Aguero, said to be from the ridiculously named town of Tirteafuera and a graduate of the newly founded University of Osuna. Under this doctor's sham protection Sancho goes hungry in the midst of abundance. He is hounded by petitioners at all hours, and receives a letter from the Duke warning of potential dangers from within and without. This makes real the very conditions that Machiavelli warned about in *The Prince*. While Sancho is making his rounds of the island as guardian of the realm he receives a letter from the Duke warning of impending plots against him. On the fictional island of Barataria – Sancho's ideal *república* – he is confronted by what would seem to be real-world dangers. The Duke writes advising him as follows:

It has come to my attention, Señor Don Sancho Panza, that certain enemies of mine and of the ínsula will launch a furious attack, but I do not know on which night; it is advisable to keep watch and stay on guard so that they do not catch you unprepared. I have also learned through trusted spies that four persons in disguise have come to that place to take your life, for they fear your cleverness; keep your eyes open, be aware of who comes to speak to you, and do not eat anything that is offered to you. I shall be sure to come to your aid if you find yourself in difficulty, and in everything you will act with your customary intelligence. (760–1)

A mi noticia ha llegado, señor don Sancho Panza, que unos enemigos míos y desa ínsula la han de dar un asalto furioso no sé qué noche: conviene velar y estar alerta, porque no le tomen desapercebido. Sé también por espías verdaderas que han entrado en ese lugar cuatro personas disfrazadas para quitaros la vida, porque se temen de vuestro ingenio: abrid el ojo y mirad quién llega a hablaros, y no comáis de cosa que os presentaren. Yo tendré cuidado de socorreros si os viéredes en trabajo, y en todo haréis como se espera de vuestro entendimiento. (II, 47, p. 390)

The irony, of course, is that the most Machiavellian character in the episode is the Duke himself, who has arranged for these masquerading traitors and phoney foreign enemies to stage an attack on the 'island.'

The moment is inconvenient, to say the least. Sancho is given 'armas defensivas y ofensivas,' and while he protests that the business of defence ought to belong to Don Quijote, he is nonetheless suited with shields and a lance: 'They immediately brought two full-length shields that they had been carrying and placed them over [Sancho's] nightshirt, not allowing him to put on any other clothing, one shield in front and the other behind, and they pulled his arms through some space they had made, and tied the shields on very carefully with cords, leaving him walled in and boarded up, as straight as a spindle and unable to bend his knees or take a single step. When they had him in this state, they told him to walk, and lead them, and encourage them all, for with him as their polestar, their lighthouse, and their lamp, their affairs would have a happy conclusion' (805–6) (al momento le trujeron dos paveses, que venían proveídos dellos, y le pusieron encima de la camisa, sin dejarle tomar otro vestido, un pavés delante y otro detrás, y por unas concavidades que traían hechas le sacaron los brazos, y le liaron muy bien con unos cordeles, de modo que quedó emparedado y entablado, derecho como un huso, sin poder doblar las rodillas ni menearse un solo paso. Pusiéronle en las manos una lanza, a la cual se arrimó para poder tenerse en pie. Cuando así le tuvieron, le dijeron que caminase y los guiase y animase a todos, que siendo él su norte, su lanterna y su lucero, tendrían buen fin sus negocios; II, 53, pp. 441–2). The moment is an inversion of some of the earliest chapters in the novel, when Don Quijote constructs his own makeshift suit of armour and later has himself dubbed a knight. The urgency attached to it stands in sharp contrast to the illusory battles that Don Quijote fights in Part I. Moreover, Sancho is clearly armed against his will. 'What do I have to do with arming?... And what do I know about arms or coming to anybody's aid? These things are better left to my master, Don Quixote, who in the wink of an eye would dispatch and see to them' (805) (¿Qué me tengo de armar ... ni qué sé yo de armas ni de socorros? Estas cosas mejor será dejarlas para mi amo don Quijote, que en dos paletas las despachará y pondrá en cobro, que yo, pecador fui a Dios, no se me entiende nada destas priesas; II, 53, p. 441).

This experience reinforces Sancho's critique of aristocratic pride and ambition. He confides to his donkey: 'When ... I had no other thoughts but mending your harness and feeding your body, then my hours, my days, and my years were happy, but after I left you and climbed the towers of ambition and pride, a thousand miseries, a thousand troubles, and four thousand worries have entered into my soul' (807) (Cuando ... no tenía otros pensamientos que los que me daban los cuidados de remendar vuestros aparejos y de sustentar vuestro corpezuelo, dichosas eran mis horas, mis días y mis años; pero después que os dejé y me subí sobre las torres de la ambición y de la soberbia, se me han entrado por el alma aden- tro mil miserias, mil trabajos y cuatro mil desasosiegos; II, 53, p. 444). The conclusion that Sancho draws from his experience on the island is that he prefers the freedoms of his past life to the obligations and discomforts of his existence as 'governor': 'let me return to my old liberty; let me go and find my past life, so that I can come back from this present death' (808) (dejadme volver a mi antigua libertad; dejadme que vaya a buscar la vida pasada, para que me resucite de esta muerte presente; II, 53, p. 444). Gov- erning is just not for him, he concludes, adding that he is by nature better suited to other activities. 'I was not born to be a governor, or to defend ínsulas or cities from enemies who want to attack them. I have a better understanding of plowing and digging, or pruning and layering the vines, than of making laws or defending provinces and kingdoms. St. Peter's fine in Rome: I mean, *each man is fine doing the work he was born for*. I'm bet- ter off with a scythe in my hand than a governor's scepter' (808; emphasis mine) (Yo no nací para ser gobernador, ni para defender ínsulas ni ciudades de los enemigos que quisieren acometerlas. Mejor se me entiende de mí de arar y cavar, podar y ensarmentar las viñas, que de dar leyes ni de defender provincias ni reinos. Bien se está San Pedro en Roma: quiero decir, *que bien se está cada uno usando el oficio para que fue nacido*. Mejor me está a mi una hoz en la mano que un cetro de gobernador; II, 53, p. 444; emphasis mine). It might well be that Sancho simply had the wrong idea about governing and viewed it as the easy way to a comfortable life. While his career began under Don Quijote's tutelage, he has in other respects absorbed the example and expectations of the Dukes. And if Plato speculated that the true philosopher would be uncorrupted by riches or the attractions of a life of luxury, then Sancho's peasant wisdom certainly seems to have its limits.

Seen from one perspective, those limits might be seen to lie in a failure to grasp the principles of political rationalism and its complex relationship to essentializing ways of thinking about the self. Recall that one of the central ideas of the *Republic* is that each person in the state ought to do one thing, and that this ought to be the thing for which that person is best suited. (Juan Huarte de San Juan wrote the *Examen de ingenios* with a similar principle in mind.) But Plato also recognizes that the 'rational' ideas he holds about the distribution of social roles are likely to be unpersuasive and even objectionable. Thus he puts forward an ancient, chthonic pseudo-myth, according to which the differences among individuals were said to have been forged within the earth itself. This is a 'pseudo-myth' rather than a 'noble lie' because Plato plainly recognizes its provisional and pragmatic function as 'a fairy story like those the poets tell and have persuaded people to believe about the sort of thing that often happened "once upon a time"' (*Republic*, 414c).[42] The myth is as follows: 'I shall try to persuade first the Rulers and Soldiers, and then the rest of the community, that the upbringing and education we have given them was all something that happened to them only in a dream. In reality they were fashioned and reared, and their arms and equipment manufactured, in the depths of the earth, and Earth itself, their mother, brought them up, when they were complete, into the light of day' (*Republic*, 414d–e). But Sancho grafts political rationalism onto a peasant work ethic. When, on his rounds of the island, he tries to ensure that there are only industrious workers in his realm, not freeloaders, just as he would propose to eliminate any beehive of its drones, who are apt to eat all the honey that the worker-bees produce: 'It's my intention to clear this ínsula of all kinds of filth, as well as people who are vagrants, idlers, and sluggards, because I want you to know, my friends, that shiftless, lazy people are to the nation what drones are to the hive: they eat the honey that the worker bees produce. I intend to favor those who labor, maintain the privileges of the gentry, reward the virtuous, and, above all, respect religion and the honor of the clergy' (774) (Es mi intención limpiar esta ínsula de todo género de inmundicia y de gente vagamunda, holgazanes y mal entretenida; porque quiero que sepáis, amigos, que la gente baldía y perezosa es en la república lo mesmo que los zánganos en las colmenas, que se comen la miel que las trabajadoras abejas hacen. Pienso favorecer a los labradores, guardar sus preeminencias a los hidalgos, premiar los virtuosos y, sobre todo, tener respeto a la religión y a la honra de los religiosos; II, 49, p. 406).

But there is a valid question to be asked about whether Sancho's ultimate rejection of his governorship represents an ascent to a still higher form of wisdom (i.e., to self-knowledge, which may or may not involve politics), or a regression to something considerably more base. In the end, Sancho's views about human nature – his own, in particular – are underpinned by folk wisdom rather than by rational support or progressive ideas. The framing of Sancho's conclusion seems ultimately to remit us to an essentialist view of the self rather than to a rational view of the state or to a progressive view of society. This essentialism is corroborated when Sancho takes the opportunity to brag about his lineage: 'I'm from the lineage of the Panzas' (808) (Yo soy del linaje de los Panzas; I, 53, p. 445). Framed in these terms, Sancho's abdication would seem to dampen the politically progressive idea that even a peasant could be an effective ruler. For in Sancho's abdication from the governorship of Barataria it would seem that the character who stands as the novel's primary example of social transformation rejects not only the idea of social mobility but the very idea of social fashioning.

There is no doubt that Sancho's conclusion flirts with the deeply bred conservatism of a society that was fiercely attached to status distinctions and that had come to esteem the ignorant and unlettered classes only as long as their ancestry was decreed free from Jewish or Muslim blood. (Cervantes' one-act farce *El retablo de las maravillas* deals with this issue in a way that aligned these pervasive beliefs with the power of a fiction which everyone shares but few if any acknowledge.) And yet Sancho's essentialist turn appears paradoxical for a novel that seems to be progressive and experimental in its very core. Why then Sancho's abdication? One answer would be that just as Sancho makes this essentialist turn he also undergoes a growth in self-awareness. Cervantes seems not to want to sacrifice humanist hopefulness – however ironic in its formulations – to the cynicism bred of an intransigent caste society. But a more plausible reason might be that Sancho too experiences a version of the problem of 'status inconsistency.' Truth be told, this is an inversion of the problem of status inconsistency. Whereas status inconsistency as it pertains to aristocrats indicates a discrepancy between the merits of high social rank and of true virtue, Sancho appears to be virtuous and yet is deprived of the kinds of pleasures that he believes ought to accompany a governor's dignified social role. He believes the social myth, even while he experiences its discrepancies from the bottom up. For their part, the Duke and the Duchess are only making sure that Sancho's life is as unpleasant as that of Plato's guardians. While others may own lands and build finely furnished houses for themselves, the guardians are to live like 'hired mercenaries quartered in the city with nothing to do but perpetual guard-duty' (*Republic*, 419–20a).

And yet because all these episodes are indeed fictions staged by the Duke and the Duchess, there is always another frame to be taken into account. Would Sancho have relinquished the governorship of his coveted island had he not been subjected to the torments arranged by this indulgent pair of aristocrats? On one level the answer is simple: the unpleasantness Sancho experiences is not randomly structured. It is meant to be a hyperbolic version of the difficulties associated with the life of those who are called from humble roots to noble rule, and perhaps even to suggest an extreme version of the hardships that Plato's guardians were expected to endure according to the *Republic*. Yet there is another level, beyond what the sources say: the machinations of the Duke and the Duchess are fictions, calculated so as to produce conditions so unpleasant that Sancho would prefer to give up the governance of his promised island. Sancho's experience is determined to be exactly the opposite of the sweetness promised by the Duke: 'If you try it once, Sancho … you'll long to eat it again, because it is a very sweet thing to give orders and be obeyed' (728) (Si una vez lo probáis, Sancho, comeros heis las manos tras el gobierno, por ser dulcísima cosa el mandar y ser obedecido; II, 42, p. 356).

The Laws of Sancho

Sancho does not leave Barataria without enacting some legislation, which gains him a measure of the fame that Don Quijote had desired since the early chapters of Part I. His laws come to be known as 'Las constituciones del gran gobernador Sancho Panza.' They are a mix of economic regulations (e.g., statutes controlling the price of footwear) and public ordinances designed to enforce moral standards and expunge various kinds of fraud.

> Sancho spent the afternoon issuing some ordinances concerning the good government of what he imagined to be an ínsula, and he ordered that there were to be no speculators in provisions in the nation, and that wine could be imported from anywhere, as long as its place of origin was indicated, so that

it could be priced according to its value, quality, and reputation, and whoever watered it or changed its name would lose his life.

He lowered the price of all footwear, especially shoes, because it seemed to him they were sold at an exorbitant price; he put a cap on the salaries of servants, which were galloping unchecked along the road of greed; he imposed very serious penalties on those who sang lewd and lascivious songs, either by night or by day. He ordered that no blind man could sing verses about miracles unless he carried authentic testimonies to their truth, because it seemed to him that most of the ones blind men sang were false, bringing those that were true into disrepute.

He created and appointed a bailiff for the poor, not to persecute them but to examine them to see if they really were poor, because in the shadow of feigned cripples and false wounds come the strong arms of thieves and very healthy drunkards. In short, he ordained things so good that to this day they are obeyed in that village and are called 'The Constitution of Great Governor Sancho Panza.' (797)

Aquella tarde la pasó Sancho en hacer algunas ordenanzas tocantes al buen gobierno de la que él imaginaba ser ínsula, y ordenó que no hubiese regatones de los bastimentos en la república, y que pudiesen meter en ella vino de las partes que quisiesen, con aditamento que declarasen el lugar de donde era, para ponerle el precio según su estimación, bondad y fama, y el que lo aguase o le mudase el nombre, perdiese la vida por ello.

Moderó el precio de todo calzado, principalmente el de los zapatos, por parecerle que corría con exorbitancia; puso tasa en los salarios de los criados, que caminaban a rienda suelta por el camino del interese; puso gravísimas penas a los que cantasen cantares lascivos y descompuestos, ni de noche ni de día; ordenó que ningún ciego cantase milagro en coplas si no trujese testimonio auténtico de ser verdadero, por parecerle que los más que los ciegos cantan son fingidos, en perjuicio de los verdaderos.

Hizo y creó un alguacil de pobres, no para que los persiguiese, sino para que los examinase si lo eran, porque a la sombra de la manquedad fingida y de la llaga falsa andan los brazos ladrones y la salud borracha. En resolución, él ordenó cosas tan buenas, que hasta hoy se guardan en aquel lugar, y se nombran 'Las constituciones del gran gobernador Sancho Panza.' (II, 51, pp. 432-3)

These passages make allusion to pressing economic issues and to contemporary trade regulations. Those include restrictions placed on the profits of re-sellers (*regatones*) of items of necessity, the regulation of the wine trade, and restrictions on the circulation of certain kinds of songs.

The framework of Sancho's 'constituciones' also owes some general debts to Antonio de Guevara's *Relox de príncipes*, as well as to some of the proposals of the contemporary *arbitristas*. Within the context of the *Quijote*, the idea of an *arbitrio* is familiar from the opening of Part II, where Don Quijote offers his own plan (*arbitrio*) for what was perceived as the most pressing international problem plaguing Spain, viz., the threat posed by 'El Turco.' But in contrast to the pragmatic orientation of all of Sancho's laws, Don Quijote's *arbitrio* is utterly fanciful. His proposal it is to round up all the knights errant of Spain, a mere dozen of which would in his view suffice to defeat the Turkish forces. But, truth be told, Don Quijote's *arbitrio* is in the service of an ulterior motive, which is to underscore the decline in knight-errantry by contrasting the *caballeros* of true valour (who no longer exist) with those contemporary *caballeros* whose interest lies principally in the pursuit of luxury. (Later in Part II, the Duke and the Duchess are envisioned so as to match Don Quijote's view of the decadence that has overtaken the knightly class. They would do well to give some heed to Machiavelli's warning: 'Princes who give more heed to luxury than to arms often lose their principality.')[43]

> Most knights today would rather rustle in damasks, brocades, and the other rich fabrics of their clothes than creak in chain mail; no longer do knights sleep in the fields, subject to the rigors of heaven, wearing all their armor head to foot; no longer does anyone, with his feet still in the stirrups and leaning on his lance, catch forth winks, as they say, as the knights errant used to do. (456)

> Los más de los caballeros que agora se usan, antes les crujen los damascos, los brocados y otras ricas telas de que se visten, que la malla con que se arman; ya no hay caballero que duerma en los campos, sujeto al rigor del cielo, armado de todas armas desde los pies a la cabeza; y ya no hay quien, sin sacar los pies de los estribos, arrimado a su lanza, sólo procure descabezar, como dicen, el sueño, como lo hacían los caballeros andantes. (II, 1, p. 48)

Who was more virtuous and valiant than the famed Amadís of Gaul? Who more intelligent than Palmerín of England? Who more accommodating and good-natured than Tirant lo Blanc? Who more gallant than Lisuarte lo Greece? Who more combative with the sword than Don Belianís? Who more interpid than Perión of Gaul, or more audacious in the face of danger than Felixmarte of Hyrcania, or more sincere than Esplandián? Who bolder than Cirongilio of Thrace? Who more courageous than Rodamonte? Who more invincible than Roland? And who more elegant and courteous than Ruggiero, from whom the modern-day Dukes of Ferrara are descended, according to Turpin in his *Cosmography*? All these knights-errant, and many others I could mention, Señor Priest, were knights-errant ... [These] are the ones I would like for my scheme; if they were part of it, His Majesty would be well served and save a good deal of money, and the Turk would be left tearing his beard. (465–6)

¿quién más honesto y más valiente que el famoso Amadís de Gaula?; ¿quién más discreto que Palmerín de Inglaterra?; ¿quién más acomodado y manual que Tirante el Blanco?; ¿quién más galán que Lisuarte de Grecia?; ¿quién más acuchillado ni acuchillador que don Belianís?; ¿quién más intrépido que Perión de Gaula, o quién más acometedor de peligros que Felixmarte de Hircania, o quién más sincero que Esplandián?; ¿quién mas arrojado que don Cirongilio de Tracia?; ¿quién más bravo que Rodamonte?; ¿quién más prudente que el rey Sobrino?; ¿quién más atrevido que Reinaldos?; ¿quién más invencible que Roldán?; y ¿quién más gallardo y más cortés que Rugero, de quien decienden hoy los duques de Ferrara, según Turpín en su *Cosmografía?* Todos estos caballeros, y otros muchos que pudiera decir, señor cura, fueron caballeros andantes ... Déstos, o tales como éstos, quisiera yo que fueran los de mi arbitrio, que, a serlo, Su Majestad se hallara bien servido y ahorrara de mucho gasto, y el Turco se quedara pelando las barbas. (II, 1, p. 49)

The point of recalling Don Quijote's *arbitrio* in its larger context is to say that the 'constitutions' produced by Sancho on Barataria offer a model of virtuous rule that links neither to an imaginary heroic project nor to the decadent self-interest of the class of nobles represented by the Dukes. And yet there is one feature of Sancho's laws that remains unaccounted for by these various interpretations, regardless of whether it is modelled on the proposals of the *arbitristas* or is an example of practical thinking whose true counterpart is (or ought to be) 'theory' rather than Don Quijote's fantastical ideas. One thrust of Sancho's laws is reminiscent of Plato's *Republic* in their opposition to various kinds of 'fictions,' and specifically to fraudulent fictions. Among Sancho's *ordenanzas* is a prohibition on singing about false miracles by blind men, as well as a prohibition against anyone who might feign a physical disability. Creating the ordered state that has gained Sancho fame as a good legislator means, among other things, putting an end to the abuses of fiction, those in the service of fraud and impostures. But we should hasten to add that this political project is conceived within a frame that is itself fictional rather than theoretical or practical. This is the manifestly fraudulent fiction instituted by the Dukes; still there is Cervantes' own fiction, which aspires to be true.

In the journey on Clavileño Sancho learns the virtue of humility in the face of arrogance and pride. Don Quijote is an ally in this project. In spite of the pride that he himself so often exhibits in the face of his enemies, Don Quijote counsels Sancho on the value of humility in matters of politics: 'Those who are not of noble origin should bring to the gravity of the position they hold a gentle mildness which, guided by prudence, may save them from malicious gossip ... Take more pride in being a humble virtuous man than in being a noble sinner ... Blood is inherited and virtue is acquired' (730) (Los no de principios nobles deben acompañar la gravedad del cargo que ejercitan con una blanda suavidad que, guiada por la prudencia, los libre de la murmuración maliciosa ... La sangre se hereda, y la virtud se aquista, y la virtud vale por sí sola lo que la sangre no vale; II, 42, p. 358). But as we have seen above, there comes a moment of disillusionment when Sancho accepts the fact that he is not well-suited for political life. The implications of this disillusionment weigh heavily on the modern reader, since they would seem to suggest that governing is for nobles, and that humble folk ought to resign themselves to their 'natural state' (estado natural) and devote themselves to manual labour. Indeed, Sancho himself seems to accept this conclusion:

> Make way, Señores, and let me return to my old liberty; let me go and find my past life ... I'd rather eat my fill of gazpacho than suffer the misery of a brazen doctor who starves me to death, and I'd rather lie down in the shade of an oak tree in summer and wrap myself in an old bald sheepskin in winter, in freedom, than lie between linen sheets and wear sables, subject to a governorship. God keep your graces, and tell my lord the duke that I was born naked, and I'm naked now; I haven't lost or gained a thing; I mean, I came into this governorship without a *blanca*, and I'm leaving without one, which is very different from how the governors of other ínsulas leave. Now move aside and let me go. (808)

> Abridme camino, señores míos, y dejadme volver a mi antigua libertad; dejadme que vaya a buscar la vida pasada ... más quiero hartarme de gazpachos que estar sujeto a la miseria de un médico impertinente que me mate de hambre, y más quiero recostarme a la sombra de una encina en el verano y arroparme con un zamarro de los pelos en el invierno, en mi libertad, que

acostarme a la sujeción del gobierno entre sábanas de holanda y vestirme de martas cebollinas. Vuestras mercedes se queden con Dios, y digan al duque mi señor que, desnudo nací, desnudo me hallo: ni pierdo ni gano; quiero decir, que sin blanca entré en este gobierno, y sin ella salgo, bien al revés de como suelen salir los gobernadores de otras ínsulas. Y apártense: déjenme ir. (II, 42, pp. 444–5)

But we ought to keep in mind that the political 'experiment' on Barataria is not in the control of a philosopher, much less of a philosopher-king. It is staged by some aristocrats whose primary interest seems to be their own pleasure. The Duchess lives with the Duke in what is described as a 'casa de placer' (II, 31, p. 273); this is their country estate, their home for relaxation and leisure enjoyment. Indeed, the first time that the Duchess appears in the novel she is described as 'a graceful lady on a snow white palfrey or pony adorned with a green harness and a silver sidesaddle ... dressed in green, so elegantly and richly that she seemed the very embodiment of elegance. On her left hand she carried a goshawk, which indicated to Don Quixoe that she was a great lady and probably the mistress of all the other hunters' (6753) (una gallarda señora sobre un palafrén o hacanea blanquísima, adornada de guarniciones verdes y con un sillón de plata ... vestida de verde, tan bizarra y ricamente, que la misma bizarría venía transformada en ella. En la mano izquierda traía un azor, señal que dio a entender a Don Quijote ser aquella alguna gran señora, que debía serlo de todos aquellos cazadores; II, 30, p. 268).

Moreover, the Duchess recognizes who Don Quijote is in part because she herself has read a good number of the romances of chivalry, including Part I of *Don Quijote*. Thus they attend to him 'with great pleasure and a desire to know him, intending to follow that turn of mind and acquiesce to everything he said, and, for as long as he stayed with them, treat him like a knight errant with all the customary ceremonies found in the books of chivalry, which they had read and of which they were very fond' (655) (con grandísimo gusto y con deseo de conocerle le atendían [a Don Quijote], con presupuesto de seguirle el humor y conceder con él en cuanto les dijese, tratándole como a caballero andante los días que con ellos estuviese, con todas las ceremonias acostumbradas en los libros de caballerías, que ellos habían leído, y aun les eran muy aficionados; II, 30, p. 270). It is understood that the political experiment that she and the Duke arrange on Barataria is an illusion conditioned by ignoble motives. But the problem is rather that they create an illusion whose illusory character remains concealed, and that they thereby create a false equivalence between the images of truth and truth itself. The result seems to validate Don Quijote's fictions while it establishes a purely ideological context for politics.

But ever since chapter 5 of Part I, when the books in Don Quijote's library are judged and some are condemned to be burned, Cervantes associates categorical judgments with a form of absolute authority that must have smacked of the Inquisition, its ideology, and its practices. In Part II he introduces another version of this same problem, which arises when judgments are predicated on a denial of their own fictitious conditions. In such instances we are clearly in the sphere of ideology. If the classical understanding of iconoclasm involves the violent suppression of images, literally by breaking them, then ideology revolves around the wilful denial of the imagistic character of all discourse for the sake of political ends. Here is one great difference between Cervantes and Plato. Cervantes does not present us with a way of distinguishing true and false myths, or between true and false fictions, if such a thing can be said. He is rather concerned with maintaining an awareness of the imagistic, which is to say fictional, character of *all* discourse. Judgment must be political. The experiment on Barataria is indeed but a preamble to politics. Coming to terms with the role ideology plays in it is essential preparation for the development of a vision of the reformed republic that Cervantes seemed so ardently to desire.

7 Imagining the Nation

Politics in *Don Quijote* is at once everywhere and nowhere. It is everywhere in the sense that Cervantes is endlessly experimenting with ways to negotiate between the speculative interests of a political 'theory' (in saying the way things ought to be, under conditions that could be considered ideal but may be impossible) and the interests of political 'practice' (where it is necessary to respond to the way things are, often in a set of complex and constraining local conditions). There is no one privileged form of expression for this negotiation, still less a specialized form of discourse proper to the domain of politics as a space 'between' theory and practice. Perhaps this is why Cervantes' relationship to politics has so often gone unnoticed. The spaces in between the discourses of theory and practice themselves turn out to reflect the pull of interests defined by theory and practice, and yet Cervantes takes pains to ensure that each one is always seen from the critical vantage point afforded by the other. The vehicle for this critical activity is nothing other than what we have come to call 'literature.' But I should hasten to add that 'literature' is by no means the name of a single form of language. Cervantes' engagement with politics ranges over all the literary speech-genres that enter into the *Quijote* and that mark it as a supremely polyphonic text. The discourse of myth allows Cervantes to explore the speculative resources and limitations of one set of communitarian ideals; the genre of the travel report affords a view of the roots of theory in practice; rhetorical speeches and argumentation *in utramque partem* introduce forms of discourse that explore the nature and limits of polemics; and finally, the fictional exploration of 'other worlds,' whether utopian or dystopian in character, imaginary and play-acted or dreamt, serves the ends of political speculation and of imminent critique in equal measure.

Especially in their engagement with questions of verisimilitude drawn from the rereading of Aristotle's *Poetics*, Renaissance literary theorists devoted considerable effort to the task of finding a place for literature in between the fantasies of adventure romances and the empirically oriented, and increasingly fact-based world of history writing. One of my arguments thus far has been that concentration on these debates has left the broader political stakes implicit in such questions unaddressed, and that Cervantes' involvement in questions about the 'possible' and 'probable' speaks principally to the issue of how to find ways to imagine what *ought* to be. But the oscillation within politics between theory and practice is ancient; what is new in Cervantes is the recourse to literature as a way of avoiding the premature foreclosure that would result from the confinement of politics to one or the other of these domains. (For Plato, the recourse to image and myth had a different function, namely to allow for speech about a polis that could never exist in the here and now.) After having looked at the discursive roots of theory, what can be said of Cervantes' relationship to the local contexts and conditions within which politics was embedded, which were often tied to their own versions of what 'ought to be'? If political thinking in classical antiquity and the Renaissance typically revolved around the idea of a city-state, the context of the *Quijote* was one in which the politics of the nation and of the nation's empire held enormous sway. But what was the nation for Cervantes?

Here it seems that politics in the *Quijote* is in a special sense nowhere, that its political geography is largely unspecified, and that the 'polis' refers to no territorial community at all. Some of this has to do with the political geography of the novel. What earlier generations of critics traced as 'The Route of Don Quijote' (La ruta del *Quijote*) covers La Mancha and the Sierra Nevada, some parts of Aragón, and leads eventually to Barcelona, but it passes through no capital city, nor any principal seat of political power. The book's topography is not just disunified, but seems to render the polis unimaginable as a territorial entity. Barcelona is the only city that Don Quijote visits, and his experiences there are strange, even humiliating. The great port city is indeed quite unlike the rural villages and countryside he has visited until then. His way through the world is itinerant and errant, and the early modern city as an urban centre is something quite alien to him. It might seem that Barataria, the faux island-realm, is in some respects more real as a polis than 'Spain' itself; however false, Barataria is nonetheless intelligible as the imaginary place that corresponds to Don Quijote's books; for readers it is identifiable as the creation of specific characters, the Duke and the Duchess, who occupy a determinate position with respect to it.

To think of the polis in relation to territories and borders is crucial, but politics is equally a matter of human associations within whatever place may be at issue. Together, geographical territories and human associations establish some of the most fundamental parameters for politics. They help determine who is a member of a given polis and who is not, and they enable the polis to imagine itself in relation to those it excludes (e.g., barbarians, poets, women, various ethnic or religious 'others,' etc.). With the exception of some remarks in Don Quijote's speech to the goatherds and a glancing reference in the episode of the *rebuznos*, however, what would appear to be one of the most basic features of political life – politics as the incorporation of individuals in a particular kind of association or political community – seems to be absent from Cervantes' text. The sharing of a meal among friends, which I have alluded to earlier, suggests the ideal of an ethical community that lies outside the scope of the political.[1] The questions of companionship and friendship, as exemplified in the relationship between Don Quijote and Sancho, likewise present important alternatives to political forms of association. Some might say that they are ideal, idealized forms of political association. But what about political community? What place might the polis have in relation to other, equally powerful forms of community, including the ones based on kinship, religion, and race that were at the centre of no less powerful interests in Spain? To explore such questions requires attending to a surprising truth: that political community in the conventional sense, whether on a large or a small scale, is largely absent in the *Quijote*. This is so in spite of the fact that at nearly every official level Spain was obsessed with the project of creating a coherent and unified national state out of a great diversity of regional histories, languages, races, and religious beliefs. 'The confusion surrounding lineages is great' says Don Quijote with respect to one version of this problem, near the beginning of Part II (494) (Es grande la confusión que hay entre los linajes'; II, 6, p. 83). Given Cervantes' scepticism vis-à-vis 'official' projects to homogenize the nation, but finding no viable alternatives ready to give, it might well seem that Cervantes would have us wonder whether political community is possible at all.

The question of political community in the early modern sense was raised on a doctrinal level by thinkers like Vitoria who spoke of the *populus* of each republic. Vitoria's close colleague, Domingo de Soto, wrote eloquently about what the *ius gentium* could and must provide over and above the law of nature, viz., a responsiveness to obligations created through consensus and community. So too, the neo-scholastic philosopher

Francisco Suárez in the *Treatise On Laws* draws distinctions between the law of nature and international law and frames careful arguments around the nature of civil power and political obligations.[2] Their work offers clear antecedents to that of Grotius and Pufendorf. But the formation of the modern state is not a matter of theory alone.[3] The matter of practical formation took on a specific cast at this time, when the political state became all but identical to the nation. As historians Charles Tilly and Immanuel Wallerstein among others have made clear, the nation is de facto the dominant and overarching modern state institution.[4] Not surprisingly, most modern political theory presupposes territories that are organized as sovereign nation-states. But this was not always the case, as many of the most influential thinkers of the Renaissance can testify. Machiavelli, for instance, wrote *The Prince* presupposing a *city*-state, not a nation, in spite of the fact that he regarded Fernando El Católico as an exemplary 'new prince,' the 'foremost king of Christendom.'[5] In considering the Mediterranean world of the fifteenth century and most of the sixteenth, Fernand Braudel observed that political life in fact belonged to its towns, and to the city-states scattered around the Mediterranean's shores.[6] While there were already a few territorial states by the end of the fourteenth century, these were relatively few and fairly homogeneous – the kingdom of Naples, the Byzantine empire, and of greatest importance here, the possessions united under the crown of Aragón. But, as Braudel went on to note, these states were in many cases merely the extensions of powerful cities: Aragón was in a sense a byproduct of the dynamic rise of Barcelona (*The Mediterranean*, 1:657).

While post-Machiavellian political writers increasingly took the territorial nation as their fundamental point of reference, and were often required to do so because of the questions raised by the newly encountered lands of the Americas, Benedict Anderson has argued that the very idea of a 'nation' was always an anomaly.[7] His insight lends clarity to the concept of the 'nation' just as it generates a critique of its foundations and consequences.[8] A nation is conceived as limited and sovereign. Even if the individual citizens of the smallest nation never come to know most of their compatriots, it is in the idea of the nation that each person imagines living in community. As Anderson went on to argue, the nation is limited largely because it is territorially bound; beyond it lie other nations. Colonialism (hence empire) presupposes the territorial integrity of the nation and its ability to control other territories, including other nations. In the sixteenth century there already existed a body of international law of regulations, treaties, ambassadorial exchanges, protocols, and the like, including between Christian and Islamic States.[9] Debates over questions of territorial rights involving Spain and its rivals within this context place us far away from the utopian ideal of a mythical time on earth when there were no territories or possessions at all. To take but two salient examples, the responses of Domingo de Soto to his Salamanca colleague Francisco Vitoria on the question of colonial dominion argued in favour of the claim to rightful possession on the basis of propinquity to territorially bounded space.[10] Much earlier, Guicciardini explained that the seizure of Navarre by Fernando el Católico was necessary in order to complete his territories and seal the integrity of his kingdoms at the Pyrenees.[11]

Furthermore, the nation was imagined as sovereign. Even though most nations were established during a time when divinely ordained, dynastic realms were crumbling, there remained a desire to institutionalize some overarching, metaphysical ground for human freedom at the political level.[12] The fact that the hereditary and hierarchical basis of monarchical states began to come under pressure during the late sixteenth and early seventeenth centuries is worth recalling because of the way in which it opened up questions about the 'horizontal' relationship among subjects comprising a community. The Hapsburgs managed to amass and expand their dynastic power by a series of opportunistic marriages, captures, and negotiations, but still could not establish the idea of a Spanish nation without finding a way to create the image among subjects that they shared essential bonds and existed in community with one another. Not only in Spain but throughout all of Europe, as Anderson suggests, the nation was conceived as a community because it was felt as rooted in deep, horizontal relationships, relationships akin to a fraternity.[13] This 'imagined' sense of community helped establish the nation not just as legal entity but as a form of political association whose basis lay in a set of relationships that were stronger than legality could define. As the venerable historian and essayist Ernest Renan remarked, the 'nation' depends upon large-scale solidarity, 'constituted by the feeling of sacrifices that one has made in the past and is prepared to make in the future. It presupposes a past; it is summarized, however, in the present by a single tangible fact, namely, consent, the clearly expressed desire to continue a common life.'[14] In Vitoria's thinking, no modern state could be based on the apparatus of power alone; power must be rooted in the community – or the idea of it – which is in Vitoria's words *pars rei publicae*.[15]

The fraternal basis of nationality contributed to the sense that the nation was not at bottom political at all, but was the political embodiment of kinship ties. This idea was ancient. In fact, it was among the grounds to which Plato appealed when attempting to legitimize the differences among individuals in the ideal state. Plato tells in the *Republic* that all men and women were originally formed and nurtured deep inside the earth, and recommends that now in their policy-making they 'must think of the land they live in as their mother'; they must defend their 'motherland' against invasion and should think of their fellow citizens 'as brothers born of the same mother earth.'[16] The project of 'imagining' a polis required for Plato considering how best to make an integrated city out of the differences among human beings. The idea of a common fraternity, rooted in the earth, is an origin myth that serves this end.[17]

The political community of the nation may well be imagined, and even 'imaginary.' Indeed, one of my tasks in this chapter will be to discuss the relationship between the political imaginary of the nation and the fantasy-structures of literary romance. But the nation is of course not just imaginary. Nations have histories, cultural roots, and legal standing.[18] As political entities, they mobilize armies, declare wars, and negotiate truces; they exist in a context that is by definition inter-national. The preliminary materials of *Don Quijote*, Part II, make it clear that this inter-national context directly informed Cervantes' self-image and his reputation as a writer. The nation brings with it a certain sense of pride, which the modern writer helps extend and to which he is attached. The *aprobación* of the licenciate Márquez Torres to Part II describes Cervantes' works as unique 'both for our nation and for foreign ones,' among which he specifically mentions Spain's continental rivals France, Germany, and Flanders ('Bien diferente han sentido de los escritos de Miguel de Cervantes, así nuestra nación como las estrañas, pues como a milagro desean ver el autor de libros que con general aplauso, así por su decoro y decencia como por la suavidad y blandura de sus discursos, han recebido España, Francia, Italia, Alemania y Flandes'; II, p. 30).[19] In Spain, the international context was especially important because of Spain's expansive imperial ambitions. Those ambitions called for a new body of law, or at the very least for the adaptation of existing laws to new circumstances. In the sixteenth century, both Vitoria and Suárez addressed specific questions in a legal context that was essentially the law of nations. And they did so even while commenting on Aquinas, in whom they sought to find a precedent for the modern law of nations in the ancient principle of the *ius gentium*.[20]

Nations were also supported by the enlargement of secular society and by secular cultural practices, many of which allowed for the enhanced administrative control of diverse cities and regions. Some secular developments, such as the invention of the printed book, brought with them the possibility of new, centrally controlled administrative procedures.[21] It goes without saying that *Don Quijote* would have been impossible without the existence of print culture.[22] This is not just an empirical fact about the book's existence, but speaks as well to the circulation of the texts that informed and shaped it, to their reception, to Don Quijote's reading, and to Cervantes' engagement with the printed work of his rival, Alonso Fernández de Avellaneda. The legend of the circulation of the first Part of the *Quijote* in print is of some note as well. Sansón Carrasco puts the run of Part I at 12,000 copies; Don Quijote says it was 30,000.[23] It is less obvious, but nonetheless true, that modern politics, which is to say *national* politics, would have been impossible without print. Homi Bhabha's account of 'nationness' as a form of social and textual affiliation for one, certainly presupposes the existence of printed texts.[24] In the longer view, seen as a condition of possibility rather than as a cause, print culture also supported the development of relatively stable vernaculars – the forerunners of national languages – which were necessary for the centralized administration of disparate lands and for establishing a sense that diverse individuals were commonly bound by something very deep. In more practical terms, the spread of printing and the stabilization of the vernacular created a need for the professional classes that I have mentioned earlier – the young lawyers, bureaucrats, planners, and problem-solvers who were critically important to the implementation of laws and the administration of 'national' policies.

Nations depend upon what Saskia Sassen has described as an 'assemblage' of territories, authorities, and rights.[25] But the assemblage of these three elements in the form of the early modern nation would have been impossible without the existence and dissemination of regularized legal codes.[26] In Spain, the effort at legal regularization that had begun with the Catholic kings (and even before them, with John II of Castile) continued throughout the later Middle Ages and early modern period in the form of compilations such as the *Ordenanzas reales de Castilla* (1484), the *Leyes de Toro* (1505), the all-important *Nueva recopilación* of 1567, and the redeployment of the venerable *Fuero Juzgo* under Philip II. As Richard Kagan has argued, these efforts at coordinated legislation were designed to produce 'national' unity. The *Nueva recopilación* (*New Collection of Laws*) promulgated by Philip II, was the work of the *letrados*, Galíndez de Carvajal and López de Alcocer among them. As a collection, it reproduced many of the ancient Spanish laws, along with their authors' names and dates, arranged systematically by subject.[27] Efforts at legal regularization produced a tremendous increase in the number of professionals who needed to be trained to interpret and apply a vast and growing body of statutes.[28] Spain was in fact one of the first truly 'administered' modern states. As noted above, the Inquisition worked by means of a highly bureaucratized apparatus, but the spread of the new legal culture was wide in secular contexts as well. As Diego Hurtado de Mendoza wrote in the very opening pages of the *Guerra de Granada*, 'The Catholic kings placed the governance of justice and public matters in the hands of lettered men ... whose expertise was knowledge of legal writings ... This way of governing, established then with less diligence, has been extended over all Christendom, and is today at the height of its authority and power: such is its sway over common life.'[29] Already in 1566 a scribe working in the *cancillería* of Valladolid, Gabriel Monterroso y Alvarado, would complain that 'lawsuits and conflicts among the populace [were] growing daily ... the world is so engulfed in these disputes that almost nothing is resolved except by the cloth of legal judgment.'[30] And yet the administration of polities on a national level, along with the regulation of civil life, was crucial to the efforts to form a political community for all of Spain.

One can detect many ways in which these circumstances reverberate in *Don Quijote*. Some have already been referred to above. Recall Don Quijote's disdain for the new classes of courtly knights and legal graduates. And yet the politics reflected in *Don Quijote* seems anomalous with respect to the idea of the 'nation' as a political entity. The reasons are hardly obscure. The 'unification' of the Iberian Peninsula following the defeat of the last Moorish king in 1492 provided the territorial basis for the establishment of a nation, but this was ultimately insufficient for the construction of a coherent political community. It was a condition of possibility but not more.[31] In the aftermath of 1492 the nation had yet to be 'produced.' Spain was thus the site of vigorous efforts to 'manufacture' the sense of a collective (national) identity precisely because its own existence as a political whole was so fragile and new. Spanish Absolutism, characterized by Perry Anderson as the paragon of all European absolutist states, was a manifestation of the ways in which the effort to produce a nation was organized and controlled at the highest levels. Indeed, those efforts reached far beyond what is recognized as politics *strictu sensu*, to the very forms of affiliation that Bhabha and others, since at least Renan in the nineteenth century, pointed to as crucial to the creation of 'nationness.'[32]

I suggested above that the very possibility of uniformity at the legal level in Spain was the existence of a common vernacular. In 1492, the humanist grammarian Antonio de Nebrija said famously in the *Gramática de la lengua española* that language is the handmaiden of empire. Nebrija was not alone, and was in fact preceded by a host of Italian antecedents on related matters of language and cultural hegemony.[33] Nebrija's remark is nonetheless often cited as a turning point in Spanish cultural history because it bridges language and politics in a way that seems to presuppose a unified nation as a political entity that could embark on still larger, imperial endeavours. (It was indeed odd that Charles V did not know Spanish when he ascended to the Spanish throne; in1518 the Cortes urged him to learn the language as rapidly as possible.) But Nebrija's was in fact a forward-looking, aspirational remark. It was territorial expansion that in turn gave Spaniards the opportunity to press claims to linguistic supremacy in unprecedented ways. Of course, Spanish expansion in the New World also raised a series of questions about the deeper logic of community and the rights of those who were subject to imperial rule, as the debates between Las Casas and Vitoria clearly showed. What might one make of the vast differences among the peoples of the globe while arguing that all the territory of the earth belonged in the first instance to the Creator? Did the indigenous people of the New World, so unlike the Spaniards in many of their practices, have souls? To whom did jurisdiction over them belong, and on what basis?

Moreover, the newly unified Spanish 'nation' was rife with fears about its possible disintegration. Threats from within and without seemed to loom increasingly large as Spain's global power reached its peak. Quevedo's 1609 diatribe, *España defendida*, offered a hyperbolic defence of Spain against her real and imagined European enemies. His rhetoric was extreme, but such a defence was not atypical in the long course of conflicts between Spain and its Protestant adversaries. While the spread of printed vernacular writings served to enhance the sense that individuals within a given territory were bound by some essential things – by the idea of a common past or *aetatem patriae*, by the outlook toward a shared future, by a common faith and, of course, by a common language – it seems that the sense of a national consciousness was often more authentically articulated from perspectives outside of Spain's territorial borders than from within.[34]

It was from Vienna that Cristóbal de Castillejo took notice of the global reach of the Spanish tongue: 'Now Spain has conversation in so many parts, not just of the world that was formerly known, but outside of it, for it is in the Indies, and widely, that Spanish is spoken and taught, just as Latin was, with the aim of understanding and enhancing it in all possible ways.'[35] Amado Alonso argued in a well-known study comparing 'Spanish' as a language and the idea of 'Spain' as a nation, that the term *español* was a neologism in Spanish, as was *patria*. His claim was that the idea of *patria* had emerged during the fifteenth century to describe a native affiliation with a supraregional political territory.[36] Some, including José Antonio Maravall, have taken issue with this idea, and have argued that both the notion of a *patria* and the idea of a *nación* have a history that goes back to classical antiquity and runs through the Middle Ages before it was 're-vived' in the Renaissance.[37] But Amado Alonso's claim has rather to do with the consciousness of nation and with the awareness of *patria* in the early modern Spanish context, not with their absolute *novelty* in the Spanish context. The matter of language as a hegemonic instrument was in wide circulation, especially in Italy's relation to the Roman Empire. It passed to Spain from there.[38] The point is that many writers, such as Francisco de Medina in introducing Herrera's monumental *Anotaciones* to Garcilaso's poetry (1580), did, in fact, speak of 'nuestra patria,' and of 'nuestra lengua' as Spanish. That prologue likewise conceives of the national language as 'the Spanish language' (el lenguaje español). Similarly, *patria* had a very long heritage, and was recreated in part as a humanist 'imitation' of an ancient idea. And while *patria* may always describe what Maravall aptly characterizes as a 'place of attachment or insertion' (lugar de afincamiento o de inserción), its role in early modern Spain was to bind a sense of territory to a belief in common ancestry.[39]

And yet, regionalism remained stubbornly in place, and especially the increasingly dominant regionalism of Castile. 'Castellano' was in fact never fully displaced by 'español.' Even in texts where the term 'español' was invoked, 'castellano' continued to carry a preponderant weight (a case in point is the *Gramática castellana* published in Antwerp by the humanist Cristóbal de Villalón in 1558). The Spanish version of Sannazaro's *Arcadia* (1547) took Castilian as the privileged, literary version of the Spanish language, comparable to the Tuscan dialect in Italy, as did Juan de Valdés's *Diálogo de la lengua*.[40] It is, in fact, the term Cervantes chooses in the *Viaje del Parnaso* when describing his own achievements as a writer, as it is in the Prologue to the *Exemplary Novels*.[41] Covarrubias's famous thesaurus, the *Tesoro de la lengua castellana, o española* (which, in 1611, was the first thesaurus of any of the modern European languages) settles for both terms, though not quite in equal measure. He glosses 'Castilla' as a region of 'nuestra España.' Why? In part, this was because the regional pre-eminence of Castile made strongest sense in the larger context of a Spanish nation. Indeed, Covarrubias and his family were quite actively involved in producing a sense of Spain as a homogeneous political and territorial entity in linguistic and ethnic terms. As Jacques Lezra has shown, numerous members of the Covarrubias family served in the Hapsburg government, where they were involved in a variety of administrative projects designed to shore up a sense of national unity, including the recovery and redeployment of the Visigothic *Fuero Juzgo*.[42] The particular member of the family who compiled the *Tesoro*, Sebastián de Covarrubias, was also an administrative official, working in Cuenca as a *consultor* to the Inquisition and as a tax administrator in Valencia.[43]

The preoccupations over Spanish vs. Castilian, and whether the language was to be called either or both, are set within a national context that was imagined as homogeneous, whole, and closed, in spite of much evidence to the contrary. That said, 'Spanish' and 'Castilian' were clearly dominant over the many regional peninsula languages as well as over all the unofficial, hybrid forms of speech. In the case of the *Diálogo de la lengua*, Valdés questions the authority of the humanist grammarian Antonio Nebrija on the grounds that he was born in Andalucía.[44]

Indeed, the normativizing intent of the very conception of a 'national' language was to exclude regional languages and to guard against encroachment of the hybrid forms of speech that were prevalent in so many of the social and political 'contact zones' characteristic of Spain's international situation – the places where Spanish came directly in touch with the various forms of Arabic and Turkish that were spoken in the nearby Mediterranean, especially in North Africa's Barbary coast as well as in parts of southern Spain.[45] Diego de Haedo's *Topografía de Argel* speaks of 'el hablar franco de Argel, casi una jerigonza o, a lo menos, un hablar de negro boçal traído a España de nuevo' (the common parlance of Algiers, almost a gibberish, or, at the least, the talk of a black man, recently brought to Spain, who does not know any language other than his own).[46] This is, in fact, what the Captive in *Don Quijote* calls 'the bastard tongue' (la bastarda lengua) used in Barbary (I, 41, p. 498). There is a further passage in the Captive's story that transmits this more complex sense of the mixing of languages in such zones of contact. The Captive relates that while he was a prisoner in Algiers, he would go to the garden outside the home of Zoraida, the beautiful daughter of the wealthy and powerful Agi Morato, in the hope that she might speak to him.[47] Just prior to his escape the Captive encounters her father; the two communicate in a language that is described as specifically *other* than national, where 'national' has both political and racial/ethnic overtones: 'One day before my departure I went there, and the first person I met was her father, who spoke to me in the language used between captives and Moors throughout Barbary, and even in Constantinople;

it is not Moorish or Castilian, *not the language of any nation, but the mix-ture of all tongues*, and with it we can understand one another' (353) (Un día, antes de mi partida, fui allá, y la primera persona con quién encontré fue con su padre, el cual me dijo, en lengua que en toda la Berbería, y aun en Costantinopla, se halla entre cautivos y moros, que ni es morisca, ni castellana, *ni de otra nación alguna, sino una mezcla de todas las lenguas* con la cual todos nos entendemos; I, 41, p. 496; emphasis added).

The question of the Captain's escape from Algiers and return to Spain with Zoraida raises the question of the status of the *moriscos* and *mudé-jares* in Spain, about which I will have more to say below. But strictly, re-garding the question of language and nation, it bears noting that Cervantes' own experiences in captivity all but precluded a monological or monolin-gual conception of what Spain might be *because* of its inter-national and inter-ethnic involvements. But the matter also goes to the roots of the Spanish language, which so often attest to the admixture of Arabic words. When Sancho asks Don Quijote what *albogues* are (a pipe-like musical instrument), Don Quijote explains that this and all other Spanish words beginning in *al-* are from Arabic, or more specifically, that they are of *morisco* origin: 'This word *albogues* is moorish, as are all those in our Cas-tilian tongue that begin with *al*, for example *almohaza, almorzar, alhom-bra, alguacil, alhucema, almacén, alcancía*, and other similar words ... I have told you this in passing because it came to mind when I happened to mention *albogues*' (901) (Este nombre *albogues* es morisco, como lo son todos aquellos que en nuestra lengua castellana comienzan en *al*, conviene a saber: *almohaza, almorzar, alhombra, alguacil, alhucema, almacén, al-cancía*, y otros semejantes ... Esto te he dicho, de paso, por habérmelo reducido a la memoria la ocasión de haber nombrado *albogues*; II, 68, p. 550).[48] To have understood something about the mixed and hybrid na-ture of the 'national' language, it was not necessary for Cervantes to have spent time in captivity in Algiers.[49] And yet among the results of Cer-vantes' exposure to the hybrid culture in North Africa was certainly a sense of the precarious and unstable range of 'national' affiliations beyond what any official stance could acknowledge: 'In Barbary they call the Moors from Aragón *Tagarinos* and the ones from Granada *Mudéjares*: in the kingdom of Fez the *Mudéjares* are called *Elches*, and these are the peo-ple used most by the king in war' (352) (*Tagarinos* llaman en Berbería a los moros de Aragón, y a los de Granada, *mudéjares*; y en el reino de Fez lla-man a los mudéjares *elches*, los cuales son la gente de quien aquel rey más se sirve en la Guerra; I, 41, p. 495). Linguistic complexity emerges from forms of cultural hybridity involving complex crossings and exchange. The beautiful Morisca Zoraida interlaces what Spanish she has learned from her nursemaid with phrases from her local Arabic; she speaks of the Virgin Mary as 'Lela Marién' and of Christian prayers as 'la zalá cristianesca' (I, 40, p. 489); similarly, the Captain refers to reverential gestures as 'zalemas a uso de moros' (I, 40, p. 487). Algiers was a notoriously mixed city, where Berbers and Andalusians along with renegade Greeks and Turks were thrown together as if at random.[50] Although the official language of the Turkish regency in Algiers was a blend of Arabic, Persian, and Osmanli Turkish, the influx of slaves from many parts of the world made it such that nearly everyone in Algiers, including the Christian captives, spoke the lingua franca. In the context of such geopolitical and linguistic mixing, it goes almost without saying that the notion of a national language, equivalent to a native language, was bound to be fraught. The Captive speaks to Zoraida in Arabic (I, 37, p. 463), and what Zoraida knows of the Christian faith was taught to her in Arabic by a slave nursemaid, which is to say, by a Christian woman who had either been taken into captivity or born of a captive in Algiers. Zoraida counts as a 'sister in Christ' in terms of a kinship deriving from a common mother.[51] But according to statutes of purity of blood she was not a Christian at all.

In sum, the relatively recent and somewhat precarious formation of 'Spain' as a territorially based political entity, together with the nearby presence of linguistic and ethnic contact zones in North Africa, southern Spain, and the Mediterranean, meant that official measures were required if there was to be any sense of a national political consciousness. Not least of these was the enforcement of homogeneity in religious teaching and practice, the prosecution of those who espoused heterodox beliefs, and enforced adherence to racialized ideas of kinship among those who regarded themselves as old-stock, pure-blooded Christians.[52] Sancho Panza offers an unwittingly hyperbolic view of these attitudes as he boasts of having 'four fingers' worth of Old Christian lard on my soul' (my translation) (sobre el alma cuatro dedos de enjundia de cristianos viejos; II, 4, p. 71). The aim of these official efforts, and their alignment with popular views, was the creation of a peninsula-wide political entity that could be recognized as having the form of a nation. But while Spain clearly did become a nation in official, legal terms, its existence as such was largely dependent upon the desire of powerful groups – principally those originating in Castile and to the north – to project a regional identity, grounded in religions conviction and based on claims to genealogical primacy, over others on the peninsula and in the New World. The idea of Spain as a political community, expressed soulfully as the idea of 'nuestra España,' as in the case of Co-varrubia mentioned above, is not uncommon from the later fifteenth century onwards.[53] Sansón Carrasco offers elaborate praise of Don Quijote in II, 7, as a hero of the 'Spanish nation,' in spite of the fact that the idea of a 'nation' is incongruous with the chivalric framework he also invokes: 'O flower of errant chivalry! O resplendent knight of arms! O honor and paragon of the Spanish nation! May it please Almighty God that the person or persons who impede or hinder your third sally never emerge from the labyrinth of their desires' (500) (¡Oh flor de la andante caballería; oh luz resplandeciente de las armas; oh honor y espejo de la nación española! Plega a Dios todopoderoso, donde más largamente se contiene, que la persona o personas que pusieren impedimento y estorbaren tu tercera salida, que no la hallen en el laberinto de sus deseos; II, 7, p. 89). Indeed, the degree to which any sense of a national 'community' in early modern Spain was both imagined and invented remains remarkable.

Some of the strongest forms of political attachment in Spain were, in fact, far more local than the idea of a nation would suggest. Many were, in fact, oriented around the city as the 'patria natural.'[54] Political theorists such as Castrillo tend to regard the city, not the nation, as the highest form of community ('la más noble de todas las compañías').[55] The notion of the ancient *politeia* was of course conceived as city-state and, as the notion of the *ciudadano* says in all but literal terms, it was in relation to the city that the citizen was conceived as a political subject in early modern Spain.[56] According to Castrillo, citizens enjoy relative equality in their relationships; they experience a form of civic friendship and share a range of customs that work together to help preserve society. While the region of Castile may have generated much of the energy behind the invention of a larger, national political consciousness, Castile was itself a community of cities, not a community of the realm. Its own political unconscious bore traces of its prior existence as one among many different Iberian kingdoms. In fact, as many as eight different 'kingdoms' were represented in the Castilian Cortes even after the fall of Granada and the supposed 'unification' of the peninsula: Castile, León, Toledo, Murcia, Córdoba, Jaén, Seville, Granada. In the trail of official documents that can be followed across the sixteenth century, reference to the eight kingdoms was only gradually displaced – first by reference to 'the kingdoms of Castile, and of León, and of Granada,' then by the term 'estos reinos' (these kingdoms) and only much later by 'Castile' *tout court.*[57] Surprisingly, all three Philips – II, III, and IV – held to the principle of the separateness of the individual kingdoms.

As late as 1619 Sancho de Moncada cited the regional diversity of Spain – a diversity rooted in the territorial adjacency of formerly autonomous kingdoms – as a reason to establish university instruction in what today we would call the discipline of 'political science.' This was, in fact, the first plan for any such instructional program in Spain, and possibly in Europe as well. He further argued that education in political science ought to go beyond a reading of the classics because Spain was itself an assemblage of diverse political and cultural entities, not reducible to any one source: 'Spain is a republic of kingdoms of many different qualities ... as many kingdoms as of contrasting complexions that it is almost impossible to find a common measure among the ancient ones, without injuring some part of it.'[58] In point of fact, the idea of the *nación* tended to conjure up allegiances to the regional entities that Moncada hints at in this passage more strongly than to any consolidated, peninsular political community. The balance of power among the various regions of Spain was nonetheless uneven. Saavedra Fajardo, for instance, complained in the *Locuras de Europa* that many national burdens tended to fall unfairly on Castile.[59] Surprisingly, perhaps, influential powers in Castile regarded the greater political entity called 'Spain,' along with its empire, as parasitic, a drain upon its leadership and resources. Petitions for the support of Portugal and Aragón in 1593 were met with sharp criticism by the likes of Francisco de Monzón, the *procurador* of Madrid.[60] In fact, Castile felt that it had been unfairly burdened with the defence of all Christendom, not just of Spain. In 1596 Valcárcel complained that 'the cause and defense of the Catholic faith is common to all of Christendom, and if these wars serve that purpose it is not up to Castile to bear all the burden, while all the other kingdoms, princes, and republics look on.'[61]

Cervantes' engagement with the politics of community, national and otherwise, takes place within this complex set of circumstances. But Cervantes refracts the public discourse about national politics so as to bring out a powerful set of tensions between the 'imagined community' of the modern secular nation and forms of community based on religion, kinship, and race.[62] As Braudel remarked, before the nationalisms of the nineteenth century, people tended to feel united by the bonds of religions belief (*The Mediterranean*, 2:824). But rather than offer a polarized set of views that would pit the politics of the nascent secular nation-state against the politics of religion and race – which quite clearly ran together at many points – Cervantes asks a more fundamental set of questions: what is it that people imagine as binding them together and, by contrast, what is it that drives them apart? Why does it seem necessary to push some groups out in order for others to form strong bonds? To this he adds a second-order question: what allows people to imagine that they exist as a community when in fact they do not? The farcical interlude (*entremés*) *El retablo de las maravillas* is perhaps Cervantes' most direct engagement with these questions. In this one-act play everyone operates within the space of a collective 'fantasy,' namely that they are all equally of 'pure blood.' But that fantasy turns out to have no support other than the fact that it is a set of mutually reinforcing beliefs that allow certain obvious truths, truths known to virtually all, to go unchallenged. The power of the fantasy seems to persist and to shore up a political bond based on a shared set of 'untruths.'

But the question of political community, and the fantasies that sustain it, reaches much farther than this short farce might suggest. To pursue these questions further requires attending to various instances of community in the *Quijote*, however provisional or unreal or divided they may be, as well as to instances where community seems to be undermined or conspicuous by its absence. These are, in turn, some of the places where Cervantes diverges markedly from classical political theory (the ideas of Plato and Aristotle), from Renaissance humanism, and from the politics of pragmatic power (*Realpolitik*) that led Machiavelli to admire Cesare Borgia and Fernando El Católico, even if ambivalently. In Cervantes, the question of community is inseparable from the collective political imaginary, which is something quite different from Plato's ideal republic. Moreover, he does not look for politics to be realized in a movement from 'imaginary' to 'real' but rather sees that the politics of the 'real' rests on a set of sometimes quite fantastical beliefs. While the work of politics may well involve negotiation between the imaginary and the real, Cervantes understands that politics is no more a matter of moving from one to the other than *Don Quijote* is itself a story about a character's failed attempt to bring the imaginary and the real into alignment. Politics remains quixotic to the extent that it is driven by fantasies about how entities such as the nation are shaped, about who its essential members are, and about the meaning that is attached to idea of participation in a whole.[63] I propose to discuss next the project of imagining the nation in Golden Age Spain drawing support from the structure of literary romance. Moreover, Cervantes' critical engagement with romance – in the way he shapes a series of romance-like episodes in *Don Quijote*, Part II – acts in the service of a critique of the national political imaginary. This considerably enlarges the critical response to romance of the kind levelled by the Canon of Toledo in Part I, which concentrates on issues of artistic unity and questions of verisimilitude. The episodes in question in Part II have little to do with verisimilitude and much to do with the need to apply pressure against the imaginary force of the national romance.

An opportune place to pursue this discussion is with the episode of Ricote and his daughter, Ana Félix, in chapters 53–5 and 63–5 of Part II, which in certain respects mirrors the episode of the Capitive and Zoraida from Part I. It is no accident that these events follow immediately after Sancho leaves his governorship. Recall that even Sancho never quite knows what it is he is governing – whether an island, a city, a village, or some other kind of place.[64] With the encounter with Ricote, the political experiment of Barataria yields to what seem to be the real-world political events that culminated during the years 1609–13: the official expulsion of the converted Muslims (moriscos) who had until then been living in Spain legally. The concrete politics of Barataria were imaginary in the pejorative sense of the term; they were fraudulent in their very framing. By contrast, the Ricote episode makes apparent reference to 'real' politics by alluding to one of the official means by which Spain endeavoured to establish itself as a homogeneous community at the national level.[65] Official policy attempted to produce a unified population and to establish political community by direct intervention. Holding aside for a moment the impracticality of accomplishing any such goal by fiat, official policy was hardly uncomplicated. The 'expulsion' of the moriscos, in fact, took place over a number of years and was the culmination of a series of regional actions between 1609 and 1613, the very years during which Cervantes was writing Part II of the Quijote. By certain estimates some 300,000 moriscos were forced to leave Spain, with consequences for the agrarian economy that have been the subject of much commentary. The official act of expulsion most often referred to was made by the Consejo de Estado on 30 January 1608, initially with application to Valencia. It was extended nationally on 1 April 1609, for 'reasons of state,' which is to say for official 'convenience' as well as for reasons of national security. This hardly seems surprising given the recent conquest of Morocco by Muley Cidán, a sworn enemy of Spain. Moreover, as Henri Lapeyre perspicuously noted, the day on which Philip III signed the decree of expulsion of the moriscos was the very day the Twelve Years Truce was also ratified. In fact, the edict of expulsion may have been a way of compensating groups that were opposed to the peace with Protestant countries.[66] It is certainly a reminder that Spain had also been busy dealing with the threat of Protestantism, especially in the Lowlands.

These immediate events had a long and significant prior history, beginning with a series of 'pragmatic sanctions' (*pragmáticas*) in 1566–7 leading to the uprising of the *moriscos* of the Alpujarras in 1568–9. The pragmatic sanctions prohibited speaking or writing in Arabic, enforced the wearing of Castilian dress, and banned all Muslim cultural and religious practices such as ritual bathing.[67] The sanctions ran directly against the agreements signed by the Catholic kings in 1492, which promised the defeated Muslims their right to language and religion. J.H. Elliott aptly described the events of the 'terrible year' that immediately preceded the Alpujarras revolt as a moment when Spain was drawn to shift its attention from the threats of Protestantism to the dangers posed by the unruly 'alien' population within its borders. In fact, it could be said that the *moriscos* played a necessary role in the process of nation-building by presenting a kernel of racial otherness within Spain, whose eradication could then be construed as a key to national cohesion. It was on Christmas night of 1568 – the same year in which a sea route was cut through the Bay of Biscay, and when Philip's son and heir, Don Carlos, was arrested and died – that a band of Morisco outlaws led by a certain Fárax Abenfárax broke into the city of Granada announcing that the Alpujarras had risen in revolt. Their incursion marked the beginnings of rebellion throughout the kingdom of Granada. Until then Spain had built strong defences against the advance of Protestantism; now it was endangered from within.[68]

Cervantes recognized both the immediacy and the historical complexity of these events. We know that the Valle de Ricote, to which the character Ricote's name obviously refers, is located in the region of Murcia, and was one of the last places from which any large group of *moriscos* was expelled. The government official responsible for the formal edict, the Viceroy Bernardino de Velasco, Count of Salazar, is in fact mentioned by name in *Don Quijote*, II, 55. But Cervantes was also writing in response to the construction of a political 'imaginary' around the issues of nationhood and community. He understood that the political decisions of the years 1609–13 ignored the fact that the unity and stability of the nation were being created in the imagination just as much as by official state acts. As if commenting on this very point, the Ricote episode in the *Quijote* reveals the astounding degree to which any political community relies on a set of imaginary, even 'fantastical' beliefs. The idea that Ricote is Sancho's neighbour (his *vecino*, which is to say, from his *vecindad*) is one of these ideas. The forgiveness of Ricote and Ricote's daughter that permits her marriage to Don Gaspar Gregorio by the Viceroy is another. Furthermore, the romance plot having to do with Ricote's return to Spain, the recovery of the hidden fortune he had left behind, and the disclosure of his daughter's true identity, suggest the kind of narrative structures that were necessary in order to support the idea of a well-integrated national community in the face of tangible evidence to the contrary. Indeed, it would seem that the project of establishing a nation-state on the basis of the 'happy' re-incorporation of its excluded, internal others would require nothing less than what the fantasy-structure that romance could provide.[69] Unlike the Platonic ideal, which creates the discursive image of a polis that is whole but that could never be constructed within the domain of the real, the fantasy-structure of romance allows for an image-ideal to insinuate itself at the level of the real because it gives 'meaning' to things that could not otherwise be accepted – by proposing a 'brotherhood' of mankind, by cultivating a sentimental attachment to the other as 'exotic,' or by heroizing the acts of generosity that allow political conflicts to be ignored. Romance is, in Fredric Jameson's analysis, a narratively structured wish-fulfilment dream that can play a crucial role in supporting the 'political unconscious' of a given historical moment.[70] But the difference between Jameson's notion and what we see in the *Quijote* is that the kernel of the 'unconscious' is not, in Cervantes' case, a set of class relations, but rather the idea of a nation, in which religious, ethnic, and regional differences, more than class conflict, could be incorporated as part of a political totality. It was in terms just like these that some of the conflicting political interests at work in early modern Spain could be imaginatively resolved.[71]

To say this is also to recognize the degree to which the alliance between literary romance and the workings of the national political imaginary provoked a critical response from Cervantes. Later in this chapter, I will turn to Cervantes' re-purposing of the bucolic setting of the pastoral, by a process of inversion of its basic form, toward similarly critical ends. In both cases some of the contradictions that are 'resolved' through literary fantasy are hiding in plain sight. The 'human' bond between Sancho and Ricote has, for instance, often been noted by critics, but not the fact that it depends on a fantastical geography. Ricote recognizes Sancho as a dear friend and neighbour in II, 54 ('mi caro amigo … mi buen vecino' [447]), but if Ricote is from anywhere near the valley of his namesake then he and Sancho must, in fact, be from very different parts of Spain. In I, 8, where Sancho is first introduced, we learn that he is a neighbour of Don Quijote's, which is to say that he must be from 'a place in La Mancha' (un lugar de la Mancha), just like Don Quijote. The Valle de Ricote, located within the region of Murcia, lies in southeastern Spain. Indeed, the question of where Sancho's encounter with Ricote in II, 54, takes place raises some further questions about the relationship between real and fictional geographies and the political implications they carry. We know that the estates of the Duke and the Duchess lie somewhere in Aragón. But Sancho explains that he has just left the governorship of an *island* nearby: 'And where is this ínsula?' asked Ricote. 'Where?' responded Sancho. 'Two leagues from here, and it's called ínsula Barataria.' 'That's amazing, Sancho,' said Ricote. 'Ínsulas are in the ocean; there are no ínsulas on terra firma.' 'What do you mean?' replied Sancho. 'I tell you, Ricote my friend, I left there this morning, and yesterday I was there governing to my heart's content' (815) ('¿Y dónde está esa ínsula?' '¿Adónde?' respondió Sancho. 'Dos leguas de aquí, y se llama la ínsula Barataria.' 'Calla, Sancho' dijo Ricote, 'que las ínsulas están allá dentro de la mar; que no hay ínsulas en la tierra firme.' '¿Cómo no?' replicó Sancho. 'Dígote, Ricote amigo, que esta mañana me partí della, y ayer estuve en ella gobernando a mi placer'; II, 54, pp. 452–3).

When Ricote first appears he is dressed as a pilgrim and is heard speaking a language that Sancho scarcely understands. Cervantes was no doubt aware of a 1590 edict prohibiting Spaniards from wearing the pilgrim's habit,[72] so the description of Ricote's habit seems politically charged, to say the least. There is a moment in the *Persiles* that echoes such concerns in an even more direct way, namely in the dialogue between 'Antonio' (Diego de Villaseñor) and his father in *Persiles*, III, 9.[73] Ricote asks Sancho for money not in Spanish but in a bastardized form of German: 'Guelte, Guelte' (from *Geld* or, in dialect, *gueltre*). This use of dialect – of so-called *germanía* – is not without significance insofar as it suggests a political affinity based on the brotherhood of Germans.[74] The interchanges between Sancho and Ricote continue by means of gestures: '"I don't understand ... what you're asking of me, good people." Then one of them took a purse from his shirt and showed it to Sancho, who then understood that they were asking for money, and he, placing his thumb on his throat and extending his hand upward, gave them to understand that he did not have any money at all' (810) ('No entiendo ... qué es lo que me pedís, buena gente.' Entonces uno de ellos sacó una bolsa del seno y mostrósela a Sancho, por donde entendió que le pedían dineros; y él, poniéndose el dedo pulgar en la garganta y estendiendo la mano arriba, les dio a entender que no tenía ostugo de moneda; II, 54, p. 447). Ricote is imagined as Sancho's neighbour, but has spent years in exile and now has returned not as a true religious pilgrim but with the intention of recovering the fortune he left behind when he was forced to flee Spain.[75] In fact, Ricote invites Sancho to accompany him on the search for his treasure in a way that appeals to the promise of adventure and of reward that has motivated Sancho's attachment to Don Quijote from the very start ('Really, Sancho, come to your senses and decide if you want to come with me, as I said, and help me take out the treasure I hid; the truth is there's so much it can be called a treasure, and I'll give you enough to live on, as I said' [815]) (Calla, Sancho, y vuelve en ti, y mira si quieres venir conmigo, como te he dicho, a ayudarme a sacar el tesoro que dejé escondido; que en verdad que es tanto que se puede llamar tesoro, y te daré con que vivas, como te he dicho; II, 54, p. 453).

Ricote's deeper story is grounded in the contemporary politics of the nation and its attempted official constitution as a homogeneous religious and ethnic entity. As a false pilgrim returning to Spain, Ricote calls to mind the kind of xenophobia that led to the placement of severe restrictions on pilgrims precisely because they were foreigners.[76] The *moriscos* are among those who would thwart the cause of national homogeneity; they are the 'serpent' within the otherwise virtuous polis:

> You know very well, O Sancho Panza, my neighbor and friend, how the proclamation and edict that His Majesty issued against those of my race brought terror and fear to all of us; at least, I was so affected, I think that even before the time granted to us for leaving Spain had expired, I was already imagining that the harsh penalty had been inflicted on me and my children. And so I arranged, as a prudent man … to leave the village alone, without my family, and find a place where I could take them in comfort and without the haste with which I and others were leaving, because I saw clearly, as did all our elders, that those proclamations were not mere threats, as some were saying, but real laws that would be put into effect at the appointed time. (813)

> Bien sabes, ¡oh Sancho Panza, vecino y amigo mío!, como el pregón y bando que Su Majestad mandó publicar contra los de mi nación puso terror y espanto en todos nosotros; a lo menos, en mí le puso de suerte que me parece que antes del tiempo que se nos concedía para que hiciésemos ausencia de España, ya tenía el rigor de la pena ejecutado en mi persona y en la de mis hijos. Ordené, pues, a mi parecer como prudente … de salir yo solo, sin mi familia, de mi pueblo, y ir a buscar donde llevarla con comodidad y sin la priesa con que los demás salieron; porque bien vi, y vieron todos nuestros ancianos, que aquellos pregones no eran sólo amenazas, como algunos decían, sino verdaderas leyes, que se habían de poner en ejecución a su determinado tiempo. (p. 450)[77]

Strangely, Ricote expounds some of the most extreme views in support of the case for the expulsion of the *moriscos* as well as a series of 'rationalized' reasons for it, viz., that it was ordered for their own good, that the expulsion offered a legal way to protect the *moriscos* from the possibility of uncontrollable violence against them: 'I was forced to believe this truth because I knew the hateful and foolish intentions of our people, and they were such that it seems to me that it was divine inspiration that moved His Majesty to put into effect so noble a resolution, not because all of us were guilty, for some were firm and true Christians ... but because it is not a good idea to nurture a snake in your bosom or shelter enemies in your house' (813) (Forzábame a creer esta verdad saber yo los ruines y disparatados intentos que los nuestros tenían, y tales, que me parece que fue inspiración divina la que movió a Su Majestad a poner en efecto tan gallarda resolución, no porque todos fuésemos culpados, que algunos había cristianos firmes y verdaderos; pero eran tan pocos que no se podían oponer a los que no lo eran, y no era bien criar la sierpe en el seno, teniendo los enemigos dentro de casa. Finalmente, con justa razón fuimos castigados con la pena del destierro, blanda y suave al parecer de algunos, pero al nuestro, la más terrible que se nos podía dar; pp. 450–1).

By stark contrast, the romance-like story of Ricote's return to Spain reflects the nostalgic fantasy of an original political 'home,' a genuine *patria*, from which he had been driven. His politics of the nation depends on the imagination of a territorial homeland. He regards Spain as his 'patria natural' in spite of the fact that Protestant Germany affords greater 'libertad de conciencia' (freedom of conscience) and offers a degree of shelter and protection he could not imagine finding in Spain. (This detail is especially important given the fact that Ricote admits to being less committed to the Christian faith than other members of his family.) Critics have spent a surprising amount of time speculating about the meaning of the phrase 'libertad de conciencia,' wondering whether it might refer to the licentious behaviour reputed to be common among *moriscos*, or to matters of religious conscience. The sense of the phrase seems clear from Ricote's comments about his ambivalent religious commitment. He means to say that (Protestant) Germany offers greater religious freedom than (Catholic) Spain. And yet he feels a personal bond to the place of his birth, which is his *patria natural*. For him, the attachment to the *patria* supersedes the family associations from which the 'political' sphere is often imagined as arising:

No matter where we are we weep for Spain, for, after all, we *were born here and it is our native country*; nowhere do we find places in Africa where we

hoped to be received, welcomed, and taken in, that is where they most offend and mistreat us. We did not know our good fortune until we lost it, and the greatest desire in almost all of us is to return to Spain; most of those, and there are many of them, who know the language as I do, abandon wives and children and return, so great is the love they have for Spain. (813; emphasis added)

Doquiera que estamos lloramos por España, que, en fin, *nacimos en ella y es nuestra patria natural*; en ninguna parte hallamos el acogimiento que nuestra desventura desea, y en Berbería, y en todas las partes de Africa, donde esperábamos ser recebidos, acogidos y regalados, allí es donde más nos ofenden y maltratan. No hemos conocido el bien hasta que le [*sic*] hemos perdido; y es el deseo tan grande que casi todos tenemos de volver a España, que los más de aquellos, y son muchos, que saben la lengua como yo, se vuelven a ella, y dejan allá sus mujeres y sus hijos desamparados: tanto es el amor que la tienen; y agora conozco y experimento lo que suele decirse: que es dulce el amor de la patria. (II, 54, p. 451; emphasis added)

Ricote's desire for 'home' as captured by the *nostos* of the romance form (and beyond that, of course, of the epic), is driven by a powerful sense of dislocation. He has, in fact, suffered the effects of multiple dislocations, not only from Spain, where he had managed to establish a very successful business as a shopkeeper,[78] but also from a host of other countries in Europe, including France, Italy, and Germany, where he had travelled in search of a place to settle upon, having been forced from his *patria natural*. He addresses Sancho in a lingua franca that suggests a shared European consciousness that, given Europe's political and religious wars, was at least as fictitious as the idea of a Spanish national community ('Español y tudesqui, tuto uno: bon compaño'; II, 54, p. 450). How odd indeed that Sancho's 'neighbour' would speak to him in a common European dialect rather than in a local idiom. In contrast to the forced, official reality of the nation-state, Ricote's is the fantasy of political community based on kinship and solidarity. It is not just imagined as national, but also as European and local. It is indeed a fantasy, and yet in this brief moment it moves to Sancho to reciprocate by returning Ricote's gesture of companionship. The scene is set in a festive atmosphere of a carefree country meal, accompanied by plenty of wine. The suggestion is that the two might share a more authentic and intimate form of community than what Sancho had experienced on Barataria, where his life was miserable in spite of the fact that everyone spoke 'Spanish.'

They began to eat with great pleasure, savoring each mouthful slowly, just a little of each thing, which they picked up with the tip of a knife, and then all at once, and all at the same time, they raised their arms and the wineskins into the air, their mouths pressed against the mouths of the wineskins and their eyes fixed on heaven, as if they were taking aim; they stayed this way for a long time, emptying the innermost contents of the skins into their stomachs, and moving their heads from one side to the other, signs that attested to the pleasure they were receiving ...

The skins were tilted four times, but a fifth time was not possible because they were now as dry and parched as esparto grass, something that withered the joy the pilgrims had shown so far. (812)

Comenzaron a comer con grandísimo gusto y muy de espacio, saboreándose con cada bocado, que le tomaban con la punta del cuchillo, y muy poquito de cada cosa, y luego, al punto, todos a una, levantaron los brazos y las botas en el aire; puestas las bocas en su boca, clavados los ojos en el cielo, no parecía sino que ponían en él la puntería; y desta manera, meneando las cabezas a un lado y a otro, señales que acreditaban el gusto que recebían, se estuvieron un buen espacio, trasegando en sus estómagos las entrañas de las vasijas...

Cuatro veces dieron lugar las botas para ser empinadas; pero la quinta no fue posible, porque ya estaban más enjutas y secas que un esparto, cosa que puso mustia la alegría que hasta allí habían mostrado. (II, 54, p. 449)

As they eat cheese and drink prodigious quantities of wine, Cervantes does not forget to mention the fact that Ricote and his friends also gnaw on ham bones, as if to flaunt Ricote's rejection of non-Christian ethnic practices.[79] And while they do drink ample quantities of wine, the suggestion is that the idea of a community that would include both Sancho and Ricote is the product of a relatively alert consciousness, not enthusiasm generated in a drunken dream:[80]

Spanish, German, we're all one, my good buddy.
And Sancho answered: Good buddy indeed, by God!

And he burst into a laughter that lasted for an hour, and then he did not remember anything that had happened to him in his governorship; for during the time and period when one eats and drinks, cares tend to be of little importance. Finally, the end of the wine was the beginning of fatigue that overcame everyone and left them asleep on their tables and cloths; only Ricote and Sancho were awake, because they had eaten more and drunk less than the others; Ricote moved away with Sancho to sit at the foot of a beech tree, leaving the pilgrims deep in their sweet sleep. (812–13)

Español y tudesqui, tuto uno: bon compaño.
Y Sancho respondía: *Bon compaño, jura Di!*

Y disparaba con una risa que le duraba un hora, sin acordarse entonces de nada de lo que le había sucedido en su gobierno; porque sobre el rato y tiempo cuando se come y bebe, poca jurisdición suelen tener los cuidados. Finalmente, el acabársele el vino fue principio de un sueño que dio a todos, quedándose dormidos sobre las mismas mesas y manteles; solos Ricote y Sancho quedaron alerta, porque habían comido más y bebido menos; y, apartando Ricote a Sancho, se sentaron al pie de una haya, dejando a los peregrinos sepultados en dulce sueño. (II, 54, p. 450)

The suggestion of a common European identity, no less than the idea of a national identity, butts up against the deep allegiance to other forms of community whose roots seem deeper than the nation. In Ricote's case, this is the community of the 'nation' in the root sense, i.e., the community to which he belongs by birth and kinship rather than because of the place where one lives. Not only at the lexical level, though certainly there as well, any political idea of the nation as a community had to deal with the weight of kinship structures: the *nación* has its roots in *natio*, and even the strongest principles of political unification were bound to have trouble eliminating those roots.[81] In Cervantes, the roots of the nation in the ethnic sense of the *nación* as a 'people' are everywhere to be found. But there is particular resonance with the understanding of 'nation' as the 'others'; to wit, in Spain it was the 'marranos' who became the *nación* (just as in Portugal they became the *nação*, and in France the *nation*).[82] In the passage just cited, the spare ham bones are a pregnant detail signalling Ricote's awareness of the need for ethnic dissembling. In I, 9, the Arabic historian belongs to 'aquella nación de mentirosos.' Cide Hamete is everywhere the potentially subversive 'other' within Cervantes' text, whose deflections of authority and truthfulness are, in turn, the source of a deft literary subversion of official policies of exclusion. So too is Cervantes' sly allusion at the close of Part I to the so-called leaden books of Sacromonte (the *libros plúmbeos*). As is now well known, those books were part of an elaborate hoax designed to produce the impression of a deep-level affinity between Christians and Muslims, and so to suggest that political conflicts might be overcome, and expulsion avoided, by the revelation of archaic affinities between the two religions.[83]

In the sequel to the Ricote episode, Ana Félix describes herself as 'not of Turkish nationality, or a Moor, or a renegade' (879) (ni soy turco de nación, ni moro, ni renegado; II, 63, p. 526). It is the fate of the *nación qua* 'race' (by birth) that moves the lament of the Ricote's daughter, Ana Félix: 'I was born to Morisco parents and am of that nation, more unhappy than wise, upon whom a sea of afflictions has lately poured down' (829) (De aquella nación más desdichada que prudente, sobre quien ha llovido estos días un mar de desgracias, nací yo, de moriscos padres engendrada; II, 63, p. 527). In such instances, the racialized sense of *nación* supersedes the political virtues of mercy and justice:

> 'One must not place hope,' said Ricote, who was present at this conversation, 'in favors or gifts, because with the great Don Bernardino de Velasco, Count of Salazar, whom His Majesty made responsible for our expulsion, prayers are in vain, as are promises, gifts, and lamentations, for although it is true that he mixes mercy with justice, he sees that the entire body of our nation is contaminated and rotten, and he burns it with a cautery rather than soothing it with an ointment; and so, with prudence, sagacity, diligence, and the fear he imposes, he has borne on his strong shoulders the weight of this great plan, and put it into effect ... So that none of our people can stay behind or be concealed, like a hidden root that in times to come will send out shoots and bear poisonous fruits in Spain, which is clean now, and rid of the fears caused by our numbers.' (891–2)

> No – dijo Ricote, que se halló presente a esta plática – hay que esperar en favores ni en dádivas, porque con el gran don Bernardino de Velasco, conde de Salazar, a quien dio Su Majestad cargo de nuestra expulsión, no valen ruegos, no promesas, no dádivas, no lástimas; porque, aunque es verdad que él mezcla la misericordia con la justicia, como él vee que todo el cuerpo de nuestra nación está contaminado y podrido, usa con él antes del cauterio que abrasa que del ungüento que molifica; y así, con prudencia, con sagacidad, con diligencia y con miedos que pone, ha llevado sobre sus fuertes hombros a debida ejecución el peso desta gran máquina ... porque no se le quede ni encubra ninguno de los nuestros, que, como raíz escondida, que con el tiempo venga después a brotar, y a echar frutos venenosos en España, ya limpia, ya desembarazada de los temores en que nuestra muchedumbre la tenía. ¡Heroica resolución del gran Filipo Tercero, y inaudita prudencia en haberla encargado al tal don Bernardino de Velasco! (II, 65, pp. 539–40)

Sancho's decision is quite different. Having learned from his experiences on Barataria to resist the temptations of wealth, ambition, and power, he decides not to accompany Ricote on his search for treasure; he also recognizes that to do so would amount to an act of treason.[84] For good or for ill, Sancho's renunciation of the governorship of Barataria brings with it allegiance to king and country.

The Ricote episode continues, after interruption, with a second 'historical' echo of Sancho's governorship on Barataria. Recall that the culminating moment of Sancho's rule arrives when the island comes under attack. In the case of Ricote and Ana Félix, the culminating moment occurs in Barcelona when an alarm signals an attack by Algerian corsairs. The one, on Barataria, is purely fictional, while the other is the fictionalized rendering of many such historical attacks. The suggestion is that of an encounter of supreme enemies, but unlike the clash between Don Quijote and the Biscayan in I, 8, this scene pits the forces of a 'nation' against more ambiguous North African pirate forces. I say 'more ambiguous' not because the threat was not real but because the pirates operating in the region were not always aligned along national lines. As Fernand Braudel wrote in his landmark study of the Mediterranean world in the era of Philip II, privateering had its own customs, agreements, and negotiations, and everyone from the richest to the most destitute was caught up in the web of piracy cast over the entire region (*The Mediterranean*, 2:865–6). Not surprisingly, piracy shows up in a number of Cervantes' works including *La ilustre fregona*, *El amante liberal*, and *La Española inglesa*. International laws and treaties notwithstanding, virtually the entire Mediterranean was an arena of conflict among warring civilizations, with piracy as one of the principal means by which it was carried out.[85]

Moreover, it is in the continuation of the Ricote episode that the handsome young captain of the Algerian corsair is revealed not to be a young man or even a pirate, but the daughter of Ricote, the beautiful and exotic *morisca*, Ana Félix. As Ana Félix tells her tale we also learn that her lover, Don Gaspar Gregorio, is being held prisoner by the Algerian king, and that she has risked the return to Spain in order to retrieve her father's treasure so as ransom him. Thanks to Ricote's enormous treasure and to the intervention of the renegade who accompanies her, the means are in place to carry out the rescue. But returning Don Gaspar Gregorio to Spain is hardly enough. Given the transgressions of Ricote and his daughter, not to mention the legal obstacles that would impede the union between a *morisca* and a Christian Spaniard about to inherit a title of nobility, a happy conclusion to the episode would require a truly extraordinary act of official justice, so extraordinary in fact that it could only have been imaginary. The episode unfolds so as to bring just this fact into relief. Recall that just before the episode concludes Ricote observes that the Viceroy is impervious to supplication. But one of Ricote's friends, Don Antonio Moreno, is also a friend of the Viceroy and intervenes on behalf of the lovers; the necessary permissions are rapidly granted, thanks no doubt to certain gifts and favours.[86]

Although we never know for certain that they do marry, the very idea of a union between a Christian aristocrat and a *morisca*, and by implication the suggestion of a nation made whole, could only have been conceived under the sign of the mytho-poetic structure of romance. Romance puts the imaginary logic of the wish-fulfilment dream in place of the truth-telling and speculative powers of myth. Roberto González Echevarría has argued in relation to this episode that romance supports the fantasy of an official act of justice, one enacted at the highest national level, that would never have been possible and that allows for the reconciliation of the interests of love and the law.[87] And while I believe that this moment is better thought of as a reconciliation of personal and political forms of 'happiness' that allows for the image of a unified nation, the point nonetheless remains that it takes the highest authority to sanction the otherwise impossible union of Ana Félix and Don Gaspar Gregorio.

But before the Ricote episode concludes with the official sanction of the Viceroy, Cervantes introduces the example of another outlaw of historical proportions. This is the figure Roque Guinart, whose activities suggest the picture of a leader of a small community that lives by alternative laws. Luis Vives, for one, was explicit about the solidarity among pirates and thieves: 'they have established among themselves a certain kind of society founded on rules that allow them to sustain peace and concord among themselves.'[88] Roque's group resembles the *cofradía* of *pícaros* in *Rinconete y Cortadillo*. Modelled after the infamous Catalan bandit Roca Guinarda (also known as Rocaguinarda), in the text he is a friend of Don Antonio Moreno, which is to say that he has connections among those who are able to influence high-level officials, including the Viceroy.[89] Cervantes includes Roque Guinart, it is often said, in the spirit of a contrast between 'quixotic' pursuits and real-world matters, notably to indicate the persistent problem of Catalan banditry and the challenges it presented for national security. (Braudel remarked that in the era of Philip II there were 'brigands everywhere ... banditry on land that is the counterpart of piracy on the sea ... It was a long established pattern of behavior in the Mediterranean. Its origins are lost in the mists of time,' *The Mediterranean*, 2:743.) But in this episode the sea piracy of the Ana Félix adventure is inverted; it is relocated to the land and made problematic in its own way: in II, 60, Don Quijote and Sancho encounter bandits who have been hung from the trees, apparently as an example of quick-and-dirty 'justice,' while Roque seems also to benefit society.

Catalonia was not only a region facing the Mediterranean, but a part of Spain bordering France, where Protestant elements were a factor. Roberto

González Echevarría also observed that Catalan brigands were viewed as particularly dangerous by the crown because they often had close contacts with French Huguenots. Roque Guinart represents a political threat as a potential ally of Spain's enemies abroad, not merely a social threat. He jeopardizes the integrity of the state and the very foundation of laws.[90] Don Quijote nonetheless greets him as an equal: 'O valorous Roque, whose fame reaches far beyond the borders of your land!' (853) (¡Valeroso Roque, cuya fama no hay límites en la tierra que la encierren! II, 60, p. 496). Roque Guinart has excerpted himself from the official political community insofar as that community is founded on law. But as an outlaw leader of another community his presence raises the question of whether there could be a community founded not on the law but on allegiance to transgression of the laws in the name of social justice. It is, in fact, the question that Don Quijote implicitly raises from the very beginning of the text by virtue of his own attempts to revive chivalric justice in a world that is bound by laws and legal procedures. The encounter between Don Quijote and Roque appears as a meeting of equals, but these are inverted equals, and Don Quijote is detained in benign captivity by Roque for several days.

Why describe this as 'benign' captivity? The issue goes to Cervantes' engagement with yet another fantasy-frame that provides an imaginary alternative to political life. Roque and his men live principally within a forest. The marginality of this landscape with respect to the urban centres where political activity was organized resonates with the 'happy' bucolic alternative to organized political life.[91] The three days Don Quijote spends with Roque seem like an eternity of pleasure, days that might well be spun out into three hundred happy years: 'Don Quixote spent three days and nights with Roque, and if it had been three hundred years, there would have been no lack of things to observe and marvel at in the way he lived: they awoke here and ate there; at times they fled, not knowing from whom, and at other times they waited, not knowing for whom. They slept on their feet, interrupting their slumber and moving from one place to another. It was always a matter of posting spies, listening to scouts, blowing on the locks of their harquebuses' (861) (Tres días y tres noches estuvo don Quijote con Roque, y si estuviera trecientos años, no le faltara qué mirar y admirar en el modo de su vida: aquí amanecían, acullá comían; unas veces huían, sin saber de quién, y otras esperaban, sin saber a quién. Dormían en pie, interrompiendo el sueño, mudándose de un lugar a otro. Todo era poner espías, escuchar centinelas, soplar las cuerdas de los arcabuces, aunque traían pocos, porque todos se servían de pedreñales; II, 61, p. 505). Roque's is an inverted world in which 'virtue' is achieved by circumventing the official (lawful) standards of virtue. And yet even in so doing he finds himself grappling with some of the moral issues raised by his life outside the law. He considers how tangled and potentially hopeless these inversions of virtue can become; in this case they seem to have brought about the moral transformation of a compassionate man into someone ruled by vengeance: 'Our manner of life must seem unprecedented to Señor Don Quixote: singular adventures, singular events, and all of them dangerous; don't wonder that it seems this way to you, because really, I confess, there is no mode of life more unsettling and surprising than ours. Certain desires for revenge brought me to it, and they have the power to trouble the most serene heart; by nature I am compassionate and well-intentioned, but, as I have said, my wish to take revenge for an injury that was done to me threw all my good inclinations to the ground' (858) (Nueva manera de vida le debe de parecer al señor don Quijote la nuestra, nuevas aventuras, nuevos sucesos, y todos peligrosos; y no me maravillo que así le parezca, porque realmente le confieso que no hay modo de vivir más inquieto ni más sobresaltado que el nuestro. A mí me han puesto en él no sé qué deseos de venganza, que tienen fuerza de turbar los más sosegados corazones; yo, de mi natural, soy compasivo y bien intencionado; pero, como tengo dicho, el querer vengarme de un agravio que se me hizo, así da con todas mis buenas inclinaciones en tierra; II, 60, p. 501).[92] Moreover, the life of Roque's good-natured community of thieves cannot fully insulate itself from national politics, nor from the politics of empire. In fact, the group clashes with representatives of 'official' Spain, viz., with members of the infantry accompanying the wife of the Viceroy of Naples, Doña Guiomar de Quiñones.

But given the fact that Roque's generosity seems to be a sufficient counterweight to his lawless actions, are we to conclude that this virtuous inversion of virtue presents an alternative model for politics? Or is there something yet more complex to the particular form of fantasy that supports the image of the virtuous brigand in this episode? We do well to note that the territory for this experiment is not just outside the space of the city (or, for that matter, outside the nation) but is instead the forest, within which Roque presents the fantasy of a virtuous inversion of the political virtues of the *civitas*. Various kinds of 'exterior' spaces and marginal positions have often been mobilized for the critique of politics; they reach back at least to the beginning of Plato's *Republic* where the characters head toward the port of Piraeus, outside the city of Athens proper.[93] There they confront the threats to the life of the polis, while hoping to refashion the republic along more virtuous lines. In Jacques Rancière's interpretation, the specific threat to the city in Plato derives from the lust for possession and profit represented by maritime interests; at the beginning of the *Republic* the interlocutors move dangerously close to the port, but the dialogue takes place along the way; it is situated in-between, in a place that is neither the city nor the seacoast. In the case of Cervantes, the organization and the values of this alternative space in the Roque Guinart episode are inversions of the pastoral alternative to city life, and so are double inversions of the critique of the values of the polis. Roque Guinart does not belong to the city-state and so cannot be considered an ordinary criminal; he cannot be treated in the way the galley slaves are dealt with in Part I. But neither can he be counted among the city's foreign military enemies; he is not, for instance, en enemy of war since he is not included in what Cicero called 'the number of lawful enemies.'[94] He seems to inhabit a space where obligations do not hold. As Cicero outlined in great detail, it is principally a share in obligation (in duties, *officiis*) that defines membership in the polis. Citizens, he explained in *De officiis*, owe much to one another on account of what they share, ultimately because they are participants in the fellowship of the whole human race.[95]

In sum, it might be tempting to see the inverted pastoral of the Roque episode as offering an alternative both to the potential corruption of the city and to the refusal of community that some versions of the pastoral entail. (As we have already had occasion to note, Marcela wins freedom at a cost that is the refusal of the social itself.)[96] There is no lack of generosity in what Roque does, and beyond that there is an adherence to the redistribution of justice. From within the inverted world, he and his small community of bandits attempt to answer the charge that the freedom of the pastoral and the virtues of the countryside require isolation from civic life. Roque is not just a land-based pirate, and yet the inverted pastoral of this episode hardly offers the 'redemption' of community in the image of a higher ideal outside the law. Piracy, whether at sea or on land, stands outside the web of obligations that bind human beings in the city. Roque leads a small society of which he cannot himself fully be a part. His life is troubled by fear and mistrust. Ironically, Roque needs to be on guard against the same official who has enabled the reunions of Ricote, Ana Félix, and Don Gaspar Gregorio – the Viceroy: 'Roque spent the nights away from his men, in locations and places they did not know, because the many edicts issued by the viceroy of Barcelona against his life made him uneasy and apprehensive, and he did not dare trust anyone, fearing his own men might kill him or turn him in to the authorities: a life, certainly, that was disquieting and troublesome' (861) (Roque pasaba las noches apartado de los suyos, en partes y lugares donde ellos no pudiesen saber dónde estaba; porque los muchos bandos que el visorrey de Barcelona había echado sobre su vida le traían inquieto y temeroso, y no se osaba fiar de ninguno, temiendo que los mismos suyos, o le habían de matar, o entregar a la justicia: vida, por cierto, miserable y enfadosa; II, 61, p. 505). The idea of a community that is at once whole and just and therefore secure seems to be impossible except in relation to a dream. This is not Plato's philosophical dream of an ideal state, but the incoherent dream of an ideal community existing outside political life.

Practical circumstances call for a different, more pragmatic solution. Cervantes recognizes this. Taken together, Roque's fame and his generosity earn him the protection of Doña Guiomar. She assures their safe passage, just as Cicero said that it was morally required of every individual to assist wanderers on their way:[97] Roque in turn assures Don Quijote's safe transit to Barcelona amid the threat of violence between two warring Catalonian clans, the Nyerros and the Cadells. The arrangements that Roque makes have such standing that they are committed to writing.[98] This is a far cry from the free-lance life quixotically pursued by his group of sometimes virtuous bandits. It is nonetheless an institutional arrangement that simply serves the interests of all involved.

8 Civil Society, Virtue, and the Pursuit of Happiness

In days of yore, this was wisdom: to draw a line between public and private
rights, between things sacred and things common, to check vagrant union, to
give rules for wedded life, to build towns, and grave laws on tables of wood.

Horace, 'Ars Poetica'[1]

A conventional way to distinguish the politics of modernity, beginning in
the sixteenth and seventeenth centuries, from what came before it is this:
in modernity the political sphere is conceived as coextensive with the public sphere and is thought to be limited to it. The converse is also widely
accepted as true: that the 'public' sphere in its modern formation is fundamentally political; what we know as 'private' life is thought to be largely
invisible to it. Whether this is true or not, the appearance of a public-political
sphere is part of what sets the early modern world apart from the feudal
society of the High Middle Ages, eventually providing the foundation for
the liberal-democratic separation of the public and private realms of life.
Jürgen Habermas invokes just such an account of the emergence of the
modern political sphere as a foundation for his early work, *The Structural
Transformation of the Public Sphere*: 'In the fully developed Greek city-
state,' he writes, 'the sphere of the *polis*, which was common (*koine*) to the
free citizens, was strictly separated from the sphere of the *oikos*; in the
sphere of the *oikos*, each individual is in his own realm. The public life,
bios politicos, went on in the market place (*agora*) ... A public sphere in the
sense of a separate realm distinguished from the private sphere cannot be
shown to have existed in the feudal society of the High Middle Ages.'[2] The
configuration of the modern public-political sphere was driven by two
new kinds of 'traffic' (*Verhehr*). One of these, the long-range traffic in
commodities, clearly had its basis in the material world. The other – the

traffic in 'news' – was at once material and discursive.[3] Habermas's argument is that the forms of rationality that became normative for modernity required conditions in which various kinds of transactions and exchanges could occur with some degree of reliability and transparency, but also required conditions in which news, opinions, and information could be exchanged with relative freedom. In principle, these all helped assure a greater degree of security than had been known before. Moreover, they helped shift the fear that was implicit in Machiavellian and Hobbesian political principles to the ground of mutual benefits and profit, to 'commodity,' to the 'traffic' of business, and to common interests.

We may set aside for the moment the fact that Hapsburg Spain in the sixteenth and seventeenth centuries was hardly a state in which ideas could circulate freely, and that Cervantes wrote under conditions that required indirect and oblique approaches to nearly all controversial matters. Those are matters I will take up in the following chapter. That there were systems of exchange for all sorts of things, public and private, remains without question. Moreover, the notions of traffic and of commodity had been introduced directly into debates about politics and government beginning with the 1604 Spanish translation of Justus Lipsius's work of ten years earlier, *Los seys libros de las Políticas o Doctrina civil (Politicorum sive civilis doctrinae libri sex)*.[4] Well before Hobbes's *De Cive*, which speaks about the origins of 'civill government,'[5] Lipsius argued that 'mutuall commoditie and profit' (understood in a broad sense, and not strictly in economic terms) were essential to the security of 'civil life.' Certainly in the background of these writings were the *quaestiones civiles* of forensic oratory, but what Lipsius calls 'civil life' is something else, viz., 'that which we lead in the society of men, one with another, to mutuall commoditie and profit, and common use of all [*multa commoda sive usum*].'[6] The matter of 'society,' broadly understood as including all forms of 'association,' is intimately linked to it: 'Civil life consisteth in society, society in two things, traffic [*commercio*] and government.'[7] In the interest of general happiness, well-being, and a stable polis, he warns, 'Let it be permitted to violate, and infringe the law of contracts, and you may take away the use of trafficke [commerce] from amongst men. It is then a most wicked and treacherous part, to breake faith, sith that it preserveth our life' (*Six Bookes*, IV, 9, p. 80 and II, 14, p. 35).

But the very idea that the politics of the early modern age distinguished itself as new because of the separation of the public and private realms seems not quite so clear. The reasons are as much a matter of historical fact as of the self-understanding of early modern political subjects. As is the case with much of what is claimed about the sixteenth and seventeenth centuries as specifically 'modern,' many of the ideas on the political stage involved a notional return, oftentimes quite explicitly, to the political constructs of antiquity. The early modern polis was routinely conceived as comparable to the *res publica* of Rome. Early modern political thinkers were also well aware that an appeal to the models of antiquity could provide sources of legitimation for what were, in fact, very different political arrangements, in very different historical times. In the *Discourses on Livy* (1551), for instance, Machiavelli is deeply conscious of the ways in which the ancient Roman Republic itself drew strength from a return to its earlier beginnings. The *Discourses* – the counterpart to *The Prince* insofar as the work on Livy treats of republics rather than of principalities – describes what is, in essence, the crab-like movement of successful states.[8] The return to the examples of the past provides one of the best assurances of sustainable forward motion (e.g., 'In Order for a Religion or a Republic to Have Long Life, It Is Often Necessary to Bring It Back to Its Beginnings').[9] But so, too, Machiavelli urges the prince to read histories and to follow examples of great figures from the past who, he reasons, will inevitably have followed great men before them.[10] Lipsius himself makes it clear that his advice is given 'according to precepts of ancient authors, declared also in their own words' (*Six Bookes*, I, 1, p. 1).

But a greater reason for rethinking conventional views about the politics of modernity is that they tend to frame discussions of the polis around the idea that at the limit of the political realm lies a separate sphere of existence, non-political life, 'private' life. They are conceived as contrastive, sometimes opposing contexts for the pursuit of human aims. One view is that these are of unequal value, and that 'private' life and the forces that drive it, including the passions and personal desires, must be 'raised up' to the level of the political.[11] Another, central to liberal modernity, holds that they must remain separate, and that the private sphere must be protected from the encroachment of the state.

Recent work, particularly that of Giorgio Agamben in *Homo Sacer*, has gone to some lengths to contest these views. Drawing on the work of Foucault, Agamben has argued that modernity was the beginning of the time when politics in the formal sense – in the formation of an organized state – came to extend its reach even as far as natural life ('bare life'). In modernity, he claims, the scope of the political became total: everything, including life itself, came to be construed politically. At issue in this notion is the difference between the simple fact of living and living with regard to some end or good (that which 'exists for the sake of a good life').[12] As the opening sections of Aristotle's *Politics* make clear, the *politikos* is classically charged only with care of *politically* qualified life; such things as reproduction and subsistence are left to the head of the family and of the estate. Those are subjects, as I will discuss below, that Aristotle treats in an accompanying work, the *Economics*. But how are the affairs of the household (the *oikos*) related to pursuit of coordinated public ends? What is their relationship to politics?

Such arguments might be framed in another way: that the modern turn towards the body provides a public, evidentiary basis for practical politics.[13] This is consistent with a world in which the requirements for visible proof were paramount in many spheres. From Shakespeare's *Othello* to Descartes's *Meditations* and Anselmo's foolish curiosity in *Don Quijote* there is a decisive interest in the power of 'ocular proofs.' Likewise, 'experience' comes to play an increasing role in the literature of advice to princes and counsellors.[14] (Fadrique Furió Ceriol's text on counsel, *El consejo y consejeros del príncipe*, is a central example.) Evidentiary politics, in turn, promises to establish fairness and security as public matters. The seventeenth-century writ of habeas corpus, around which a much older principle came to be formalized, offers rather telling evidence in support of this view. What the precise wording of the writ demands is that there be a body to present for judgment: 'habeas corpus ad subjiciendum.'[15] We might contrast modern, evidentiary politics with a world in which binding oaths, promises, and beliefs could all be based firmly on things unseen. Don Quijote, for instance, demands that the Toledan merchants swear to the superlative beauty of Dulcinea even without having seen her: 'Halt, all of you, unless all of you confess that in the entire world there is no damsel more beauteous than the empress of La Mancha, the peerless Dulcinea of Toboso.' The merchants answer clearly: 'Señor Knight, we do not know this good lady you have mentioned; show her to us, for if she is as beautiful as you say, we will gladly and freely confess the truth you ask of us' (Todo el mundo se tenga, si todo el mundo no confiesa que no hay en el mundo todo doncella más hermosa que la emperatriz de la Mancha, la sin par Dulcinea del Toboso ... Señor caballero, nosotros no conocemos quién sea esa buena señora que decís; mostrádnosla: que si ella fuere de tanta hermosura como significáis). And Don Quijote retorts, 'If I were to show her to you ... where would the virtue be in confessing so obvious a truth? The significance lies in not seeing her and believing, confessing, affirming, swearing, and defending that truth?' (39) (Si os la mostrara ... ¿qué hiciérades vosotros en confesar una verdad tan notoria? La importancia está en que sin verla lo habéis de creer, confesar, afirmar, jurar y defender; I, 4, p. 100).

From the perspective of an increasingly rationalized, public sphere, valuations of the body that resist the reach of organized politics are bound to appear archaic and, for some readers of the *Quijote* such as Vladimir Nabokov, objectionable.[16] Consider the many drubbings that Don Quijote takes in Part I, but that seem to have little psychological impact until we reach Part II. Consider as well the fact that Sancho's identity is initially conceived around his appetite and bodily mass. The fear instigated by the strange sound of the fulling mills in I, 20, may well be a psychological state, but its effects are quite physical: the fear causes Sancho to lose control of his bowels. And yet these characters move about in a world where at least something of what Agamben says seems to be true: that many bodies in the *Quijote* have been brought under the authority of a political will, in the sense that they have become directly subject to the power of the state. The galley slaves in Part I are chained together, and are forcibly marched toward the Spanish galleons, where they will be obliged to serve the imperial will as punishment for their crimes. In this instance, Don Quijote attempts to answer official state power with unofficial force; curiously, the galley slaves respond to their circumstances discursively: each one offers some form of circumlocution as a way of saying, while not saying, what it is he has been accused of – one of excessive 'love' for things possessed by another; another for betraying a friend by 'singing' about his crimes, etc.

As we have seen above, it is only much later, in Part II, when Don Quijote advises Sancho on how to best govern his island, that he himself argues that a special kind of care for the body – in the form of grooming, discipline, and the cultivation of good manners – is an essential part of politics. To govern well requires of Sancho a bodily regimen to which he is unaccustomed. After having feasted at Camacho's wedding, Sancho is allowed to eat almost nothing on Barataria. The exigencies of governance countermand his natural desires. Don Quijote advises Sancho on how to groom himself and polish his manners if he is to enter the official sphere of politics. His recommendations to Sancho regarding the comportment suitable for a governor stand in marked contrast to the relatively rough way in which he and Sancho engage the world in most of the preceding chapters. The asceticism that informs Don Quijote's penance in the Sierra Morena invokes the tradition of disciplining of the heroic body as a way to purify, strengthen, and ennoble it. But his eventual recognition that the body is in fact political – as he does preceding Sancho's governorship – is also informed by a humanist ideal in which public and private virtues ought to be regarded as reflections of one another. That framework was one in which talk about the body, and especially talk about the political body, is meant to be continuous with talk about the soul: 'What I have said to you so far are the teachings that will adorn your soul; now listen to the ones that will serve to adorn your body' (732) (Esto que hasta aquí te he dicho son documentos que han de adornar tu alma; escucha ahora los que han de servir para adorno del cuerpo; II, 42, p. 360).[17]

What the concentration on the body – evidentiary or otherwise – leaves aside is a set of issues that have to do with the claims that other forms of 'qualified life' might make, including claims that the highest human values, and indeed human happiness itself, might have to be pursued outside of, or on the borders of, politics.[18] This is something quite different from the inversion of civic virtues explored in the episode of Roque Guinart. Rather, it seems to resonate with the thought that on leaving Barataria Sancho does not just leave government but hopes to leave political life itself, seeking happiness for himself in the return to a simple life, lived in a rural context, close to the earth. The implication is that politics may not in the end be all-encompassing with respect to the most important values for human beings. There are claims to be made in relation to social values such as friendship and generosity (liberalidad) that seem to flourish outside, if not against, the contexts of institutionalized politics. Such possibilities matter for subjects who aim independently or informally to pursue some of the very same things that 'official' politics aims to provide (e.g., justice, true nobility, insulation from the vagaries of fortune, happiness in the broadest sense). This is not inconsistent with one of the more ironic insights of Plato's Republic: that the goal of politics may have to be found somewhere other than in the city.

For Plato, of course, the question is whether the good for human beings can, in fact, be accommodated by the polis as it might ever exist, or whether the pursuit of happiness as a form of the good is bound to be inconsistent with actual political life. When Seneca writes of the private life it is in part because he wonders whether any commonwealth is fit for the wise.[19] Plato seems to have reached a deeply contradictory conclusion about such matters. Human beings have desires, only some of which are consistent with the good, are rational, and may lead to 'justice' in the soul. But those rational desires cannot fully be satisfied in just any polis. They would require an ideal state with an ideal constitution, which is to say that they would require the kind of state and constitution that a philosopher, and not a politician, might develop. As Alasdair MacIntyre put it in speaking of the classical virtues in relation to the polis, 'what is satisfying is attainable only by philosophy and not by politics.'[20] It follows that the truly virtuous individual may always be looking elsewhere, that he or she may not fully be a member of any state, and that a virtuous life may have to be led on the borders of politics. And yet the fact remains that the concept of the virtues is for Plato a political concept; his account of the virtuous individual is inseparable from his account of the virtuous citizen. The question that nags, of course, is whether such an individual can be satisfied as a citizen of any state in *this* world.

There is a long line of thinking that resists the notion that virtue and politics are irreconcilable and insists instead that the well-ordered state – the Priest's *república bien concertada* of I, 32 – offers the best possible framework for the realization of true human happiness. This thinking has deep roots in Aristotle's *Politics* and his *Nicomachean Ethics*. Both are committed to the idea that human beings require a framework of justice and laws if they are to attain the good, that human happiness must be ful- filled within the context of the polis. This positions political life, and in some instances the state itself, above individual life and higher than non- political forms of association. 'Even if the end is the same for a single man and for a state,' writes Aristotle, 'that of the state seems at all events some- thing greater and complete whether to attain or preserve; though it is worth while to attain the end merely for one man it is finer and more god- like to attain it for a nation or for city-states.'[21] The final book of Cicero's *Republic*, the 'Somnium Scipionis,' is similarly explicit on this matter. There is nothing more worthy, writes Cicero, than political life: 'to that supreme god who rules the universe nothing (or at least nothing that hap- pens on earth) is more welcome than those companies and communities of people linked together by justice that are called states.'[22] This is likewise a central thought of *De officiis*: 'if wisdom is the greatest virtue ... then the obligation stemming from the sense of community must undoubtedly be the greatest.'[23] The tradition according to which human ends are best real- ized in the state has a very long life; it extends at least through Hegel, who in very different historical circumstances argued that the highest form of ethical life is to be found not within the cosmopolitan world of civil soci- ety but within a specific national state.[24]

But is it indeed the case that all human ends – never mind the highest ends – must in fact constitute themselves in the state?[25] Along with the family, 'civil society' *(societas civilis)* is the realm that has made the strongest claim as a framework for the pursuit of human happiness that is not necessarily political. Neither the modern state nor private life now seems imaginable without civil society; its existence seems to lend a degree of stability to a variety of endeavours that human beings conduct in association with others, endeavours that are neither strictly private nor officially political. And yet to talk about civil society in relation to Cervantes might well seem odd. For what we understand as 'civil society' is generally regarded as having been formed in the eighteenth century as a network of institutions, agencies, and groups emerged within the framework of the nation-state in order to secure individual needs and protect individual rights. Central among these was the right to acquire property, which was a formalized version of arrangements long recognized as binding.[26] Cicero for instance wrote that 'property becomes private either through long occupancy (as in the case of those who long ago settled in unoccupied territory) or through conquest (as in the case of those who took it in war) or by due process of law, bargain, or purchase, or by allotment ... in each case some of those things which by nature had been common property became the property of individuals.'[27] In modernity, civil society was the realm in which commodity exchange and social labour became relatively free from government directives, but also a realm in which reliable laws and institutions could help make the workings of labour, the processes of exchange, and the holding of property all more stable and secure.[28] Moreover, civil society allowed for the pursuit of certain social values – sociability itself among them – that could not be framed as political in the conventional sense but which were not limited to the sphere of the individual or the family. Marriage was one such institution, which had been regularized through the decrees made by the Council of Trent, where clandestine marriages were prohibited and the authority of the nobility regarding the marriage of their subjects limited.[29]

The question as regards Cervantes, writing in the long shadow of the Council of Trent and only one year after the publication of Lipsius's *Politicorum* in Spanish, is this: what happens to the prospects for personal happiness and security when allegiances to traditional, inherited principles of value and nobility begin to shift? What happens when the traditional virtues are torn away from any corresponding social order? If one function of the state is to help guard against the unwelcome consequences of 'fortune' (by, among other things, the even-handedness of justice) then what security can be introduced into affairs that are conducted among individuals in civil association with one another? If the expansion of commerce and exchange was a way in which individuals could gain some measure of control over their own happiness, then what could be done to help protect against the new, 'secularized' forms of bad fortune? And what could be done to help align earned forms of happiness with the desire to see true virtue rewarded and those rewards in turn reflected in the social order?

As I hope to make clear over the course of what follows, many of Cervantes' characters find themselves involved in just these questions while in pursuit of happiness within contexts that are neither purely private nor formally political. They strive to make sense of their prospects, sometimes within the context of the family (e.g., as fathers and sons, or as married partners), sometimes as friends or lovers, and almost always in association with others.[30] They raise the kinds of questions for which the more robust institutions of civil society would eventually provide some answers. The novel, it could be said, becomes the dominant genre of civil society. Meanwhile, these characters inhabit a literary world in which exemplary narratives, novellas, pastoral novels, sentimental romances, and adventure tales afforded a variety of generic opportunities for the discursive exploration of these unresolved questions. Indeed, many of the genres in question came to serve as vehicles for a collateral concern about how to conceive the 'virtues,' both personally and socially, including questions about whether virtue and happiness could be, or ought to be, aligned.[31] These are consistent with concerns about whether the virtues needed to be framed strictly within the context of politics or imagined outside it, and whether they needed to be conceived according to inherited, 'traditional' paradigms of value, or could be constructed in less conventional ways, including in relation to various paradigms of exchange, which Lipsius called 'traffic.'

Whereas Spain was once regarded as tardy in relation to modern social and economic developments, conventional ideas about the 'tardiness' of Spanish culture have been contested by historians of many stripes, many who have argued quite persuasively for the role of Spanish merchants and traders in the development of an early bourgeoisie in Spain. And as Ralph Bauer has more recently suggested, the circulation of reports from the New World and of stories told by captives returned from Algiers and North Africa provided the basis for a mercantilist system of knowledge exchange.[32] In the case of those held captive, there was also a network of exchange in which freedom was literally bought with the ransom money paid for their release by various religious groups.

Exempla

The shifting landscape of 'exemplary' literature, which is one of the sites where the novel eventually took root, was overwhelmingly influenced by these factors. That changing terrain was marked by a long series of debates, many influenced by Cicero and his humanist heirs, over what true virtue and nobility are, how they may be pursued, demonstrated, measured, and investigated narratively, where they vie against political claims, and whether they can be aligned with happiness.[33] The series of 'exemplary' figures arrayed in Machiavelli's *The Prince* – from Cesar to Cesare Borgia – also raised new questions about the necessary *mis*alignment of moral exemplarity and political success. Indeed, the very sense of what exemplary literature could accomplish in technical and formal terms, as a means of investigation and of argument, came under considerable pressure, to which Cervantes responds in many of the narratives interpolated into the *Quijote*. In the classical sense, models of virtuous action could be demonstrated through historical and fictional *exempla*, i.e., through the actions of specific characters in particular narrative contexts designed to epitomize or illustrate certain principles.[34] The implication was that moral paradigms of broad validity could be extrapolated from such cases. But especially insofar as something may 'turn' or 'hinge' on the narrative outcome of a plot, exemplary literature could also put the question of the virtues into play; it could allow for a genuine investigation of the 'truth' about various virtues and values such as *liberalidad,* friendship, fairness, and so on. And it could do so in part by concentrating on the points where different underlying frameworks diverge. Hence the puzzling, nearly counterexemplary nature of much of what presents itself in Cervantes under the rubric of 'exemplary' literature. Indeed, Cervantes' new way with examples suggests that there is in the end no clear path from the task of limning the virtues in an abstract sense to the work of imagining them as elements of a possible social praxis.[35]

Many of the narratives involving questions of virtue and value, both in *Don Quijote* and in the *Exemplary Novels*, are indeed framed around paradoxical propositions or circumstances, not unlike the sophismata of late medieval philosophy, in which puzzling premises were designed to bring some larger truth into focus.[36] Erasmus's *Praise of Folly* intersects with this tradition in a way that is clearly of importance to Cervantes. That Folly should speak, and should speak wisely, is perhaps the fundamental paradox of Erasmus's text, a paradox nonetheless designed to illustrate the truth. Among Cervantes' texts, the man who believes he is made of glass ('El licenciado vidriera'), or the contradictory idea of an English Spanish lady ('La española inglesa'), the fiction of talking dogs ('El coloquio de los perros'), or of a husband who creates the conditions for his wife's infidelity by trying to prove that she is faithful (in the interpolated story in the *Quijote*, 'El curioso impertinente') are all presented as puzzling and paradoxical.[37]

And yet in most such instances there is no clear sense that any general, underlying principle or idea is in the end available for elucidation. Rather, they are incitements to reframe established views in relation to contradictory circumstances, either because their protagonists are irreducible mixtures of virtue and vice, or because their status in civil society is irreconcilable with their moral qualities, or because their actions are resolved formally while the moral issues that have been raised remain pending. They clearly call for something other than simple imitation by the reader.[38]

Consider again the difficult case of Marcela in Part I of *Don Quijote*, which is at once an unusual exemplum and an investigation of questions about female autonomy and independence in relation to society. Vivaldo tries to frame this story as an exemplum centring on Grisóstomo's innocent suffering and Marcela's alleged hard-heartedness. As Vivaldo rescues the papers on which Grisóstomo's last verses are written, he offers the following remarks for the benefit of Ambrosio and Grisóstomo's other friends: 'By giving life to these papers, you can have Marcela's cruelty live on *as an example to those who live in future days*, so that they can flee and run from similar dangers ... from this lamentable history one can learn how great was the cruelty of Marcela, the love of Grisóstomo, and the steadfastness of your friendship, as well as the final destination of those who madly gallop along the path that heedless love places in front of them' (93; emphasis added) (Haced, dando la vida a estos papeles, que la tenga siempre la crueldad de Marcela, *para que sirva de ejemplo, en los tiempos que están por venir*, a los vivientes, para que se aparten y huyan de caer en semejantes despeñaderos ... de la cual lamentable historia se puede sacar cuánto haya sido la crueldad de Marcela, el amor de Grisóstomo, la fe de la amistad vuestra, con el paradero que tienen los que a rienda suelta corren por la senda que el desvariado amor delante de los ojos les pone; I, 13, p. 179; emphasis added). And yet the case is considerably more complex than this. It is not at all clear that Marcela is simply the culpable, counterexemplary figure who causes pain without regard for others. She offers a spirited defence of herself and disclaims any responsibility for Grisóstomo's suffering, let alone his death. And while many of those listening to Vivaldo might be inclined to accept his sense of the situation, Don Quijote for one does not.[39] Marcela leaves those around her with a sense of wonder and awe and filled with admiration as much for her intelligence here as for her beauty when she appeared on the scene.[40]

And yet we also know that Marcela is not simply unable to live in society, and certainly not unwelcome in it; she is committed to a life apart as a resolute expression of autonomy. If hers is an example of 'virtue' then it represents a form of virtue that pits itself categorically against the public social world, in which obligations to others are unavoidable. (Marcela is echoed much later by Don Quijote, who upon leaving the estates of the Duke and the Duchess in II, 58, associates an ideal form of freedom with the absence of all attachments and obligations.) We are, of course, driven to ask whether such a life, lived in isolation from all others, can in fact be free in any true sense, no matter how beautiful or pure. But at this stage in the novel the question is not at all decided. Even as Vivaldo argues strenuously against her, others choose to follow Don Quijote and pursue her.

Politics or Virtue?

Against Marcela's solitary freedom, humanist views were committed to the idea that virtue and nobility could not be wholly private, but needed to be placed in action, proved in the world, and shaped in such a way that they might form part of a web of obligations. In some accounts, the dialogue between virtue and politics meant that qualities such as generosity (*liberalidad*) and friendship could exert a positive form of pressure against existing political frames, that they could be applied critically against reigning conceptions of the political, and especially against an imperial state that masks its warring intentions under the cover of virtue.

But even to speak of the virtues in the political context is likely to seem strange in modern times. Machiavelli did so, but always with the condition of semblance in place. One reason for this difficulty is that in the classical tradition of the virtues, moral psychology is understood as woven of character, action, and context, all laced together in story-like forms. There is no 'science' of the virtues in the modern sense. Plato's *Meno*, for example, attempts to approach the question of the virtues *more geometrico*, only to conclude that this is impossible. Indeed, Plato seems to have understood that neither virtue in itself, nor any of the virtues conceived individually (e.g., courage, justice) can be defined as one thing. Any time a single conclusion about virtue is reached – for instance, that virtue consists essentially in justice – the result turns out to contain irreducible complexities within it. Hence the frequent recourse to examples in the Platonic dialogues in response to what seem to be requests for simple definitions, e.g., 'What is the nature of virtue?' Especially in Aristotle the very conception of what it means to be courageous, or loyal, or just, or otherwise virtuous, is inseparable from an understanding of characters acting in particular contexts.[41] Not surprisingly, the kind of moral education thought necessary for the cultivation of virtue was for centuries linked to the literature of examples, whether in the Homeric poems, popular fables, or in the narrative exempla of the Middle Ages and early Renaissance.[42] This remained true even as the specific virtues became increasingly codified and fixed, both in number and in kind.

A pivotal figure in the modern transformation of the literature of examples and the classical framework of the virtues was indeed Machiavelli, who looked to a wide range of models of political practice, but who also proposed to tell the unvarnished truth about human nature and to argue pragmatically about how to act politically. According to those views – which are not inconsistent with Hobbes's more systematic and 'scientific' approach to politics – human beings are fundamentally dangerous, and always at risk of conflict with one another. A state could be made whole and stable by appealing to common fears. *The Prince* may offer many narrative fragments that seem to work as examples – as 'eventful instantiations of general rules,' in Nancy Struever's phrase – but these are in fact designed to generalize from strategic interests. The principle seems to be epitomized in one of the chapter headings of the *Discourses on Livy*: 'Although men may deceive themselves in general questions, they do not do so in the particulars.'[43] No wonder Machiavelli's examples are in the service of what seem to be counterintuitive conclusions.[44] The 'virtues' are preserved, though only in appearance, as means to achieve pragmatic goals. Consider the matter of generosity: 'A republic or a prince,' Machiavelli writes, 'should *seem* to do out of generosity what must be done out of necessity' (*Discourses*, I, 51, p. 126; my emphasis). The exercise of generosity, as with the other virtues, requires the exercise of a corresponding vice (in this case, parsimony). The logic is as follows. Generosity exercised in modesty is likely to go unnoticed; to be perceived as generous requires a great deal of sumptuous display. But this is bound to make the generous person hated by many, even if praised by a few. Therefore, 'a wise prince, seeing that he is unable to practice ostentatious generosity without harming himself, must not mind acquiring a reputation for miserliness ... Parsimony is one of the vices that permit him to rule' (74–5). Cyrus, Caesar, and Alexander are all offered as models of this new, inverted exemplarity.

One of Cervantes' most explicit set of pronouncements on the subjects of virtue, value, and the civic role of literature is made in connection with the question of exemplarity in the Prologue to the *Exemplary Novels*. Those remarks are juxtaposed to what appear to be some offhand comments about opportunities for diversion in the *república*. Cervantes makes a nod to conventional notions of moral exemplarity while acknowledging that the stories in his collection may not be exemplary in any standard way. ('I have called them *exemplary*, and if you look carefully there is not a single one from which some worthwhile example cannot be derived; and if it wouldn't mean going on about this subject, perhaps I could show you the tasty and honest fruit than can be picked from them, all together and each one on its own') (Heles dado nombre de *ejemplares*, y si bien lo miras, no hay ninguna de quien no se pueda sacar algún ejemplo provechoso; y si no fuera por no alargar este sujeto, quizá te mostrara el sabroso y honesto fruto que se podría sacar, así de todas juntas, como de cada uno de por sí.)[45] At the same time, he describes his ensemble of stories as a kind of billiard table (a 'mesa de trucos') that has been placed in the public square ('en la plaza de nuestra república') for recreational purposes. The image very nearly duplicates one that the Priest invokes in *Don Quijote*, Part I, in explaining how the books of chivalry might have been allowed to be published in spite of the many untruths they seem to contain. The answer draws on the idea that the well-ordered state needs to include some things that do not directly contribute to political life. Games and other social diversions are among them: 'These books are intended to amuse our idle minds; and just as in harmonious republics games such as chess and ball and billiards are permitted for the entertainment of those who do not have to, or should not, or cannot work, so too the printing of such books is permitted, on the assumption, which is true, that no one will be so ignorant as to mistake any of these books for true history') (Que esto se hace para entretener nuestros ociosos pensamientos; y, así como se consiente en las repúblicas bien concertadas que haya juegos de ajedrez, de pelota y de trucos, para entretener a algunos que ni tienen, ni deben, ni pueden trabajar, así se consiente imprimir y que haya tales libros, creyendo, como es verdad, que no ha de haber alguno tan ignorante que tenga por historia verdadera ninguna destos libros; I, 32, p. 397).

In this Prologue, however, the argument about honest recreation is followed by a defence of the moral rectitude of the collection that can only be described as hyperbolic. Having already lost the use of one hand in the battle of Lepanto, Cervantes offers the other as collateral to guarantee the moral integrity of the collection: 'If by some chance the reading of these novels were to lead the reader to some evil desire or thought, I would rather cut off the hand with which I wrote them than see them published. I am no longer of an age to be toying with the other life') (Que si por algún modo alcanzara que la lección destas novelas pudiera inducir a quien las leyera a algún mal deseo o pensamiento, antes me cortara la mano con que las escribí, que sacarlas en público. Mi edad no está ya para burlarse con la otra vida [64]). This is remarkable. For when taken together the

Exemplary Novels and the *Quijote* seem to provide as many examples of characters gone bad as of clearly virtuous lives. Marcela is ambiguous, but even more so the two friends in the *Quijote*'s 'Tale of Foolish Curiosity,' Anselmo and Lotario, or the man who believes he is made of glass, 'El Licenciado Vidriera,' and the deceived deceiver, Ensign Campuzano in 'El casamiento engañoso,' who dreams the dialogue of the dogs while in his hospital bed. Indeed, it seems that virtuous characters hold relatively little narrative interest, and that where they do exist they are rarely able to find a happy place for themselves among others in the world.

This complexity is not inconsistent with Cervantes' own claim that he was the first to write novels (*novelar*) in Spanish.[46] But it merely redoubles the challenges that can be levelled against literature on moral and political grounds. As noted above in relation to the Canon's discourse about the books of chivalry, it is customary to think that the conceptual framework Cervantes inherited for thinking about such matters was neo-Aristotelian and Horatian, and that literature's self-defence depended on the idea that it could combine moral instruction with a kind of pleasure that would make such instruction palatable. The effort to strike a balance between virtue and pleasure as articulated in the Prologue to the *Exemplary Novels* would certainly seem to suggest this much. Moreover, one of the preliminary *aprobaciones* of the collection, signed by Fr. Juan Bautista and dated 9 July 1612, goes so far as to invoke Aquinas's concept of *eutrapelia* – a balanced form of pleasure, of pleasure in moderation – as part of its predictably conservative endorsement of the book: 'Seeing that it is a plain truth, as the angelic Doctor Thomas Aquinas writes, that *eutropelia* [*sic*] is a virtue, consisting in honest entertainment, I deem that there is true *eutropelia* in these *Novels*, because they entertain with their novelty ... and the author fulfils his purpose in them, by which he also brings honour to the Castilian language, and warns republics about the harm which may follow from certain vices, and many other benefits, and thus it seems to me that they should and ought to be granted the requested approval for publication' (Supuesto que es sentencia llana del angélico doctor Santo Tomás que la eutropelia [*sic*] es virtud, la que consiste en un entretenimiento honesto, juzgo que la verdadera eutropelia está en estas novelas, porque entretienen con su novedad, enseñan con sus ejemplos a huir vicios y seguir virtudes, y el autor cumple con su intento, con que da honra a nuestra lengua castellana, y avisa a las repúblicas de los daños que de algunos vicios se siguen, con otras muchas comodidades; y así, me parece se le puede y debe dar la licencia que pide).[47] The roots of *eutrapelia* lie in the section of Aristotle's *Nicomachean Ethics* that addresses the virtues of social intercourse, and that recommends *bene vertens,* or the quality of 'ready wit,' as the middle ground between buffonery and boorishness.[48]

Aristotle notwithstanding, a return to central, unresolved questions of Plato's *Republic* seems unavoidable: what is the place of literature in politics if virtue must be realized on the margins of the state and if the literary forms that offer its richest versions must be excluded? What good then is literature in the state? Responses such as the one put forward in the Prologue to the *Exemplary Novels* – that the stories in it contain something worthwhile to teach and, more emphatically still, that their author would just as soon cut off one of his hands than be responsible for endorsing anything non-virtuous – suggest that they may in fact be rather dangerous vis-à-vis established conceptions of literature.[49] The image of a 'mesa de trucos' does not merely conjure up the image of an innocent pastime. 'Truco' also says 'trick,' and the association with games of leisure (chess, ball-playing) suggests the sort of easily distracted, idle individual to whom Part I of the *Quijote* is addressed, the 'desocupado lector.' In *Don Quijote*, the Priest in fact says explicitly that 'pastimes,' including the reading of fictions, are intended for people who are unemployed, i.e., for those who are not contributing in some productive or useful way to the collective life of the polis.[50] The central question is how such 'idle' individuals and their 'useless' literary pursuits might be of any value at all. Whatever answers may be proposed, they are likely to come from an oblique angle.[51]

My belief is that Cervantes is far more than just the genial figure his Prologue might suggest, just as he is considerably more inventive than the Canon of Toldeo might lead us to expect. Cervantes may pay lip service to the idea that his exemplary texts all tell of 'pleasant and honest entertainments, which are rather of benefit than harm' (los ejercicios honestos y agradables [que] antes aprovechan que dañan [64]). But, as Francisco Márquez Villanueva has suggested, there is something strange about this claim, something not to be taken seriously, which is, in fact, a condition for taking such claims as they are meant – just as we have to not take the foolishness of the *Praise of Folly* literally in order to grasp its depth.[52] Notwithstanding the echoes of classical defences of literature, there is the inherent oddity, irony, and exorbitance of many of Cervantes' stories themselves. In the case of the *Quijote*, that 'oddity' pertains to the novel as a whole insofar as the principal character is himself an exorbitant experiment in the project of virtuous imitation. The secondary narratives and interpolated tales in turn refract that exorbitant experiment through the mirror of their own investigations of virtue and happiness. Especially in

Part I, each of the secondary narratives – the story of the Anselmo, Lotario, and Camila in the 'Curioso Impertinente,' for instance, as well as the narratives of the two interlaced pairs of lovers (Fernando, Dorotea, Cardenio, and Luscinda), the story of Doña Clara and Don Luis, and the portrait of the Caballero del Verde Gabán and his son the poet – seems to offer some new social or historical twist on the political questions that Cervantes explores through the figure of Don Quijote. Can virtue and nobility be aligned? Can that alignment be exemplified in literature? The latter question is especially interesting insofar as the case of Don Quijote himself shows what can go awry when trying to follow literary examples. To be sure, history binds us to ask whether the literature of example can survive the social pressures encountered by the characters in the secondary narratives of Cervantes' text,[53] but *Don Quijote* compels us to ask whether it can survive the devastations of literature itself.

In one sense, Don Quijote is a character among many. He attempts to imitate exemplars to the point where he can claim as his own a set of virtues – courage, justice, and loyalty, for instance – that are closely associated with the values of the heroic world. He hopes, in the process, to reform the state. But he is just as clearly unable to find accommodation for those virtues in the world around him. Rather than recognize that historical conditions have changed to the degree that the practice of the classical virtues relevant to a hero may no longer be relevant, his own response is to recommend a revival of the practice of knight-errantry as a way to restore virtue to its proper place. This pits virtue against history just as 'theory' and 'practice' were pitted against one another in other instances. But the project is impossible: if virtue were to prevail, history would not be as it is. Indeed, history seems in the end to be one principal reason why the quixotic effort to reform the state fails. While history may itself be a potentially great fund of examples, and while the attempt to change its course may appeal to examples, history may also be thought of as beyond the power of examples. Virtue, for its part, is given many other opportunities to stake a claim, most notably as the characters in the interpolated stories try to sort through questions of nobility, honour, and wealth in a changing world.

To speak of virtue is, of course, to speak in terms of a moral psychology that is not and never was 'scientific' in the modern sense. By contrast, the 'scientific' conception of politics tends to hold that an understanding of desires, of the good, and of political ends, can be determined on the basis of arguments from first principles, if not from the laws of nature themselves. This is a far cry from Aristotle's *Nicomachean Ethics*, which is quite clear about the difference between the practical wisdom necessary for politics and the mathematical reasoning that may be useful elsewhere.[54] Don Quijote the character is an experiment in moral psychology at a time when it was unclear just where the boundaries between morality and psychology might lie. Conventional accounts suggest that Don Quijote's mental condition results from insomnia, and this from the fact that he stays awake from dusk until dawn reading books. Not implausibly, this account mixes Galen's theory of the humours with Juan Huarte de San Juan's *Examen de ingenios*, which describes a *manía* 'which is a warm and dry distemper of the brain.'[55] This may well be the reason Don Quijote could be rendered 'cured and calm' (44) (sano y sosegado) by drinking a big jug of cold water (I, 5, p. 107). But what the account of a dry-witted Don Quijote leaves out is the particular kind of energy or 'spiritedness,' that underlies his pursuit of virtue.[56] This underlying 'spiritedness' (a quality that Plato called *thumos*) makes Don Quijote forceful while also difficult to accommodate politically. That fact, in turn, echoes one of the principal concerns of the *Examen*, viz., to improve the *república* by means of a rational approach to different kinds of 'spirit' (*ingenio*) and their uses.

Don Quijote demonstrates his sheer 'spiritedness' in nearly all of his encounters with those things he perceives to be adversarial or unjust. Think, for instance, of his precipitous response to the flocks of sheep in I, 18, which is modelled on the tragic heroism of Sophocles' *Ajax*. When it comes to the virtues, it is not so much a question of Don Quijote's pursuit of any one quality, whether in his quest for justice and mercy for the servant boy Andrés, or in his steadfast loyalty to Dulcinea, or in his valiant attempt to show courage (*ánimo*)[57] in the face of the caged lions – all of which clearly fail because the conditions for enacting them are either mistaken or wholly lacking – but of the particular force of the moral convictions driving all his actions. This moral force is the quality that propels his engagement with the world, and is something of which he is himself well aware. Consider his remarks to Sancho after freeing the galley slaves and agreeing to avoid confrontation with the Santa Hermandad:

'You are naturally a coward, Sancho,' said Don Quixote, 'but so that you will not say that I am stubborn and never do as you advise, on this occasion I want to take your advice and withdraw from the ferocity that frightens you so, but it must be on one condition: that never, in life or in death, are you to tell anyone that I withdrew and retreated from this danger out of fear, but only to satisfy your pleasure. For merely thinking that I am withdrawing and retreating from any danger, especially this one, which seems to carry with it some small shadow of fear, is enough to make me want to remain and wait here alone, not only for the Holy Brotherhood which you have mentioned and fear so much, but for the brothers of the twelve tribes of Israel, and the seven Macabees, and Castor and Pollux, and all the brothers and brotherhoods there are in the world.' (173–4)

'Naturalmente eres cobarde, Sancho' dijo don Quijote, 'pero, porque no digas que soy contumaz y que jamás hago lo que me aconsejas, por esta vez quiero tomar tu consejo y apartarme de la furia que tanto temes; mas ha de ser con una condición: que jamás, en vida ni en muerte, has de decir a nadie que yo me retiré y aparté deste peligro de miedo, sino por complacer a tus ruegos … que en sólo pensar que me aparto y retiro de algún peligro, especialmente déste, que parece que lleva algún es no es de sombra de miedo, estoy ya para quedarme, y para aguardar aquí solo, no solamente a la Santa Hermandad que dices y temes, sino a los hermanos de los doce tribus de Israel, y a los siete Macabeos, y a Cástor y a Pólux, y aun a todos los hermanos y hermandades que hay en el mundo.' (I, 23, pp. 277–8)

Both here, in his attempt to liberate the galley slaves, and also in his efforts to protect the boy Andrés from physical punishment by a harsh master, Don Quijote's 'spirited' efforts backfire.[58]

'Spiritedness' (*thumos*) may well be an element in the making of courage, though not in the fundamental way that sheer strength (*vis*) is. There is intentionality implicit in *thumos*, as there is not in strength; intentionality requires direction toward an appropriate object. Not surprisingly, Plato argues that *thumos* is higher than mere anger or rage insofar as it has affinities with the intellect.[59] When *thumos* is entirely separate from wisdom it will not contribute to justice at all, but will lead to random acts of rage and anger. But when wisely directed it can be of considerable benefit to the polis, certainly more so than mere anger. *Thumos* originates in self-concern – in the desire to protect oneself, one's family, property, etc. – but it can be of political importance insofar as the spirited individual may be led to transcend merely personal interests and to make sacrifices for the good of the whole. As David Lewis Schaefer explains in connection with Montaigne, *thumos* may lead also to the sacrifice of oneself for things such as one's honour, or the city, that are regarded as extensions of oneself. It is thumotic concern for one's own dignity that inspires the performance of noble deeds that may redound to the greater benefit of the city as a whole.[60]

The case with Don Quijote is this. Notwithstanding his frequently mistaken understanding of the situations confronting him, Don Quijote's 'spiritedness' is often excessive and misdirected. It is largely incompatible with reason or justice and manifests itself as a false form of courage – false not because he dissembles, but false because the conditions required for it are generally mistaken or lacking. His actions reactivate the *vir* in *virtus*, but in a way that makes him potentially dangerous to any state. The imbalance in his psyche is initially explained as a consequence of reading and a lack of sleep, but that explanation serves only to raise again old questions, questions about the role of literary examples in politics, questions about what should and should not be read, and how much, as well as questions about whether literary models need to be subjected to the demands of historical 'truth' if they are to be of any value at all. At one point the Priest says that all this is a matter of determining what qualities might make books suitable for inclusion in 'harmonious republics' (las repúblicas bien concertadas; I, 32, p. 397). What kind of books can in turn contribute to the formation of the 'balanced' character that could best serve the good of these republics? The figure of Don Diego de Miranda, the Caballero del Verde Gabán, might well be put forward as an example of the balanced, virtuous soul, who seems to do all things, including reading, in moderation. He would be an instance of the virtuous *paterfamilias* exemplified in Tasso's dialogue on the father of the family. The fact that Don Diego's son is a poet provides a further opportunity to engage the Platonic question of the role of literature in the state. I will have more to say about him at the end of this chapter. For now, it is enough to note that the literature of example is not a sufficient response to the persistent Platonic question about the place of literature in the state. The reasons are twofold. The first is that the domain of literature is far broader, and its implications far greater, than what can be carried by the notion of 'exemplarity.' The second is that the category of the 'example,' however limited, needs to be refracted through the lens of history, in which the conditions for the exercise of the virtues had shifted considerably from what they were imagined to be in the classical world. In Cervantes' case, this shift is especially visible because the elements of what we have come to know as civil society – as comprised of institutions distinct from the *oikos* and the state, however interwoven with them – were themselves in the course of being formed. In the process, long-established ideas about the relationship between virtue and the social contexts for happiness were called into question.

For Plato, the question was more abstract: how to understand the relationship between the well-being of the polis and the well-being of the individual soul, and how to imagine a place for the virtuous individual

within the city. The schematic answer is that in Plato there is a direct analogy between the parts of the city and the parts of the soul. The rulers, who
exemplify wisdom in the city, are deemed analogous to the intellect; the
warriors are analogous to spiritedness in the soul; and the moneymakers in
the city are analogous to the soul's faculty of desire. The inadequacy of
these analogies lies precisely in the fact that this understanding is indeed
schematic, and so forgets that each soul is bound to have within it some
measure of intellect, spiritedness, and desire.[61] The question is how to find
a balance among these elements. Plato's answer is that justice will prevail
in the soul, as it will in the state, when spirit and appetite are respectful of
reason (*Republic*, 422ff). Virtue must be considered in a similar way: there
can be no exercise of any one virtue that would, as a matter of principle,
obviate the others. The unity of the virtues is required, just as justice requires harmony in the city. (Hence 'justice' is not exclusively a political
virtue.) But Plato also recognizes that in reality – which is to say, in any
city that might actually exist – things are bound to be rather different. An
awareness of this difference drives the need to distinguish the mere appearance of virtue from whatever 'true' virtue might be.

An investigation of the difference between true and false virtues was, in
fact, one premise of the humanist critique of inherited social structures.
More's *Utopia* turns upon this issue, as do many fifteenth-century texts,
including Buonaccorso's *Controversia de nobilitate* (1428), Lorenzo Valla's
De vero falsoque bono (1429–30), and two texts entitled *De vera nobilitate*,
the first by Cristoforo Landino (who held the Chair of rhetoric and poetry
in Florence) and the second by Bartolomeo Platina, the Prefect of the Vati-
can Library.[62] A further investigation of the truth about virtue must reflect
the fact that claims of 'nobility' were caught up in growing uncertainties
within the social world about just how to identify, measure, and assess this
particular quality – was it an inherent element of moral character, or a bio-
logical inheritance, or attached to social status, or earned as one might earn
a fortune in the world? Could one acquire nobility in the way that one
might acquire wealth? The question echoes the one that Meno asks Socrates
in the dialogue of that name: 'Can you tell me, Socrates, whether virtue is
acquired by teaching or by practice; or if neither by teaching nor by practice, then whether it comes to man by nature, or in what other way?'[63] Indeed, the *Meno* begins with an explicit investigation of what 'virtue' means
and of whether it is one thing or many. (Socrates concludes that virtue must
be wisdom, which may well be more than one thing in many.) A similar set
of questions, oriented specifically around the question of inherited wealth,
has a prominent place in the dialogue between Socrates and Cephalus at the

very beginning of the *Republic*: 'Did you inherit most of your fortune ... or did you make it yourself?' asks Socrates. 'Did I make my fortune, Socrates? ... As a businessman, I am somewhere between my grandfather and my father. For my grandfather, whom I'm named, inherited about as much as I have and multiplied it several times over, while my father Lysanias reduced it to less than what it is now; for myself I shall be pleased enough if I leave these boys of mine a little more than I inherited.'[64]

What becomes crystallized as historically 'conservative,' aristocratic ideology insisted that nobility could only be inherited, not acquired. But conservative ideology was contested on many grounds. One precedent lay already in Cicero, whose own example as the 'new man' (*novus homo exemplum*) suggested that admission to the Senate should be based on 'work and virtue' together (industria ac virtus).[65] This model was taken up by Tasso in the dialogue on the father of the family mentioned above.[66] But historical facts in the early modern age continued to reveal contradictions of all sorts. Among these were the increasing numbers of individuals who had amassed substantial sums of wealth, individuals whose families who were not noble by inheritance, and who, in turn, could think of trading wealth for rank. No wonder Ricote presents such a problem, since he has considerable wealth and is a *morisco*.

By the time we reach the later chapters of Part II, Don Quijote's thoughts about virtue turn from displays of 'spiritedness' toward questions of society, nobility, manners, and humility. His 'spiritedness' is, in fact, considerably muted. Just before Sancho takes up the governorship of Barataria, Don Quijote urges him to flaunt his humble lineage so as to make his true virtue known. As we have seen above, his thought is that Sancho may potentially be 'improved' for political life. Such 'improvements' are important not only because they move in the direction of an 'ideal' alignment between the virtues of the soul and those of the body, but because Sancho's rustic comportment and appearance do not in themselves align with what this particular society had come to think of as 'virtue.' The larger point behind Don Quijote's remarks is that virtue must be earned, not just inherited, and that it must likewise be outwardly displayed if there is to be any hope of congruence between the inner and external faces of the self: 'Take pride in the humbleness of your lineage, and do not disdain to say that you come from peasants,' he says, 'because blood is inherited, and virtue is acquired, and virtue in and of itself has a value that blood does not' (730–1) (Haz gala, Sancho, de la humildad de tu linaje, y no te desprecies de decir que vienes de labradores ... porque la sangre se hereda y la virtud se aquista, y la virtud vale por sí sola lo que la sangre no vale; II, 42, p. 358).

While incorporating the wisdom of humility learned on Clavileño, this advice represents a decidedly progressive posture with respect to the question of virtue in the social world. It is consistent with what was for all intents and purposes a commonplace of humanist thinking, viz., that true nobility must be virtuous. (Echoing a Senecan tradition, much alive among Erasmian humanists, Dorotea reminds Fernando of this, verbatim, in I, 36.)[67] What surprises, of course, is that such 'progressive' views are uttered by Don Quijote, who has throughout much of the novel taken a far less sympathetic view of Sancho's rustic roots. But Don Quijote consistently speaks in favour of reform. He firmly believes that he knows what true nobility is. What he may not realize is that his image of 'true' nobility implies a critique of the 'false' nobility of the Duke and the Duchess. The fact that a character who himself poses as virtuous is blind to false virtue suggests that there may be no perspective from within the novel to determine the absolute difference between true virtue and false. Those differences are themselves historical. Indeed, Don Quijote's articulation of the principles of virtue to Sancho represents a way of engaging a long line of questions that have been raised, both explicitly and implicitly, in preceding episodes, where the question of virtue is framed specifically in relation to the circumstances of the modern social world, comprised of a nascent civil society in which personal fortunes could rise and fall and where admission to the company of those who regard themselves as noble could be gained on the basis of advantageous marriages or the acquisition of wealth.

Indeed, nearly all the characters associated with the interpolated stories of Part I have a significant awareness that the question of virtue is in flux. For many of them, the most immediate question is to discern whether nobility is inherently attached to inherited wealth and social standing, and conversely whether wealth and social standing provide guarantees of virtue. Not least for this reason, these stories need to be understood as transformations of the genre of exemplary literature that takes the uncertainties of increasingly 'modern' conditions into account. They are not simply ways of 'exemplifying' the virtues (or their opposites) but rather are ways of exploring the question of what virtue might mean in the context of a new historical world. That exploration occurs within a space that is partly but not wholly private, insofar as matters of love and honour are involved; that is partly but not wholly economic, insofar as the management of family estates and matters of inheritance and rank are at play; and that is partly but not wholly social, insofar as the association among characters, especially in Part I, begins to create the semblance of a small 'society' whose focal point is the relatively public space of the inn.

Assessing Values

All the characters of the interpolated stories struggle with the questions of virtue, nobility, value, and various forms of interpersonal association in some substantial way. They do so outside the context of the formal institutions of civil society but thereby raise questions about virtue and obligation in a more exposed way. The first and perhaps most extreme case is that of Marcela who, as we have already seen, seems unable to conceive of virtue and society together: she prizes her autonomy over anything that society might offer in exchange. She asks for nothing and gives nothing in return. In a Hobbesian world this would mean that Marcela is worth nothing. Hobbes defines human value strictly in relation to the value that can be placed on the use of power in a form of exchange ('The Value, or Worth of a man, is as of all other things, his Price; that is to say, so much as would be given for the use of his Power; and therefore is not absolute, but a thing dependent on the need and judgment of another').[68] But Marcela admits to no 'price' and will not give herself to another as part of any exchange. But it is not as though the question of worldly value never arises for her, even if she does believe she can refuse it. The orphaned Marcela is the daughter of a wealthy father ('Guillermo el rico') and of a mother whose beauty is said to be as remarkable as her daughter's. Marcela has wealth to match her beauty. Surprisingly, many of the details about her are often glossed over by commentators intent on highlighting her autonomy:

> In our village there was a farmer even richer than Grisóstomo's father, and his name was Guillermo, and God gave him not only great wealth but also a daughter, whose mother had died giving birth to her, and her mother was the most respected woman in the whole district ... Her husband, Guillermo, died of grief at the death of such a good woman, and their daughter, Marcela, was left a very rich girl, in the care of an uncle who was a priest, the vicar of our village. The girl grew, and her beauty reminded us of her mother's, which was very great ... Her uncle kept her carefully and modestly secluded, but even so, word of her beauty spread so that, for her own sake, and because of her great fortune, not only the men of our village but those from many miles around, the best among them, asked, begged, and implored her uncle for her hand in marriage. But he, a good and honest Christian, though he wanted to arrange her marriage as soon as she was of age, didn't want to do it without her consent, and didn't even care about the profit and gain from the girl's estate that he would enjoy if he delayed her marriage. (83–4)

En nuestra aldea hubo un labrador aún más rico que el padre de Grisóstomo, el cual se llamaba Guillermo, y al cual dio Dios, amén de las muchas y grandes riquezas, una hija, de cuyo parto murió su madre, que fue la más honrada mujer que hubo en todos estos contornos ... De pesar de la muerte de tan buena mujer murió su marido Guillermo, dejando a su hija Marcela, muchacha y rica, en poder de un tío suyo sacerdote y beneficiado en nuestro lugar. Creció la niña con tanta belleza que nos hacía acordar de la de su madre, que la tuvo muy grande ... Guardábala su tío con mucho recato y con mucho encerramiento; pero, con todo esto, la fama de su mucha hermosura se estendió de manera que, así por ella como por sus muchas riquezas, no solamente de los de nuestro pueblo, sino de los de muchas leguas a la redonda, y de los mejores dellos, era rogado, solicitado e importunado su tío se la diese por mujer. Mas él, que a las derechas es buen cristiano, aunque quisiera casarla luego, así como la vía de edad, no quiso hacerlo sin su consentimiento, sin tener ojo a la ganancia y granjería que le ofrecía el tener la hacienda de la moza, dilatando su casamiento. (I, 12, pp. 164–5)

But, like the cleric-uncle who raised her, Marcela operates far away from the framework of worldly values. There has been some speculation that her uncle instructed her in the ideas of Renaissance Neoplatonism.[69] Since the narrative does not say, this can only be speculation. But it seems not by mere chance that she alludes to Plato's *Symposium* on the subject of the indivisibility of love and the importance of free will: 'According to what I have heard, true love is not divided and must be voluntary, not forced' (99) (Según yo he oído decir, el verdadero amor no se divide, y ha de ser voluntario, y no forzoso; II, 14, p. 186).

Marcela's beauty is clearly a gift, and yet for her it entails no reciprocity and creates no obligations: 'Heaven made me, as all of you say, so beautiful that you cannot resist my beauty and are compelled to love me, and because of the love you show me, you claim that I am obliged to love you in return ... I cannot grasp why, simply because it is loved, the thing loved for its beauty is obliged to love the one who loves it' (98–9) (Hízome el cielo, según vosotros decís, hermosa, y de tal manera que, sin ser poderosos a otra cosa, a que me améis os mueve mi hermosura; y, por el amor que me mostráis ... no alcanzo que, por razón de ser amado, esté obligado lo que es amado por hermoso a amar a quien le ama; I, 14, p. 185–6).[70] Her idealized sense of what it would mean to exist outside the scope of all reciprocal obligations anticipates Don Quijote's rhapsodic praise of freedom from obligations much later, in II, 58. These are anti-political stances that all but directly refuse the respect for obligations so forcefully outlined in Cicero's *De officiis*. One contrastive heroine would be Zoraida, who is both beautiful and generous ('hermosa y liberal'; I, 42, p. 519).

Marcela's beauty is fortified, not to say hardened, by the strength of her will, which grants her the ability to give consent and to withhold it. It goes almost without saying that the power of 'no' is stronger than the power of 'yes,' and that Marcela is committed to 'no' as a way to limit the bonds that beauty might create. We know many things about her: that she claims complete innocence in the suicide of her lover Grisóstomo; that she has been pursued by many other men, all of whom she has discouraged and refused; and that she adamantly claims her right to live apart from the world of reciprocal obligations as an expression of her freedom. 'I was born free, and in order to live free I chose the solitude of the countryside' (99) (Yo nací libre, y para poder vivir libre escogí la soledad de los campos; I, 14, p. 186).

Marcela has been taken both as an anticipatory expression of female independence and as a hyperbolic example of wilfulness that results in the refusal of social intercourse. In her view, there is no necessary correspondence between beauty and the kind of desire that will result in an erotic bond, much less a society. But an additional problem is that there seems to be no inner-worldly way to value the very beauty that attracts so many to her. The question she raises is whether there is a way to find a place for such beauty in association with others, particularly among the company of men. She first appears to Vivaldo and the others gathered for Grisóstomo's funeral as a stunning, miraculous vision. She draws responses of wonder and awe. Her appearance is described as if it were transcendent, her beauty a value beyond all values: '[Vivaldo] was struck by a marvelous vision ... Those who had not seen her before looked at her in amazement and silence, and those who were already accustomed to seeing her were no less thunderstruck' (98) ([A Vivaldo] lo estorbó una maravillosa visión ... Los que hasta entonces no la habían visto la miraban con admiración y silencio; y los que ya estaban acostumbrados a verla no quedaron menos suspensos; I, 14, p. 185).

Marcela may be beyond price, hence outside of the worldly valuations, transactions, and protocols of exchange that may frame dutiful obligations. But this fact cuts two ways. Just as she is exalted, she is immediately demonized by Grisóstomo's close friend, Ambrosio, as a 'savage basilisk' (fiero basilisco) who has come to watch the blood pour out of the wounds that she has inflicted on those who admire her. By contrast, Ambrosio's own orientation in the matter of attachments, as proved by the example of his faithfulness to Grisóstomo, revolves around friendship, which had long been thought of as more perfect than love. Cicero was among its greatest champions, especially in *De amicitia*. But Marcela is neither friend nor lover to anyone. She reserves attachment for herself and exhibits the kind of auto-affection suggestive of Narcissus. 'The clear waters of these streams are my mirrors; I communicate my thoughts and my beauty to the trees and to the waters' (99) (Las claras aguas destos arroyos [son] mis espejos; con los árboles y con las aguas comunico mis pensamientos y hermosura; I, 14 p. 186).

Perhaps the most apt comparison with Marcela as regards the question of a value *hors commerce* – both above and below price – is Lotario's view of Camila in the 'Tale of Foolish Curiosity.' In an impasssioned speech to Anselmo, Lotario compares Camila to diamonds, ermine, gold, and a mirror of crystal-clear glass. Camila is beyond price, but also abject. She suffers from a desire, said not to be uncommon among women, that drives her to consume dirt, plaster, charcoal and, it is said, even more disgusting things. On one level her sickness seems to allude to what was believed about female hysteria and the cravings associated with pregnancy. On another level it is simply meant to suggest the contaminated nature of the love triangle, in which all actions seem to conspire toward a tragic outcome.

In contrast to the priceless beauty and sublime solitude of Marcela, or the contaminated purity of Camila, all the other figures in the intercalated episodes of Part I, including Grisóstomo, are located, for better or for worse, on a scale of worldly values and in relation to personal interests in which two very different 'terministic screens,' those of the public and the private worlds, uneasily overlap. The distraught and desperate Grisóstomo is characterized as both extremely wealthy and deserving. He has inherited a fortune that he also happens to merit.[71] But he finds no satisfactory response to his virtues in the place he seeks. He reaches the nadir of unhappiness in a love that is not returned. What then are we to make of the friendship with him that Ambrosio found so satisfying? As mentioned above, there is a tradition that idealizes friendship as a better alternative to love, but in this episode friendship seems to be no less dream-like than the pastoral ideal. Ambrosio appears to have befriended a young man who had little interest in reciprocity.

The cases of the two pairs of crossed lovers introduced into the subsequent stories of Part I – Fernando and Dorotea, Cardenio and Luscinda – all involve further investigations of the limits of exemplary discourse in contexts where virtue and nobility often seem misaligned, and where there is no single frame of values, much less any one institutional form, for resolving their disparities. The purely 'private' matters of love and betrayal, personal integrity and worth, sexual desire and coercion, are ranged against worldly matters such as status, wealth, or the possession of an estate. Central to them all are questions about what true virtue and nobility are and whether any of these qualities creates binding obligations toward others. These questions touch on the ethical roots out of which any form of public life must be built, but they also raise questions about the virtues that any citizen – any participant in civic life – ought to possess. Plato's question about the analogy between the city and the soul is not far away, even if the historical conditions are vastly different. It is of course true that the context of these narratives never involves the public spaces of a political state or even a city. But, as mentioned above, these characters are brought together within the walls of Juan Palomeque's inn. The inn can be regarded as one of civil society's early successors to the medieval castle, where destinies might cross and lives intersect around stories of virtue, fortune, and love. (The inn will eventually be superseded by the coffeehouse, which Habermas and others have identified as essential to the transactions of civil society.) And yet the inn is far freer than the castle in the sense that its doors are open to noblemen, muleteers, and prostitutes alike. It is precisely one of the kinds of space around which the civil society essential to modernity would come to conduct much of its business. Moreover, as regards questions of literature, of reading, and of what will eventually become aesthetics (as a science of 'finer feeling'), the inn is the place where a consideration of types of stories cedes to a focus on types of pleasures. As is said at the inn, the books of chivalry offer something for every kind of reader, but the point is not that they are vast in what they may treat, but that the diverse assemblage of characters at the inn, ranging from peasant labourers to clergymen and from prostitutes to innkeepers, represents the kind of public whose judgments of taste would have to be accommodated by the institutions of civil society.[72] The institution of modern literary criticism, of which the Canon and the Priest are the precursors, would certainly be among them.

The narratives in question begin with Cardenio, early in Part I, who appears in rags, utterly distraught, and seemingly madder than Don Quijote. On telling his own story it turns out that Cardenio is not just a raving lunatic but has a bona fide claim of nobility to make, as well as a tale to tell about the loss of his beloved Luscinda to Fernando, the treacherous son of Duke Ricardo. The initial point of Cardenio's complaint is this: that his unhappiness seems unjust insofar as it is vastly out of proportion to his inherent virtue and his inherited wealth. But, as he goes on to explain, the ways of the world have taught him that happiness is not something that can ever be guaranteed by wealth. 'I come from one of the finest cities of Andalucia,' he says; 'my family is noble; my parents, rich; my misfortune, so great that my parents had to weep and my family grieve, without being able to alleviate it with their wealth' (185; translation modified) (Mi patria [es] una ciudad de las mejores desta Andalucía; mi linaje, noble; mis padres, ricos; mi desventura, tanta que la deben de haber llorado mis padres y sentido mi linaje, sin poderla aliviar con su riqueza; I, 24, p. 292). But nobility of rank is in the end a relative thing, as is wealth. Cardenio's 'back-story' is this: that he entered into the service of Duke Ricardo and became friends with the Duke's younger son, Fernando, as a way to move up in the world. It is Cardenio's absence while in the service of the Duke – i.e., while exercising the civic virtue of the soldier and meeting his contracted obligations – that affords an opportunity for Fernando to betray him.

Fernando, the third-born son of one of the *grandes* (titled nobles) of Spain, is a pivotal figure in the stories of the four lovers. Notwithstanding his noble parentage, his genuine expressions of generosity (*liberalidad*), or his great friendship with Cardenio, Fernando turns out to be mightily false, both to his friend Cardenio and to the woman to whom he offers the hope of marriage, Luscinda. Clearly – emphatically, one might say – nobility of rank is no guarantee of nobility of character. Quite the contrary, as it seems to allow for moral turpitude. Fernando's case is remarkable in part because of the suggestion that his own inherent virtues, friendship and generosity among them, are betrayed by his own behaviour. As described by Cardenio, he was 'a gallant, charming youth, magnanimous and inclined to fall in love, who in a very short time showed so great a desire for my friendship that everyone spoke of it' (185) (mozo gallardo, gentil hombre, liberal y enamorado, el cual, en poco tiempo, quiso que fuese tan su amigo, que daba que decir a todos; I, 24, p. 294). But Fernando's betrayal of friendship and love is not all. The deeper insight of this story is that the problem of virtue does not originate in the modern world. On the contrary, Fernando is a supreme example of what has been called 'status inconsistency,' i.e., of the disparity between the virtue that inherited aristocratic standing would presume and the claims that social actions may warrant.[73]

Of all the figures in the interpolated stories, Fernando is most clearly drawn as a member of the older, titled classes, with all the advantages and limitations that such a status implies. Indeed, as the Duke's third-born son, in a culture where the rule of *mayorazgo* dictated that both the title and the greatest part of the family inheritance should pass to the first-born, his future is not at all secure.[74] The suggestion is that he must, like the Captive and his brothers, earn his standing. (In the case of the Captive, it is the father who makes it clear that his sons must choose a viable public career from three proverbial options: the religious-intellectual life, seafaring and commerce, or royal service in the military.)[75] Fernando, by contrast, does little by way of his actions to validate his nobility of character. His failure to honour the standards of action that would be expected of a person of his social station involves a failing of duty, of what he *owes*, to Cardenio.[76] Indeed, he flouts obligation to such a degree that he is compared to some of the most famous political traitors of all time. The suggestion is that no society, much less a viable polis, could be built around such qualities. Here is how Fernando, the betrayer of friends and lovers, appears when refracted through the hyperbolic filter of Cardenio's rage. He is like a political traitor: 'O ambitious Marius, O cruel Catalina, O wicked Sulla, O lying Galalón, O traitorous Vellido, O vengeful Julián, O greedy Judas! Traitrous, cruel, vengeful, and lying man, what disservice had been done to you by wretch who so openly revealed to you the secrets and joys of his heart!' (218) (¡Oh Mario ambicioso, oh Catilina cruel, oh Sila facinoroso, oh Galalón embustero, oh Vellido traidor, oh Julián vengativo, oh Judas codicioso! Traidor, cruel, vengativo y embustero, ¿qué deservicios te había hecho este triste, que con tanta llaneza te descubrió los secretos y contentos de su corazón? ¿Qué ofensa te hice? I, 27, p. 333). Dorotea's complaint just one chapter later closely tracks this language: that the son of a high-ranking nobleman, one of the grandees of Spain, has turned out to be a traitor: 'What he is heir to I do not know other than the treacheries of Vellido and the lies of Galalón' (230) (No sé yo de qué sea heredero, sino de las traiciones de Vellido y de los embustes de Galalón; I, 28, p. 348).

Before Fernando is finally reformed within the context of this small society, Dorotea's story introduces the matter of his further deception – not just of Cardenio and Luscinda, but of her love as well. Dorotea condemns his betrayals while taking an opportunity proudly to assert her irreproachable status as an 'old Christian' (*cristiana vieja*) from a family that has risen by degrees to the rank of *hidalgos* and perhaps as high as *caballeros*.[77] 'My parents … are farmers, simple people with no mixture of any objectionable races, what are called the Oldest of Old Christians, but so rich that their wealth and luxurious way of life are slowly gaining for them the name of gentlefolk, even of nobility' (230) (Mis padres … son labradores, gente llana, sin mezcla de alguna raza mal sonante, y, como suele decirse, cristianos viejos ranciosos; pero tan ricos, que su riqueza y magnífico trato les va poco a poco adquiriendo nombre de hidalgos, y aun de caballeros; I, 28, p. 348). Dorotea's claim to virtue is in inverse proportion to Fernando's failure to measure up to his nobility.[78] Her resistance to Fernando is one element in the picture of her 'complete' virtue ('She was so beautiful, modest, discreet, and virtuous that no one who knew her could decide in which of these she showed greater excellence of distinction' [186]; Era tan hermosa, recatada, discreta y honesta que nadie que la conocía se determinaba en cuál destas cosas tuviese más excelencia ni más se aventajase; I, 24, p. 294). It is not inconsistent with earned wealth. Her old-Christian, working family has risen from pure but quite modest beginnings, as her parents prospered by dint of their efforts.[79] At first Dorotea was kept cloistered in her parent's house, visible only to the household staff and to Fernando, but she was eventually entrusted with the care of the family's sizeable estate and is appointed its *mayordoma*.

This remarkable level of responsibility places Dorotea within the framework of activities that Aristotle addresses as part of the *Economics*, the *oikos*. But the *oikos* is not self-contained, just as in Aristotle economics accompanies politics. The circumstances nonetheless divide Dorotea between the opportunities afforded by her industriousness and the relatively limited set of options typically available for women in early modern Spain. Dorotea has complete responsibility for management of the family estate, including hiring and firing servants, keeping accounts, and procuring everything from oil and wine presses to livestock and beehives. At the very same time, she displays valued qualities of modesty, reserve, and tact with members of the household. Dorotea is at once a responsible manager of the worldly affairs of the household and decorous woman, a 'perfecta casada' in the making.

It is nonetheless worth noting that neither her worldliness nor her virtue owes much to reading. She concentrates principally on devotional books that support her chaste interior life: 'My times of leisure, after I had attended to overseers, foremen, and other laborers, I spent in activities both proper and necessary for young women, such as those afforded by the needle and pincushion and, at times, the distaff; when I left these activities to refresh my spirit, I would spend the time reading a book of devotions, or playing the harp' (231) (Los ratos que del día me quedaban, después de haber dado lo que convenía a los mayorales, a capataces y a otros jornaleros, los entretenía en ejercicios que son a las doncellas tan lícitos como necesarios, como son los que ofrece la aguja y la almohadilla, y la rueca muchas veces; y si alguna, por recrear el ánimo, estos ejercicios dejaba, me acogía al entretenimiento de leer algún libro devoto, o a tocar una arpa; I, 28, pp. 348–9). One might well contrast this brief portrait to the image of Alonso Quijano as presented at the very opening of Cervantes' novel, who reads romances of chivalry and forgets entirely about the care of his estate. Dorotea pursues reading in well-earned leisure time, as part of a virtuous interior life that is isolated from questions of worldly value and held apart from the secular concerns of the public sphere. There is no small irony, then, in the fact that Dorotea is enlisted by the Priest and the Barber in the project to bring Don Quijote back home by playing the part of an exotic princess, Micomicona, whose image is drawn from the very kinds of books that she herself had avoided reading.

Whether or not she recognizes it as also literary, Dorotea also realizes that her own story of rising status through marriage is not an unusual one.[80] She says as much to herself while contemplating the choice she must make vis-à-vis Fernando: either to accept him in a prosperous marriage to a member of a more noble family or, in all likelihood, be subject to the force of his will. The options seem unpromising. 'I had a brief dialogue with myself, saying "Yes, I shall not be the first woman who by way of matrimony has risen from a humble to a noble estate, and Don Fernando will not be the first man moved by beauty, or irrational attraction, which is more likely, to take a wife unequal to him in rank. If I cannot do anything that has not been done before, it is a good idea to accept the honor that fate offers me, even if the love he shows me lasts no longer than the satisfaction of his desire, for after all, in the sight of God I shall be his wife"' (234) (Hice un breve discurso conmigo, y me dije a mí mesma: 'Sí, que no seré yo la primera que por vía de matrimonio haya subido de humilde a grande estado, ni será don Fernando el primero a quien hermosura, o ciega afición, que es lo más cierto, haya hecho tomar compañía desigual a su grandeza. Pues si no hago ni mundo ni uso nuevo, bien es acudir a esta honra que la suerte me ofrece, puesto que en éste no dure más la voluntad que me muestra de cuanto dure el cumplimiento de su deseo; que, en fin, para con Dios seré su esposa'; I, 28, p. 353). And yet in the final analysis Dorotea's steadfastness is enough to reverse the heart and will of Fernando. As the story nears its denouement, in I, 36, it is clearly her fidelity that tempers his aristocratic pride and privilege, thus rendering him fit for incorporation into society in a way that accords with his inherent nobility.[81] Dorotea allows Fernando to realize his nobility, to display true generosity (liberalidad), and to assume the role of the benevolent leader of what David Quint has aptly called 'the little community at the inn' (Quint, Cervantes's Novel, 154). The people assembled at the inn, preoccupied by inner-worldly concerns, are very much the representatives of a 'civil society' in the making. The inn provides a space in which stories are traded and converge, and where questions of virtue and the ways of the world can be sorted out, even among individuals of very different social ranks. The person who comes to guide it, Fernando, is not an ideal governor of any sort, but a character whose standing is dependent upon the worldly influence that other members of society, not necessarily his social equals, have on him.

The problem of reconciling virtue with the ways of the world as well as the interest in aligning virtue with the collective aims of civil society would seem to be a still greater challenge in the penultimate case I consider here, that of the Captive's brother, the judge (*oidor*) Juan Pérez de Viedma. The judge is a civil servant, a representative of Spain's lower levels of political officialdom, but his daughter, Doña Clara, aspires to a marriage above her rank with Don Luis. Juan Pérez de Viedma has all the signs of distinction that attach to a modest but well-regarded public servant: he wears the robes of a civil judge and leaves no doubt that he expects the respect of others.[82] He is in fact travelling to the Indies, where he has earned an appointment to the High Court of Mexico (I, 42). His position notwithstanding, there seems to be an impossible status gap between his daughter Doña Clara and her prospective mate don Luis. Doña Clara laments, 'What ending can we expect if his father is so distinguished and wealthy that he won't think me good enough to be his son's maid, let alone his wife?' (378) (¿qué fin se puede esperar, si su padre es tan principal y tan rico, que le parecerá que aun yo no puedo ser criada de su hijo, cuanto más su esposa? I, 43, p. 525). And yet Clara does have the possibility of marrying into a higher station because she brings with her the prospect of a sizeable inheritance. The source of this inheritance is not at all trivial. It speaks to the persistence of factors wholly outside of human control in the shaping of individual and collective happiness. Unlike Dorotea, Doña Clara has neither earned her wealth in the 'modern' way, by dint of labour, nor, as a future heiress, has she come to it by traditional routes. Rather, she has a promise of wealth because of an unfortunate accident: her mother died in childbirth, and a fortune (her mother's dowry) passed to her father as a result. Insofar as Clara's worthiness is tied to inherited wealth, it is nothing that she can associate with her own character. Her happiness is neither the result of her independent efforts nor of her inherent qualities, but of an inheritance that can at best be described as a mixed blessing. Such accidents are neither political nor individual, even if they have a bearing on both forms of life.

We know this all by very indirect routes. The story about Doña Clara as a half-orphan is embedded in a stock 'recognition scene' centred around her father, more typical of romance narratives than of exemplary tales. The drama of recognition is, in fact, so powerful that it might well seem to supersede all other frames. Certainly it is a matter of great emotional consequence when the Captive meets his brother the judge and when the judge recognizes that the youth disguised as a boy is, in fact, his daughter, Doña Clara. When the matter about Clara's inheritance comes to light it seems overshadowed by these recognitions, but it is nonetheless crucial to her happy marriage to Don Luis: 'The captive also learned that her mother had died in childbirth, and that he was very wealthy because of the dowry his daughter had inherited. The captive asked their advice as to how he should make himself known, or if he ought to determine first whether his brother would feel humiliated when he saw how poor he was or would welcome him affectionately' (370) (Supo también como aquella doncella era su hija, de cuyo parto había muerto su madre, y que él había quedado muy rico con el dote que con la hija se le quedó en casa. Pidióles consejo qué modo tendría para descubrirse, o para conocer primero si, después de descubierto, su hermano, por verle pobre, se afrentaba o le recebía con buenas entrañas; I, 42, p. 516). Within this framework, the story also confronts the desires of two relatively modern, independent children, Clara and Luis, to make choices about their lives apart from their parents' wishes. They implicitly challenge what Vitoria and others, including Alonso de Castrillo, had to say about the quasi-legal status of parental authority.[83]

The deference that Don Luis shows to his future father-in-law is nonetheless remarkable for the way in which it helps diminish the tension between parental authority and the desire for autonomy among the new generation ('Señor, you already know of my parents' wealth and nobility, and also that I am their only heir, and if these seem reason enough for you to venture to make me entirely happy, then accept me as your son' [388]; Ya, señor, sabéis la riqueza y la nobleza de mis padres, y como yo soy su único heredero: si os parece que éstas son partes para que os aventuréis a hacerme en todo venturoso, recebidme luego por vuestro hijo; I, 44, p. 537). The story involves the chiasma-like crossing of two very different paradigms of happiness: on the one side, a 'modern' paradigm in which marriage can be chosen independently, even across status lines, and on the other side, a much older framework, in which fortune sometimes conspires with the authority of fathers to bring about happy consequences for the next generation. Establishing the formal associations that would be able to respond to these conflicting pressures was, of course, crucial to the formation of civil society. Likewise, finding the forms of society that would allow for obligations not just to be accepted, but to be freely accepted as responsibilities, was a crucial element in the development of civil society. Still on the horizon in Cervantes, where we can see it forming as a set of questions, rather than posed as a set of institutional answers, civil society was a development that came to serve the long-term interests of individuals and of the state in seeming equal measure.

Self-Sufficiency

In all this, there is one character who seems to model a remarkably virtuous life conducted apart from dependence on others save his immediate family: Diego de Miranda, also known as the 'Knight of the Green Overcoat' (el Caballero del Verde Gabán). He can be seen as a paragon of humanist values, as an example of the Aristotelian 'middle way,' as a counter-quixotic figure (i.e., the type of individual Don Quijote might have turned out to be had he not read so many books of chivalry), as a virtuous example of the lower ranks of the class of *hidalgos* (he is a 'caballero labrador y rico'; II, 18, p. 169), and as a veiled reference to one of Cervantes' literary rivals, Lope de Vega.[84] He is also, as mentioned above, modelled on Tasso's dialogue about the *paterfamilias*. (It is the Captain's father who struggles to find the right measure of virtue; he ends up dividing his estate among his sons before it is time so as to avoid giving it away out of excessive generosity.)[85] But what matters about the Caballero del Verde Gabán from the standpoint of politics, happiness, and civil society is this: he is a self-sufficient man, who seems to have achieved happiness without any involvement in politics and, indeed, without much involvement in the institutions of civil society either.[86] He lives in domestic contentment with his wife Cristina and their poet-son Lorenzo. The picture we have of him would seem to suggest the counter-Ciceronian idea that neither politics nor civil society may be necessary for happiness. Although Diego de Miranda may socialize with friends, his happiness seems not to depend much on others at all. Indeed, it seems on reflection that he has gained his happiness by limiting the radius of his obligations. Whether or not that limitation compromises his ethical standing is something that remains to be determined. For while he may not make any affronts to the principle of general responsibility as it might have been read from Cicero's *De officiis*, neither does he seize the opportunity to demonstrate or defend his connection to the rest of human kind.

The Caballero del Verde Gabán is one of the few figures Don Quijote encounters in an interior, domestic space. (Don Antonio Moreno, whom Don Quijote visits in Barcelona, is another.) Rather than an exemplary story, in which some question about virtue or justice or social standing hangs in the balance, either around some question of marriage or honour or inheritance, here we are offered a less dynamic profile. He nonetheless appears to be an admirable individual, whose life seems to epitomize the virtues associated with self-control. While some readers might justifiably respond that his life is lacking in interest and excitement – lacking indeed in the very 'spiritedness' that drives Don Quijote – and that nothing in his story hangs in the balance, he has nonetheless steered a virtuous middle course. In so doing he seems to have achieved a level of autonomy that allows him to minimize the role of politics and the institutions of civil society in his own life. He has no worries about whether or not to approve his son's marriage, whether his wife is faithful, or who will inherit his estate. Rather, Diego de Miranda seems to lead a contented existence with his family and friends in conditions of relative prosperity. ('I am more than moderately wealthy and ... spend my time with my wife, and my children, and my friends ... From time to time I dine with my neighbors and friends, and often I invite them to my table; my meals are carefully prepared and nicely served and in no way meager' [554]; Soy más que medianamente rico y ... paso la vida con mi mujer, y con mis hijos, y con mis amigos ... Alguna vez como con mis vecinos y amigos, y muchas veces los convido; son mis convites limpios y aseados, y no nada escasos; II, 16, p. 153.) He enjoys the entertainments one might expect of a *hidalgo*, including fishing and hunting; he is devout, generous, and modest.[87] His personal library is likewise a picture of 'exemplary' reading. It contains some books in Latin and others in Spanish, some religious and others, which he says he prefers, profane, but no books of chivalry; instead, he has many works that provide 'honest entertainment': 'I have some six dozen books, some in our Romance language and some in Latin, some historical and some devotional; books of chivalry have not yet crossed my threshold. I more often peruse profane books than devout ones, as long as the diversion is honest, and the language delights, and the invention amazes and astounds, though there are very few of these in Spain' (544; translation modified) (Tengo hasta seis docenas de libros, cuáles de romance y cuáles de latín, de historia algunos y de devoción otros; los de caballerías aún no han entrado por los umbrales de mis puertas. Hojeo más los que son profanos que los devotos, como sean de honesto entretenimiento, que deleiten con el lenguaje y admiren y suspendan con la invención, puesto que déstos hay muy pocos en España; II, 16, p. 153).

This portrait nonetheless raises a question. If happiness can be achieved privately, independent of the polis, and with little connection to civil society, why not strive to diminish the importance of others in the conduct of human affairs? Why not avoid the demands that obligation entails and instead cultivate happiness on a strictly individual scale? Seneca, who stands in the middle-distance background here, would suggest that there are two public realms, hence two commonwealths: the one (the city or fatherland) of which we are members by birth, the other (universal) which is not temporal at all. We serve the latter commonwealth best, he argues, in retirement from the world, by inquiring into the true nature of virtue.[88] Cervantes' version of a response is provided in the context of a dialogue between Don Quijote and Diego de Miranda's son Lorenzo, in which the larger category of private pleasure is subordinated to the public virtues that Don Quijote associates with knight-errantry. It is consistent with Cicero's views in *De officiis*: that an individual must contribute to the community by honouring obligations and making himself of service to others. Indeed, even Don Lorenzo's father seems to have wished that his son had studied law or theology at Salamanca. That might have placed him in line for a career as a public official; for, as his father acknowledges, they live in an age when *letras* are valued only insofar as they are coupled with noble actions:

> I, Señor Don Quixote ... have a son ... [who] has spent the last six years in Salamanca, studying Latin and Greek, and when I wanted him to go on to study other areas of knowledge, I found him so enthralled with poetry, if that can be called knowledge, that I can't make him show any enthusiasm for law, which I would like him to study, or for the queen of all study, which is theology. I would like him to be the crown of his lineage, for we live in a time when our kings richly reward good, virtuous letters, for letters without virtue are pearls in the dungheap. (555)

> Yo, señor don Quijote ... tengo un hijo ... [que] los seis ha estado en Salamanca, aprendiendo las lenguas latina y griega, y cuando quise que pasase a estudiar otras ciencias, halléle tan embebido en la de la poesía (si es que se puede llamar ciencia), que no es posible hacerle arrostrar la de las leyes, que yo quisiera que estudiara, ni de la reina de todas, la teología. Quisiera yo que fuera corona de su linaje, pues vivimos en siglo donde nuestros reyes premian altamente las virtuosas y buenas letras, porque letras sin virtud son perlas en el muladar. (II, 16, p. 154)

Not surprisingly, Don Quijote's initial response to this reasoning takes the form of a classical paean to poetry. It is an art that can, when practised well, be the source of public fame ('the man who uses and treats poetry in the requisite ways that I have mentioned will be famous, and his name esteemed, in all the civilized nations of the world' [556]; el que con los requisitos que he dicho tratare y tuviere a la poesía, será famoso y estimado su nombre en todas las naciones políticas del mundo; II, 16, p. 155). Yet Don Quijote goes on to argue that 'poetry' is not enough if it is regarded as merely beautiful and pleasing. Certainly it is not enough to think that the scope of poetry is limited to the kind of verses that the son, Don Lorenzo, seems to be writing – precious, not to say frivolous *glosas* that do nothing to advance the public good or to enhance the ends of civil society. The shallow pleasures of such poetry are easily surpassed by the claims that Don Quijote makes at the conclusion of this episode regarding the virtues of knight-errantry. Indeed, Don Quijote's answer to Don Lorenzo on the question of the nature of poetry as a 'science' transforms the discussion into a recapitulation of the debate over arms and letters from Part I. In contrast to the idle pleasures of the son's pointless glosses in verse, Don Quijote's vision of the 'science' of knight-errantry encompasses law and politics, theology and natural science, mathematics and moral philosophy. He regards it as a 'science' that encompasses the whole:

> It is a science ... that contains all or most of the sciences in the world, because the man who professes it must be a jurist and know the laws of distributive and commutative justice so that he may give to each person what is his and what he ought to have; he must be a theologian so that he may know how to explain the Christian law he professes, clearly and distinctly, no matter where he is asked to do so; he must be a physician, and principally an herbalist, so that he may know, in the midst of wastelands and deserts, the herbs that have the virtues to heal wounds ... he must be an astrologer, so that he can tell by the stars how many hours of the night have passed, and in what part and climate of the world he finds himself; he must know mathematics, because at every step he will have need of them. (570)

> Es una ciencia ... que encierra en sí todas o las más ciencias del mundo, a causa que el que la profesa ha de ser jurisperito y saber las leyes de la justicia distributiva y comutativa, para dar a cada uno lo que es suyo y lo que le conviene; ha de ser teólogo, para saber dar razón de la cristiana ley que profesa, clara y distintamente, adondequiera que le fuere pedido; ha de ser médico, y principalmente herbolario, para conocer en mitad de los despoblados y desiertos las yerbas que tienen virtud de sanar las heridas ... ha de ser astrólogo, para conocer por las estrellas cuántas horas son pasadas de la noche y en qué

parte y en qué clima del mundo se halla; ha de saber las matemáticas, porque a cada paso se le ofrecerá tener necesidad dellas. (II, 18, p. 171)

The image of a 'science of the whole' places us within range of questions about politics and governance that have been taken up in the preceding chapters. Suffice it here to say that Don Quijote's claim that literature (which he calls 'poetry') also contains all the other arts and sciences within it leaves out the obvious analogy to the polis, which is likewise a construction of the 'whole,' to which all the arts and sciences contribute. That said, the analogy leads to one of the persistent questions surrounding the 'autonomy' of literature in the modern age – including its autonomy from politics. If literature embraces all possible forms of knowledge, then is it a form of knowledge of its own? The future resonance of this question was of course beyond the historical scope of what Cervantes was able fully to conceive, but its long prior history was certainly not.

There is nonetheless Don Digeo de Miranda, in whom we glimpse a version of the settled, bourgeois, domestic way of answering the question about literature in its relationship to political life. His answer is clear: that literature may well form part of a well-balanced domestic existence, but has no essential political import. For Don Diego and his son Lorenzo, literature challenges little and disturbs nothing. It contributes to private pleasure and adds to a sense of domestic well-bring. In and of itself this may seem unobjectionable, but on reflection this settlement of the issue raises the spectre of literature held largely apart from any role in the polis. This is, or ought to be, unacceptable from both sides. On the one hand it accommodates literature as part of a life that is itself oblivious to politics. And on the other hand it underestimates the potential of literature itself. Don Diego de Miranda scarcely reads with a sense of engagement. He is not much open to provocation by any book. If we attend to what Cervantes says specifically about him, or has him say about himself, he simply 'looks over' or 'peruses' the books on his shelf ('Hojeo más los que son profanos …').

9 Free Speech?

It is no mean manifestation of Nature and Reason that man is the only animal that has a feeling for order, for propriety, for moderation in word and deed.

Cicero, *De officiis*[1]

He asks that his work not be scorned but praised, not for what he has written but for what he has omitted from his writing.

Cervantes, *Don Quijote*, II, 44[2]

At various points in the preceding chapters I have touched on the ways in which Cervantes explores the resources of myth, travel writing, controversial argumentation, exemplary narratives, and many other forms of discourse as a way to talk about questions that bear on politics. He does this in full view of the conditions of constraint that bear upon all forms of discourse. These conditions frame the outlook of the novel and inform a broad series of internal questions about what can and cannot be said or read. The lurking threat of the Inquisition, as reflected in the review of books in Don Quijote's library in Part I is of course one factor, but hardly the only one. The repression of Erasmian humanism and the marginal status of all Spanish *conversos* were also among the substantive matters of concern behind the Inquistion's activities. There is, in fact, good reason to believe that Cervantes in fact conceived the *Quijote* during a period when he was quite literally constrained (i.e., incarcerated). The suggestive phrase in the Prologue to Part I – that the book resembles a child 'begotten in a prison, where every discomfort has its place and every mournful sound makes its home' (3) (se engendró en una cárcel, donde toda incomodidad tiene su asiento y donde todo triste ruido hace su habitación; I, 1, p. 50) – certainly leads one to think so. Was the *Quijote* conceived during his incarceration in the Royal Prison in Seville in 1597, which seems most likely, or earlier, in Castro del Río in 1592? We do not know for certain. But, in the end, the matter goes well beyond whether Cervantes meant to trace the genesis of the *Quijote* to a particular period when he was in jail or, as some have suggested, the Prologue is simply intending to say that the book was born out of a whole life's worth of suffering. The passage in question also bears a literary debt to Boethius, whose *Consolation of Philosophy* was widely known to have been occasioned by his imprisonment in Ticinum.[3] So too it stands in line with the dialogue between 'Reason' and 'Sorrow' in Petrarch's *De Remediis* (SORROW: 'I lead a miserable life in prison.' REASON: 'Some have composed books in prison ... Many have chosen voluntarily to live in caves and caverns, or enclose themselves behind confining walls').[4] But, most of all, Cervantes wants to signal that he is aware of the fact that the acts of writing and of engendering – the one 'artificial'and the other 'natural' – are both constrained. Nature is hardly a domain of freedom, as the discourse on the Golden Age and some versions of pastoral suggest. And writing is in turn constrained, so the Prologue would seem to say, just as the order of nature itself is, where there seems to be no freedom at all from the basic law by which like engenders like. When read in full, the passage just cited takes Cervantes' incarceration as the image of an 'artificial' constraint that cannot be circumvented any more than the laws of nature herself: 'I have not been able to contravene the natural order; in it, like begets like. And so what could my barren and poorly cultivated wits beget but the history of a child who is dry, withered, capricious, and filled with inconstant thoughts never imagined by anyone else, which is just what one would expect of a person begotten in a prison, where every discomfort has its place and every mournful sound makes its home?' (3) (No he podido yo contravenir al orden de naturaleza, que en ella cada cosa engendra su semejante. Y, así, ¿qué podía engendrar el estéril y mal cultivado ingenio mío, sino la historia de un hijo seco, avellanado, antojadizo y lleno de pensamientos varios y nunca imaginados de otro alguno, bien como quien se engendró en una cárcel, donde toda incomodidad tiene su asiento y donde todo triste ruido hace su habitación? I, Prologue, p. 50).[5]

It is not until relatively late in Part II, when Don Quijote addresses Sancho upon his departure from the estate of the Duke and Duchess, that we hear a full-throated contrast to this acknowledgment of constraint. Here, Don Quijote sings a rhapsody to freedom. The passage is a reprise of the discourse on the Golden Age, in which Don Quijote dwells on the fantasy of living without obligations. In contrast to the discourse on the

Golden Age, it offers a post-political view rather than a pre-political theory of what 'pure' freedom might be:

> Freedom, Sancho, is one of the most precious gifts heaven gave to men; the treasures under the earth and beneath the sea cannot compare to it; for freedom, as well as for honor, one should risk one's life, while captivity, on the other hand, is the greatest evil that can befall a person ... You have clearly seen the luxury and abundance we have enjoyed in this castle that we are [now] leaving, but in the midst of those flavorful banquets and those drinks, as cool as snow, I felt as if I were suffering the pangs of hunger because I could not enjoy them with the freedom I would have had if they had become mine; the obligations to repay the benefits and kindnesses we have received are bonds that hobble a free spirit. Fortunate is the man to whom heaven has given a piece of bread with no obligation to thank anyone but heaven itself! (II, 58, p. 832).

> La libertad, Sancho, es uno de los más preciosos dones que a los hombres dieron los cielos; con ella no pueden igualarse los tesoros que encierra la tierra ni el mar encubre; por la libertad, así como por la honra, se puede y debe aventurar la vida, y, por el contrario, el cautiverio es el mayor mal que puede venir a los hombres. Digo esto, Sancho, porque bien has visto el regalo, la abundancia que en este castillo que dejamos hemos tenido; pues en metad de aquellos banquetes sazonados y de aquellas bebidas de nieve, me parecía a mí que estaba metido entre las estrechezas de la hambre, porque no lo gozaba con la libertad que lo gozara si fueran míos; que las obligaciones de las recompensas de los beneficios y mercedes recebidas son ataduras que no dejan campear al ánimo libre. ¡Venturoso aquél a quien el cielo dio un pedazo de pan, sin que le quede obligación de agradecerlo a otro que al mismo cielo! (II, 58, p. 470)

Somewhere in between the acknowledgment of the constraints of nature and of circumstance, and the utopic dream of absolute freedom, lies one of the fundamental questions of politics: how to justify the constraints that human beings construe as binding? How do we go from the 'state of nature' (sometimes viewed as a state of pure freedom) to a political state, in which human beings are asked to accept the restrictions placed upon them by others or agree to the ones they place upon themselves? When Rousseau observed that 'man is born free and everywhere he is in chains' he was invoking a later version of a very old question. Machiavelli's remarks on the bondage of the Italians (*The Prince*, ch. 26) was among his predecessors. Hobbes's view in *Leviathan* was that the only rational thing for the members of a society to do was to invest a monopoly of force in a single figure, the sovereign, as a way of protecting freedom and ensuring peace for all.

It bears remarking that Cervantes' strategy for dealing with the question of constraint tends on the one hand to reckon with external factors and to deal with them obliquely. His response to a political environment that was anything but free lies with the words he writes but also with the direction from which they are aimed, with their ability to strike at their targets sideways, from places that lie just outside the reader's main line of sight.[6] There are, at the very least, two kinds of readers, or two reading positions, required for the *Quijote*. Cervantes names one of these explicitly in the very opening words of the Prologue to Part I. This is the 'desocupado lector,' the idle and incautious reader, the kind of reader who is inclined to take things at face value. The other kind of reader, not named directly, is created by the experience of reading the book itself. This reader learns to be alert to what the *Quijote* has to say obliquely, to meanings that cannot be fully voiced aloud, and to implications that lie between the lines of whatever may be said explicitly. (As one of the epigraphs to this chapter suggests, Cervantes is well aware of the importance of what he has chosen *not* to say in this book.)[7] Moreover, this reader comes to recognize that there are numerous internal constraints placed on what can and cannot be said within the book, whether for reasons of decorum, or considerations of length, or unity of form, or considerations of verisimilitude, or the tolerance of listeners. The *Quijote* is filled nearly to obsession with talk about what should or should not be said, and when, and where, by whom, at what length, and in what register. There is ongoing comment on words that are inappropriate, about stories that are too long, details that are objectionable because they seem distracting, elements of a plot that are suspicious because they may be too fantastic, malapropisms that need correcting, proverbs that are called into question because they are brought to bear on the wrong circumstances, speeches that seem praiseworthy except that they are verbose, expressions that are too vulgar or ill-formed, whole books that are judged for their questionable historical accuracy, their moral quality, or their aesthetic qualities and, in Part II, objections about the disruptions caused by the intercalated stories in Part I. Indeed, it would be hard to think of a book more concerned with passing judgment on things said or written than the *Quijote*. It is a text that seems bound up with a deep-seated worry about what should or should not be said. This seems perplexing for a book that seems to admit so many forms of otherwise free speech, and that presents itself as a form of discourse that is not firmly attached to origins or authority. What has not been so clearly recognized is that these concerns bind the *Quijote* to a set of deeply rooted political issues insofar as they are meant not just to govern what is said but to regulate the potentially problematic generativity of discourse while engaging in the process of discursive production. These come about not for any gratuitous reason, not simply because of a concern for decorum or for the rules of literary or aesthetic 'theory,' but because of a need to deal with the limitations that seem necessary for political life, while finding ways and means to speak the truth where politics would constrain expression.

I turn first to the matter of Cervantes' indirect and multilayered response to external constraints. Francisco Márquez Villanueva writes of Cervantes' strategic and deft sidestepping way of taking up critical positions within an authoritarian context.[8] The controversial philosopher Leo Strauss spoke of a very similar state of affairs in 'Persecution and the Art of Writing.' Persecution, he said, 'gives rise to a peculiar technique of writing, and therewith to a peculiar type of literature, in which the truth about all crucial things is presented exclusively between the lines. That literature is addressed, not to all readers, but to trustworthy and intelligent readers only. It has all the advantages of private communication without having its greatest disadvantage – that it reaches only the writer's acquaintances. It has all the advantages of public communication without having its greatest disadvantage – capital punishment for its author.'[9] These conditions are apt to produce a particular kind of text, which Strauss calls 'exoteric.' The exoteric text carries two levels of meaning, one intended for the many (in Cervantes' case, the *vulgo*), and another for those 'who know' (the wise). Every book written on two or more levels – every exoteric book – contains, as it were, two teachings: 'a popular teaching of an edifying character, which is in the foreground; and a philosophic teaching concerning the most important subject, which is indicated only between the lines' (36).

Not surprisingly, Strauss's views have been resisted because they seem undemocratic. Who is to determine inclusion among the few wise individuals who 'know,' and on what basis will the 'many' be excluded? The case is somewhat different with Cervantes, where the need for an exoteric text responds to the well-established circumstance of a *converso* with Erasmian-humanist leanings. The conditions of social and political constraint under which Cervantes wrote can be located historically, and not merely in the abstract. About a hundred years earlier, under conditions of perhaps even greater political constraint, Fernando de Rojas wrote a supremely exoteric text, *La Celestina*. In the anagrammatic verses that preface *La Celestina* the author discloses his identity to the few, while the subsequent 'Síguese' suggests that the book offers a conventional moral lesson intended for the many. That conventional lesson is offered under the guise of 'exemplary' literature (where the text serves as a cautionary example advising masters to be wary of servants and warning headstrong lovers of the perils they may face). It also speaks with the authority of Petrarch's *De Remediis* on the subject of fortune. But its meaning for the few has everything to do with its author's *converso* background and, quite possibly as well, with his training in the lawyer's arts.[10] So too, in order to speak the truth under the particular conditions of constraint in early seventeenth-century Spain Cervantes had to be explicit about some things – the parody of the romances of chivalry, for instance – and evasive and indirect about others. This was only one of the ways he found it possible to release the power of literature as a form of political critique in an inhospitable political environment.

In speaking the truth through a form of discourse whose meaning had to be read 'between the lines,' Cervantes followed the example of his humanist predecessors, Erasmus foremost among them.[11] In *De Copia*, for instance, Erasmus takes due note of Socrates' suggestion that the ability to lie and the ability to tell the truth cleverly are kindred talents.[12] I will have considerably more to say about this below. But there is a longer lineage to these efforts that reaches back to humanist engagements with the Platonic dialogues and with the rhetorical tradition that they in turn engage. In Plato's dialogues, we can never be fully certain whether Socrates is speaking seriously or ironically, nor can we be sure whether he serves as Plato's mouthpiece or as a foil. This discourse is profoundly indirect.[13] At one point in the *Gorgias*, Callicles asks, point blank, 'Tell me, Socrates, are we to suppose that you are joking or in earnest? If you are serious and what you say is true, we shall have human life turned completely upside down.'[14] The Platonic dialogues are indirect in many ways. The inaudible Plato and the audible Socrates continuously refract the views of Socrates the philosopher who wrote nothing, and of a Plato who spoke only through various mouthpieces, including Socrates, the Eleatic Stranger, and their interlocutors. In Book VI of the *Republic* Adeimantus objects that Socrates leads his interlocutors astray until they contradict themselves.[15] We know from Alcibiades in the *Symposium* that Socrates was himself sometimes compared to the contradictory Sileni, figures that appeared to be ugly on the outside but beautiful within. The image was popular among humanists. As Bakhtin points out, it was central to the Prologue of Rabelais's

Gargantua; it was also cited by Erasmus in no fewer than three different works, including *The Sileni of Alcibiades*.[16]

As has long been known, Cervantes' discourse was heavily indebted to Erasmian and humanist models in which the voice of truth was often given to the least plausible of figures – to 'Folly,' for example – or was located in impossible places, such as 'utopia.'[17] Given the overbearing orthodoxies in place in Cervantes' Spain, these were among the necessary means for the articulation of the truth, not optional fictional embellishments of it. Why the fool? Cervantes had the experience of living in a world where many things boldly asserted as true were plainly false; for example: the 'truth' that so many Spaniards were of pure, old Christian blood; or, as Quevedo argued in *La España defendida* of 1609, that Spanish was the most ancient of all the modern tongues because it had its roots in Hebrew; or, as some of the ballads told, that the inhabitants of pre-Muslim Spain were the descendants of the Goths. (A mere four years after the publication of *Don Quijote*, Part II, Fray Benito de Peñalosa y Mondragón proposed that he could trace the myth of pure blood through a tribal bloodline to a Teutonic or Gothic ancestor named Tubal from the twenty-second century before Christ.)[18] This was a culture in which the discourse of the truth had been severely distorted by political attempts, at both official and popular levels, to establish it on solid ground by constructing cultural pedigrees out of fantastical ideas. Consequently, any effort to speak the truth – the true truths, the ones being concealed or falsified, not the ones proffered as valid to the many – imposed a need to speak in a way contrary to the official truth, hence to speak as if uttering foolishness and falsehoods, or by disavowing the source and authority of one's own words.

The response to external constraint in the *Quijote* is this complex and more so. It involves various strategies of what can broadly be called 'indirect discourse.' (Its links to the multivoicedness that Bakhtin associated with menippean satire will be taken up below.) We need to think of 'indirect discourse' in the *Quijote* first of all in relation to the deflected truth-claims associated with the shifting narrator, the multiplication of authorial stances, and the sidestepping of authorial views. These deflections all contribute to the scepticism that Michael McKeon has related to the novel's generic critique of romance idealism.[19] But to say that the object of Cervantes' critique is 'romance idealism' is to miss the larger political point: that these deflections of authority allow Cervantes the opportunity to speak truly without speaking directly. The figure of Cide Hamete Benengeli – the mendacious Arabic chronicler whose historical text is allegedly the source of everything that we read in the novel, and self-consciously so beginning with the interruption between chapters 8 and 9 of Part I – is one of the keys to this enterprise. Indeed, the figure of the mendacious historian-narrator is of a piece with a much wider set of discursive strategies in the novel and comes to serve as emblematic of the fact that virtually everything said in the *Quijote* can be cast under the sign of 'indirect discourse.' But indirection begins textually well before the introduction of the fictitious author device in chapter 9, with the very Prologue to Part I, where the 'author' describes the difficulty of writing a prologue, and introduces the fiction of an authorial double, who poses as a 'friend' and advises the primary author about how best to proceed in overcoming his writer's block. The 'friend's' advice has to do with the need to deflect the authority of a tradition that would constrain anyone who might aspire to write a contemporary text of importance.[20] Subsequently, Cide Hamete is one of many subnarrators; they are less creatures of an authorial voice than mechanisms for refracting that voice, for maintaining its authority at a distance. Fiction itself is an activity that remains free to the degree that it can acknowledge conditions of constraint while resisting efforts to elicit speech in a forcible way. Indeed, the *Quijote* is filled with characters who speak all too freely – or at any rate at great length – and with relatively little prompting, about all manner of things. In contrast to what has sometimes been characterized in other novelists as the problem of 'speech-forcing,' with all the Oedipal overtones that such a notion suggests,[21] and likewise in contrast to the role that Socrates plays as a speech-forcer in some of Plato's dialogues, Cervantes' characters run the risk of drowning in the sea of words that they seem to produce quite freely.

This risk would be fatal were it not for the fact that nearly everything introduced in Cervantes' text is there by virtue of indirection, or serves to place some other element of the text at an oblique angle vis-à-vis all of its other components. Some 'other' voice invariably intervenes to interrupt or divert attention, as when Don Quijote interrupts Sancho as he tells of the goats crossing the river in the story of Lope Ruiz and Torralba. Consider the many internal frames that deflect and direct what is said in other instances: Cardenio is known by his notebooks before he is ever encountered; Grisótomo is present solely in his written legacy – the 'Song of Despair' – as well as in what the characters Marcela, Ambrosio, and Vivaldo say about him, but never directly, since he is dead. What still cannot be said directly, by anyone, is that Grisóstomo took his own life; Cervantes buries the detail in the verses of his *canción*, thinking, perhaps, that the official censors would not bother to look for anything so dangerous there. Each of the pairs of crossed lovers in Part I is likewise presented obliquely before any of them gets to say anything. With Ginés de Pasamonte, later to be Maese Pedro the puppeteer, the directness of the autobiography he claims to be writing is undercut by the discursive frames that precede it – by the *Lazarillo de Tormes* in particular. Many characters, including Don Quijote himself, lapse into forms of speech that echo and allude to ballad verses, which are not their 'own,' and which are consistently offset at some slight angle of difference from the rest of the text. Don Quijote frequently falls into patterns of discourse that sound as if they are drawn directly from chivalric romances, or from pastoral novels, or steeped in Ovid, or imbued with the rhetoric of Renaissance humanist *controversia* as described above. The Captive's story contains a well-known reference to 'a certain Saavedra' that functions as an obviously indirect reference to Cervantes; but even the biographical allusiveness of this 'open secret' is deflected through the genre of literary romance (one is tempted to say *re*-deflected, because it is not in the end clear which is deflecting which, biography or romance). Following the descent into the Cave of Montesinos, the narrator remarks, with deadpan humour, that the story of Don Quijote's adventure in the cave may well have been apocryphal. Such examples could be multiplied at great length.

As for Cide Hamete, it might be better to say that this figure is a crystallization of the indirectness that lies at the novel's core, not an idiosyncratic feature or literary 'device' as has sometimes been claimed. He is not just a way for Cervantes to engage questions about historical accuracy and fictionalized histories, or to parody the ill-repute of Muslim historiographers among Christian authors during the Spanish Golden Age, but is a mechanism that allows the truth to be spoken by deflecting the directness of discourse. What is at stake in this figure as in all the many instances of indirect discourse in the *Quijote*, philosophically and otherwise, is not so much the inability to get close enough to the truth so as to arrive at certainty, or to find sufficiently accurate or authoritative sources, but the reverse, i.e., the purposeful and artful introduction of factors that obstruct any co-opting by official versions of the truth. This is not uncertainty as a deficiency, but uncertainty as a purposeful strategy.

For this reason, Cervantes' indirect discourse bears comparison with that of Descartes, whose pursuit of epistemological certainty has frequently been linked to the principle that philosophical writing must be clear, complete, and direct. This assertion of directness turns out to be part of a philosophical ideology as much as anything else. A principal component of that ideology is contained in the fiction that the two central Cartesian texts – the *Meditations* and the *Discourse on Method* – derive their authority entirely from what they themselves say, just as the *cogito* derives its authority directly from the thinking subject.[22] Nonetheless, Descartes takes care for obvious political reasons to solicit the good will of the doctors of theology of the Sorbonne as he issues the *Meditations*. And in reflections later collected under the informal title 'Cogitationes Privatae' he declares that his philosophical presence in the world is mediated and masked: 'larvatus prodeo' (I go forth concealed). Descartes claims to know the truth but recognizes that the bearer of the truth must be concealed until such time when it may be safe for it to be brought to light.[23]

Cervantes is aware that every approach to the truth must be indirect because there is no truth-centre to be attained. This is perhaps inevitable for the author of a work that incorporates lyric poetry, dialogue, epistles, novellas, political advice, proverbs, ballads, theoretical discussions of literature, and so much more. His predecessors in this enterprise are those writers who roundly embrace the indirectness of their own discourse. The multivoicedness that Bakhtin identified as a generic hallmark of the novel is part and parcel of the indirect discourse that runs throughout the *Quijote*. (Quite independent of Bakhtin, Paul Hazard wrote presciently that reading *Don Quijote* gives the reader 'the impression of listening to several voices in one and the same passage.')[24] Not surprisingly given Bakhtin's arguments about the relationship between menippean satire and the ancient dialogue tradition, first and foremost among Cervantes' predecessors in writing such a text was Plato, whose own philosophical activity was conducted through the mediation of alternating voices. (Socrates, for his part, judges multiple voicings in relation to narrative and dramatic representations, and specifically on the basis of whether the character 'imitated' is worthy or not.)[25] Among Cervantes' more proximate antecedents are Erasmus and More, both of whom adopt various forms of indirect discourse as counter-hegemonic forces that can provide a way of speaking the truth in the face of some potentially powerful political distortions of it.

In Plato, indirect discourse encompasses the dialogue form itself as well as the mediating interventions of a principal interlocutor whose stance is famously difficult to determine. Plato's indirect discourse also involves the use of image and myth. But since the question of literature's role in the state is raised explicitly in the *Republic*, an entirely reasonable question to ask is why Plato himself would choose to speak in the discourse of image and myth, rather than 'directly,' about matters of the highest philosophical importance. The Allegory of the Cave, in which the prisoners do not see the light itself but instead see only flickers of flames and shadows on the wall, says something about this. Remember that the philosopher brings the prisoners out into the light of day where they can see things directly, but then returns them to the cave. The question is: why must they be returned? In Plato's view, ordinary mortals are not able to gaze upon the ideal forms directly; only gods can do that. Mortals would in fact be blinded by the sun that illuminates the forms, says Plato, and so they must perceive the forms through their images. As noted in various places above in relation to the *Sophist*, the challenge within the image-world is to distinguish true images from false ones. In Plato's terms – as, for instance, in the discussion of images in *Republic*, 510–11 – this means discerning the difference between imagistic distortions and those images that offer accurate resemblances of the originals by preserving their just proportions.

The import of 'literature' in relation to these questions carries with it the special problem of fictionality. But sometimes the more preposterous the fiction the better, notwithstanding neo-Aristotelian concerns about ways to make marvellous things seem legitimate. Consider the example of Cervantes' talking dogs ('El coloquio de los perros'). This canine dialogue is presented as the dream-vision of a character whose own deceits have landed him in the hospital with syphilis. But within the dream-dialogue the dogs seem to say some very wise and truthful things. Of these some must be taken at face value and others in exactly the opposite sense. One brief example may suffice. Where Cipión and Berganza discuss education they come to praise the many virtues of the Jesuits, including their humility: CIPIÓN: 'They say that if Jesuits ran the world, we'd be a lot better off. For spiritual guidance, hardly anyone can touch them. They're like mirrors that reflect purity, piety, great sagacity and, finally, profound humility – the keystone of all happiness.' BERGANZA: 'Amen to that.' (CIPIÓN: yo he oído decir desa bendita gente que para repúblicos del mundo no los hay tan prudentes en todo él, y para guiadores y adalides del camino del cielo, pocos les llegan. Son espejos donde se mira la honestidad, la católica dotrina, la singular prudencia, y, finalmente, la humildad profunda, basa sobre quien se levanta todo el edificio de la bienaventuranza. BERGANZA: Todo es así como lo dices.)[26] But the cautious reader will recognize that the Jesuits were known for their boldness and that the humility is the very same 'virtue' that the dogs have used to ingratiate themselves with their masters.[27]

The need to detect the presence of many voices in one voice was a requirement for understanding the thrust of texts that were constrained in what they could say directly not so much for reasons of decorum but for reasons of political prudence, i.e., because of the need to veil their critical thrust. One of Cervantes' most important predecessor texts, the *Lazarillo de Tormes*, epitomizes just this strategy, and for just these reasons, in a deftly crafted, double-voiced prologue. The prologue takes the form of a letter directed to a recipient known only as 'Vuesa Merced' (Your Grace). The prologue-letter is a response to a request for information made by 'Your Grace' about what is simply referred to as the *caso* (the 'matter,' 'case,' or 'incident'). We know nothing about what this 'matter' is until the very end of the book, where we learn that it involves the *ménage à trois* in which Lazarillo accepts the role of the cuckolded husband whose wife sleeps with the *arcipreste*. In responding to the request from 'Your Grace' about the situation, Lazarillo replies with a scathingly critical tale about the tactics necessary for survival and success in a corrupt society. 'Your Grace' has asked for an explanation of the 'matter,' and Lazarillo responds by trumpeting the scandalous news as if it were a new discovery or a military triumph: 'I believe it fitting that such extraordinary things as these, which may never have been heard of or seen before, should come to the attention of many people, instead of being buried in the grave of oblivion.'[28] He tells not just the details of the *caso* itself, but the whole extended truth about a world of fakery and corruption: 'Since you told me that you wanted me to write down all the details of the case, I have decided not to start out in the middle but at the beginning. That way you will have a complete picture of me, and at the same time those people who received a large inheritance will see just how little they had to do with it, since fortune was favourable to them, and they will also see how much more those people accomplished whose luck was against them, since they rowed hard and well and brought their ship safely into port.'[29]

To return to Cervantes, the passage from the Prologue to Part I cited at the outset of this chapter – with its references to the book's sad origins in jail – is on one level crucial to his acknowledgment of the limiting conditions that bear upon his writing. But on another level it is completely ironic. In saying that the book is the product of his 'barren and poorly cultivated mind' (estéril y mal cultivado ingenio) Cervantes avails himself of the familiar topos of *humilitas* as a way to signal the very fruitful and productive character of the book he has written.[30] The alternation between two hyperbolic stances – between a posture of exaggerated modesty about the limitations of an unproductive mind and the constraints of having to work in jail, and a rhetoric of inflated and verbose self-confidence – is a hallmark of Cervantes' writing. Consider the pride that brims over in many of the speeches considered in the chapters above, where Don Quijote 'holds forth' at great length on a topic like the Golden Age or the relative merits of arms and letters, or the bravado that characterizes the Prologue to the *Exemplary Novels*, where he speaks of himself in the third person as the hero 'who lost his left hand in the battle of Lepanto from a harquebuz shot, a wound which might seem ugly but which he holds beautiful for having earned it on the most memorable occasion that the past centuries have seen, or that coming ones might hope to witness, while fighting under the flag of the son of the lightning rod of war himself, Charles V, of happy memory' (perdió en la batalla naval de Lepanto la mano izquierda de un arcabuzazo, herida que, aunque parece fea, él la tiene por hermosa, por haberla cobrado en la más memorable y alta ocasión que vieron los pasados siglos, ni esperan ver los venideros, militando debajo de las vencedoras banderas del hijo del rayo de la guerra, Carlos Quinto, de felice memoria.) [31] Some of this is doubtless a reflection of Cervantes' own 'spiritedness' when it comes to the glories and misfortunes of his youthful military career. As I will discuss below, some of this is also sheer showmanship, a virtuosic demonstration of the writer's ability to speak with freedom and confidence, not to mention sensibly, about a great variety of topics. It is a reflection of the rhetorical virtue associated with copious discourse. But as I will also discuss, *copia* involves equal measures of freedom and restraint. It must reconcile *abbreviatio* and *amplificatio*. Indeed, these two opposing concerns are continuously at work in Cervantes: concerns over discursive constraint are counterbalanced by the force of a discourse that is astoundingly varied, productive, and fertile; but by the same token 'copious' language can only be effective if it is restrained.

Copia

To be able to speak freely and well was a rhetorical ideal with a pedigree reaching back at least to Erasmus and before him to Quintilian and ultimately to Socrates and the sophists.[32] As Terence Cave pointed out, the phrase *copia dicendi* suggests 'a rich, many faceted discourse springing from a fertile mind and powerfully affecting its recipient … it transcends specific techniques and materials, pointing towards an ideal of "articulate energy," of speech in action.'[33] It is a disciplined form of *facundia*. Fernando de Herrera interprets it in just this context at the beginning of his crucial *Anotaciones* to the poetry of Garcilaso.[34] In Erasmus's letter of dedication to Colet, he claims to be the first to treat of this subject,[35] but we know (as he does) this is not the case; indeed in *De Copia* itself (I, ch. 2) Erasmus acknowledges important forebears, including Quintilian and the sophists. Moreover, the play between fullness and brevity is itself woven into Erasmus's writing on this subject with considerable irony and verbal agility.

He speaks, for instance, of 'that Aesopic fable about the fox and the crow which Apuleius *narrates briefly* with a wonderful economy of words, *and also amplifies as fully as possible with a great many words*, doubtless to exercise and show his genius' (12, emphasis added). Surprisingly, *copia* may in the end serve the ends of concision: 'who could speak more tersely than he who has ready at hand an extensive array of words and figures from which he can immediately select what is most suitable for conciseness?' (15). Even at the beginning of *De Copia* there is a tension between the virtues of productive discourse and its dangers. The brief treatise provides ample instruction on the various methods and mechanisms for *copia*, but commences with a warning against 'futile and amorphous loquacity … thoughts and words thrown together without discrimination' which 'obscure the subject and burden the ears of their wretched hearers' (11). The overriding precepts are themselves expressed in a tightly formed paradox: 'that you may be able in the fewest possible words so to comprehend the essence of a matter that nothing is lacking; that you may be able to amplify by *copia* in such a way that there is nonetheless no redundancy; and, the principle learned, that you may be free either to emulate laconism, if you wish, or to copy Asian exuberance, or to exhibit Rhodian moderation' (15). Moreover, Erasmus well knows, as does Cervantes, that claims to brevity can themselves be productive.[36] The story of the writer's impasse recounted in the Prologue to *Don Quijote*, Part I, for instance, proves to generate its own solution.

The difference between abundance and *brevitas* is sometimes figured as the difference in rhetoric between Cicero and Demosthenes. While Cicero was clearly the more prominent figure to contend with because he was the principal source of the Renaissance creation of a philosophically informed political rhetoric, *Don Quijote* invokes both orators in a nearly formulaic fashion while at the ducal palace – 'que fueron [Cicerón y Demóstenes] los dos mayores retóricos del mundo' (II, 32, p. 289). The Duchess, to whom he is speaking, has not heard of Demosthenes, but her husband clearly has.[37] Indeed, ever since Plutarch's *Lives*, Cicero's oratorical fertility was contrasted with Demosthenes' spare and direct style. In Plutarch's view, Demosthenes wrote 'without all embellishment and jesting, wholly composed for real effect and seriousness; not smelling of the lamp, as Pytheas scoffingly said, but of the temperance, thoughtfulness, austerity, and grave earnestness of his temper.' He places Cicero at the other end of the spectrum; Cicero is not merely prolix but exhibits a love of mockery and of laughter that was so appealing to humanists.[38] Erasmus no doubt inherited this juxtaposition from Plutarch; Cervantes may in turn have inherited these views from Erasmus, if not from Plutarch directly.

The frequent banter between Don Quijote and Sancho about the length and appropriateness and correctness of whatever is said is hardly limited to the *Quijote*. There is similar banter between Cipión and Berganza in 'The Dialogue of the Dogs.' And the issue of lengthy discourse is likewise prominent in the *Persiles*, where Periandro's exceedingly long speech told in segments succeeds principally in boring some of his listeners. (In *Persiles*, II, 21, Mauricio expresses a sense of relief when it is finished.)[39] It is essential to narrative of all kinds that the storyteller be able to carry on with the tale, i.e., to find the means of connecting the elements of a plot as well elaborating upon its central idea. But for how long, and how long is too long? When Sancho tells the story of Lope Ruiz and Torralba, those questions are pressed to the limit. Sancho begins the story with a series of circumlocutions and redundancies to which Don Quijote rapidly objects. Sancho's continuation of the story is scarcely an improvement, and so Don Quijote again interrupts to urge brevity and directness: 'Somewhere in Extremadura there was a goatherd, I mean to say a man who tended goats, and this goatherd I am telling you about in my story was named Lope Ruiz, and this Lope Ruiz was in love with a shepherdess named Torralba, and this shepherdess named Torralba was the daughter of a rich herder, and this rich herder.' 'If you tell your story this way, Sancho,' says Don Quijote, 'repeating everything you say two times, you will not finish in two days' (145) (En un lugar de Estremadura había un pastor cabrerizo (quiero decir que guardaba cabras), el cual pastor o cabrerizo, como digo, de mi cuento, se llamaba Lope Ruiz; y este Lope Ruiz andaba enamorado de una pastora que se llamaba Torralba, la cual pastora llamada Torralba era hija de un ganadero rico, y este ganadero rico; I, 20, p. 242). Then, in the interest of giving a complete and truthful account of what happened as the goatherd tried to ferry his flock across the river, Sancho presses the tolerance of his listener to the limit, enumerating the passage of each and every one of the goats, and of course the return trip of the little boat as well. The story that begins as a trifle, that Sancho hopes will not get out of control ('si no me va de la mano') rapidly runs to excess. When Don Quijote subsequently praises Sancho for having invented something absolutely new in the genre of fables, we have to recognize that Cervantes is being completely ironic. In fact, the story that never seems to end was a commonplace in the Middle Ages, and especially in the oral tradition that a character like Sancho might well have known.[40]

But there is more to say, especially on the subject of Don Quijote's insistence on a kind of brevity he himself never practises. When Sancho wants to speak his mind about the outcomes of their adventures, his salary, or his promised island, Don Quijote chastises him for speaking so much, not least because such a prolix squire is unknown in the books he has read: 'Be advised of one thing: from now on you are to refrain and abstain from speaking too much to me, for in all the books of chivalry I have read, which are infinite in number, I have never found any squire who talks as much with his master as you do with yours' (151) (Está advertido de aquí adelante en una cosa, para que te abstengas y reportes en el hablar demasiado conmigo; que en cuantos libros de caballerías he leído, que son infinitos, jamás he hallado que ningún escudero hablase tanto con su señor como tú con el tuyo; I, 20, p. 250). Thus when Sancho finally asks permission to say what is on his mind, Don Quijote obliges only on condition that he be brief: 'Señor, does your grace wish to give me leave to talk a little? After you gave me that harsh order of silence, more than a few things have been spoiling in my stomach, and one that I have now on the tip of my tongue I wouldn't want to go to waste.' 'Say it,' said Don Quijote, 'and be brief, for no speech is pleasing if it is too long' (157) ('Señor, ¿quiere vuestra merced darme licencia que departa un poco con él? Que, después que me puso aquel áspero mandamiento del silencio, se me han podrido más de cuatro cosas en el estómago, y una sola que ahora tengo en el pico de la lengua no querría que se mal lograse.' 'Dila,' dijo don Quijote, 'y sé breve en tus razonamientos, que ninguno hay gustoso si es largo'; I, 21, p. 258). With redoubled irony, Don Quijote then proceeds to expound at very great length on all sorts of things relating to knight-errantry.

Don Quijote is nonetheless not the only one to insist on brevity. Cervantes' narrators often apologize for being prolix; conversely, they complement each other for telling a tale concisely.[41] The narrator of the episode of Maese Pedro notes that 'going on can engender boredom' (la prolijidad suele engendrar el fastidio; II, 26, p. 243); yet we know full well that Don Quijote has a tendency to speak at length. The discourse on Arms and Letters in I, 38, is characterized as a 'lengthy preamble' (largo preámbulo) and the speech on the Golden Age as a 'lengthy harangue, which could very easily have been omitted' (77) (larga arenga – que se pudiera muy bien escusar; I, 11, p. 157). Sancho eventually acquires some of the discursive habits of his master; his explanation of why he decides to leave Barataria counts as a 'long discourse' (larga plática; II, 55, p. 461). The Canon's critique of the romances of chivalry contains what is arguably a reference to the rhetorical flaws of prose that fails to adhere to the aims of *copia*: 'I have never been able to read one from beginning to end because it seems to me they are essentially all the same, and one is no different from another' (411) (Jamás me he podido acomodar a leer ninguno del principio al cabo, porque me parece que, cuál más, cuál menos, todos ellos son una mesma cosa, y no tiene más éste que aquél, ni estotro que el otro; I, 47, p. 564).

These are no doubt exaggerated versions of what *copia* was meant to achieve. For *copia* was never conceived along purely quantitative lines, and certainly not as an accumulative process, but as a strategy for effective discourse in which freedom and restraint, expansiveness and concision, could be combined. It was not so much a way of generating infinite quantities of discourse, or of creating speeches out of nothing, as a way of exploring the potential nuances contained in any given idea. *Copia* could be relatively free and generative because it was rooted in a rhetoric where *verba* and *res* were not inherently bound together; it could thus avail itself of fictional licence. To read through Erasmus's text is to take a tour of the possible uses of fabulous examples ('De exemplo fabuloso'), as well as parables ('De parabola'), arguments ('De apologia'), dreams ('De somnio'), and made-up stories ('De fictis narrationibus'). All these allow a much greater freedom of *verba* from *res* than more literal-minded thinkers or strict moralists might be willing to accept. As Cave duly noted, 'the licence which Erasmus had given himself (for the sake of teaching and for the sake of youth) releases *res* from the constraints of a predetermined *sententia* so that they may flow with the devious, Protean current of *verba*' (*Cornucopian Text*, 33–4). Indeed, the seemingly infinite range and the very copiousness of rhetoric often seemed to smack of something immoral. Proteus and his tribe – Maese Pedro would certainly be a member of it – are crucial to its workings, and stand for a wide-ranging generativity, not easily limited by pedagogical or moral interests. (On some still stronger views, it is proliferation itself that is associated with evil.)[42] Socrates voices worries about the proliferative powers of the sophist and the poet in, among other places, Book III of the *Republic*. Socrates concludes, 'If we are visited by someone who has the skill to transform himself into all sorts of characters and represent all sorts of things, and he wants to show off himself and his poems to us, we shall treat him with all the reverence due to a priest and giver of rare pleasure, but shall tell him that he and his kind have no place in our city, their presence being forbidden by our code, and send him elsewhere' (398a–b). The concern was that without wisdom, or the regulation provided by reason, no degree of eloquence could have a place in the well-ordered state.[43] For some Renaissance thinkers, including the Spanish humanist Benito Arias Montano, the sophists were aligned with the 'barbarians.'[44]

As these passages may help make clear, the lingering question was not whether each of the fictive or figurative uses of *verba* was true in any literal way, but whether or not they could advance the aims of effective discourse. If productive speech is of concern politically it is because it echoes Plato's worries about the proliferation of forms of discourse that were untethered to the 'truth,' as was allegedly the case among the sophists. Similarly, it was of concern insofar as poetry was thought to multiply 'copies' of things without adherence to their originals. Sophistry and poetry are both for Socrates too close to the productivity of the craftsman who could seemingly make a world by simply holding up a mirror and turning it around: 'This same craftsman can not only make all artificial objects, but also create all plants and animals, himself included, and, in addition, earth and sky and gods, the heavenly bodies and everything in the underworld ... The quickest way is to take a mirror and turn it round in all directions; before long you will create sun and stars and earth, yourself, and all other animals and plants, furniture and the other objects we mentioned just now' (*Republic*, 598c). For Socrates, this issue is of paramount concern for the regulation of the state insofar as the proliferation of entities through language was thought to undermine those who 'know' the way things really are and who claim to rule on the basis of what they know. In Cervantes, of course, the question is how to rule when there are competing claims about the way things are, many of them generated through words and discourse, and none grounded in a possible appeal to the 'ideas.' If the *Quijote* is indeed in a deep dialogue with the *Republic*, this is one of the crucial places where they diverge; Cervantes wishes to avail himself of all the resources of *copious* discourse.

This divergence can be linked to the division between *verba* and *res* that separates the two parts of *De Copia*.[45] While Erasmus clearly intends *res* to mean something like 'thought' or 'idea,' it also means 'thing' in a way that was never fully subsumed under the notion of 'subject' or 'matter' in an ideational sense. As Cave pointed out, the shift from object (object-thing) to word (word-thing) is a form of catachresis, i.e., the 'improper' use of a term, usually where the 'proper' one is lacking.[46] Moreover, questions of *verba* are never simply about words. In short, *copia* raises worries about the proliferation of things as much as about the proliferation of words. It is in Book II of *De Copia* where Erasmus opens up the vast domain of *res*. In it there are fabulous descriptions, some of which allude to true things and others not. Linguistic satisfaction is attained when *verba*, coalescing into *res*, points toward a *sententia* (idea); at the same time, as Erasmus's treatise *De Ratione Studii* reveals, 'things' can only become apparent by virtue of language itself.[47]

These issues bear on the *Quijote*, and ultimately on the question of politics, in two significant ways. First, there is the imaginary generation and transformation of things, as Don Quijote transforms the things of the 'real' world into their fantastic equivalents, and then transforms them back via the fiction of the 'evil enchanters.' Second, there is the question of linguistic convention, which is sometimes invoked as a way to settle the divergences created by the proliferation of entities within language. Bakhtin characterized the first of these under the sign of 'regeneration.' It is manifested in the windmills that become giants, the inns that become castles, flocks of rams and sheep that become armies of knights, innkeepers that become lords of the castle, prostitutes that become noble ladies, and so forth. 'All these images form a typical grotesque carnival,' he writes, 'which turns a kitchen and banquet into a battle, kitchen utensils and shaving bowls into arms and helmets, and wine into blood. Such is the first, carnival aspect of the material bodily images of *Don Quijote*.'[48]

But the principles of internal constraint dictate that the 'carnival' in which words and things are free to generate and regenerate could not escape the pressures that are designed to constrain it. (Indeed, it is not unreasonable to conclude that 'carnival' is dependent on the rule of order and the laws of constraint.) Discourse is internally limited by ideas about decorum and plausibility inherited from all manner of sources, including the handbooks for courtiers, manuals for princes, and compendia of maxims about how best to succeed in the public world. These were relatively more benign forms of limitation than the censorship that Plato imagined in the *Republic*. The proposal that an official censor ought to be appointed to decide which books can be admitted into the state[49] is echoed directly in the discussions between the Canon of Toledo and the Curate about the books of chivalry and the *comedia* in I, 48.

> Other poets compose their works so carelessly that after they have been performed, the actors have to flee and go into hiding, fearful that they will be punished, as they often have been, for putting on pieces prejudicial to certain kings and offensive to certain families. All these difficulties, and many others I will not mention, would cease *if there were at court an intelligent and judicious person who would examine each play before it was performed, not only those produced in the capital, but also those put on anywhere in Spain, and without his approval, stamp, and signature, no magistrate anywhere would permit a play to be performed.* (418; emphasis added)

> Otros las componen tan sin mirar lo que hacen que después de representadas tienen necesidad los recitantes de huirse y ausentarse, temerosos de ser castigados, como lo han sido muchas veces, por haber representado cosas en

prejuicio de algunos reyes y en deshonra de algunos linajes. Y todos estos in-
convinientes cesarían, y aun otros muchos más que no digo, con *que hubiese*
en la Corte una persona inteligente y discreta que examinase todas las comedias
antes que se representasen (no sólo aquellas que se hiciesen en la Corte, sino
todas las que se quisiesen representar en España), *sin la cual aprobación, sello*
y firma, ninguna justicia en su lugar dejase representar comedia alguna; y, desta
manera, los comediantes tendrían cuidado de enviar las comedias a la Corte, y
con seguridad podrían representallas. (I, 48, p. 572; emphasis added)

The passage is hardly covert in its echo of Plato's censorship of tragedies
in the *Republic* on the grounds that they present the gods in an unfavour-
able light. Plato's idea of a state censor may well be ironic in a philosophical way, but Cervantes' irony makes allusion, in the manner of an all but
fully open secret, to the very conditions of censorship that were imposed
on literature in Spain and elsewhere in Europe through the *Index* and other state institutions. These are political concerns that travel under the veil
of questions about aesthetics.

As language proliferates entities, there is a corresponding demand for some
kind of regulation. Consider the matter of the *baciyelmo*, which occurs just
after the exchanges between Don Quijote and Sancho cited above about
completeness and brevity surrounding the story of Lope Ruiz and Torralba.
The episode of the *baciyelmo* creates something seemingly new, although in
fact it is a hybrid of two identifications of and names for the same object.
The initial question is whether the object in question is a shaving basin or a
helmet. One ought to be able to tell, and in fact there are experts among
those present who are called upon to offer their opinions. But the question
is equally a matter of discourse, i.e., of the way things are named; given the
divergence of opinions and names, the real task at hand is to converge upon
some way to limit the free-play by which a thing could be called either a
bacía or a *yelmo*. Appeals to the notions of 'point of view' and 'perspective'
in relation to this episode obscure the underlying issues of *verba* in relation
to *res*.[50] The neologism *baciyelmo* represents a contractual linguistic solution, an agreement made at the level of language in order to address the worrisome fact that language might itself generate very different versions of *res*.
   Beginning with Hobbes, conventions of naming and of rational agreements came to form a central part of political thought. Indeed, even when
Hobbes objects to Descartes's definition of 'reason' in favour of something far more corporeal, he found himself obliged to repeat and agree
with conventionalist arguments:

What shall we now say, if it turns out that reasoning is simply the joining together and linking of names or labels by the verb 'is'? It would follow that the inferences of our reasoning tell us nothing at all about the nature of things, but merely tell us about the labels applied to them; that is, all we can infer is whether or not we are combining the names of things in accordance with the arbitrary conventions which we have laid down in respect of their meaning. If this is so, as may well be the case, reasoning will depend on names, names will depend on the imagination, and imagination will depend (as I believe it does) on the motions of our bodily organs; and so the mind will be nothing more than motion occurring in various parts of an organic body.[51]

But there is something else to contend with as names coalesce and stabilize, something that Bakhtin describes as what happens when 'bodies and objects begin to acquire a private individual nature,' when they are 'rendered petty and homely and become parts of private life, the goal of egoistic lust and possession.' As he goes on to suggest, 'This is no longer the positive, regenerating and renewing lower stratums, but a blunt and deadly obstacle to ideal aspirations.'[52] When Bakhtin suggests that bodies and objects emerge from the freedoms of the carnival world to acquire a 'private individual nature,' we can infer that they are designated by a nomenclature that is (or imagines itself to be) not just valid in a special public domain, but stable, stabilizing, and general in a way that helps lend permanence to that domain. Not surprisingly, things seem real to individuals who are able to speak to and deal with them in the context of general public agreement about their names.

But the appeal to contractual language in reference to the episode of the *baciyelmo* is in historical terms precocious and anticipatory, to say the least. Indeed, there is little reason to believe that any sense of contract, beyond convention, was part of Cervantes' response to the possible proliferation of things out of words. That said, there *is* a clear commitment to the role of mutually supporting beliefs in relation to experiences that cannot finally be ascertained as 'true'; such is clearly the case in Part II when Don Quijote and Sancho make a compact to believe each other about what happened in the Cave of Montesinos and during the flight on Clavileño.

The restrictions on speech that originate in Plato's discussion of the proliferation of entities that falsify their relationship to originals is one of the often overlooked sources behind Renaissance concern over verisimilitude. Cervantes' preoccupation with the 'legitimate marvellous' can be traced to this same underlying tradition. Among the most important links in this chain is Tasso's *Discorsi del Poema Eroico*, which in turn cites Mazzoni's *Difesa di Dante* on the two types of imitation proposed in Plato's *Sophist*, the 'icastic' and 'phantastic.' The problem of concern to Tasso is that Mazzoni follows Plato in associating the poet with the sophist, i.e., the one who multiplies false images and non-existent entities: '[Mazzoni] calls the kind that imitates things present here or past icastic and the kind that imitates non-existent things phantastic. And this latter he chooses to call perfect poetry, which he places under the sophistic faculty, whose subject is the false and the non-existent.'[53] This is unacceptable to Tasso, as no doubt it was to Cervantes. Tasso's aim, in fact, was to make sure that the poet is held apart from the sophist. He does so by two means. One involves the incorporation of the poet into the category of truth-tellers who have insights into causes beyond the natural world. Here, Tasso's point is that actions regarded as marvellous and implausible in themselves may be legitimate sources of truth if we look beyond their causes; we must, for example, recognize that human beings have from time immemorial accepted the fact that 'God and his ministers, and by his permission demons and magicians' have performed acts not possible for human beings.[54] Poets, he says, may operate in the same fashion. Consequently, 'one same action can then be both marvelous and verisimilar: marvelous when regarded in itself and confined within natural limits, verisimilar when considered apart from these limits in terms of its cause, which is a powerful supernatural force accustomed to performing such marvels.'[55] Even in Plato there are clear examples of impossibilities that are unobjectionable because they are drawn into the dialogues from the store of myths to serve as sources of philosophical arguments and as elements in dialectical 'proofs.' Consider the myth of the cicadas or the story of the fantastical Ring of Gyges, which could make its bearer invisible to those around him. Plato uses it as the basis of a dialectical experiment, as Socrates asks his interlocutors to imagine what might happen if one such ring were given to a moral person and another to an immoral one (*Republic*, 359–60).

The other line of response involves the claim that this same example from Plato can help illustrate, viz., that poetry is directly allied with rhetoric and dialectic and that, as such, it plays an essential role in disclosing the truth in ways necessary for the health of any 'republic.'[56] This is indeed part of what Cervantes' Canon of Toledo means to say when he contemplates a type of fiction that will display 'all the characteristics contained in the sweet and pleasing sciences of poetry and rhetoric' (414) (todas aquellas partes que encierran en sí las dulcísimas y agradables ciencias de la poesía y de la oratoria; I, 47, p. 567). For any kind of poetry to be valued in this way, it must of course be distinguished from the false images propounded by the sophists and their ilk. On this very point Tasso writes that he 'cannot conceive either that poetry is to be placed under the sophist's art or that the fantastic is the most perfect kind of poetry.' As he goes on to say, 'even if I did concede that poetry like the sophistic art creates idols, and not merely idols but god ... I still would not concede that the sophist's art and the poet's are the same. I say, therefore, that poetry surely belongs under dialectic with rhetoric, which, as Aristotle says, is the other child of the dialectical faculty.'[57] The argument is akin to Don Quijote's discourse on the Golden Age, which offers a 'false' image insofar as it refers to a time that never existed, and yet is true insofar as it helps to think about the world as it is and how it ought to be. Indeed, the entire quixotic project can be viewed in this way: while we know that some of the heroes that Don Quijote has read about in the books of chivalry did exist and others did not, the point is less this distinction than the truths that are disclosed by virtue of Don Quijote's (sometimes fantastical) ideas. The interest in the 'legitimate marvellous' is less a compromise than a surprisingly subtle way of allowing 'poetry' to speak truthfully and thereby to find a place for it within the 'republic.'

We already know from Don Quijote's response to the Caballero del Verde Gabán that poetry is potentially an all-encompassing enterprise, the site of knowledge that is true and vast. Yet the Canon cannot conceive of such a thing except as comprised of many specific, subspecializations: 'The writer can show his conversance with astrology, his excellence as a cosmographer, his knowledge of music, his intelligence in matters of state, and perhaps he will have the opportunity to demonstrate his talents as a necromancer, if he should wish to. He can display the guile of Ulysses, the poetry of Aeneas, the valor of Achilles, the misfortune of Hector, the treachery of Sinon, the friendship of Euralyus, the liberality of Alexander, the valor of Caesar, the clemency of Trajan, the fidelity of Zopyrus, the prudence of Cato, in short all those characteristics that make a noble man perfect, sometimes placing them all in one individual, sometimes dividing them among several' (413) (Ya puede [el poeta] mostrarse astrólogo, ya cosmógrafo excelente, ya músico, ya inteligente en las materias de estado, y tal vez le vendrá ocasión de mostrarse nigromante, si quisiere. Puede mostrar las astucias de Ulixes [sic], la piedad de Eneas, la valentía de Aquiles, las desgracias de Héctor, las traiciones de Sinón, la amistad de Eurialio, la liberalidad de Alejandro, el valor de César, la clemencia y verdad de Trajano, la fidelidad de Zopiro, la prudencia de Catón; y, finalmente, todas aquellas acciones que pueden hacer perfecto a un varón ilustre, ahora poniéndolas en uno solo, ahora dividiéndolas en muchos; I, 47, pp. 566–7). What the Canon never contemplates is whether, or how, the poet's knowledge might be akin to that of the philosopher-king, who must know something beyond what any other member of the polis might individually be able to master.

Not surprisingly, then, the Canon attempts to exert a lower-level form of control over the proliferation of discourse by censuring literature that fails to respond to narrower demands for 'truth' and 'knowledge.' The fantastic adventures of the romances of chivalry provoke his outrage as much because they are full of physical and geographical impossibilities – which he simply calls 'lies' – and because they fail to give those lies the appearance of truth: 'The more truthful the fiction, the better it is, and the more probable and possible, the more pleasing' (421) (Que tanto la mentira es mejor cuanto más parece verdadera, y tanto más agrada cuanto tiene más de lo dudoso y possible; I, 47, p. 565).[58] As the historian of ancient literary theory Wesley Trimpi put it, 'in striving to give an accurate factual account, a literary fiction may become inappropriately committed to verisimilarly exact representation.'[59]

The Canon's companion, the Priest, launches a similar set of charges – within the space of a similarly crowded discourse – about the ways in which some contemporary plays let fantasy run out of control. The result seems to be a distortion of the fundamental purpose of the theatre: 'I have seen plays in which the first act began in Europe, the second in Asia, and the third concluded in Africa, and if there had been four acts, the fourth would have ended in America, making it a play that took place in all four corners of the earth. And if mimesis is the principal quality a play should have, how can it possibly satisfy anyone of even average intelligence if the action is supposed to occur in the days of King Pepin and Charlemagne, but the central character is the Emperor Heraclius, who entered Jerusalem bearing the cross, and conquered the Holy Sepulchre, like Godffrey of Bouillon, where there is an infinite number of years between one and the other ... The worst thing is ignorant folk who say that this is perfect' (416) (He visto comedia que la primera jornada comenzó en Europa, la segunda en Asia, la tercera se acabó en Africa, y ansí fuera de cuatro jornadas, la cuarta acababa en América, y así se hubiera hecho en todas las cuatro partes del mundo? Y si es que la imitación es lo principal que ha de tener la comedia, ¿cómo es posible que satisfaga a ningún mediano entendimiento que, fingiendo una acción que pasa en tiempo del rey Pepino y Carlomagno, el mismo que en ella hace la persona principal le atribuyan que fue el emperador Heraclio, que entró con la Cruz en Jerusalén, y el que ganó la Casa Santa, como Godofre de Bullón, habiendo infinitos años de lo uno a lo otro ... es lo malo que hay ignorantes que digan que esto es lo perfecto, y que lo demás es buscar gullurías; I, 48, p. 570).

What impresses most about these critiques is not just that they adhere to a relatively narrow, empirically oriented notion of the truth of literature, and that Cervantes struggles against these to allow literature a much wider berth, but that they themselves lose sight of the broader bases of their own arguments. Both the Priest and the Canon blame the flaws of contemporary literature on the 'ignorant masses' and their 'barbaric' tastes. But the additional point is that these more educated and tasteful critics, the Canon and the Priest themselves, have lost sight of what a good literary education might yield: insight into the political importance of literature, which is to say insight into a form of discourse whose value depends neither on the simple representation of facts nor on the artful transformation of lies into apparent truths. Those deeper possibilities have nonetheless not wholly disappeared from what they say. The underlying sense of what the Canon intends is that literature *ought* to have a place in the state, and that it *could* serve the polis in allowing the highest and most capacious faculties of the mind to flourish. In the case of the Priest, the idea is that drama ought to hold a mirror up to life in a way that tells the truth about it.

Ever since Plato, there has been discussion about whether the polis ought to be ruled by those in control of philosophical discourse, and concomitantly whether philosophy was in some special way different from other, more specific types of language. We can recognize that there are various domains of expertise and, correspondingly, various forms of discourse, each pertaining to some knowledge-domain. In the *Republic* (475b) Socrates suggests that a philosopher must have a passion for 'wisdom of every kind,' but he subsequently draws the conclusion that the highest of all wisdom is knowledge of the good. (This, of course, leaves unsaid whether the good is independent of all other things, a form unto itself, or plural and valid only for particular domains.) At the same time there is the question, beginning with Plato, of whether philosophy ought to be a specialized discourse. The closely related matter is whether one discourse ought to stand for and synthesize the great diversity of elements that comprise the state. Is literature that form of discourse? Is philosophy? This question is intensified in relation to early modern political discourse, which increasingly wanted to be specialized, and which Cervantes resists in the development of a much more fluid literary-political practice. In

Cervantes there are nonetheless certain internal voices, such as those of the Canon and the Priest, that point in the direction of a more specialized *theory* of literary discourse. But it is equally these internal voices that Cervantes' literary practice ultimately resists. That practice suggests that the role of literature in relation to politics is more complex than any of the standard defences of literature may portray. Indeed, literature itself offers some of the most resourceful ways to shunt many of the defences offered on its behalf.

As I have been arguing throughout this book, we are no more likely to find a single articulation of the political meaning of literature in Cervantes than we are to find a single statement in Plato about the meaning of the Platonic dialogues. In fact, quite the contrary seems far closer to the truth: that the expectation of a 'theoretical' argument of the kind the Canon and the Priest seem to want is bound to blind us to the fact that the genuine well-being of the 'republic' requires something closer to critical insight than to theory. For Plato, the formulation of 'insight' took a form that would have been inconceivable to Cervantes, viz., insight into the 'true nature' of things in their essential forms (in ideas). This was possible only in relation to belief in a residual 'memory' of the original forms imprinted in the soul. Whereas the Platonic view has come to be associated with a form of essentialism that invites authoritarian politics, Cervantes' humanist roots had alerted him to the far more ironic dimensions of Plato's literary critique. For Cervantes, 'memory' meant something quite different from what Plato meant, as the example of Don Quijote goes to show: what Don Quijote reads in the books of chivalry and what he assumes about the ideal state were never forgotten by him, while the world around him seems to have little recollection of how things might ever have been and looks increasingly to the evaluation of evidence as the basis for a better future. That said, it is also clear that to approach the need for insight from the standpoint of an increasingly scientific world generated its own peculiarly modern set of risks. It would also be too easy for an idea of literature to overvalue the truth as the representation of things that are best known by perception. This is an issue that the novel in particular had to contend with in establishing itself as the literary genre of 'experience'; it did so in a context where the standard of literary truth became aligned with the truth of experience. But there was also the risk that access to a form of truth beyond experience might be conceived as outside of literature's grasp, on a plane where experience might not count. From the place where Cervantes stood, such questions about truth were just as problematic as the division between theory and practice. The appeal to empirical truths smacked of a politics that would confine speech to that which could be said explicitly, while the appeal to the powers of sheer insight or intuition could be blind to the fact that discourse inevitably plays a role in shaping whatever 'experience' might be.

One plausible response to these risks lies in the recognition that literature is not the discourse of discourses, where everything and anything can freely be said – whether about love or astrology, history or politics, society or its outcasts – but is rather a place where frames can be found for the negotiation of the many different discourses that might figure in the state.[60] Literature is neither synthetic nor subordinate. Scholars thus far have focused principally on the ways in which Cervantes sought to balance concerns about truth with the formal-aesthetic interests that centre on literature's imaginative capabilities. My contention has instead been that Cervantes works at the very point where the 'philosophical' and the 'literary' converge with a discursive understanding of the political. The matter is not just, as I have argued, that literature is inflected by contemporary political conditions (although that is certainly true). The matter is also that literature offers a way to articulate what philosophy may know about the possibilities of politics, but may be unable to say in a satisfactory way. The same holds true, mutatis mutandis, for politics. Even when politics takes its bearings by the elements of 'nature,' as in Hobbes, or by the 'real truth of things' – according to *la verità effetuale della cosa,* as Machiavelli put it – political theory was never intended simply to provide a true and complete vision of the world of facts but was meant to propose such things as a vision of the common good, of effective leadership, or the ways to pursue peace among nations. Literature in Cervantes is equally about the world and about what that world might be. In this conjuncture, what 'might be' remains important insofar as literature also provides a way to understand the world as it is.

Notes

1 Introduction

1 Hobbes writes: 'The true and perspicuous explication of the Elements of Laws, Natural and Politic, which is my present scope, dependeth upon the knowledge of what is human nature, what is a body politic, and what it is we call a law.' *The Elements of Law: Human Nature and De Corpore Politico*, ed. J.C.A. Gaskin (Oxford: Oxford University Press, 1994), 21.

2 See 'The Classical Doctrine of Politics' and 'Dogmatism, Reason, and Decision: On Theory and Praxis in Our Scientific Civilization' (both, 1963), in *Theory and Practice*, trans. John Viertel (Boston: Beacon Press, 1973). Habermas's formulation of the difficulty of linking theory and praxis in modernity is grounded in his understanding of Marx's work as a form of critique; see 'Between Philosophy and Science: Marxism as Critique' in *Theory and Practice*. Heidegger's attempted retrieval of Aristotelian *phronēsis* in lectures given in the1920s and 1930s was also crucial; it helped spark Hannah Arendt's reconsideration of the political as well as debates about Hegel's attempt to recover ancient insights into politics without betraying modernity.

3 *Tractado de república* (1521). See ch. 23: 'Que trata cómo la ciencia que toca cerca de la gobernación de los hombres y de los pueblos es la más excelente de todas las ciencias' (reprinted, Madrid: Instituto de Estudios Políticos, 1958), 170.

4 See José Antonio Maravall, 'Un primer proyecto de facultad de ciencias políticas en la crisis del siglo XVII (El "Discurso VIII" de Sancho de Moncada),' in *Estudios de historia del pensamiento español: El siglo del barroco,* 2nd ed. (Madrid: Cultura Hispánica, 1984), 135.

5 See Jean-Pierre Dédieu, *L'Administration de la foi* (Madrid: Casa de Velásquez, 1989).

6 Fernand Braudel notes that most *letrados* were graduates of Salamanca or Alcalá de Henares. See *The Mediterranean and the Mediterranean World in the Age of Philip II*, trans. Siân Reynolds (Berkeley: University of California Press, 1995), 2:682, and Diego Hurtado de Mendoza, *Guerra de Granada*, ed. Bernardo Blanco-González (Madrid: Castalia, 1970), 105. One of its earliest monarchs, Fernando El Católico, was a model for Machiavelli in *The Prince*.

7 See William Byron, *Cervantes: A Biography* (New York: Doubleday, 1978), 33.

8 Maravall's views about just such matters display the clear influence of Max Weber's work on 'rationalization': 'Un Estado moderno, tal como quedó hecha su traza por los Reyes Católicos, supone una administración en la que un cuerpo organizado de hombres, con una técnica, es decir, con unos conocimientos adecuados a la práctica de los negocios públicos, aplican el ordenamiento jurídico que se extiende a todos y dispone de una fuerza para hacerlo cumplir.' Maravall, *El humanismo de las armas en 'Don Quijote'* (Madrid: Instituto de Estudios Políticos, 1948), 40–1.

9 On the history and development of this institution, see Pedro Barbadillo Delgado, *Historia del ilustre Colegio de Abogados de Madrid* (Madrid: Aldus, 1956).

10 'La experiencia como manera de llegar a conocer el desarrollo de los hechos políticos … como conocer los hechos políticos para gobernarlos.' Maravall, 'Empirismo y pensamiento político,' in *Estudios de historia del pensamiento español: El siglo del barroco*, 20. Cervantes accepts the authority of experience as one basis for politics, but also regards it as insufficient. *Experiencia* in the empirical sense is essential to the desire for proof in the 'Curioso impertinente' episode, and is associated with the notion of 'experiment,' as, for instance, where Anselmo wants to 'experiment with truth' (278) (hacer experiencia de la mesma verdad; I, 33, p. 406). As driven by *curiositas*, Anselmo is manifestly bereft of wisdom, and so his 'experiment' produces disastrous results.

11 Forcione is especially sensitive to this issue in Cervantes' *Novelas ejemplares*: 'Cervantes's treatment of the problem of knowledge places him in the central stream of humanist thought, originating in the writings of certain fifteenth-century Florentine thinkers and statesmen for whom the only true wisdom is that which manifests itself in beneficial civic action, and reaching its most influential expression in the sixteenth-century humanist reform movement.' *Cervantes and the Humanist Vision* (Princeton: Princeton University Press, 1982), 314–15.

12 See Quentin Skinner, *Reason and Rhetoric in the Philosophy of Hobbes* (Cambridge: Cambridge University Press, 1996).

13 Suárez's *De Legibus ac Deo Legislatore* was published in 1612. For Vitoria, see *Political Writings*, ed. Anthony Pagden and David Lawrance (Cambridge: Cambridge University Press, 1991). On de Soto, see Venancio D. Carro, *Domingo de Soto y el derecho de gentes* (Madrid: Bruno del Amo, 1930).

14 Cervantes' engagement with these questions adds something important to familiar accounts of humanism in the context of Renaissance literature and literary theory. Such accounts do not often consider the political implications of humanism. See, nonetheless, Angel Gómez Moreno, *España y la Italia de los humanistas* (Madrid: Gredos, 1994), 153–66, and for an earlier period that takes account of Italian civic humanism, Ottavio di Camillo, *El humanismo español del siglo XV* (Valencia: Torres, 1976).

15 On the question of obliquity in Cervantes and the Spanish Golden Age, see David R. Castillo, *(A)wry Views: Anamorphosis, Cervantes, and the Early Picaresque* (West Lafayette, IN: Purdue University Press, 2001).

16 'Uno de aquellos juristas hijos de universidad de Bolonia y padres de la burocracia estatal moderna que tan decisivamente contribuyeron al triunfo de la monarquía frente al poder señorial de los caballeros medievales.' Vicente Lloréns, 'Historia y ficción en el "Quijote,"' in *Literatura, historia, política* (Madrid: Revista de Occidente, 1967), 162. With characteristic Cervantean irony, Sansón Carrasco is in the end appointed one of the executors of Alonso Quijano's estate.

17 Forcione, *Cervantes, Aristotle and the 'Persiles'* (Princeton: Princeton University Press, 1970); E.C. Riley, *Cervantes's Theory of the Novel* (Oxford: Clarendon Press, 1962).

18 González Echevarría, *Love and the Law in Cervantes* (New Haven: Yale University Press, 2005). See also José Canalejas, *Cervantes y el derecho* (Zaragoza: Universidad de Zaragoza, 1905).

19 One important exception is Barry Ife, *Reading and Fiction in Golden Age Spain* (Cambridge: Cambridge University Press, 1985). Ife deals with Plato at some length.

20 Paul Oskar Kristeller, 'Renaissance Platonism,' in *Renaissance Thought and Its Sources* (New York: Columbia University Press, 1979), 50–65; he does mention Chrysoloras's proposal for a translation of the *Republic*, which would have been the first. James Hankins gives an expansive treatment in *Humanism and Platonism in the Italian Renaissance*, 2 vols (Rome: Edizioni di Storia e Letteratura, 2003), reaching similar conclusions. Hankins focuses on Chrysoloras's rendering of Plato's arguments about the 'divided line' (2:78–82). His account of Castiglione's relation to politics in Plato's *Republic* and in Aristotle (2:493–509) is more germane to the questions raised here.

21 The recent study of the political interest of the Neoplatonists, Dominic O'Meara's *Platonopolis* (Oxford: Clarendon Press, 2003), is illuminating on the broader question of Plato's reception. The *Republic* was known to Huarte de San Juan, who cites it along with other dialogues (including the *Ion*) in the *Examen de ingenios*. See Hans Baron, *The Crisis of the Early Italian Renaissance* (Princeton: Princeton University Press, 1966). Among Garin's works in English, see *Italian Humanism: Philosophy and Civic Life in the Renaissance*, trans. Pete James (Westport: Greenwood Press, 1975). Hankins's work on Garin and Baron is itself illuminating. See *Humanism and Platonism*, 1:573–90, and his introduction to *Renaissance Civic Humanism* (Cambridge: Cambridge University Press, 2000).

22 The tradition of humanist dialogue in Spain was of tremendous and equal importance. One helpful account is that of Angel Gómez Moreno, *España y la Italia de los humanistas*, especially pp. 197–214 ('La recuperación del diálogo'). By contrast, Jesús Gómez points out some fundamental divergences between sixteenth-century dialogue in Spain and the tradition derived from Plato. See *El diálogo en el renacimiento español* (Madrid: Cátedra, 1988). My contention is that Cervantes worked against the grain of the tradition that Gómez Moreno foregrounds.

23 See, for example, Iris Murdoch, *The Fire and the Sun: Why Plato Banished the Poets* (London: Oxford University Press, 1977), G.R.F. Ferrari, *Listening to the Cicadas* (Cambridge: Cambridge University Press, 1987), Christopher Janaway, *Images of Excellence* (Oxford: Clarendon Press, 1995), and Myles Burnyeat, *The Theatetus of Plato* (Indianapolis: Hackett, 1990).

24 Kahn, *Plato and the Socratic Dialogue: The Philosophical Use of a Literary Form* (Cambridge: Cambridge University Press, 1996). Daniel Boyarin's innovative critique of the monologism associated with Plato draws on Bakhtin and the Lucianic tradition; see *Socrates and the Fat Rabbis* (Chicago: University of Chicago Press, 2009).

25 It is, in fact, a vision of literature as 'critique' in the way that the Frankfurt-school thinkers used that term. See Horkheimer, 'Traditional and Critical Theory' in *Critical Theory: Selected Essays*, trans. Matthew J. O'Connell and others (New York: Continuum, 2002).

26 In a related context, Homi Bhabha describes the 'splitting' of the national subject as constitutive of the 'space of the people.' See *The Location of Culture* (London and New York: Routledge, 1994), 209–17.

27 Huarte explains in the 'Proemio' that his discrimination of types of *ingenio* is 'para que las obras de los artífices tuviesen la perfección que convensa al uso de la república.' *Examen de ingenios*, ed. Guillermo Serés (Madrid: Cátedra, 1989), 149. For a review of the broader literature, see Ronald W. Truman,

Spanish Treatises of Government, Society and Religion in the Time of Philip II (Leiden: Brill, 1999), José Antonio Maravall, *Carlos V y el pensamiento político del renacimiento* (Madrid: Instituto de Estudios Políticos, 1960), and Quentin Skinner, *The Foundations of Modern Political Thought* (Cambridge: Cambridge University Press, 1978).

28 The literature on humanism in Spain is vast, though discussions of politics in relation to humanism are relatively few when compared with discussions of the humanist literary theory in Spain. Following Américo Castro's *El pensamiento de Cervantes* (1925) and his 'Erasmo en tiempos de Cervantes,' *Revista de filología española* 18 (1931), 329–89, works that relate most directly to my subject are Angel Gómez Moreno, *España y la Italia de los humanistas* and the essays in *L'humanisme dans les letters espagnoles*, ed. Augustin Redondo (Paris: Vrin, 1979); of these, see especially Alberto Blecua, 'La Littérature apothegmatique en Espagne' (119–31), and Francisco Rico, 'Humanisme et dignité de l'homme' (31–50). Marcel Bataillon's work continues to be indispensable: *Erasmo y España*, 2nd ed., trans. Antonio Alatorre (Mexico: Fondo de Cultura Económica, 1966), along with Alban Forcione, *Cervantes and the Humanist Vision* (Princeton: Princeton University Press, 1982), and *Cervantes and the Mystery of Lawlessness* (Princeton: Princeton University Press, 1984). Yet as Francisco Márquez Villanueva noted, there still remains much to be said about Cervantes' humanism and his relationship to Erasmus. See *Cervantes en letra viva* (Barcelona: Reverso, 2005), 53.

29 As José Antonio Maravall has pointed out, there was nonetheless the desire for an understanding of causes that expressed itself in increasingly empirical terms. See 'Empirismo y pensamiento político,' in *Estudios de historia del pensamiento español: El siglo del barroco*, 15–38.

30 In addition to González Echevarría's *Love and the Law*, see Jesús Rodríguez-Velasco, 'Esfuerzo: La caballería, de estado a oficio (1524–1615)' in *Amadís de Gaula, quinientos años después: Estudios en homenaje a Juan Manuel Cacho Blecua*, ed. José Manuel Lucía Megías, María Carmen Marín Pina, and Ana Carmen Bueno (Alcalá de Henares: Centro de Estudios Cervantinos, 2008), 661–89.

31 See Nancy Struever, *The Languages of History in the Renaissance: Rhetoric and Historical Consciousness in Florentine Humanism* (Princeton: Princeton University Press, 1970).

32 Ernesto Grassi elaborates on this perception at length in his discussion of rhetoric as the ground of society in *Rhetoric as Philosophy: The Humansit Tradition*, trans. John Michael Krois and Azizeh Azodi (Carbondale: Southern Illinois University Press, 2001).

33 For Erasmus's views on the scholastics as 'barbarians,' see *De antibabarborum liber*; and for 'El Brocense,' see the account of the 1558 *Organum dialecticum et rhetoricum* in Antonio Martí, *La preceptiva retórica española en el siglo de oro* (Madrid: Gredos, 1972), 62–83. The Erasmian position is echoed in Juan Maldonado's *Paraenesis ad litteram* ('Exhortación a las buenas letras contra la turba de los gramáticos, 1529'), ed. Eugenio Asensio and Juan Alcina Rovira (Madrid: Fundación Universitaria Española, 1980). On Nebrija in this context, see Francisco Rico, *Nebrija frente a los bárbaros* (Salamanca: Universidad de Salamanca, 1978).

34 Spoken by the character Tirsi in Book IV of *Galatea*, ed. Francisco López-Estrada and María Teresa López García-Bedoy (Madrid: Cátedra, 1995), 438. Similarly, Periandro in *Los Trabajos de Persiles y Sigismunda* speaks of nature as the 'mayordoma del verdadero Dios' (chief assistant to the true God). *Los trabajos de Persiles y Sigismunda*, ed. Juan Bautista Avalle-Arce (Madrid: Castalia, 1969), III, 11, p. 352.

35 See Vives, *De Concordia et Discordia Humani Generis*, trans. Laureano Sánchez Gallego as *De Concordia y Discordia* (México, DF: Séneca, 1940).

36 I take this matter up in relation to Hobbes in chapter 9 below.

37 Bacon, translation of *De augmentis scientiarum* (*The Advancement of Learning*), in *The Works of Francis Bacon*, ed. James Spedding, Robert Leslie Ellis, and Douglas Denon Heath, (London: Longman, 1858), 5:17.

38 Skinner, *Reason and Rhetoric in the Philosophy of Hobbes*. Skinner also examines the thorough training in humanist rhetoric that enabled Hobbes later to draw on its resources for politics. Victoria Kahn offers a complementary view in her treatment of Hobbes in *Rhetoric, Prudence and Skepticism in the Renaissance* (Ithaca: Cornell University Press, 1985). Kahn demonstrates how Hobbes's texts (especially *Leviathan*) often engage in rhetorical actions that either modify or contravene their explicit claims.

39 See also Giuseppe Toffanin, *Machiavelli e il Tacitismo* (Naples: Guida, 1972). On Tacitism in Spain, see José Antonio Maravall, 'Los 'Comentarios políticos' del tacitista Juan Alfonso de Lancina,' in *Estudios de historia del pensamiento español: El siglo del barroco*, 437–53.

40 Hobbes, *The Elements of Law, Natural and Politic*, Part I: *Human Nature*, ed. J.C.A. Gaskin (Oxford: Oxford University Press, 1999), 34–9.

41 Philip Pettit, *Made with Words: Hobbes on Language, Mind, and Politics* (Princeton: Princeton University Press, 2008), 13, 24–39.

42 The first is by Robert Adams, *The Prince: A Revised Translation* (New York: W.W. Norton, Norton Critical Edition, 1992), 43; the second by Peter Constantine, *The Prince, A New Translation*, ed. Albert Russell Ascoli (New York: Random House – Modern Library, 2007), 72–3. The version of this

passage offered by Christian Detmold ('the real truth of the matter') does a bit better; *The Prince* (New York: Washington Square Press, 1963), 66. For ease of reference, I follow the Constantine translation throughout.

43 Nancy Struever, *Theory as Practice: Ethical Inquiry in the Renaissance* (Chicago: University of Chicago Press, 1992), 217.

44 I am indebted to the account given in O'Meara, *Platonopolis*, 171–84.

45 See O'Meara, *Platonopolis*, 171.

46 Ascoli and Kahn, introduction to *Machiavelli and the Discourse of Literature*, ed. Albert Ascoli and Victoria Kahn (Ithaca: Cornell University Press, 1993), 2.

2 What the Canon Said

1 'Yo hallo por mi cuenta que son perjudiciales en la república estos que llaman libros de caballerías' (I, 47, p. 564; translation mine).

2 Erasmus, *The Education of a Christian Prince*, in *The Erasmus Reader*, ed. Erika Rummel (Toronto and London: University of Toronto Press, 1990), 255.

3 On the circulation of Plato's views about the dangers of reading, see Barry Ife, *Reading and Fiction in Golden Age Spain* (Cambridge: Cambridge University Press, 1985).

4 Critics such as E.C. Riley, *Cervantes's Theory of the Novel* (Oxford: Clarendon Press, 1962), have long recognized that Cervantes had no theory of the genre he is asserted to have begun; this is in part because the novel was a newly emergent form of discourse situated at the limit of the genres that Cervantes had in view.

5 Cervantes, *Novelas ejemplares*, ed. Juan Bautista Avalle-Arce (Madrid: Castalia, 1982), 1:64.

6 *The Council of Trent, Eighteenth Session*, ed. and trans. J. Waterworth (London: Dolman, 1848), 133.

7 See Giovanni Ferrari, *City and Soul in Plato's Republic* (Chicago: University of Chicago Press, 2005), and Nicholas White, *A Companion to Plato's Republic* (Indianapolis: Hackett, 1979).

8 See José Antonio Maravall, *Estado moderno y mentalidad social: Siglos XV a XVII* (Madrid: Revista de Occidente, 1972): 'El político sabrá en qué medida, para alcanzar ciertos efectos psicológicos y morales en sus súbditos, de acuerdo con la política que tenga programada, tendrá que servirse de unos y otros recursos físicos, lo que quiere decir que, en principio, tiene medios para actuar sobre el estado sanitario de la población' (264). Ife discusses Guevara's *Aviso de privados y doctrina de cortesanos* in *Reading and Fiction*, 15, 33–4.

9 Huarte de San Juan draws on the analogy of the specificity of the various crafts, 'para que las obras de los artífices tuviessen la perfección que convenía

al uso de la república.' *Examen de ingenios*, ed. Guillermo Serés (Madrid: Cátedra, 1989), 49.

10 'En el mundo no hay cosa más esclarecida que la buena gobernación para la salud de nuestra compañía humana.' Ed. Enrique Tierno Galván (Madrid: Instituto de Estudios Políticos, 1958), 164. For an excellent overview of this text and its importance, see Manuel Alberto Montoro Ballesteros, 'El "Tractado de República" de Alonso de Castrillo (1521),' *Revista de estudios políticos* 58 (1973), 107–52.

11 Roberto González Echevarría points out the level of descriptive detail common in legal proceedings and offers this episode as one among several examples in *Love and the Law in Cervantes* (New Haven: Yale University Press, 2005), 30 and passim.

12 'Con la Santa Hermandad no hay usar de caballerías, que no se le da a ella por cuantos caballeros andantes hay dos maravedís' (I, 23, p. 277) (You can't use chivalries with the Holy Brotherhood because they wouldn't give two *maravedís* for all the knights errant in the world, 173).

13 'La justicia de Peralvillo que, asaeteado el hombre, le formaban proceso.' A similar allusion appears in Luis Vélez de Guevara: 'El ventero se quiso poner en medio, y dió con él en Peralvillo,' in *El Diablo cojuelo*, ed. A.R. Fernández and Ignacio Arellano (Madrid: Castalia, 1988), 146.

14 Among discussions of Cervantes' relationship to rhetorical practice, few treat his relationship to humanist rhetorical ideals. Alberto Blecua deals with Cervantes and rhetoric in relation to the *Persiles* in 'Cervantes y la retórica,' in *Lecciones cervantinas*, ed. Aurora Egido (Zaragoza: Caja de Ahorros de Zaragoza, Aragón y Rioja, 1985), 131–47. Luisa López Grigera, in *La retórica española en el siglo de oro* (Salamanca: Ediciones Universidad de Salamanca, 1994), proceeds by an analysis of tropes, figures, parts of discourse, and the like. Antonio Martí treats Cervantes' relationship to rhetoric as an aspect of poetics; see *La preceptiva retórica española en el siglo de oro* (Madrid: Taurus, 1972).

15 'Que los príncipes y grandes señores deven mucho advertir en elegir buenos juezes para que administren justicia; porque en esto consiste todo el bien de la república.' Antonio de Guevara, *Relox de príncipes*, in *Obras completas*, ed. Emilio Blanco (Madrid: Turner, 1994), 2:651. Virtually all of Book III ('En la cual se trata de las particulares virtudes que los príncipes han de tener, es a saber: de la justicia, de la paz, de la magnificencia, etc.') is relevant. Guevara introduces the entire work by explaining that 'el fin de tener relojes es por ordenar las repúblicas, mas este *Relox de príncipes* enséñanos a mejorar las vidas' (30).

16 On Venice as an 'ideal republic' admired by humanists for its tradition of stable governance, see Eco Haitsma Mulier, *The Myth of Venice and Dutch*

Republican Thought in the Seventeenth Century, trans. Gerard T. Moran (Assen: Van Gorcum, 1980), and 'The Language of Seventeenth-Century Republicanism in the United Provinces,' in Anthony Pagden, ed., *The Languages of Political Theory in Early Modern Europe* (Cambridge: Cambridge University Press, 1987), 179–95.

17 Thanks largely to Macrobius's 'Commentary,' the final part of *De Republica*, the so-called Somnium Scipionis, was an especially important element in the episodes of the Cave of Montesinos and the flight on Clavileño in *Don Quijote*, Part II; both episodes also draw on Plato's *Republic* as a subtext. The term 'republic' also calls to mind the writings of Jean Bodin (*Les six livres de la republique*) which, though banned in Spain, were known in their infamy; likewise it suggests an influential set of Spanish political ideas, including those of Guevara himself, that had emerged during the time of Charles V, no doubt supported by Erasmus's personal friendship with Charles V. See José Luis Abellán, *El Erasmismo español* (Madrid: Espasa Calpe, 1982), 132–40.

18 These may have been designed to help Charles V, a non-Spaniard, secure a national base for his imperial rule.

19 See José Antonio Maravall, *Carlos V y el pensamiento político del renacimiento* (Madrid: Instituto de Estudios Políticos, 1960), 250.

20 'Algo tan necesariamente plural que en su propia definición entra, para él, la referencia a otras repúblicas.' Maravall, *Carlos V y el pensamiento político*, 252.

21 See Venancio D. Carro, *Domingo de Soto y el derecho de gentes* (Madrid: Bruno del Amo, 1930), 60, 64.

22 In *De Optima Politia* (*On the Ideal Government*) of 1529. See the Latin-Spanish edition of Nuria Belloso Martín (Pamplona: EUNSA, 2003), especially pp. 93, 143. 'El Tostado' points explicitly to Plato's ideal of a republic governed by a philosopher-king, though he is careful to specify that the kind of wisdom needed by anyone who would rule in such a republic is legal wisdom (68). He nonetheless makes an important distinction between law-making and government: 'La forma de gobierno es un cierto orden según el cual los ciudadanos deben juntarse para constituir la ciudad; se dice que es ley cierta regla que se impone a los mismos ciudadanos que ya son tales' (93). Don Quijote makes passing reference to 'El Tostado' in conversation with the bachelor Sansón Carrasco in II, 3.

23 'Un orden según el cual han de arguparse los ciudadanos para constituir una ciudad ... Este orden consistirá en que coloquen sobre sí a un solo hombre para que gobierne siempre, o en que vayan gobernando todos por tiempos iguales, o en que gobiernan los virtuosos o los que aventajan en poder a los demás' (Castrillo, *Tratado de república*, 37); see also Ballesteros, 'El "Tratado de república,"' 144.

24 Augustine, *De civitate Dei*, book 19, ch. 7; see Castrillo, *Tractado de república*, 14–15.

25 The mentions are scattered throughout: in I, 22, 48, 49; and in II, 12.

26 Translation mine. 'Hizo cosas de mucho esfuerzo, y particularmente en aquella guerra de Antequera hizo hechos dignos de perpetua memoria, sino que esta nuestra España tiene en tan poco el esfuerzo, por serle tan natural y ordinario … no como aquellos romanos y griegos, que al hombre se le aventuraba a morir una vez en toda la vida le hacían en sus escriptos inmortal y le trasladaban a las estrellas.' *El Abençerraje: novela y romancero*, ed. Francisco López-Estrada (Madrid: Cátedra, 2003), 131–2.

27 Riley, *Cervantes's Theory of the Novel*, and Alban Forcione, *Cervantes, Aristotle and the 'Persiles'* (Princeton: Princeton University Press, 1970).

28 On the fusion of Aristotle and Horace, see Bernard Weinberg, *A History of Literary Criticism in the Italian Renaissance* (Chicago: University of Chicago Press, 1961), 1:111–55 ('Ars Poetica: Confusion with Aristotle').

29 See the discussion in Sarah Beckjord, *Territories of History* (University Park: Pennsylvania State University Press, 2007), 15–41. Vives's influence on rhetorical theory has been discussed by Martí in *La preceptiva retórica*, 32–4.

30 Weinberg, 'From Aristotle to Pesudo-Aristotle,' in *Aristotle's Poetics and English Literature*, ed. Elder Olson (Chicago: University of Chicago Press, 1965), 1955.

31 See Weinberg, *A History*, 1:293.

32 '¿Qué diré más dela Poesía? Sino que *es tan prouechosa ala* [sic] *República Christiana, quanto dañosos los libros de caballerías*, que no siruen otra cosa, sino de corromper los ánimos delos mancebos y donzellas … pues de algunos no se puede sacar fruto, que para el alma sea de prouecho, sino todo mentiras y vanidades.' *Arte poética en romance castellano* (Madrid: CSIC, 1944), 42–3; emphasis added. See also Weinberg, *A History*, 1:252–3.

33 'Su intención … en esse primer lugar del tercero de *República*, no es vituperar a la poesía, sino a los poetas … En el lugar segundo del *Epinomis* confiesso que reprehende a la misma arte poética, mas conuiene romper más esta cáscara y sacar del todo el meollo que está dentro, para lo cual es de aduertir el fin que Platón en esse diálogo tuvo, que fué buscar la sabiduría cierta, que niega estar en las más de las artes y más principales; y, auiendo dicho que la tal sabiduría no tenía su assiento en la arte de curar, caçar, regir y gouernar y nauegar, ni en otra alguna de las artes imitantes, dize que ni en la Política. Y da la causa: porque no proceden por partes scientíficas y euidentes, sino por conjeturales. Assí que, si Platón dize mal de la Poética en esse lugar, es por lo que reprehende a la Medicina y a la Política y a las demás; y las quales no sólo no son malas,

pero son digníssimas y muy importantes.' *Philosophía antigua poética*, ed. Alfredo Carballo Picazo (Madrid: CSIC, 1953), 84–5. The reference to the *Epinomis* is to a text that was long believed to be the 13th book of Plato's *Laws*. Early modern editions were published in Basle (1534 and 1556) and Louvain (1551). An English text is available in Plato, *Philebus and Epinomis*, trans. A.E. Taylor, ed. Raymond Klibansky (London: Thomas Nelson and Sons, 1956). The connection between El Pinciano and the Aristotelian basis of the Canon's ideas has long been known. See Sanford Shepard, *El Pinciano y las ideas literarias del siglo de oro* (Madrid: Gredos, 1962), 209–14. My emphasis is on the Platonic-political dimension.

34 See especially Wesley Trimpi, *Muses of One Mind: The Literary Analysis of Experience and Its Continuity* (Princeton: Princeton University Press, 1983). For Boethius, as for many others, the hypothesizing function was vested in rhetoric: 'The dialectical discipline examines the thesis only; a thesis is a question not involved in circumstances. The rhetorical [discipline], on the other hand, investigates and discusses hypotheses, that is, questions hedged in by a multitude of circumstances.' Boethius, *De topicis differentiis*, IV, 1205c–d, trans. Eleanor Stump (Ithaca: Cornell University Press, 1978), 79. See also Thomas Sloane, *On the Contrary: The Protocol of Traditional Rhetoric* (Washington, DC: Catholic University of America Press, 1997), 96.

35 This was published in Ficino's *Commentaria in Platonem* (1496).

36 The challenge lies in the fact that Plato never says what 'just proportion' means in the realm of images, though he was careful to avoid what would become the Aristotelian distinction between form (ideas) and matter (their visible or material realizations). For a detailed discussion of these issues, especially in relation to *Sophist*, 240a–e, see Stanley Rosen, *Plato's 'Sophist'* (New Haven: Yale University Press, 1983), 147–69, and 186–203.

37 See the discussion in Arthur F. Kinney, *Continental Humanist Poetics* (Amherst: University of Massachusetts Press, 1989), 315–17.

38 Lloréns, 'Historia y ficción en el "Quijote,"' in *Literature, historia, política* (Madrid: Revista de Occidente, 1967): 'Cervantes había reiterado a lo largo de su obra que la verosimilitud no basta para trazar la linea divisoria entre fábula e historia. La realidad – y allí estaba su propia vida para probarlo – puede ser tan inverosímil como lo inventado' (159).

39 Lloréns, 'Historia y ficción,' 159.

40 'I ... have felt a certain temptation to write a book of chivalry in which I followed all the points I have mentioned, and, to tell the truth, I have already written more than a hundred pages' (414) (Yo ... he tenido cierta tentación de

hacer un libro de caballerías, guardando en él todos los puntos que he significado; y si he de confesar la verdad, tengo escritas más de cien hojas; I, 48, p. 567).

41 *Republic*, trans. Desmond Lee, 2nd ed. (London: Penguin, 2007); I cite throughout according to Book and Stephanus pagination, here X, 608a.

42 'Con el justo fin de combatir opniniones tan *perjudiciales*.' Rivadeneira, *Tratado de la religión y virtudes que debe tener el príncipe cristiano para gobernar y conservar sus estados, contra lo que Nicolas Maquiavelo y los políticos deste tiempo esneñan*, in *Obras escogidas del Padre Pedro de Rivadeneira*, ed. Don Vicente de la Fuente (Madrid: M. Rivadeneyra, 1868), BAE, XL, 454; my emphasis. Rivadeneira's chief complaint is against Machiavelli's political atheism.

43 See Dopico-Black, 'Canons Afire: Libraries, Books, and Bodies in Don Quixote's Spain,' in *Cervantes' Don Quixote: A Casebook*, ed. Roberto González Echevarría (New York: Oxford University Press, 2005), 103.

44 The Toledan humanist and poet Alvar Gómez de Castro left a memoir on the dual principles of censorship, one applying to works in Latin and the other to works in Spanish. The text was published in *Revista de Archivos, Bibliotecas y Museos* 8 (1903), 218–21. Among the vernacular books expurgated as a result of these decrees were in fact some books of chivalry, along with books of amorous poetry. See Henry Kamen, *The Spanish Inquisition: A Historical Revision* (London: Wiedenfeld and Nicolson, 1997), 114–15.

45 See Edward Glaser, 'Nuevos datos sobre la crítica de los libros de caballerías en los siglos XVI y XVII,' *Anuario de estudios medievales* 3 (1966), 393–410. An inventory of the Escorial's holdings lists some 139 printed books that the Inquisition had seized but not burned. See Dopico-Black, 'Canons Afire,' 106. It is worth noting that in the 1616 Valencia printing of *Don Quijote*, II, the following passage in chapter 36 was expurgated: 'que las obras de caridad que se hacen tibia y flojamente no tienen mérito ni valen nada' (II, 36, p. 320) (works of charity done half-heartedly have no merit or value; my translation). The 1632 *Expurgatory Index* of Cardinal Zapata ordered the passage deleted from all other printings, and in Spain the passage was not reinstated until the 1839–40 Barcelona editions of Antonio Bergnes.

46 Sancho will turn to the Old Testament in a much more comic way in II, 22, when he cites the biblical Adam as the first person ever to have scratched his head.

47 See Judges 13–16, passim. This biblical story may also have inspired Cervantes for the episode of Don Quijote's encounter with the lions in II, 17.

48 Vives, *De tradendis disciplinis*, trans. Foster Watson, *Vives: On Education* (Cambridge: Cambridge University Press, 1913), 304.

49 The sixteenth-century 'Dictamen' attributed to Zurita was published in *Revista de Archivos Bibliotecas y Museos*, 3rd series, 8 (January–June, 1903), 218–21, by Manuel Serrano y Sanz from an original in the Biblioteca Nacional, Madrid. Zurita's dubious authorship was subsequently addressed and the document republished by P.E. Russell in 'Secular Literature and the Censors: A Sixteenth-Century Document Re-Examined,' *Bulletin of Hispanic Studies* 59 (1982), 219–25.

50 Consider the related substitution, in I, 5, of books of chivalry, as physical objects, for their effects on Don Quijote's madness; or the resolution of disputed questions of taste, in II, 13, by the identification of a leather thong and an iron nail in a barrel of wine. One might also think of the social significance of the substitution of signs for things in the episode of the *rebuznos*.

51 The distinction between eikastic and phantasmatic images (between icons and phantasms) is explained in Plato's *Sophist*, which I discuss further in chapter 5 below.

52 The specific idea of exile to the fantastical Islands of the Lizards seems to draw from Antonio de Torquemada: 'Una mujer cometió un delito muy grave, por el cual fue condenada en destierro para una isla deshabitada de las que comúnmente llaman Las Islas de los Lagartos.' *Jardín de flores curiosas*, ed. G. Allegra (Madrid: Castalia, 1983), 182–3.

53 I would likewise note that the notion of natural law requires both certain 'theoretical' beliefs and a world to which those beliefs must refer.

54 On this, see Donald Gilbert-Santamaría, *Writers on the Market: Consuming Literature in Early Seventeenth-Century Spain* (Lewisburg: Bucknell University Press, 2005).

55 Cf. Horace, *Odes*, 3.1, vv. 1–2: 'Odi profanum / vulgus et arceo' (I hate the ignorant crowd and keep them far away).

56 The need for leisure is, in turn, justified because human beings cannot sustain themselves for long without some form of recreation: 'The bow cannot always be pulled taut, and it is not in the nature of human frailty to endure without honest recreation' (418) (No es posible que esté continuo el arco armado, ni la condición y flaqueza humana se pueda sustentar sin alguna lícita recreación; I, 48, p. 572).

57 Hobbes, *Leviathan*, ed. C.B. Macpherson, (Harmondsworth: Penguin, 1968), I, ch. 3, p. 99.

58 I discuss the question of writing under constraint in chapter 9. On the purely aesthetic issues involved, see Alan Trueblood, 'Sobre la selección artística en el *Quijote*: "lo que he dejado de escribir" (II, 44),' *Nueva Revista de Filología Hispánica* 10 (1956), 44–50.

3 Views from Nowhere

1 See, for example, Rivadeneira, *Tratado de la religión y virtudes que debe tener el príncipe cristiano para gobernar y conservar sus estados, contra lo que Nicolas Maquiavelo y los políticos deste tiempo esneñan*, in *Obras escogidas del Padre Pedro de Rivadeneira*, ed. Don Vicente de la Fuente, BAE, vol. 60 (Madrid: M. Rivadeneyra, 1868): 'Nicolas Maquiavelo fue hombre que se dió mucho al estudio de la policía y gobierno de la república y de aquella que comunmente llaman razón de estado. Escribió algunos libros, en que enseña esta razón de estado' (455; I have modernized the accents). Rivadeneira contrasts the 'false reason of state' (razón falsa de estado) with the 'law of God' (la ley de Dios).

2 The mention of Lycurgus, who was known from Plutarch's account in the *Greek Lives*, corroborates the possibility that the very opening of the *Quijote* may well have been inspired by Plutarch. There is certainly a resonance between Cervantes' first chapter and the first paragraph of Plutarch's biographical sketch of Lycurgus: 'Even allowing for the fact that there is nothing indisputable to be said about Lycurgus the legislator, since there are divergent accounts of his family, his travels abroad, his death, and above all precisely what he achieved with regard to the laws and the constitution, there is particularly little agreement about when the man lived. Some people, including the philosopher Aristotle, say that he was contemporary with Iphitus and helped him arrange the Olympic truce ... Others, however, such as Eratosthenes and Apollodorus, use the list of successive Spartan kings to work out when he lived, and demonstrate that he preceded the first Olympiad by quite a few years ... Nevertheless, in spite of such a confused record, I shall try, in the course of my narrative of the man, to follow these accounts which have attracted the least controversy and have the most distinguished witnesses on their side.' *Greek Lives*, trans. Robin Waterfield (Oxford: Oxford University Press, 1998), 9.

3 'So, according to that, you want to make a new man'? 'I wanted to put in the good and leave out everything bad' (Vos querrades, según eso, hazer un mundo nuevo? Querría dexar en él lo bueno y quitar de él todo lo malo). *Diálogo de las cosas ocurridas en Roma (Diálogo de Lactancio y el arcediano)*, ed. José F. Montesinos (Madrid: La Lectura, 1969), 115.

4 A notable plan for radical political reform, published not long after *Don Quijote*, Part II, was Fernández de Navarrete, *Conservación de monarquías* (1619).

5 Paul, Epistle to the Ephesians, 4:24.

6 As cited in Maravall, *El humanismo de las armas en Don Quijote* (Madrid: Instituto de Estudios Políticos, 1948), 87. Cf. Maravall on Don Quijote's

complete internal reform: 'Don Quijote se considera logrado, porque se ha rehecho por dentro, porque se ha renovado según un cuadro de virtudes morales realmente ejemplar, no ya para su profesión caballeresca, sino para el hombre en general. Se ha convertido en *hombre Nuevo* ... Don Quijote quiere dar universal ejemplo de cómo se puede ser otro del que se era' (91). The entire essay also appears in his *Utopía y contrautopía en el Quijote* (Madrid: Pico Sacro, 1976), 111–48.

7 Regarding theory as a 'view from nowhere,' as my chapter title suggests, I am indebted to Thomas Nagel, *The View from Nowhere* (New York: Oxford University Press, 1989.

8 Cicero, *De oratore*, trans. E.W. Sutton and H. Rackham (Cambridge, MA: Harvard University Press, Loeb Library, 1976), I. viii, 30–2, 34; pp. 23–7. Antonio de Guevara's influential *Relox de príncipes* offered a related endorsement of the pragmatic importance of rhetoric: 'Vean, pues, agora los príncipes y grandes señores quánto les va en saber bien hablar y ser eloqüentes; porque no vemos otra cosa cada día sino a uno que es bajo por linaje, la cloqüencia lo haze alto en fortuna.' *Relox de príncipes*, in *Obras completas,* ed. Emilio Blanco (Madrid: Turner, 1994), 2:502.

9 Aristotle, *Rhetoric*, 3.11. See also the very lengthy description in *Don Quijote* I, 18, from which I excerpt briefly here: 'In his imagination he saw what he did not see and what was not there, and in a loud voice he began to say: "That knight you see there in the gold-colored armor, who bears on his shield a crowned lion kneeling at the feet of a damsel, is the valiant Laurcalco, lord of the Badge of Silver ... Now turn your eyes in the other direction, and you will see in front of and at the head of the other army the ever victorious and never defeated Timonel of Carcajona ..." Lord save me! What a number of provinces he mentioned and nations he named, attributing to each one, with marvelous celerity, the characteristics that belonged to it, so absorbed and immersed was he in his lying books! Sancho Panza hung on his words but said none of his own, and from time to time he turned his head to see if he could see the knights and giants his master was naming' (127–9) (Viendo en su imaginación lo que no veía ni había, con voz levantada comenzó a decir: 'Aquel caballero que allí ves de las armas jaldes, que trae en el escudo un león coronado, rendido a los pies de una doncella, es el valeroso Laurcalco, señor de la Puente de Plata ... Pero vuelve los ojos a estotra parte y verás delante y en la frente destotro ejército al siempre vencedor y jamás vencido Timonel de Carcajona ... ¡Válame Dios, y cuántas provincias dijo, cuántas naciones nombró, dándole a cada una, con maravillosa presteza, los atributos que le pertenecían, todo absorto y empapado en lo que había leído en sus libros mentirosos! Estaba Sancho Panza colgado de sus palabras, sin hablar ninguna, y de cuando en cuando volvía la

cabeza a ver si veía los caballeros y gigantes que su amo nombraba'; I, 18, pp. 219–22). Don Quijote's speech is also a supreme example of abundance (*copia*) in words. See Terrence Cave, *The Cornucopian Text* (Oxford: Oxford University Press, 1979), and chapter 9 below.

10 Juan Luis Vives, 'On the Causes of the Corruption of the Arts,' trans. Wayne Rebhorn, in *Renaissance Debates on Rhetoric* (Ithaca: Cornell University Press, 2000), 83.

11 See Myriam Yvonne Jehenson and Peter N. Dunn, *The Utopian Nexus in Don Quixote* (Nashville: Vanderbilt University Press, 2006).

12 There was a long medieval tradition in which fables were thought to disclose the truth in its most immediate forms. See Ernesto Grassi, *Rhetoric as Philosophy: The Humanist Tradition*, trans. John Michael Krois and Azizeh Azod (1980; rpt. Carbondale: Southern Illinois University Press, 2001), 84.

13 Plato, *Statesman*, 268d, p. 144, trans. J.B. Skemp (London: Routledge 1961). This dialogue may well have been influential for Castrillo's writings about the Golden Age in the *Tractado de república*.

14 Blumenberg, *Work on Myth*, trans. Robert M. Wallace (Cambridge, MA: MIT Press, 1985), 149.

15 This question remains a point of contention for the relationship between literary and philosophical discourse, even within a broad understanding of what philosophy might be. Slavoj Žižek, for instance, writes that 'the synchronous symbolic order fills out the void of its "origins" by means of a *narration*: fantasy has, by definition, the structure of a *story* to be narrated … It has its roots in the philosophical conflict between Hegel and Schelling concerning the way to present [*darstellen*] the Absolute: through *logos* or *mythos*, through logical deduction or through the narration of God's "ages"?' *For They Know Not What They Do: Enjoyment as a Political Factor* (London: Verso, 1991), 211.

16 Plato, *Protagoras*, trans. W.K.C. Guthrie (Harmondsworth: Penguin, 1956), 320c, p. 52.

17 Regarding the 'surplus of meaning' associated with myth in classical philosophy, see M.M. McCabe, 'Myth, Allegory and Argument in Plato,' in A. Barker and M. Warner, eds, *The Language of the Cave*, Aperion 25 (Edmonton, AB: Academic Printing and Publishing, 1992), 47–68.

18 See Grassi, *Rhetoric as Philosophy*.

19 John [*sic*] Scotus, *De divisione naturae*, 5.4; I owe the reference to Grassi, *Rhetoric as Philosophy*, 69–70. I will explain in connection with the episode on Clavileño that Plato recognized theory as having both public and private dimensions. While he saw a role for the private *theoros*, especially in the non-ideal polis, he tended to emphasize the formation of civic *theoros*, and

this as a kind of story meant for public circulation and political insight. See Andrea Nightingale, *Spectacles of Truth in Classical Greek Philosophy* (Cambridge: Cambridge University Press, 2004), 136.

20 It is true, as Geoffrey Stagg and other commentators have noted, that the myth of the Golden Age is not strictly speaking a part of the literary pastoral, nor vice-versa. Don Quijote associates the two by a logic of adjacency, and not without reason, since the setting of the mythical Golden Age is often that of an idyllic landscape. See Stagg, 'Illo tempore: Don Quijote's Discourse on the Golden Age and Its Antecedents,' in *'La Galatea' de Cervantes: Cuatrocientos años después*, ed. Juan-Bautista Avalle-Arce (Newark: Juan de la Cuesta, 1985), 71–90.

21 *Metamorphoses*, trans. Mary Innis (Harmmondsworth: Penguin, 1955), I, pp. 31–2.

22 Noël Salomon, *La vida rural castellana en tiempos de Felipe II* (Barcelona: Planeta, 173), 144.

23 There they take up questions of origins and 'inventions,' questions such as who was the original inventor of playing cards, or who was the first person ever to scratch his head. Those conversations clearly evoke the degradation of the power of myth at the hands of a historico-scientific interest in determining matters of fact.

24 See Cicero, *On Obligations*, trans. P.G. Walsh (Oxford: Oxford University Press, 2000), Book II, par. 73. Jehensen and Dunn also discuss this connection in *The Utopian Nexus*, 115.

25 'The trees of these mountains are my companions, the clear waters of these streams my mirrors' (99) (Los árboles destas montañas son mi compañía, las claras aguas destos arroyos mis espejos; con los árboles y con las aguas comunico mis pensamientos y hermosura; I, 14, p. 186).

26 See Jehensen and Dunn, *The Utopian Nexus*, 133.

27 Cicero, *On Obligations*, I, 151, p. 51.

28 'Camacho is rich, and can buy whenever, and wherever, and whatever he desires' (596) (Camacho es rico, y podrá comprar su gusto cuando, donde y como quisiere; II, 21, p. 201).

29 Castrillo writes of the social and political organization of bees: 'Pues escribir algo de República ... contaré para doctrina nuestra el concierto y las condiciones de las abejas, que parescerá cosa no poco maravillosa ver tan gran ejemplo en tan pequeño animal.' *Tractado de república*, ed. Enique Tierno Galván (Madrid: Instituto de Estudios Políticos, 1958), 29.

30 Ibid., 32–3.

31 Aristotle, *Politics*, 1253a; Hobbes, *De Cive*, ch. 5 ('Of the causes, and first beginning of civill government'), *Leviathan*, ch. 17, pp. 6–12. Its first

appearance in Hobbes seems to be in *The Elements of Law* (1640; xix, 4–5). See also Charles Butler's popular 1609 work entitled *The Feminine Monarchie or a Treatise Concerning Bees, and the Due Ordering of Them*, republished in 1623 as *The Feminine Monarchie, or The History of Bees: Shewing Their Admirable Nature, and Properties, Their Generation, and Colonies, Their Government, Loyaltie, Art, Industrie, Enemies, Warres, Magnanimitie, &c. Together With the Right Ordering of Them From Time to Time; And the Sweet Profit Arising Thereof.* See Craig McFarlane, 'Political Animals: Bees,' http://www.theoria.ca/theoria/archives/2008/06/political-animals-bees.html.

32 Hobbes, *The Elements of Law, Natural and Politic*, Part I, *Human Nature*, ed. J.C.A. Gaskin (Oxford: Oxford University Press, 1999), 79, 110. See also the section of *Leviathan*, 'Of the Natural Condition of Mankind.'

33 Hobbes, *Leviathan*, ch. 13, p. 186.

34 That principle was articulated as early as the thirteenth century by Brunetto Latini, who described politics as 'the highest and the loftiest activity of men. It is that which teaches us how to rule a people, a state, or a group in times of war and peace. It teaches us all the arts and occupations [*mestiers*] that man needs. And it achieves this in two ways; one is through work [*oeuvre*] the other is through words [*paroles*]. What it achieves through work occurs through the occupations of blacksmith, weaver, farm worker … all occupations that man needs … What man achieves through *words* occurs through his mouth and tongue.' Latini, *Li livres du tresor*, ed. F.J. Carmody (Berkeley: University of California Press, 1949), 21. Ernesto Grassi discusses the passage in *Rhetoric as Philosophy*, 72–3.

35 Aristotle, *Nicomachean Ethics*, trans. David Ross (Oxford: Oxford University Press, 1998), IV, 1, p. 80.

36 In approaching such issues, Cervantes may well have had Aristotle's emphasis on 'right giving' in mind.

37 See Benedict Anderson, *Imagined Communities*, 2nd ed. (London: Verso Books, 2006), 67–8.

38 See Alban Forcione, 'Sancho Panza and Cervantes' Embodiment of Pastoral,' in *Literature, Culture and Society in the Modern Age: In Honor of Joseph Frank*, ed. Edward J. Brown et al. (Stanford: Department of Slavic Languages and Literatures, Stanford University, 1991), 1:57–75.

39 Cervantes returns to these questions in Part II in the context of Don Quijote's advice to Sancho as he prepares to govern the 'island' of Barataria.

40 'It is from God's act when he set it in motion that it has received all the virtues it possesses, while it is from its primal chaotic condition that all the wrongs and evils arise in it – evils which it engenders in turn in the living creatures within it. When it is guided by the Divine Pilot, it produces much good and

but little evil in the creatures it raises and sustains. When it must travel on without God, things go well enough in the years immediately after He abandons control, but as time goes on and forgetfulness of God arises in it, the ancient condition of chaos also begins to assert its sway. At last, as this cosmic era draws to its close, this disorder comes to a head. The few good things it produces it corrupts with so gross a taint of evil that it hovers on the very brink of destruction, both of itself and of the creatures within it' (*Statesman*, 273b–d).

41 'En aquella primera edad y en aquel siglo dorado todos vivían en paz. Cada uno curava sus tierras, plantava sus olivos, cogía sus frutos, vendimiava sus viñas, segava sus panes y criava sus hijos; finalmente, como no comían sino de sudor proprio, vivían sin perjuyzio ageno. ¡O! malicia humana, ¡o!, mundo traydor y maldito, que jamás dexas las cosas permanescer en un estado … aviendo passado dos mil años del mundo sin saber qué cosa era mundo, Dios permitiédolo y la malicia humana lo inventando, los arados tornaron en armas, los bueyes en cavallos, las aguijadas en lanças … finalmente el sudor que sudavan en provecho de su hazienda tornaron a derramar sangre en daño de su república.' Antonio de Guevara, *Relox de príncipes*, 215.

42 'Una España desgarrada en sus entrañas mismas por las violencias de las guerras civiles y de las revueltas populares.' Ballesteros, 'El "Tractado de República" de Alonso de Castrillo (1521),' *Revista de estudios políticos* 58 (1973), 122.

43 The phrase in question is 'dichosa edad y dichoso siglo' (I, 2, p. 80).

44 Though, in preparing for his second *salida*, he does find it necessary to gather some basic monetary resources: 'Dio luego orden don Quijote en buscar dineros, y, vendiendo una cosa, y empeñando otra, y malbaratándolas todas, llegó una razonable cantidad' (I, 7, p. 126).

45 'Los romanos no compraron el mundo por dineros, mas con la virtud señorearon a todos los que tenían los dineros.' *Tractado de República*, 206; see Ballesteros, 'El "Tractado de República,"' 135.

46 In *Humanist Educational Treatises*, ed. and trans. Craig W. Kallendorf (Cambridge, MA: Harvard University Press, I Tatti Library, 2002), 69–71.

47 See Aristotle, *Nicomachean Ethics*, IV, 1123a; also II, 1107b and IV, 1122a.

48 Plato, *Republic*, II, 372a–373a.

49 Cicero, *De inventione*, 1.2, 88–9.

50 In so doing, we are reminded of the fact that Aristotle's own account of mimesis in the *Poetics* began from the consideration of imitation as a natural phenomenon. On the wider implications of mimesis and conflict in these and related episodes, see René Girard, *Deceit, Desire, and the Novel: Self and Other in Literary Structure*, trans. Yvonne Freccero (Baltimore: Johns

Hopkins University Press, 1965), and Cesáreo Bandera, *Mímesis conflictiva: ficción literaria y violencia en Cervantes y Calderón* (Madrid: Gredos, 1975).

4 Controversies

1 *Vives on Education: A Translation of De Tradendis Disciplinis*, trans. Foster Watson (Cambridge: Cambridge University Press, 1913), 180. The passage cited here introduces Vives's chapter on rhetoric.
2 See Vives, *De ratione dicendi*, in *Opera omnia*, ed. G. Mayans (1872–86; rpt. London: Gregg Press, 1964), 2:207.
3 See Garcilaso de la Vega, 'Egloga' III, v. 40.
4 At the very end of Part II, the pen of Cide Hamete speaks about a reconcilia-tion of the competing demands of *armas* (action) and *letras* (writing): 'For me alone Don Quijote was born, and I for him; he knew how to act, and I to write; the two of us alone are one' (939) (Para mí sola nació Don Quijote, y yo para él; él supo *obrar* y yo *escribir*; solos los dos somos para en uno; II, 74, p. 592; emphasis added).
5 There are two types of rhetoric exemplified in these speeches: the first imagis-tic and directive, the second argumentative. Ernesto Grassi writes of the primacy of poetic language (as revelatory and metaphorical) over argumenta-tive, deductive, rational speech. See Grassi, *Rhetoric as Philosophy: The Humanist Tradition*, trans. John Michael Krois and Azizeh Azod (1980; rpt. Carbondale: Southern Illinois University Press, 2001), 80.
6 Mikhail Bakhtin, *Problems of Dostoevsky's Poetics*, trans. Caryl Emerson (Minneapolis: University of Minnesota Press, 1984). He notes that typical of all forms of the menippea is syncrisis – the comparison and contrast, of stripped-down statements of 'ultimate positions in the world,' often in a structure of parallel clauses (116).
7 Ibid., 120. Bakhtin notes that the founder of the diatribe was Bion Borys-thenes, who was also a founder of the menippea. He goes on to suggest that it was the diatribe, and not classical rhetoric, that was a major influence on Christian sermonizing.
8 He speaks of the non-synthetic form of debate as drawn from 'los antiguos oradores, en cuyas contiendas el acusador era el primero que dezía, y después el defensor.' *Diálogo de la dignidad del hombre*, ed. María Luisa Carrón Puga (Madrid: Cátedra), 120.
9 Cicero, *Orator*, trans. G L. Hendrickson (Cambridge, MA: Harvard University Press, Loeb Library, 1939), xiv. 46 ('ad copiam rhetorum, in utramque partem ut ornatius et uberius dici posset'). In *De finibus* Cicero writes that 'Aristotle first instituted the practice of rhetoric as well as dialectic; and Aristotle first

instituted the practice of speaking on either side concerning individual matters.'
See A.A. Long, 'Cicero's Plato and Aristotle,' in *Cicero the Philosopher*, ed.
J.G.F. Powell (Oxford: Clarendon Press, 1995), 37–61. On *in utramque partem*
argumentation in the context of the dialogue tradition in Spain, see Jesús
Gómez, *El diálogo en el renacimiemto español* (Madrid: Cátedra, 1988), 66–7.

10 Cicero, *De Oratore*, trans. E.W. Sutton and H. Rackham (Cambridge, MA:
Harvard University Press, Loeb Library, 1948), I. 31, 142–3; emphasis added.
Cicero also describes argument *in utramque partem* as 'in regular use among
philosophers, and chiefly those who make a practice of arguing at extreme
length either for or against any proposition whatever laid before them' (*De
Oratore*, 1.263).

11 Erasmus, *On the Art of Writing Letters* (*De Conscribendis Epistolis*), in
Collected Works of Erasmus, vol. 25, ed. J.K. Sowards (Toronto and London:
University of Toronto Press, 1985), 44. I discuss Cervantes' engagement with
the Demosthenes – Cicero controversy in chapter 9 below.

12 Hobbes, *Leviathan*, ch. 12, p. 179.

13 See W.K.C. Guthrie, *The Sophists* (Cambridge: Cambridge University Press,
1971), 316–19. Some of the notions in the anonymous *Dissoi Logoi* (*Double
Arguments*) bear a remarkable resemblance to the ideas placed in the mouth of
the Protagoras who appears represented as a character in Plato's dialogue of
that name. See Charles Trinkaus, 'Protagoras in the Renaissance,' in *Philosophy and Humanism: Essays in Honor of Paul Oskar Kristeller*, ed. Edmund
Mahoney (New York: Columbia University Press, 1976), 194.

14 Plato, *Protagoras*, in *Protagoras and Meno*, trans. Adam Beresford (London:
Penguin, 2005), 332d.

15 See Long, 'Cicero's Plato and Aristotle,' 43–4.

16 *De Oratore*, 1.34, 157–9. Among many other sympathetic views from the
Roman rhetorical tradition, see especially Quintilian, *Institutio Oratoria*, X.
v. 19–20.

17 Erasmus, *On the Art of Writing Letters*, 43.

18 Erasmus followed Plato in warnings about the dangers of over-controversializing.
See, for example, Erasmus's letter to Carondelet, 5 January 1523, in the
Selected Writings ed. John C. Olin, 3rd ed. (New York: Fordham University
Press, 1987), especially notes 190 and 199; see also Olin, p. 104.

19 See, for example, Plato, *Sophist*, 232e.

20 Erasmus, *On the Art of Writing Letters*, 44.

21 In *Humanist Educational Treatises*, ed. and trans. Craig W. Kallendorf
(Cambridge, MA: Harvard University Press, I Tatti Library, 2002), 37.

22 Castiglione, *The Book of the Courtier*, trans. Charles S. Singleton (Garden
City: Doubleday, 1959), 69. 'Ben so io che tutti conoscete quanto s'ingannano

i Francesi pensando che le lettere nuocciano all'arme. Sapete che delle cose grandi ed arrischiate nella guerra il vero stimulo è la Gloria ... E che la vera gloria sia quella che si commenda al sacro tesauro delle lettere, ognuno po comprendere, eccetto quegli infelici che gustate non l'hanno.' *Il Libro del Cortegiano*, ed. Bruno Maier (Torino: Unione Tipografico-Editrice, 1964), 160.

23 For Bruni 'the active life is superior in public service.' Cited in Victoria Kahn, *Rhetoric, Prudence and Skepticism in the Renaissance* (Ithaca: Cornell University Press, 1985), 37.

24 Vergerio, 'The Character and Studies Befitting a Free-Born Youth,' in *Humanist Educational Treatises*, 75.

25 Erasmus's *Querela Pacis* (*A Complaint of Peace*) stands clearly in the background.

26 *Paraclesis* among them; see Sloane, *On the Contrary: The Protocol of Traditional Rhetoric* (Washington, DC: Catholic University of America Press, 1987), 11.

27 I discuss the matter of *copia* at greater length in chapter 9 below.

28 Gadamer, *Dialogue and Dialectic: Eight Hermeneutical Studies on Plato*, trans. P. Christopher Smith (New Haven: Yale University Press, 1980), 128.

29 'Una larga arenga que se pudiera muy bien excusar' (I, 11, p. 157).

30 'One of the objections people make of the history,' said the bachelor, 'is that its author put into it a novel called *The Man Who Was Recklessly Curious*, not because it is a bad novel or badly told, but because it is out of place and has nothing to do with the history of his grace Señor Don Quixote' (477–8) ('Una de las tachas que ponen a la tal historia,' dijo el bachiller 'es que su autor puso en ella una novela intitulada *El Curioso impertinente*; no por mala ni por mal razonada, sino por no ser de aquel lugar, ni tiene que ver con la historia de su merced del señor don Quijote'; II, 3, p. 63).

31 'You are all of an age to choose a profession or, at least, to select an occupation that will bring you honor and profit when you are older' (335) (Vosotros estáis ya en edad de tomar estado, o, a lo menos, de elegir ejercicio, tal, que cuando mayores, os honre y aproveche; I, 39, p. 474).

32 No doubt, this non-convergence reflects Cervantes' own attempts to negotiate between a soldier's calling and a writer's ambition. See Anthony J. Cascardi, 'Cervantes' Two Hands,' in *Cervantes y su mundo*, ed. A. Robert Lauer and Kurt Reichenberger (Kassel: Edition Reichenberger, 2005), 3:41–60.

33 Thomas O. Sloane, *Donne, Milton, and the End of Humanist Rhetoric* (Berkeley: University of California Press, 1985), and *On the Contrary*.

34 See Sloane, *Donne, Milton*, 211, 215. The waning of the dialogic ideal may be understood in relation to the inherent instability of *controversia*, but also to

the rise of print culture and, mainly elsewhere in Europe, to the influence of Ramism. Print may work counter to the humanist movement by deemphasizing conditions of speech that are grounded in the social matrix. No doubt the predilection for printed texts diminished the pedagogical importance of arguing *in utramque partem* since it weakened the importance of rhetorical education in general.

35 *Leviathan*, ch. 12, p. 171.

36 Colie, *Paradoxia Epidemica: The Renaissance Tradition of Paradox* (Princeton: Princeton University Press, 1966).

37 The idea of a *consensus omniorum* is unlikely to yield the cohesion that a 'commonwealth' ought to have. I explain in chapter 7 that Cervantes was responding to a very different set of ideas about what would be required to make a 'nation,' and to make a nation whole.

38 Hobbes, *De Corpore Politico*, ed. J.C.A. Ghaskin (Oxford: Oxford University Press, 2008), VI, 15, p. 207.

39 *Leviathan*, Introduction, 82.

40 The locus classicus on linguistic perspectivism in Cervantes is Leo Spitzer, 'Linguistic Perspectivism in the *Don Quijote*,' in *Linguistics and Literary History* (1948; rpt. Princeton: Princeton University Press, 1974), 41–85. The argument that Cervantes' 'perspectivism' projects a future reader not anywhere contained within the book is convincingly made by Wlad Godzich and Nicholas Spadaccini, 'Popular Culture and Spanish Literary History,' in *Literature among Discourses* (Minneapolis: University of Minnesota Press, 1986), 41–61.

5 The Practice of Theory

1 Cervantes was doubtless aware of various versions of Cicero's claim (*De officiis*, I.31.114) that the truly wise person is the one who recognizes that all the world's a stage. Tacitus functioned as a proxy for Machiavelli in allowing the darker implications of this view to be placed in circulation.

2 This is admittedly to schematize Plato's nuanced and changing attitudes toward *theoria*. For a more detailed account, see Andrea Nightingale, *Spectacles of Truth in Classical Greek Philosophy* (Cambridge: Cambridge University Press, 2004).

3 See Nightingale: 'Distancing us from our traditional world-view, it encourages us to accompany the mythic philosopher on his journey to the Forms.' Ibid., 96.

4 See ibid., 142.

5 Ibid., 118.

6   This insight is, in the end, as important for 'practice' as it is for 'theory.' As
    we shall see in regard to Don Quijote's advice to Sancho and Sancho's
    governorship on Barataria, Cervantes was well aware of the risks involved in
    any attempt to displace 'theory' by an experiment in 'practice,' if only because
    'practice' is never wholly innocent. Just as the limits of 'theory' need to be
    probed, so too the idea of 'practice' needs to be investigated for the ways in
    which it too is a discursive construct. In the case of Barataria, the island itself
    is clearly a theatrical affair staged by the Duke and the Duchess.

7   The practice of a philosophical critique of Europe from exotic and sometimes
    fantastic extra-European locations extends widely, from Lucian's *True History*
    to Montaigne's essay on the cannibals and Montesquieu's *Lettres Persanes*.

8   Antonio de Guevara is one of many who note the need for keen observation, in
    his account of Phetonio's voyage in the *Relox de príncipes*, which I discuss
    below. As Nightingale notes, there were many cultural and historical factors
    that contributed to the emergence of *theoria* in the fourth century BCE: the
    development of writing, social tensions between an aristocratic class and the
    demos, the professionalization of many disciplines and occupations, the creation
    of schools of higher education, the rise of imperial politics, and the decline of
    the city-state. These conditions were remarkably similar to those in which
    Cervantes found himself, in spite of enormous local differences. Cervantes was
    powerfully aware that he was living in the midst of a culture in crisis. His critical
    orientation toward these historical factors was supported by his affinity with the
    humanist interest in philosophical reform. This put Cervantes well within range
    of a position that was close to the sense of *theoria* evident in Plato's texts.

9   Alban Forcione discusses this figure in connection with Cervantes' *El
    licenciado vidriera* in *Cervantes and the Humanist Vision* (Princeton:
    Princeton University Press, 1982), 309–12, where the point is the need to
    temper theory by knowledge from experience. I discuss the critique of theory
    by practice in the chapter to follow ('Theory Brought down to Earth').

10 '[Los tebanos] acordaron de enviar allá a un filósofo entre ellos muy estimado,
    que avía nombre de Phetonio, y mandáronle que pidiese las leyes a los
    lacedemonios y que mirase bien qué tales eran sus costumbres y ritos.' *Relox
    de príncipes*, ed. Emilio Blanco (Madrid: Turner, 1994), 538.

11 'Yo he estado allá más de un año mirándolo todo muy por menudo.' *Relox de
    príncipes*, 538.

12 'Porque los philósofos somos obligados a mirar no sólo lo que se haze, pero
    aun saber por qué se haze.' Ibid.

13 'Sabed, tebanos, que ésta es la respuesta de mi embaxada, conviene a saber:
    que los lacedemonios en esta horca ahorcan a los ladrones, con este cuchillo
    degüellan a los traydores, con esta mordaza atormentan a los parleros, con

estos açotes castigan a los vagabundos, con estos grillos detienen a los sediciosos y con estas esposas atan a los juzgadores; finalmente digo, que yo no os traygo por escripto las leyes, pero tráygoos los instrumentos con que se conservan las leyes' (ibid.). His 'theoretical' point, based on observation, is that written laws mean nothing without enforcement. Perhaps this is why Sancho insists on enforcement in the ordinances he enacts on Barataria, which become known after him as 'The Constitutions of the Great Governor Sancho Panza' ('Las constituciones del gran gobernador Sancho Panza').

14 'Esta peregrinación ha de ser curiosa i prudente, no descuidada o nescia, como suele ser la de hombres ociosos y vagabundos ... es una cierta i averiguada regla para conoscer un hombre si ha sacado provecho de su peregrinación o no ... mirar lo que dice en sus conversaciones de las tierras por donde ha peregrinado; porque si condena a bulto las tierras estrangeras, i a bulto loa las suias, esse tal es hombre apassionado, o descuidado, o mal mirado, o nescio, o loco; en tal ánimo no cabe distinción de cosas o no hai distinción, no puede haver elección, sin elección no hai prudencia, todo falta, do prudencia falta.' Furió Ceriol, *El concejo y consejeros del príncipe*, ed. Diego Sevilla Andrés (Valencia: Institución Alfonso el Magnánimo), 133–5.

15 Aristotle, *Protrepticus* (*An Exhortation to Philosophy*), 44b; a reconstruction of the text in English is available by Anton-Hermann Chroust (Notre Dame: University of Notre Dame Press, 1964).

16 'Nombre griego, vale especulación, meditación y contemplación, del verbo θεωρείν, *animo contemplari.*' Covarrubias, *Tesoro de la lengua castellana, o española,* ed. Felipe C.R. Maldonado, rev. Manual Camarero (Madrid: Castalia, 1995), 916b, s.v. *teórica.*

17 Cicero writes it in Greek in the *Letter to Atticus*, 12, 6. 1. See also the use of *contemplativus* (opp. *practicus*) as a rendering of *theoreticus* as attested in Lewis and Short, *Latin Dictionary* (Oxford: Clarendon Press, 1962).

18 This is true not only in Cervantes, nor only in Spain. In his 1598 dictionary, *A worlde of wordes, or most copious, dictionaire in Italian and English*, for example, John Florio gives no independent listing for anything like 'theory' but does gloss *theorica astronomia* as 'that part of Astronomy chat giueth the view of the motions of the planets by their Orbes.' See http://www.pbm .com/~lindahl/florio1598/.

19 'El Coloquio de los perros,' in *Novelas ejemplares*, ed. Juan Bautista Avalle-Arce (Madrid: Castalia, 1987), 3:270. 'The Dialogue of the Dogs,' trans. David Kipen (Brooklyn, NY: Melville House, 2008), 50–1.

20 In *Famous Utopias of the Renaissance*, ed. Frederic White (1946; rpt. New York: Hendricks House, 1955), 6. This less modern translation preserves a better sense of the original than some more colloquial English versions.

21 Michel de Montaigne, *Essays*, trans. Donald Frame (Stanford: Stanford University Press, 1957), 150.

22 'Del famoso reino de Candaya, que cae entre la gran Trapobana [*sic*] y el mar del Sur, dos leguas más allá del cabo Comorín, fue señora la reina doña Maguncia, viuda del rey Archipiela, su señor y marido' (II, 38, p. 332).

23 The *Lusíadas*, well known in Spain, can itself be read as part travel report, inside of which is the account of a fanciful journey to the celestial spheres, X, 91; it may have been one of Cervantes' points of reference for the flight on Clavileño.

24 See Thomas Hart, 'Renaissance Dialogue and Narrative: *The Viaje de Turquía*,' *Modern Language Review* 95 (2000), 112.

25 Pedro Mártir de Anglería, *Décadas del nuevo mundo*, ed. Ramón Alba (Madrid: Ediciones Polifemo, 1989), 9.

26 For example, in pointing out the similarity between the episode of the Knight of the Lake and the adventure in the Cave of Montesinos, Forcione writes, 'The episode of the Cave of Montesinos contains some striking formal parallels to the debate between the Canon and Don Quixote, which would suggest that there are deeper thematic links between the two scenes … In addition to the similarity of the journeys to the other world, which in the former case Don Quixote narrates as an adventure typical of the books of chivalry and in the present case recounts as a real experience … there is in both episodes a frame of literary debate surrounding the vision and reflecting critically upon it. Don Quixote is guided to the cave by the humanist Cousin, a "famous scholar much given to the reading of books of chivalry." The literary ideals of this young man bear the stamp of the Renaissance critical movement.' *Cervantes, Aristotle and the 'Persiles'* (Princeton: Princeton University Press, 1970), 137–8.

27 Lucian, *The True History*, in *The Works of Lucian of Samosata*, trans. Henry Watson Fowler and Francis George Fowler (1905; rpt. Forgotten Books, n.p., 2007), 303. The denial of truthfulness takes the familiar form of the so-called Cretan liar's paradox: 'I now make the only true statement you are to expect – that I am a liar' (302). On paradox in Cervantes, see Charles Presberg, *Adventures in Paradox* (University Park: Pennsylvania State University Press, 2001). For the wider context, see Rosalie Colie, *Paradoxia Epidemica: The Renaissance Tradition of Paradox* (Princeton: Princeton University Press, 1966), and Steven Hutchinson, 'Mapping Utopias,' *Modern Philology* 85 (1987), 170–85.

28 The remark has a source in Virgil, *Aeneid*, VI, 264–7: 'Ye gods, who hold the domain of spirits! Ye voiceless shades … Suffer me to tell what I have heard; suffer me of your grace to unfold secrets buried in the depths and darkness of

the earth.' Trans. H.R. Fairclough (Cambridge, MA: Harvard University Press, 1999).

29 The passage continues: 'And after eight days again his disciples were within, and Thomas with them: then came Jesus, the doors being shut, and stood in the midst, and said, Peace be unto you. Then saith He to Thomas, Reach hither thy finger, and behold my hands; and reach hither thy hand, and thrust it into my side: and be not faithless, but believing. And Thomas answered and said unto him, My Lord and my God. Jesus saith unto him, Thomas, because thou hast seen Me, thou hast believed: blessed are they that have not seen, and yet have believed.' John 20:26–9 (King James version).

30 Vives, *De tradendis disciplinis*, in *Vives: On Education*, trans. Foster Watson (Cambridge: Cambridge University Press, 1913).

31 See especially chapter 99 of *Las Sergas* and María Rosa Lida de Malkiel, 'La visión de trasmundo en las literaturas hispánicas,' in Howard Rollin Patch, *El otro mundo en la literatura medieval*, trans. Jorge Hernández Campos (México, DF: Fondo de Cultura Económica, 1956). The episode is echoed in the *Persiles*, III, 18. Just as the pilgrims are about to reach Rome the generous and wise Soldino warns of an impending fire. He leads them to his hermitage and invites them into what looks like a dark cave only to reveal, in its centre, a beautiful field full of flowers and fruit-bearing trees. Here again are the Elysian fields of Don Quixote's fantasy, achieved now not by an impetuous leap into murky waters, but through painstaking work. Soldino explains: 'I built the hermitage with my own hands and with my constant effort I dug the cave … Here I am lord of myself' (my translation) (Yo levanté aquella ermita, y con mis brazos y con mi continuo trabajo cavé la cueva … Aquí soy yo señor de mí mismo), ed. Juan Bautista Avalle-Arce (Madrid: Castalia, 1969), 395. This is treated in Ruth El Saffar, 'Persiles' Retort: An Alchemical Angle on the Lovers' Labors,' *Cervantes* 10 (1990), 31.

32 The relevant textual echoes are Virgil, 'Conticuere omnes intentique ora tenebant' (*Aeneid*, II, 1); and Cervantes, 'Callaron todos, tirios y troyanos' (*Don Quijote*, II, 26, p. 239). On this passage, see the edition of *Don Quijote* by Rudolph Schevill and Adolfo Bonilla in the *Obras completas de Miguel de Cervantes Saavedra* (Madrid: Bernardo Rodriguez, Gráficas Reunidas, 1914–41).

33 The very first words of the *Republic*, spoken by Socrates, are 'I went down [*katebên*] yesterday with Glaucon …' (katebên chthes eis Peiraia meta Glaukônos …), *Republic*, 327a. This 'descent' may itself resonante with the prior tradition of mythical and epic descents.

34 In *Don Quijote*, II, 24, the episode is described as questionable by the fictional chronicler Cide Hamete; the reader is asked to make a prudential

judgment about its veracity: 'No me puedo dar a entender ni me puedo persuadir que al valeroso don Quijote le pasase puntualmente todo lo que en el antecedente capítulo queda escrito ... Tú, lector, pues eres prudente, juzga lo que te pareciere' (734) (I cannot believe, nor can I persuade myself, that everything written in the preceding chapter actually happened in its entirety to the valiant Don Quixote ... You, reader, since you are a discerning person, must judge it according to your own lights [614]). Knowing that the visions were obviously part of a dream, the further meaning of this remark is that the reader must determine what *sense* to make of what Don Quijote claims he saw.

35 This fourth-century *Commentary on Scipio's Dream* was, in fact, one of the basic sources for medieval scholasticism. Aristotle addresses related questions in the *Historia animalium* and the *Parva naturalia*. A compendium is available in *Aristotle on Sleep and Dreams*, ed. David Gallop (Warminster: Aris and Phillips, 1996).

36 Macrobius, *Commentary on the Dream of Scipio*, ed. and trans. W.H. Stahl (New York: Columbia University Press, 1952), 90.

37 Virgil, *Aeneid*, VI, 893–6. Macrobius's 'Commentary' would have provided Cervantes with additional support for his engagement with these ideas by surrounding Virgil's figure of the two gates with references to Homer and to Porphyry's commentaries on Homer.

38 The Cousin says 'Yo, señor Don Quijote de la Mancha, doy por bien empleadísima la jornada que con vuestra merced he hecho, porque en ella he granjeado cuatro cosas' (Señor Don Quixote of La Mancha, I consider the journey I have made with your grace very worthwhile, because I have derived four things from it). Among them is 'haber sabido lo que se encierra en esta cueva de Montesinos, con las mutaciones de Guadiana y de las lagunas de Ruidera, que me servirán para el *Ovidio español* que traigo entre manos' (having learned what is inside the Cave of Montesinos, along with the mutations of the Guadiana and the Lakes of Ruidera, which will be of great use to me in the *Spanish Ovid* that I have in hand); another is 'entender la antiguedad de los naipes, que, por lo menos, ya se usaban en tiempo del emperador Carlomagno, según puede colegirse de las palabras que vuesa merced dice que dijo Durandarte, cuando al cabo de aquel grande espacio que estuvo hablando con él Montesinos, él despertó diciendo *Paciencia y barajar*' (having realized the antiquity of cards, which were in use during the time of the Emperor Charlemagne, as one can deduce from the words your grace says Durandarte said when, after that long period of time when Montesinos was talking to him, he awoke and said 'Have patience and shuffle the deck'); still another is 'haber sabido con certidumbre el nacimiento del río Guadiana, hasta ahora ignorado de las gentes' (having learned the truth regarding the origins of the Guadiana River, unknown to anyone until now [615; II, 24, p. 224]).

39 Polydore Vergil, 'Letter to Lodovico Odassio of Padua' (1499), in *On Discovery*, ed. and trans. Brian Copenhaver (Cambridge, MA: Harvard University Press, 2002), 4–5.

40 See Giuseppe Mazzotta, *Cosmopoiesis* (Toronto and London: University of Toronto Press, 2001), 89.

41 'El que mira la historia de los antiguos tiempos atentamente, y lo que enseñan guarda, tiene luz para las cosas futuras, pues una misma manera de mundo es toda.' Luis Cabrera de Córdoba, *De historia*, ed. Santiago Montero Díaz (Madrid: Instituto de Estudios Políticos, 1948), 11.

42 The Grossman translation reverses the meaning of the Spanish by having Don Quijote say that he wishes to remain at home. As for the reference to Archbishop Turpin, see *Don Quijote* I, 49, where the Canon says: 'I cannot deny, Señor Don Quixote, that some of what your grace has said is true, especially with regard to Spanish knights errant; by the same token, I also wish to concede that there were Twelve Peers of France, though I cannot believe they did all those things that Archbishop Turpin writes about them' (427) (no puedo yo negar, señor don Quijote, que no sea verdad algo de lo que vuestra merced ha dicho, especialmente en lo que toca a los caballeros andantes españoles; y, asimesmo, quiero conceder que hubo doce Pares de Francia, pero no quiero creer que hicieron todas aquellas cosas que el arzobispo Turpín dellos escribe; I, 49, p. 582). The possible connection between the minaret of the mosque of Granada, known as 'Turpin's Tower,' and the so-called leaden books of Sacromonte is discussed by Barbara Fuchs in *Mimesis and Empire: The New World, Islam, and European Identities* (Cambridge: Cambridge University Press, 2001), 113–17.

43 Roberto González Echevarría treats this in *Love and the Law in Cervantes* (New Haven: Yale University Press, 2005).

44 'I saw my donkey, and riding him, dressed like a Gypsy, was Ginés de Pasamonte, the lying crook that my master and I freed from the chain' (481) (Venía … en hábito de gitano aquel Ginés de Pasamonte, aquel embustero y grandísimo maleador que quitamos mi señor y yo de la cadena; II, 4, p. 67).

45 The character may have been inspired by Jerónimo de Pasamonte, whose biography was remarkably parallel to Cervantes' own.

46 The *Commentaria in Platonem* (Florence, 1496).

47 See John Muckelbauer, 'Sophistic Travel: Inheriting the Simulacrum through Plato's The Sophist,' *Philosophy and Rhetoric* 34 (2001), 225–44.

48 Ficino lingers on this last passage, which is crucial to the distinction between icons and phantasms: 'There are two kinds of imitation. One kind looks at something that is true. Committed to using the true as its exemplar, it fabricates likeness, just as a painter and others do. The other kind has not yet gazed upon the true and yet strives to fabricate images of it. In the process,

however, it produces phantasms that appear perhaps to resemble realities but are not true likenesses. We must put the sophist in the latter kind.' The translation is from Michael Allen, *Icastes: Marsilio Finico's Interpretation of Plato's Sophist (Five Studies and a Critical Edition with Translation)* (Berkeley: University of California Press, 1989), 228.

49 The criminality of the sophist is sometimes linked to the proliferation of evil itself. Forcione points to implications of this proliferation for the picaresque in *Cervantes and the Mystery of Lawlessness* (Princeton: Princeton University Press, 1984), 25.

50 Luis Vaz de Camões, *Os Lusíadas*, trans. Landeg White (Oxford: Oxford University Press, 1997), X, 91, p. 215.

51 On hyperbole as an element of a baroque aesthetic, see Christopher Johnson, *Hyperboles: The Rhetoric of Excess in Baroque Literature and Thought* (Cambridge, MA: Harvard Department of Comparative Literature, 2010).

52 Lucian, *Icaromenippus, An Aerial Expedition*, in *The Works of Lucian of Samosata*, 458. In addition, the episode resonates with a central question raised by a text that was long believed to be the 13th book of Plato's *Laws*, the *Epinomis*: what 'science' is best able to teach the highest forms of wisdom and piety? The answer proposed by the *Epinomis* is astronomy, which surprises because the early astronomers had a reputation for impiety. An English text is available in Plato, *Philebus and Epinomis*, trans. A.E. Taylor, ed. Raymond Klibansky (London: Thomas Nelson and Sons, 1956). Early modern editions were published in Basle (1534 and 1556) and Louvain (1551). The Greek text was also part of Aldus's 1513 Venice edition of Plato's works. An edition of the Greek with a series of indispensable studies is Leonardo Tarán, *Academica: Plato, Philip of Opus, and the Pseudo-Platonic* Epinomis (Philadelphia: American Philosophical Society, 1975). One implication of this claim is that one learns best on the basis of ironic practice. On the atheism of astronomers, see Plato, *Laws*, XII, 967a–d, and the discussion in Tarán, *Academica*, 98–114.

53 Cicero, *De republica*, VI, 20–2, pp. 90–1.

54 Macrobius, *Commentary on the Dream of Scipio*, trans. William Harris Stahl (New York: Columbia University Press, 1952), 216. Macrobius is a likely source for the fanciful comments on geography in *Don Quijote*, I, 29, where Dorotea pretends to be a princess from the kingdom of Micomicón and is said to have journeyed all the way from Guinea (Ethiopia) to seek Don Quijote's help.

55 *Discourses on Livy*, trans. and ed. Julia Conaway Bonadella and Peter Bonadella (Oxford: Oxford University Press, 1997), II, 14, p. 187.

56 'Rodeamos la tierra, medimos las aguas, subimos al cielo, vemos su grandeza, contamos sus movimientos, y no paramos hasta Dios, el cual no se nos esconde. Ninguna cosa hay tan encubierta, ninguna hay tan apartada, ninguna

hay puesta en tantas tinieblas, do no entre la vista del entendimiento humano.' Pérez de Oliva, *Diálogo de la dignidad del hombre*, ed. José Luis Abelllán (Barcelona: Ediciones de Cultura Popular, 1967), 118.

57 *Discourse on Livy*, trans. Julia Conway Bonadella and Peter Bonadella (Oxford: Oxford University Press, 1997), 26.

58 See II, 41, where Don Quijote assures Sancho, 'Sancho, my friend, the ínsula I have promised you is neither movable nor transitory: it has roots growing so deep in the depths of the earth that three pulls will not tear it out or move it from where it is now' (719) (Sancho amigo, la ínsula que yo os he prometido ni es movible ni fugitiva: raíces tiene tan hondas, echadas en los abismos de la tierra, que no la arrancarán ni mudarán de donde está a tres tirones; II, 41, p. 346).

59 *Nicholas of Cusa on Learned Ignorance*, trans. Jasper Hopkins (Minneapolis: Arthur J. Banning Press, 1981), 117.

6 Politics Brought down to Earth

1 More, *Utopia*, in *Famous Utopias of the Renaissance*, ed. Frederic White (New York: Hendricks House, 1955), 33.

2 The work on the subject of nationhood is vast. In examining its complexities beyond the basic historical level, I have found especially helpful Benedict Anderson's 1983 *Imagined Communities* (2nd ed. London: Verso, 2003), and Homi Bhabha's *The Location of Culture* (London and New York: Routledge, 1994). I discuss both at greater length in chapter 7.

3 Amado Alonso points out that 'tierra' here indicates the 'patria regional' while in similar contexts 'patria' suggests 'tierra nacional.' See *Castellano, español, idioma nacional* (Buenos Aires: Instituto de Filología de la Facultad de Filosofía y Letras de la Universidad de Buenos Aires, 1938), 36. I take up these issues further in relation to national identity in chapter 7.

4 Antonio de Guevara is a likely influence on these chapters; his *Menosprecio de corte y alabanza de aldea* is particularly important in this context. See Horacio Chiong Rivero, 'Insula de buen gobierno: el palimpsesto guevariano en "Las Constituciones del gran gobernador Sancho Panza,"' *Cervantes* 28 (2009), 135–65. On the practical politics of the island, see also Daniel Nemser, 'Governor Sancho and the Politics of Insularity,' *Hispanic Review* 78 (2010), 1–23.

5 The question of one's dress as an authentic or inauthentic reflection of identity has a special connotation within the cultural context in which Cervantes wrote. In a world where *conversos* were obliged to pass as Old Christians, it was said by some that merely adopting the comportment of an Old Christian would gain one the identity. In the *Libro de todas las cosas*, for example, Quevedo remarks that a Jew or a Moor can become a hidalgo by adopting the comportment of

the Old Christians: 'Para ser caballero o hidalgo, aunque seas judío y moro, haz mala letra, habla despacio y recio, anda a caballo, debe mucho y vete donde no te conozcan, y lo serás.' *Libro de todas las cosas* in *Los sueños, Cartas del caballero de la Tenaza, Capitulaciones de la vida de la corte, Libro de todas las cosas* (Paris: Michaud, Biblioteca Eeconómica de Clásicos Castellanos, n.d.), 249; I have modernized the accents. Barbara Fuchs discusses related issues in *Passing for Spain* (Urbana and Chicago: University of Illinois University Press, 2003).

6 Suárez, *De Legibus ac Deo Legislatore* (1612; rpt. London, 1679), III: 2, 3. The matters that go beyond natural law are those of consensus and political community.

7 See Vitoria, 'On Law,' lect. 121, article 3, in *Political Writings*, ed. Anthony Pagden and Jeremy Lawrance (Cambridge: Cambridge University Press, 1991), 158–60.

8 On the farcical nature of Sancho's governorship, see Anthony Close, *Cervantes and the Comic Mind of His Age* (Oxford: Oxford University Press, 2000).

9 Bataillon, *Erasmo y España*, 2nd ed., trans. Antonio Alatorre (Mexico: Fondo de Cultura Económica, 1966), 784.

10 The dangers of fame as a corrupting force in the 'republic' and the need for good judges are prominent themes in Antonio de Guevara's *Relox de príncipes*.

11 Norbert Elias, *Power and Civility*, trans. Edmund Jephcott (New York: Pantheon, 1982), 236–7.

12 This observation is key in Leo Straus's 'The Problem of Socrates,' in *The Rebirth of Classical Political Rationalism*, ed. Thomas Pangle (Chicago: University of Chicago Press, 1989), 106.

13 See Marjorie Grice-Hutchinson, *The School of Salamanca* (Oxford: Clarendon Press, 1952).

14 See Michael McKeon, *The Origins of the English Novel, 1600–1740* (Baltimore: Johns Hopkins University Press, 1987).

15 *La vida de Lazarillo de Tormes* (Madrid: Mestas, 1999), 12; trans. Michael Alpert in *Two Spanish Picaresque Novelas* (Harmondsworth: Penguin, 1969), 24.

16 Don Quijote's 'justification' for this inconsistency is framed so as to overlook the role of the Duke and the Duchess. 'I say all this ... so that you do not attribute the kindness you have received to your own merits, but give thanks first to heaven for disposing matters so sweetly, and then to the greatness that lies in the profession of knight errantry' (730) (Todo esto digo ... para que no atribuyas a tus merecimientos la merced recibida, sino que des gracias al cielo, que dispone suavemente las cosas, y después darás a la grandeza que en sí encierra la profesión de la andante caballería; II, 42, p. 357).

17 In I, 20, Don Quijote explicitly mentions the fact that Gandalín in *Las Sergas de Esplandián* is made a count.

18 Olaus Magnus, archbishop of Uppsala. His *Historia de Gentibus Septentrionalibus* (1555) was doubtless of importance for Cervantes in the writing of the *Persiles*.

19 Botero's book was in part an ode to the natural beauty of the newly discovered islands. *Relaciones*, trans. Diego de Aguiar (Valladolild: Herederos de D. Fernández de Córdoba, 1603). 'Será cosa conveniente … descubrir las islas que están esparcidas y derramadas por todo este inmenso piélago, obra … de mayor entretenimiento y gusto por la variedad de las mismas islas y por la infinita diversidad de sus calidades y naturalezas, porque, aunque verdaderamente parece que en el continente plugo a la divina majestad mostrarnos junta en cuerpo la hermosura y belleza de la tierra, en las islas nos la han querido también mostrar y descubrir en muchas y diversas formas distintas y repartidas: éstas, pequeñas; aquéllas, grandes; unas desiertas y otras pobladas; aquéllas fértiles, y éstas, estériles; campesinos y silvestres.' This is cited by Francisco López Estrada from the 1603 edition in his *Tomás Moro y España* (Madrid: Universidad Complutense, 1980), 66.

20 *Los trabajos de Persiles y Sigismunda*, ed. Juan Bautista Avalle-Arce (Madrid: Castalia 1969), I, 22, pp. 149–50; *The Trials of Persiles and Sigismunda: A Northern Story*, trans. Celia Weller and Clark Colahan (Berkeley: University of California Press, 1989), 96–7.

21 For details on the category of the *novus homo*, see by Ronald Syme, *The Roman Revolution* (Oxford: Oxford University Press, 1960), as well as T P. Wiseman, *New Men in the Roman Senate* (Oxford: Oxford University Press, 1971), and H.H. Scullard, 'The Political Career of a "Novus Homo,"' in *Cicero*, ed. T.A. Dorey (New York: Basic Books, 1965), 1–25.

22 See Childers, *Transnational Cervantes* (Toronto and London: University of Toronto Press, 2006).

23 José Antonio Maravall's study of the picaresque hinges largely on the claim that the picaresque was a literature of social critique. See *La literatura picaresca desde la historia social* (Madrid: Taurus, 1986).

24 This may also be Cervantes' way of commenting ironically on Antonio de Guevara's idea in the *Relox de príncipes* that one ought to be suspicious of anyone who seeks the office of judge: 'a big indication is to see whether he sought out the position of judge. Because whoever of his own will tries to take charge of the conscience of another must not hold his own in high regard' (muy gran indicio es ver si él procuró aquel oficio de justicia. Porque el hombre que de su propia voluntad procura encargarse de conciencia ajena, no deve tener en mucho la suya propia). *Relox de príncipes*, ed. Emilio Blanco (Madrid: Turner, 1994), 660.

25 The *Dicta* is the name given to *Disticha, de Moribus Catonis*, which was widely used since the Middle Ages as an elementary Latin textbook. On the connection to Cervantes, see Elias L. Rivers, 'Don Quixote's Fatherly Advice, and Olivares's,' *Cervantes* 18 (1998), 75.

26 Machiavelli writes: 'Anyone who reads Xenophon's life of Cyrus can see in Scipio's actions how much glory his imitation of Cyrus brought him, and to what extent Scipio conformed with what Xenophon wrote about Cyrus in matters of chastity, openness, humanity, and liberality.' *The Prince*, trans. Peter Constantine (New York: Modern Library, 2007), 71. The reference was widespread. Erasmus mentions it in *De Copia* more as an example of education than as an example of history. *On Copia of Words and Ideas*, trans. Donald B. King and H. David Rix (Milwaukee: Marquette University Press, 1963), 71. On the *Cyropaedia* more generally, see Christopher Nadon, *Xenophon's Prince* (Berkeley: University of California Press, 2001).

27 See also Guevara's *Aviso de privados o despertador de cortesanos* (1539). On the influence of Guevara on the episodes of Sancho's governorship, see Rivero, 'Insula de buen gobierno.'

28 Luis Murillo enumerates many of the additional potential sources in vol. 3 of his edition of *Don Quijote*, 124–5.

29 There is a rich literature addressing this issue. See especially Allan H. Gilbert, *Machiavelli's Prince and Its Forerunners: The Prince as a Typical Book Regimine Principum* (Durham, NC: Duke University Press, 1938), and Albert Russell Ascoli, 'Machiavelli's Gift of Counsel,' in *Machiavelli and the Discourse of Literature*, ed. Albert Russell Ascoli and Victoria Kahn (Ithaca: Cornell University Press, 1993), 219–57.

30 See Donald Bleznick, 'Don Quijote's Advice to Governor Sancho Panza,' *Hispania* 40 (1957), 62–5.

31 There are, of course, biblical resonances of the need for justice and mercy, ranging from Psalms (101:1) to the Gospels (Matthew 23:13; Luke 11:42).

32 *De Civilitate* went through more than twelve editions in 1530 alone and was widely translated throughout the 1530s. See Erika Rummel, ed., *The Erasmus Reader* (Toronto and London: University of Toronto Press, 1990), 101.

33 The concern about flattery shows up in More's reference to 'the fawnings and flatteries of those who propose to fix their own interests' (*Famous Utopias*, 11). More's source was Plutarch's 'How to Tell a Flatterer from a Friend,' *Moralia*, I, ed. and trans. Frank Cole Babbitt (Cambridge, MA: Harvard University Press, 1927), 265–395. The *Moralia* had been translated into Spanish and published in Salamanca in 1571.

34 *The Book of the Courtier*, trans. Charles S. Singleton (Garden City: Double-day, 1959), 30.

35 It should nonetheless be noted that there are indeed practical jokes in *The Courtier* (as, for example, in II, 85–6).

36 'I visit the market squares, as your grace advises, and yesterday I found a marketwoman who was selling hazelnuts, and I saw that she had mixed a *fanega* of fresh hazelnuts with a *fanega* of ones that were old, worthless, and rotten' (796) (Yo he visito las plazas, como vuestra merced me aconseja, y ayer hallé una tendera que vendía avellanas nuevas, y averigüéle que había mezclado con una hanega de avellanas nuevas otra de viejas, vanas y podridas; II, 51, p. 431).

37 Murillo, *A Critical Introduction to Don Quijote* (New York: Peter Lang, 1988), 202.

38 Cervantes may also be alluding here to the meagre provisions offered to prisoners.

39 This may also be traced to a story about the life of St Nicholas of Bari, collected in the *Legenda Aurea* of Jacobus de Vorágine. See *Leyenda de los santos* (Madrid and Rome: Universidad Pontificia Comillas and Institutum Historicum Societatis Iesu, 2007).

40 The cases all involve petty crimes and minor offences, rather like those brought before the judge in Cervantes' *entremés*, *El juez de los divorcios*.

41 'So graves penas proybió Licurgo a los lacedemonios que las mugeres no saliessen fuera de sus casas si no era entre año los días señalados de fiestas, ca dezía él que las mugeres o avían de estar en los templos orando a los dioses, o avían de estar en sus casas criando a sus hijos; porque andar las mugeres por los campos a passear o por las plaças a ruar, ni a ellas es honesto, ni a sus casas provechoso.' *Relox de príncipes*, ed. Emilio Blanco (Madrid: Turner, 1994), 538.

42 Aristotle likewise writes about certain cosmological myths that were added to the tradition with a view to the persuasion of the multitude: 'the other traditions have been added in mythical form for the persuasion of the multitude and for their legal and social uses.' *Metaphysics*,1074b, trans. Richard Hope (Ann Arbor: University of Michigan Press, 1960), 265.

43 Machiavelli, *The Prince*, 68.

7 Imagining the Nation

1 On these ethical implications, see Alban Forcione, 'Sancho Panza and Cervantes' Embodiment of Pastoral,' in *Literature, Culture, and Society in the Modern Age: In Honor of Joseph Frank*, ed. Edward J. Brown et al. (Stanford: Department of Slavic Languages and Literatures, Stanford University, 1991), 57–75.

2 On de Soto, see Venancio D. Carro, *Domingo de Soto y el derecho de gentes* (Madrid: Bruno del Amo, 1930). Suárez's *Tractatus de Legibus ac Deo Legislatore*

(1612) was influential in the wider European context in part because of a 1679
London edition.

3 Maravall takes a similar position in 'The Origins of the Modern State,'
   Cahiers d'Histoire Mondiale 6 (1961), 794–5.

4 See especially Wallerstein's *The Modern World System* (New York: Academic
   Press, 1947–80), and the essays in Charles Tilly, ed., *The Formation of
   National States in Western Europe* (Princeton: Princeton University Press,
   1975).

5 Machiavelli, *The Prince*, trans. Peter Constantine (New York: Modern
   Library, 2007), 103. It is worth recalling that in *Don Quijote*, II, 33, the
   Duchess presents Sancho with a state to rule in the form of an island-city. It
   may be that the reference involves an allusion to Naples, a Spanish colony and
   an island that was not an island. See Braudel, *The Mediterranean and the
   Mediterranean World in the Age of Philip II*, trans. Sîan Reynolds (New
   York: Harper and Row, 1972–3), 1:160–1.

6 Braudel, *The Mediterranean*, 2:657. Joseph Strayer's thesis that the origins of
   the sovereign modern state were medieval has been regarded by some as a
   'soft' claim, offering too wide a berth to the notion of the 'state.' For Strayer's
   views, see *On the Medieval Origins of the Modern State* (Princeton: Princeton
   University Press, 1970), 10.

7 Benedict Anderson, *Imagined Communities*, 2nd ed. (London: Verso, 2003).

8 The literature on the subject is vast. My views are indebted to Wallerstein, *The
   Modern World System*; to various essays gathered in *Nation and Narration*, ed.
   Homi Bhabha (London: Routledge, 1990), especially Ernest Renan, 'What Is a
   Nation?'; to Timothy Brennan, 'The National Longing for Form'; to Homi
   Bhabha *The Location of Culture* (London: Routledge, 1994); and to Pheng
   Cheah, *Spectral Nationality* (New York: Columbia University Press, 2003).

9 See Braudel, *The Mediterranean*, 2:865–6, and Timothy Hampton, *Fictions of
   Embassy: Literature and Diplomacy in Early Modern Europe* (Ithaca: Cornell
   University Press, 2009).

10 De Soto writes: 'It is undeniable that harbors, rivers, gold and silver mines
   belong to the people who own the territory in which they lie. The sea
   bordering a land belongs to the owners of the territory, and they can therefore
   reserve the right of fishing there, and forbid it to others. In this way the King
   of Spain and Portugal can forbid foreigners (and in fact does forbid them) to
   catch sea-carp (*turdos*) along the shore of Turdetania, commonly known as
   the Algarve, and to fish near the shores of Spain.' See Bernice Hamilton,
   Political Thought in Sixteenth-Century Spain (Oxford: Clarendon Press,
   1963), 104.

11 See Maravall, 'The Origins of the Modern State,' 793.

12 This desire may help explain the Enlightenment notion of a form of sovereignty that could be attached to the people as a whole.

13 In *The Politics of Friendship* (London: Verso, 2005) Jacques Derrida notes that the two, kinship and politics, may not be so distinct after all.

14 Renan, 'What Is a Nation?' 19.

15 Cited in Maravall, 'Origins,' 805.

16 *Republic*, 414e. I follow the translation of Desmond Lee (London: Penguin, 1974).

17 This is the point of the subsequent passage in the *Republic* (415a–c) which tells that during the forming process God added gold into the mixture of the rulers, silver into the auxiliaries, and iron and copper into the composition of the farmers and workers. The idea of universal brotherhood also draws on the New Testament notion of a brotherhood in Christ, as in Matthew 23:8: 'But do not be called Rabbi; for One is your Teacher, and you are all brothers.'

18 As Timothy Hampton argued for France, the early modern nation is also literary in its formation. See *Literature and Nation in the Sixteenth Century* (Princeton: Princeton University Press, 2001), 9, and also Richard Helgerson, *Forms of Nationhood: The Elizabethan Writing of England* (Chicago: University of Chicago Press, 1992).

19 Also in the preliminary materials to Part II, Cervantes is described by Josef de Valdivielso as the 'honor and glory of our nation, wonder and envy of foreign ones' (my translation) (honra y lustre de nuestra nación, admiración y invidia de las estrañas; II, p. 29). One should also note Cervantes' fanciful invocation of the book's success, and of his fame in China (in the dedicatory letter to the Conde de Lemos of *Don Quijote*, II).

20 They did so well before Grotius and Pufendorf began to refashion Aquinas's views of natural law for that same purpose.

21 Popular impressions notwithstanding, the Spanish Inquisition was modern in its procedures and tactics, and not in this respect a relic of the Middle Ages.

22 Printing was introduced into Alcalá de Henares well before it became established in Madrid. But by 1561, when Madrid had become the new capital, printing had also taken root there. Philip II established a Royal Press (Imprenta Real) in 1594. See Colin Clair, *A History of European Printing* (London: Academic Press, 1976), 185–94, 'Sixteenth Century Spanish Printing.' By 1500, there were already some 20 million printed books in Europe. The estimate is widespread. See Bill Katz, *Dahl's History of the Book* (Metuchen, NJ: Scarecrow Press, 1995).

23 Sansón Carrasco in II, 3; Don Quijote in II, 16.

24 See the chapter 'DissemiNation' in *The Location of Culture* (London: Routledge, 1994), 201.

25 Sassen, *Territory, Authority, Rights: From Medieval to Global Assemblages* (Princeton: Princeton University Press, 2006).

26 Alfred Weber has written extensively on this topic. See *La Crisis de la idea moderna del estado en Europa* (Madrid: Revista de Occidente, 1932).

27 See Maravall, 'Origins,' 803–4.

28 See Kagan, *Lawyers and Litigants in Castile, 1500–1700* (Chapel Hill: University of North Carolina Press, 1981).

29 'Pusieron los Reyes Católicos el gobierno de la justicia y cosas públicas en manos de letrados … cuya profesión eran letras legales … Esta manera de gobierno, establecida entonces con menos diligencia, se ha ido extendiendo por toda la cristiandad, y está hoy en el colmo de poder y autoridad: tal es su profesión de vida en común.' Diego Hurtado de Mendoza, *Guerra de Granada*, ed. R. Blanco-González (Madrid: Castalia, 1970), 105. See also Maravall, 'Origins,' 807.

30 Cited in Kagan, *Lawyers and Litigants*, 3.

31 One of the central ingredients in the legal construction of the modern state, the notion of political rights as claims that bind the agents of the state to specific groups of people, was alien to it. I have found especially helpful Charles Tilly's 'Reflection on the History of European State-Making,' in Tilly, ed., *The Formation of National States in Western Europe*, 36.

32 I am thinking especially of the excerpt from Renan, 'What Is a Nation?' in Homi Bhanba, ed., *Nation and Narration* (London and New York: Routledge, 1990), 8–22. Among the things that concern Renan are those that border on the imaginary – language and 'spirit' – and not merely territory or legal standing in the international context.

33 See Angel Gómez Moreno, *España y la Italia de los humanistas* (Madrid: Gredos, 1994), 121–32, 'Lengua y hegemonía en Europa.'

34 Appeal to the 'common,' whether as the shared or the vulgar, is notably not a part of Plato's politics. On the contrary, it is a part of politics that Plato tried to resist. In the words of one recent thinker, Jacques Rancière, 'the *demos* [for Plato] is the intolerable existence of the great beast which occupies the stage of the political community without ever becoming a single subject.' *On the Shores of Politics*, trans. Liz Heron (London: Verso, 1995), 12.

35 'Ya que España reina y tiene conversación en tantas partes no solamente del mundo sabido antes, pero fuera dél, que es en las Indias, y tan anchamente se platica y enseña la lengua española según antes la latina, a propósito es entendella y adornalla por todas vías.' Castillejo, 'Dedicatoria,' *Diálogo entre el autor y su pluma*, cited in Amado Alonso, *Castellano, español, idioma nacional* (Buenos Aires: Instituto de Filología, Facultad de Filosofía y Letras, Universidad de Buenos Aires, 1938), 24. The matter has received ample

critical attention, especially in relation to sixteenth-century humanism. See, for example, Angel Gómez Moreno, *España y la Italia de los humanistas*, 121–32 ('Lengua y hegemonía en europa').

36 The formation of a collective political consciousness on the Iberian Peninsula depended on the existence of a national language 'como instrumento de la nación y, en cierto modo como su símbolo, y visto en parangón con los otros idiomas nacionales.' Alonso, *Castellano, español*, 29–30.

37 See Maravall, *Estado moderno y mentalidad social: Siglos VI a XVII*, I (Madrid: Revista de Occidente, 1972), 457–525. Alvaro de Luna speaks of the 'amor natural que cada uno ha a su tierra.' Luna, 'Libro de las claras e virtuosas mujeres,' in *Opúsculos literarios de los siglos XIV a XVI* (Madrid: A. Paz y Melía, 1892), 131–2, 138, 269. Recent work on the subject, with a special view towards Spain's empire, is Tamar Herzog, *Defining Nations: Immigrants and Citizens in Early Modern Spain and Spanish America* (New Haven: Yale University Press, 2003).

38 See Gómez Moreno, *España y la Italia de los humanistas*, 121–32, 'Lengua y hegemonía en Europa.'

39 Maravall, *Esatado moderno y mentaliad social*, 457. The name most closely associated with the peninsula, Iberia, was never associated with language, no matter how ancient it was.

40 The full title is *Arcadia de Jacobo Sannazaro traduzida nuevamente en nuestra Castellana lengua Española, en prosa y verso como ella estava en su primera lengua toscana.* Juan de Valdés, *Diálogo de la lengua*, ed. Cristina Barbolani (Madrid: Cátedra, 1998), 123.

41 In the *Viaje del Parnaso*: 'Yo he abierto en mis Novelas un camino / por do la lengua castellana puede / mostrar con propiedad un desatino,' in *Obras completas*, vol. 1, ed. Angel Valbuena Prat (Madrid: Aguilar, 1970), IV, 25–7, p. 90; and in the 'Prólogo' to the *Novelas ejemplares*, 'soy el primero que he novelado en lengua castellana.' Ed. Juan Bautista Avalle-Arce (Madrid: Castalia, 1982), 1:64.

42 The *Fuero Juzgo* has its roots in the Visigothic *Liber iudiciorum*. Covarrubias even includes his family name in his definition of the *fuero juzgo* in the *Tesoro*.

43 See Jacques Lezra, 'La Mora Encantada: Covarrubias in the Soul of Spain,' *Journal of Spanish Cultural Studies* 1 (2000), 5–27, here p. 9. As Eric Graf noted in this regard, Cervantes' text in turn questions the idea of 'national identity' promoted by Castilians such as the Covarrubias and their Hapsburg patrons. Graf, 'When an Arab Laughs in Toledo: Cervantes's Interpellation of Early Modern Spanish Orientalism,' *Diacritics* 24 (1999), 74.

44 'No se puede negar que era andaluz, y no castellano, y que scrivió aquel su *Vocabulario* con tan poco cuidado que parece averlo escrito por burla' (124).

45 I adapt the notion of 'contact zones' from Mary Louise Pratt's 1991 essay 'Arts of the Contact Zone,' in *Mass Culture and Everyday Life*, ed. Peter Gibian (London: Routledge, 1997), 61–72, and her *Imperial Eyes* (London: Routledge, 1992).

46 Haedo, *Topografía e historia general de Argel* (Madrid: Sociedad de Bibliófilos Españoles, 1927), 1:116. See also María Antonia Garcés, *Cervantes in Algiers* (Nashville: Vanderbilt University Press, 2002), 145.

47 It is well established that Agi Morato is modelled after Hāŷŷī Murād, whom Cervantes may have known from the *Topografía de Argel*.

48 Barbara Fuchs provides an illuminating discussion of this passage in its wider context in *Exotic Nation: Maurophilia and the Construction of Early Modern Spain* (Philadelphia: University of Pennsylvania Press, 2009), 24–6.

49 Homi Bhabha proposes this as the underlying condition for 'national' identity: 'The nation fills the void left in the uprooting of communities and kin, and turns that loss into the language of metaphor.' *The Location of Culture*, 200.

50 See Braudel, *The Mediterranean*, 2:884 and Haedo, *Topografía*, 1:116.

51 See Marc Shell, *Children of the Earth: Literature, Politics, and Nationhood* (New York: Oxford University Press, 1993), 29.

52 See Albert Sicroff, *Les Controverses des status de 'pureté de sang' en Espagne du XVe au XVIIe siècle* (Paris: Didier, 1960).

53 See Pierre Vilar, 'Patria y nación en el vocabulario de la guerra de la independencia española,' in *Hidalgos, amotinados y guerrilleros* (Barcelona: Grijalbo, 1982), 223. See also I.A.A. Thompson, 'Castile, Spain and the Monarchy: From *patria natural* to *patria nacional*,' in *Spain, Europe and the Atlantic World*, ed. Richard L. Kagan and Geoffrey Parker (Cambridge: Cambridge University Press, 1995), 159.

54 For a modern treatment of related issues, see Shell, *Children of the Earth* and Herzog, *Defining Nations*.

55 Castrillo, *Tratado de república* (1521; rpt. Madrid: Instituto de Estudios Políticos, 1958), 19.

56 Already chroniclers like Diego de Valera called the royal faction of those belonging to the city the 'citizens.' See Maravall, 'Origins,' 795.

57 See Thompson, 'Castile, Spain and the Monarchy,' 136.

58 'España es república de Reynos muy diferentes en qualidades ... tantos Reynos así de contrarias complexiones, es casi imposible admitir medio alguno de los antiguos, sin daño de algunas partes de él.' The 'Discurso VIII' is reprinted in Maravall, 'Un primer proyecto de facultad de ciencias políticas en la crisis del siglo XVII (El 'Discurso VIII' de Sancho de Moncada'),' in *Estudios de historia del pensamiento español: El siglo del barroco* (Madrid: Cultura Hispánica,

1975), 158. In a recent essay, Jean-Pierre Dédieu argues that over the long run the project of nation building in Spain involved dis-aggregation and segregation, and that the problematic aggregation of kingdoms in the phase I am referring to here was but a moment in a larger process. See 'Comment l'état forge la nation,' in *Le sentiment national dans l'Europe méridionale aux XVIe et XVIIe siècles*, ed. Alain Tallon (Madrid: Casa de Velázquez, 2007), 51–74.

59 'Cuanto mayor es la potencia de los príncipes, es menor la libertad de la nación dominante, y mayores sus gastos para sustentar las conquistas.' Saavedra Fajardo, *Locuras de Europa* (Madrid: Atlas, 1944), 108. Cervantes clearly understood *nación* as indicating a racial and ethnic basis of community that could not be imagined as viable into the future.

60 Monzón criticized demands made 'para la defensa del buen gobierno y paz y quietud del reino de Portugal, todo el caudal que para esto sea necesario se saque del mismo reyno, y lo mismo para los reynos de la corona de Aragón.' See Thompson, 'Castile, Spain and the Monarchy,' 143.

61 'La religión católica y la causa y defensa de ella es común a toda la cristiandad, y si estas guerras importan para esto, no toca a los reynos de Castilla llebar toda la carga, estándose los demás reynos, príncipes y repúblicas a la mira.' Thompson, 'Castile, Spain and the Monarchy,' 143, n. 53.

62 A discussion of related issues that calls these distinctions into question is Immanuel Wallerstein, 'The Construction of Peoplehood: Racism, Nationalism, Ethnicity,' in Etienne Balibar and Wallerstein, *Race, Nation, Class: Ambiguous Identities* (London: Verso, 1991), 71–85.

63 Barbara Fuchs convincingly argues that romance plays a major role in this enterprise. See *Passing for Spain: Cervantes and the Fictions of Identity* (Urbana: University of Illinois Press, 2003).

64 'He had never bothered to find out if it was an island, city, town, or village that he was governing' (810) (que él nunca se puso a averiguar si era ínsula, ciudad, villa o lugar la que gobernaba; II, 54, p. 447).

65 The bibliography on this subject as it plays out in Cervantes is extensive. I have benefitted especially from Francisco Márquez Villanueva, *Personajes y temas del Quijote* (Madrid: Taurus, 1975), 229–335, as well as *El problema morisco (desde otras laderas)* (Madrid: Ediciones Libertarias, 1991); Steven Hutchinson, *Cervantine Journeys* (Madison: University of Wisconsin Press, 1992), 184–8; and Miguel Herrero García, *Ideas de los españoles en el siglo XVII*, (Madrid: Gredos, 1966), 563–96.

66 Henri Lapeyre, *Géographie de l'Espagne morisque* (Paris: S.E.V.P.E.N., 1959), 51. Pierrre Chaunu offers an excellent review of the debates over the numbers of *moriscos* expelled in his review-essay of Lapeyre, 'Minorités et conjuncture: L'expulsion des morisques en 1609,' *Revue Historique* 221 (1961), 81–98.

67 The details are remembered in, among other places, Diego Hurtado de Mendoza, *Guerra de Granada*, 108–9.

68 Elliott, *Imperial Spain* (New York: St Martin's Press, 1963), 227–8.

69 William Childers addresses related issues in his discussion of internal colonization in Spain in *Transnational Cervantes* (Toronto and London: University of Toronto Press, 2006). On connections between the *morisco* question and pastoral fantasy in Cervantes, see also Javier Irigoyen-García, '"¡Qué si destas diferencias de música resuena la de los albogues!" Lo pastoral y lo morisco en Cervantes,' *Cervantes* 28 (2008), 119–46.

70 See especially the chapter on Joseph Conrad, 'Magical Narratives,' in Jameson, *The Political Unconscious* (Ithaca: Cornell University Press, 1981). Jameson's analysis of romance in turn refers to Northrop Frye's *Anatomy of Criticism* (Princeton: Princeton University Press, 1957). Claudio Guillén's discussion of literature as 'historical contradiction' with special reference to *El Abencerraje* and the 'Moorish novel' is consistent with this line of thought. See *Literature as System* (Princeton: Princeton University Press, 1971).

71 For a related view, see González Echevarría, *Love and the Law in Cervantes* (New Haven: Yale University Press, 2005), and Anthony J. Cascardi, *Ideologies of History in the Spanish Golden Age* (University Park: Pennsylvania State University Press, 1997).

72 See Françoise Crémoux, *Pélerinages et miracles à Guadaloupe au XVIe siècle* (Madrid: Casa de Velásquez, 2001), 103

73 This place, Quintanar, is one that Cervantes refers to several times in the *Quijote*. Juan Haldudo is said to be from the general area ('el vecino del Quintanar'; I, 4, p. 97).

74 The relationship between Germany and *germanía* (also found in 'Rinconete y Cortadillo') is not trivial. Its etymology suggests a union of German siblings as well as a brotherhood among the speakers of a language. See Covarrubias, *Tesoro de la lengua castellana, o española*, 56b, s.v. *Alemania*. On the creation of a *lingua franca* out of the mixture of tongues in Cervantes, see Elvezio Canonica, 'La conciencia de la comunicación interlingüística en las obras dramáticas y narrativas de Cervantes,' in *Cervantes: Estudios en la víspera de su centenario*, ed. K. Reichenberger (Reichenberger: Kassel, 1994), 19–42.

75 On the transnational context of pilgrimage in Cervantes, with special emphasis on the *Persiles*, see Childers, *Transnational Cervantes*.

76 The xenophobic tendency was longstanding. The Catholic kings, for example, wanted no foreigners in ecclesiastical posts in their kingdom. See Maravall, 'Origins,' 806.

77 Cf. Damián Fonseca, *Justa expulsión de los moriscos de España* (1612), cited in Márquez Villanueva, *Personajes y temas*, 240.

78 This is not uncomplicated; aside from the toponymical reference, 'Ricote' means 'filthy rich.'

79 'They stretched out on the ground, and with the grass as their tablecloth, they set out bread, salt, knives, nuts, pieces of cheese, and bare ham-bones that could not be gnawed but could still be sucked' (812) (Tendiéronse en el suelo y, haciendo manteles de las yerbas, pusieron sobre ellas pan, sal, cuchillos, nueces, rajas de queso, huesos mondos de jamón, que si no se dejaban mascar, no defedían el ser chupados; II, 54, p. 449).

80 The emphasis on the wine cannot be overlooked: 'What stood out most on the field of that banquet, however, were six wineskins, for each of them took one out of his bag; even the good Ricote, transformed from a Morisco into a German or Teuton, took out his own wineskin, comparable in size to the other five' (812) (Lo que más campeó en el campo de aquel banquete fueron seis botas de vino, que cada uno sacó la suya de su alforja: hasta el buen Ricote, que se había transformado de morisco en alemán o en tudesco, sacó la suya, que en grandeza podía competir con las cinco; II, 54, p. 449). In 'Sancho Panza and Cervantes' Embodiment of Pastoral,' Forcione reads the episode as a moment of bucolic happiness, where Cervantes transcends the literary pastoral and moves toward a Christian ethic of friendship.

81 Marc Shell treats the subject over a wide range of cases in *Children of the Earth*.

82 See Shell, *Children of the Earth*, 32, 215.

83 See Thomas Case, 'Cide Hamete Benengeli y los *libros plumbeos*,' *Cervantes* 22 (2002), 9–24.

84 'I think it would be treason against my king if I helped his enemies' (815) (Haría traición a mi rey en dar favor a sus enemigos; II, 54, p. 452).

85 Privateering was, in fact, often undertaken by a city acting on its own authority, independent of national allegiances (Braudel, *The Meiterranean*, 2:869; Garcés, *Cervantes in Algiers*, 30).

86 The suggestion is that gifts and favours might enable the intervention at court: 'By means of favors and gifts, many difficult issues can be resolved' (891) (Por medio del favor y de las dádivas, muchas cosas dificultosas se acaban; II, 65, p. 539).

87 In *Love and the Law* he argues that the reunion of Ricote and his daughter also amounts to the reintegration of an outlaw, in the legal sense, back into the nation. The legal context is not obviated by the issues of nation and ethnicity. Ricote is an outlaw, first, for having ignored the edict of expulsion, and second for having concealed a fortune within Spanish borders at the very time when the nation was short of cash. Given Spain's financial plight and the edict against the *moriscos*, Ricote would have to be regarded as nothing less than a

traitor. In fact, he travels with a band of fake pilgrims who are attempting to export some of the wealth that the *moriscos* had been forced to leave in Spain when they fled.

88 Vives, from the beginning of book IV of *De concordia et discordia in humano henere*, trans. Laureano Sánchez Gallego (Mexico, DF: Séneca), 341.

89 On the subject of the influence of the brigands among the nobility and, vice-versa, the support lent to the brigands by the nobles, see Braudel, *The Mediterranean*, 2:749.

90 See *Love and the Law*, 164.

91 In Spain the countryside was also the imaginary ground for a moral critique of the court, as in Antonio de Guevara's well-known *Menosprecio de corte y alabanza de aldea*.

92 Don Quijote's response adheres strictly to the rhetorical features of Roque's statement, which he finds surprising: 'Don Quixote was amazed to hear Roque speak so well and so reasonably, because he had thought that among those whose profession it was to rob, kill, and steal, there could be no one who was well-spoken' (858) (Admirado quedó don Quijote de oír hablar a Roque tan buenas y concertadas razones, porque él se pensaba que, entre los de oficios semejantes de robar, matar y saltear no podía haber alguno que tuviese buen discurso; II, 60, p. 501).

93 Cf. Jacques Rancière, who regards this in quite the opposite way. For him, Plato's politics is anti-maritime. 'Athens has a disease that comes from its port, from the predominance of maritime enterprise governed entirely by profit and survival.' *On the Shores of Politics*, trans. Liz Heron (London: Verso, 2007), 1. He goes on to associate empirical politics (including the fact of democracy) with maritime politics and the desire for possession. He posits that 'in order to save politics it must be pulled aground among the shepherds' (1).

94 Cicero, *De officiis* (*On Obligations*), trans. Walter Miller (Cambridge, MA: Harvard University Press, 1968), 3:107 (p. 384).

95 Cicero, *On Obligations*, 1:50, p. 52. See also Daniel Heller-Roazen, *The Enemy of All: Piracy and the Law of Nations* (New York: Zone Books, 2009), 13–22.

96 Recall how Marcela echoes Gelasia of *La Galatea* VI: 'I was born free and ground myself in freedom' (Libre nascí y en libertad me fundo). Marcela: 'I was born free, and in order to live free I chose the solitude of the countryside'; Marcela goes on: '[My intention] was to live perpetually alone and have only the earth enjoy the fruit of my seclusion and the spoils of my beauty' (99–100) ([Mi intención] era vivir en perpetua soledad, y de que sola la tierra gozase el fruto de mi recogimiento y los despojos de mi hermosura. Yo nací libre, y para

poder vivir libre escogí la soledad de los campos; I, 14, p. 186). Underlying her Neoplatonic beauty and remarkable independence is the profile of a narcissist, for whom any form of relationship with others is impossible to conceive: 'The trees of these mountains are my companions; I communicate my thoughts and my beauty to the trees and to the waters … I have wealth of my own and do not desire anyone else's; I am free and do not care to submit to another: I do not love or despise anyone' (99–100) (Los árboles destas montañas son mi compañía; las claras aguas destos arroyos, mis espejos; con los árboles y con las aguas comunico mis pensamientos y hermosura … tengo riquezas propias y no codicio las ajenas; tengo libre condición y no gusto de sujetarme: ni quiero ni aborrezco a nadie; I, 14, pp. 186–7). Her narcissism is predicated upon a form of autonomy that neither loves nor hates others, because it refuses to recognize the affects: 'I have wealth of my own and do not desire anyone else's' (100) (Tengo riquezas propias y no codicio las ajenas; tengo libre condición y no gusto de sujetarme: ni quiero ni aborrezco a nadie; I, 14, p. 187).

97 Cicero, *On Obligations*, 1:51, citing verses by Ennius: 'The friendly soul who shows one lost the way / Lights, as it were, another's lamp from his. / Though he has lit another's, his own still shines.' Trans. P.G. Walsh (Oxford: Oxford University Press, 2000), 19.

98 'He dispatched the letter with one of his squires, who changed his bandit's clothes for those of a peasant, and entered Barcelona, and delivered it to the person to whom it was addressed' (861) (Despachó estas cartas con uno de sus escuderos, que, mudando el traje de bandolero en el de un labrador, entró en Barcelona y la dio a quien iba; II, 60, p. 505).

8 Civil Society, Virtue, and the Pursuit of Happiness

1 'Ars Poetica,' trans. H.R. Fairclough (Cambridge MA: Harvard University Press, 1970), vv. 396–9: 'fuit haec sapientia quondam, / publica privatis secernere, sacra profanis, / concubitu prohibere vago, dare iura maritis, / oppida moliori, leges incidere ligno' (482–3).

2 Jürgen Habermas, *The Structural Transformation of the Public Sphere*, trans. Thomas Burger with Frederick Lawrence (Cambridge MA: MIT Press, 1993), 3.

3 'Wir meinen die Elemente des neuen Verkehrszuhammenhangs: den *Waren- und Nachrichtenverkehr*, den der frühkapitalistische Fernhandel schafft.' *Strukturwandel der Öffentlichkeit* (Neuwied am Rhein and Berlin: Luchterland, 1965), 25.

4 The Spanish translation, by Bernardino de Mendoça, was published in Madrid in 1604. Insofar as Lipsius treats mainly of principalities, the work is meant to 'compete' with, or rather to temper, Machiavelli.

5 Hobbes, *De Cive* (1651; rpt. Whitefish, MT: Kessinger, 2004), 48–53.

6 English translation, 1594, *Six Bookes of Politickes or Civil Doctrine*, I, 1, p. 1. I cite the reprinted Latin edition of the *Politicorum* (Hiledesheim: Georg Olms Verlag, 1998), 2. Castrillo's treatise on the republic likewise addresses elements of the polis on the order of 'civil society' in chapter 26, dealing with 'mercaderes y oficiales.' *Tractado de república* (1521; rpt. Madrid: Centro de Estudios Políticos, 1958), 198–205.

7 *Six Bookes*, I, 1, p. 16. 'Vita civilis in societas est: Societas in duabus rebus, Commercio et Imperio' (*Politicorum*, 71). The notions of 'civil order' and 'civil powers' as opposed to a divine order and ecclesiastical powers were, of course, much older, but continued to be influential in the writings of Vitoria and others. See, for example, Vitoria's lecture 'De Potestate Civili' of 1528 ('Of Civil Power') in *Political Writings*, ed. Anthony Pagden and Jeremy Lawrence (Cambridge: Cambridge University Press, 1991), 1–44. Lipsius was able to temper the harshness of Machiavellian ideas and was especially influential in Spain. See Theodore G. Corbett, 'The Cult of Lipsius: A Leading Source of Early Modern Spanish Statecraft,' *Journal of the History of Ideas* 36 (1975), 139–52, and Jeremy Robbins, 'The Art of Perception,' *Bulletin of Spanish Studies* 82 (2005), 41–2. Halvard Leira aptly describes the influence of Lipsius: 'His works could be found in the libraries of both Richelieu and Olivares, and, in what was probably *the* most important textbook for diplomats of the 17th and early 18th century, Juan de Vera y Figueroa's *Embaxador*, the author drew heavily on Lipsius' ideas, particularly the division that Lipsius made in the *Politica*, between the dissimulation and deceit that could be necessary in the public life of Princes (and ambassadors) and the strict morality that should govern their private lives. Lipsius also corresponded directly with several prominent Spanish statesmen … Lipsius' particular popularity in Spain could be explained partly by his affinity with the Spanish scholastics, like Vitoria, partly, as … the double strand of militarism and piety that dominated Spanish statecraft, and that led to a search for theories that harmonised Machiavellian themes and religious values.' 'Justus Lipsius, Political Humanism and the Disciplining of 17th Century Statecraft,' *Review of International Studies* 34 (2008), 669–92.

8 Guicciardini offers the contrasting view. 'Quanto si ingannono coloro che a ogni parola allegano e Romani' (How wrong it is to cite the Romans at every turn). *Ricordi*, ed. R. Spongano (Florence: Sansoni, 1951), 110.

9 Machiavelli, *Discourses on Livy*, trans. Julia Conaway Bonadella and Peter Bonadella (Oxford: Oxford University Press, 1997), III, 1, pp. 246ff.

10 Machiavelli, *The Prince*, trans. Peter Constantine (New York: Modern Library, 2007), 70.

11 See Albert O. Hirschman, *The Passions and the Interests* (Princeton: Princeton University Press, 1977). Hirschman explains that the 'passions' could be tempered by 'interests,' which could, in turn, benefit the political order.

12 Aristotle, *Politics*, 1252b, trans. Ernest Barker (London: Oxford University Press, 1952), 5.

13 As Agamben puts it, 'It is not the free man and his statutes and prerogatives, nor even simply *homo*, but rather *corpus* that is the new subject of politics.' *Homo Sacer: Sovereign Power and Bare Life*, trans. Daniel Heller-Roazen (Stanford: Stanford University Press, 1998), 124.

14 See, for example, the emphasis on experience in Fadrique Furió Ceriol's *El consejo y consejeros del príncipe* (1559), which was influential enough to have been reworked in English as *Of Councils and Counselors*, by Thomas Blundeville (1570).

15 A standard reference on the subject is William Blackstone, *Commentaries on the Laws of England* (Oxford, 1765–9). The recent work on the subject by Paul D. Halliday, *Habeas Corpus: From England to Empire* (Cambridge, MA: Harvard University Press, 2010), is of special importance.

16 Vladimir Nabokov, *Lectures on Don Quixote* (San Diego: Harcourt Brace Jovanovich, 1983).

17 The language tracks Marcela's in Part I: 'Honor and virtue are adornments of the soul, without which the body is not truly beautiful' (99) (La honra y las virtudes son adornos del alma, sin las cuales el cuerpo, aunque lo sea, no debe de parecer hermoso; I, 14, p. 186).

18 With specific reference to Cervantes and to Don Quijote as living on the margins of the law, see Roberto González Echevarría, *Love and the Law in Cervantes* (New Haven: Yale University Press, 2005).

19 Seneca, 'On the Private Life,' in *Moral and Political Essays*, ed. John Cooper and J.F. Procopé (Cambridge: Cambridge University Press, 1995), 172–80. The essay is a fragment, preserved in the principal manuscript source of Seneca's essays appended to chapter 27 of *On the Happy Life*.

20 MacIntyre, *After Virtue*, 2nd ed. (Notre Dame: University of Notre Dame Press, 1984), 140–1.

21 Aristotle, *Nicomachean Ethics*, 1094a, trans. David Ross (Oxford: Oxford University Press, 1980), 2. See also *Politics*, 1253a: 'Man, when perfected is the best of animals; but if he be isolated from law and justice he is the worst of all.'

22 Cicero, *The Republic*, trans. Niall Rudd (Oxford: Oxford University Press, 1998), 88. Cicero nonetheless held open the idea that there are certain kinds of virtue, intimately tied to the good (e.g., friendship, as outlined in *De amicitia*), that flourish outside the state.

23 Cicero, *On Obligations*, trans. P.G. Walsh (Oxford: Oxford University Press, 2000), I, 153, pp. 51–2.

24 Hegel writes: 'It is part of education, of thinking as the consciousness of the single in the form of the universality, that the ego comes to be apprehended as a universal person in which all are identical. A man counts as a man in virtue of his manhood alone, not because he is a Jew, Catholic, Protestant, German, Italian, etc. This is an assertion which thinking ratifies and to be conscious of it is of infinite importance. It is defective only when crystallized, e.g., as a cosmopolitanism in opposition to the concrete life of the state.' *Philosophy of Right*, trans. T.M. Knox (Oxford: Oxford University Press, 1967), 134.

25 The notion endures until at least Marx. See *The Marx-Engels Reader*, ed. Robert C. Tucker (New York: Norton, 1978), 17–18.

26 This, at least, was the conception made famous by Hegel's *Philosophy of Right* and that was transferred, via Marx, to many subsequent analyses of the modern world. See Z.A. Pelczynski, ed., *The State and Civil Society: Studies in Hegel's Political Philosophy* (Cambridge: Cambridge University Press, 1984). The modern notion of 'civil law' (*ius civile*) nonetheless has ancient roots.

27 *De Officiis*, trans. Walter Miller (Cambridge, MA: Harvard University Press, Loeb Library, 1968), I: 21, p. 23; emphasis added.

28 Habermas, *The Structural Transformation of the Public Sphere*, 74.

29 'The Council of Trent, The Eighteenth Session': *The Canons and Decrees of the Sacred and Oecumenical Council of Trent*, ed. and trans. J. Waterworth (London: Dolman, 1848), 192–232; available electronically at http://history .hanover.edu/texts/trent/ct18.html.

30 The solitary Marcela is an exception in this regard.

31 Tasso's dialogue 'Il Padre di Famiglia' tries to do just this. Tasso in turn refers to Aristotle's *Economics* (where the relevant passage is ch. 8, 1346a). The reference, in the very concluding line of 'Il Padre di Famiglia,' is both to what can be learned at court and what can be learned from Aristotle. See the 'Il Padre' in *Tasso's Dialogues*, trans. Carnes Lord and Dain A. Trafton (Berkeley: University of California Press, 1982), 148.

32 Bauer, *The Cultural Geography of Colonial American Literatures* (Cambridge: Cambridge University Press, 2003).

33 See especially Cicero, *Tusculan Disputations*, book V. Trans. J.E. King (Cambridge, MA: Harvard University Press, Loeb Library, 1927), 424–547.

34 On this tradition in the early modern age, see especially John D. Lyons, *Exemplum: The Rhetoric of Example in Early Modern France and Italy* (Princeton: Princeton University Press, 1989), and Timothy Hampton, *Writing from History* (Ithaca: Cornell University Press, 1990).

35 Cf. Struever, *Theory as Practice: Ethical Inquiry in the Renaissance* (Chicago: University of Chicago Press, 1992), 213. Struever takes praxis in a considerably more literal sense. Nonetheless, it is clear that Cervantes' novelistic approach to the exemplum builds on, and in this case is built out of, issues arising with respect to the Italian novella. As Struever points out, the novellas in the *Decameron* already problematize the exemplum: 'Where the exemplum acts as a translucent illustration of moral maxims, the novella demands only a starting point for moral inquiry; it demands the formulation of a further moral response' (148).

36 A 'sophisma' is understood as a sentence puzzling in its own right on the basis of a certain assumption, designed to bring some abstract issue into sharper focus. See the *Cambridge History of Later Medieval Philosophy*, ed. N. Kretzman et al. (Cambridge: Cambridge University Press, 1982).

37 The label 'curioso' also refers to the strange and rare quality of the story.

38 See Karlheinz Stierle, 'L'Histoire comme example,' *Poétique* 10 (1972), 176–98.

39 Don Quijote: 'Let no person, whatever his circumstance or condition, dare to follow the beautiful Marcela lest he fall victim to my fury and outrage. She has shown with clear and sufficient reasons that she bears little or no blame in the death of Grisóstomo' (101) (Ninguna persona, de cualquier estado y condición que sea, se atreva a seguir a la hermosa Marcela, so pena de caer en la furiosa indignación mía. Ella ha mostrado con claras y suficientes razones la poca o ninguna culpa que ha tenido en la muerte de Grisóstomo; I, 14, p. 188).

40 'Leaving all those present filled with admiration as much for her intelligence as for her beauty' (100–1) (dejando admirados, tanto de su discreción como de su hermosura, a todos los que allí estaban; I, 14, p. 188).

41 MacIntyre gives a rich account of this point in *After Virtue*.

42 Coluccio Salutati is one among many who pointed out the deficiency of teaching precepts without exemplary images in his letter to Juan Fernández de Heredia. *Epistolario di Coluccio Salutati*, II (Rome: Istituto Storico Italiano, 1893), 289–302, 460. On this letter, see Nancy Struever, *The Language of History in the Renaissance* (Princeton: Princeton University Press, 1970).

43 *Discourses*, I, 47, p. 119. This particularism is reflected in Guicciardini, who declares on the basis of historical evidence that 'it is a great error to speak of things of this world absolutely and indiscriminately, and to deal with them, as it were, by the book. In nearly all things we make distinctions and exceptions because of the differences in their circumstances. These circumstances are not covered by one and the same rule.' *Maxims and Reflections (Ricordi)*, ed. Robert Bowers (Gainesville, FL: Scholar's Facsimiles, 1955), sig. c7v.

44 See Struever, *Theory as Practice*, 148.

45 I cite the edition of Juan Bautista Avalle-Arce, *Novelas ejemplares* (Madrid: Castalia, 1982), 1:63–4. Translations from the Prologue are my own.

46 'Yo soy el primero que he novelado en lengua castellana.' *Novelas ejemplares*, 1:64.

47 *Novelas ejemplares*, 1:55. For St Thomas on *eutrapelia*, see *Summa*, 2a 2ae q. 168, art 2. See also Bruce Wardropper, 'La *eutrapelia* en las *Novelas ejemplares* de Cervantes,' *Actas del Séptimo CAII* (1982), 1:153, 169; Joseph R. Jones, 'Cervantes y la virtud de la eutrapelia,' *Anales Cervantinos* 20 (1985), 19–30; and Franscico Márquez Villanueva, *Cervantes en letra viva* (Barcelona: Reverso, 2005), 87–8.

48 Aristotle writes: 'Such, then, is the man who observes the mean, whether he be called tactful or ready-witted. The buffoon on the other hand, is the slave of his sense of humor … The boor, again, is useless for such social intercourse; for he contributes nothing and finds fault with everything.' *Nicomachean Ethics*, trans. David Ross (Oxford: Oxford University Press, 1980), IV, 8 (p. 104).

49 Cervantes also echoes the *Lazarillo*, another dangerous book posing as something more innocent. The anonymous author of the *Lazarillo* cites Pliny as the source of the idea that 'no hay libro, por malo que sea, que no tenga alguna cosa buena.' *La Vida de Lazarillo de Tormes* (Madrid: Mesta, 1999), 11.

50 The image also corresponds closely to one dimension of the 'carnival square' as described by Mikhail Bakhtin in *Problems of Dostoevsky's Poetics*, ed. and trans. Caryl Emerson (Minneapolis: University of Minnesota Press, 1984), 128–9.

51 On the matter of 'oblique' views in Cervantes and Golden Age Spain, see David R. Castillo, *(A)wry Views: Anamorphosis, Cervantes, and the Early Picaresque* (West Lafayette, IN: Purdue University Press, 2001).

52 As Márquez writes, one detects the scent of something concealed here; the phrase is, in fact, an echo of Erasmus's *Moria* and Folly's invitation to join forces with liberating laughter and madness. 'Respira aquí la verdad obfuscada, puesto que esto no es sino un nuevo eco de la *Moria* erasmista y de su invitación con otras palabras a pactar con la locura y risa liberadora' (*Cervantes en letra viva*, 86–7). Márquez goes on to argue that this position is at the core a form of Christian foolishness.

53 See Hampton, *Writing from History*.

54 See Anthony J. Cascardi, 'Two Kinds of Knowing in Plato, Cervantes, and Aristotle,' *Philosophy and Literature* 24 (2000), 406–23.

55 Huarte de San Juan's *Examen de ingenios*, ed. Guillermo Serés (Madrid: Cátedra, 1989); see especially the second 'Proemio,' 178–80. Otis Green

discusses the Cervantes-Huarte connection at length in 'El *Ingenioso Hidalgo*,' *Hispanic Review* 25 (1957), 175–93, though without recognizing the political concerns of either.

56 Citing Aristotle, El Pinciano's character Fadrique aligns the essence of virtue with a form of 'spirit.' 'La virtud no es otra cosa que una fuerça del alma.' *Philosophía antigua poética*, ed. Alfredo Carballo Picazo (Madrid: CSIC, 1953), 22–3.

57 The title of II, 17, speaks explicitly of Don Quijote's *ánimo*, which Grossman renders as 'courage.' Though it is more, *ánimo* may well imply courage, in part through a long history that roots in the sense of 'spirit' as a 'breath' that proceeds from the soul (*ánima*) of a living being. Cf. Covarrubias, *Tesoro de la lengua castellana, o española* (1611), ed. Felipe C.R. Maldonado, rev. Manual Camarero (Marid: Castalia, 1995), 95, s.v. *ánimo, animar*.

58 The episode involving Andrés may be meant as a counter-example to what Tasso writes in 'Il Padre di Famiglia' about the fair treatment that fathers, as masters, owe to servants. *Tasso's Dialogues*, 100–3.

59 I am indebted to the excellent discussion of 'spiritedness' in relation to anger in Stanley Rosen's *Plato's 'Republic': A Study* (New Haven: Yale University Press, 2005), 155–8.

60 See Schaefer, *The Political Philosophy of Montaigne* (Ithaca: Cornell University Press, 1990), 253.

61 As Ferrari has pointed out, this is schematic even for Plato. See Ferrari, *City and Soul in Plato's Republic* (Chicago: University of Chicago Press, 2005).

62 This tradition of inquiry had an enormous range of influence. John Tiptoft's (ca. 1460) translation of Buonaccorso da Montemagno's *Controversia de Nobilitate* (*The Declamation of Noblesse*) intersects directly with it.

63 *Meno*, 70a, trans. W.K.C. Guthrie (Harmondsworth: Penguin, 1956), 115.

64 *Republic*, I, 330b, trans. Desmond Lee, 2nd ed. (London: Penguin, 1974). The passage raises the question of the appropriate measure of generosity, which is germane to the episode of the father of Captive and his brothers in *Don Quijote*.

65 'Industriae ac virtuti.' *Pro Sestio*, lxvi, 137, in *Cicero: The Speeches*, trans. R. Gardner (Cambridge, MA: Harvard University Press, 1966), 226. On the category of the *novus homo*, see the references in chapter 6, n. 21, above.

66 'Il Padre di Famiglia,' 139–41.

67 'True nobility consists of virtue' (317) (La verdadera nobleza consiste en la virtud; I, 36, p. 451). The passage has innumerable classical and humanist resonances, including with Seneca's *Moral Epistles*, XLIV: 'animus facit nobilem.' *Ad Lucilium Epistulae Morales*, I (Rome: Typis Regiae Officinae

Polygraphicae, 1937), 154. Forcione emphasizes the point in relation to the *Novelas ejemplares* in *Cervantes and the Humanist Vision* (Princeton: Princeton University Press, 1982), 250.

68 Hobbes, *Leviathan*, ed. C B. MacPherson (Harmondsworth: Penguin, 1975), I, 10, pp. 151–2.

69 See María Rosa Lida de Malkiel, *La originalidad artística de La Celestina*, 2nd ed. (Buenos Aires: Eudeba, 1970), 671. Don Quijote speaks in similarly Neoplatonic language: 'Beauty, in and of itself, attracts the desires of all who look upon it and recognize it, and royal eagles and high-flying birds swoop down for it as if it were savory bait' (598) (La hermosura por sí sola atrae las voluntades de cuantos la miran y conocen, y como a señuelo gustoso se le abaten las águilas reales y los pájaros altaneros; II, 22, p. 203).

70 This topic is much debated by Leonido and Tirsi in *La Galatea*, IV.

71 'Grisóstomo inherited a big estate, goods as well as lands, no small amount of livestock both large and small, and a large amount of money; the boy became master of all of this, and the truth is he deserved it all, for he was a good companion and a charitable man and a friend of good people' (83) (Quedó heredado en mucha cantidad de hacienda, ansí en muebles como en raíces, y en no pequeña cantidad de ganado, mayor y menor, y en gran cantidad de dineros; de todo lo cual quedó el mozo señor desoluto, y en verdad que todo lo merecía, que era muy buen compañero y caritativo y amigo de los Buenos; I, 12, p. 163).

72 Virtually all of I, 32, provides relevant evidence in this regard.

73 See Michael McKeon, *The Origins of the English Novel, 1600–1740* (Baltimore: Johns Hopkins University Press, 1987).

74 González Echevarría offers an insightful analysis of this matter in *Love and the Law*.

75 'There is a proverb in our Spain, one that I think is very true … [which] says: "The Church, the sea, or the royal house" … whoever wishes to be successful and wealthy should enter the Church; or go to sea as a merchant, or enter the service of kings in their courts … It is my desire that one of you should pursue letters, another commerce, and the third should serve the king in war … In a week's time I shall give each of you his entire share in cash, down to the last penny, without cheating you out of a cent' (335; my translation) (Hay un refrán en nuestra España, a mi parecer muy verdadero, [que] dice: 'Iglesia, o mar, o casa real'… Es mi voluntad, que uno de vosotros siguiese las letras, el otro la mercancía, y el otro sirviese al rey en la guerra, pues es dificultoso entrar a servirle en su casa; que, ya que la guerra no dé muchas riquezas, suele dar mucho valor y mucha fama. Dentro de ocho días, os daré toda vuestra parte en dineros, sin defraudaros en un ardite, como lo veréis por la obra.

Decidme ahora si queréis seguir mi parecer y consejo en lo que os he propuesto; I, 39, p. 474). The implication is that by making themselves worthy
and rich they will also be deserving of the full inheritance the father promises
in good faith to give them ('sin defraudaros en un ardite'). The father's story is
recognizable as a fable-like tale, so much so that in I, 42, the Priest compares
it to the stories that old women might tell while sitting beside the fire in
winter.

76 Cardenio asks aloud: 'Who could imagine that Don Fernando, an illustrious
and intelligent nobleman under obligation to me for my services ... would, as
they say, bother to burden his conscience by taking from me my only sheep?'
(218–19) (¿Quién pudiera imaginar que don Fernando, caballero ilustre,
discreto, obligado de mis servicios ... se había de enconar, como suele decirse,
en tomarme a mí una sola oveja? I, 27, pp. 333–4).

77 'Hidalgos, y aun de caballeros' (I, 28, p. 348).

78 Dorotea says: 'I am your vassal, but not your slave; the nobility of your blood
does not have nor should it have the power to dishonor and scorn the
humbleness of mine; I, a low-born farmer, esteem myself as much as you, a
noble lord, esteem yourself. Your force will have no effect on me, your wealth
will hold no value for me, your words will not deceive me, and your sighs and
tears will not soften me' (23) (Tu vasalla soy, pero no tu esclava; ni tiene ni
debe tener imperio la nobleza de tu sangre para deshonrar y tener en poco la
humildad de la mía; y en tanto me estimo yo, villana y labradora, como tú,
señor y caballero. Conmigo no han de ser de ningún efecto tus fuerzas, ni han
de tener valor tus riquezas, ni tus palabras han de poder engañarme, ni tus
suspiros y lágrimas enternecerme; I, 28, pp. 351–2).

79 Her father, 'the rich Clenardo' (240) (el rico Clenardo), is named only once (I,
29, p. 259), but this is enough to prove who she is to Cardenio.

80 See David Quint, *Cervantes's Novel of Modern Times* (Princeton: Princeton
University Press, 2003).

81 'The valiant heart of Don Fernando – it was, after all, fed by illustrious blood
– softened and let itself be vanquished by the truth he could not deny even if
he had wished to; the indication that he had surrendered and ceded to the
good advice offered to him was that he bent down and embraced Dorotea,
saying to her: "Arise, Señora; it is not right for the woman I have in my heart
to kneel at my feet; if, until now, I have not demonstrated what I say, perhaps
it was ordained by heaven so that I, seeing the fidelity of your love for me,
would esteem you as you deserve to be esteemed"' (319–20) (El valeroso
pecho de don Fernando (en fin, como alimentado con ilustre sangre) se
ablandó y se dejó vencer de la verdad, que él no pudiera negar aunque
quisiera; y la señal que dio de haberse rendido y entregado al buen parecer

que se le había propuesto fue abajarse y abrazar a Dorotea, diciéndole: 'Levantaos, señora mía, que no es justo que esté arrodillada a mis pies la que yo tengo en mi alma; y si hasta aquí no he dado muestras de lo que digo, quizá ha sido por orden del cielo, para que, viendo yo en vos la fe con que me amáis, os sepa estimar en lo que merecéis'; I, 36, p. 454). Quint points out that the story of a prideful nobleman who is tempered by the passion of a virtuous woman becomes a common theme of the modern novel. Among many examples, Jane Austen's *Pride and Prejudice* stands out.

82 The description of his robes in I, 41 is telling. *Oidores* were well paid; ca.1600, *oidores* in Valladolid earned over 300,000 *maravedíes* annually. See Richard Kagan, *Students and Society in Early Modern Spain*, ch. 5, 'The Letrado Hierarchy,' also at http://libro.uca.edu/students/students5.htm.

83 Vitoria, 'De Potestatis Civilis' ('On Civil Power'), sec. 24, 'The commands of parents and husbands are binding in the same manner as civil laws.' *Political Writings*, 43–4. Castrillo, *Tractado de república*, 50–8 ('De la obediencia').

84 Helena Percas de Ponseti suggested that this may be a satirical portrait of Lope de Vega. See *Cervantes y su concepto del arte* (Madrid: Gredos, 1975), 2:332–82.

85 His son reports: 'He truly would have been [rich] if he had been as skilled in preserving his wealth as he was in spending it. This propensity for being generous and openhanded came from his having been a soldier in his youth, for soldiering is a school where the stingy man becomes liberal, and the liberal man becomes prodigal, and if there are any soldiers who are miserly, they are, like monsters, very rarely seen. My father exceeded the limits of his generosity and bordered on being prodigal, something of little benefit to a man who is married and has children who will succeed to his name and position. My father had three sons, all of an age to choose a profession. Seeing, as he said, that he could not control his nature, he decided to deprive himself of the means and cause of his being prodigal and a spendthrift by giving up his estate, without which Alexander himself would have seemed a miser' (334) (Verdaderamente lo fuera [rico] si así se diera maña a conservar su hacienda como se la daba en gastalla. Y la condición que tenía de ser liberal y gastador le procedió de haber sido soldado los años de su joventud, que es escuela la soldadesca donde el mezquino se hace franco, y el franco, pródigo; y si algunos soldados se hallan miserables, son como monstruos, que se ven raras veces. Pasaba mi padre los términos de la liberalidad, y rayaba en los de ser pródigo: cosa que no le es de ningún provecho al hombre casado, y que tiene hijos que le han de suceder en el nombre y en el ser. Viendo, pues, mi padre que, según él decía, no podía irse a la mano contra su condición, quiso privarse del instrumento y causa que le

hacía gastador y dadivoso, que fue privarse de la hacienda, sin la cual el mismo Alejandro pareciera estrecho; I, 39, pp. 472–3).

86 This is a crucial element in Tasso's dialogue 'Il Padre di Famiglia,' 57–8.

87 'My pastimes are hunting and fishing, but I keep neither hawk nor grey-hounds, openly some tame decoy partridges or a few bold ferrets ... I hear mass every day; I distribute alms to the poor but do not boast of doing good works, so as not to allow hypocrisy and vainglory into my heart ... I attempt to bring peace to those whom I know are quarreling; I am devout to Our Lady, and trust always in the infinite mercy of the Lord our God' (554) (Mis ejercicios son el de la caza y pesca; pero no mantengo ni halcón ni galgos, sino algun perdigón manso, o algún hurón atrevido ... oigo misa cada día; reparto de mis bienes con los pobres, sin hacer alarde de las buenas obras, por no dar entrada en mi corazón a la hipocresía y vanagloria ... procuro poner en paz los que sé que están desavenidos; soy devoto de nuestra Señora, y confío siempre en la misericordia infinita de Dios nuestro Señor; II, 16, p. 153).

88 Seneca, 'On Private Life,' 175.

9 Free Speech?

1 *De Officiis*, trans. Walter Miller (Cambridge, MA: Harvard University Press, 1968), I. iv. 14, p. 15.

2 *Don Quijote*, 738. 'Pide no se desprecie su trabajo, y se le den alabanzas, no por lo que escribe, sino por lo que ha dejado de escribir' (II, 44, pp. 366–7).

3 Ticinum is modern Pavia. The literary device whereby the author of the prologue receives assistance from a friend is similarly Boethian. *The Consolation of Philosophy* begins as the narrator marks a pause in his lament on the fickleness of fortune: 'My dutiful pen was putting the last touches to my tearful lament, when a lady seemed to position herself above my head.' This 'lady' is Philosophy herself. *The Consolation of Philosophy*, trans. P.G. Walsh (Oxford: Oxford University Press, 1999), 3.

4 *Petrarch's Remedies for Fortune Fair and Foul*, trans. Conrad H. Rawski (Bloomington: Indiana University Press, 1991), 3:145.

5 There are also echoes of Ovid's *Tristia* in what Cervantes writes here.

6 On topics related to the sideways glance, See Castillo, *(A)wry Views: Anamorphosis, Cervantes, and the Early Picaresque* (West Lafayette, IN: Purdue University Press, 2001).

7 For a conventional view of this passage, see Alan Trueblood, 'Sobre la selección artística en el *Quijote*: "lo que he dejado de escribir" (II, 44),' *Nueva revista de filología hispánica* 10 (1956), 44–50.

8 Márquez Villanueva, *Cervantes en letra viva* (Barcelona: Reverso, 2005), 43–5.

9 Strauss, *Persecution and the Art of Writing* (Glencoe, IL: Free Press, 1952), 24.

10 See Stephen Gilman, *The Spain of Fernando de Rojas* (Princeton: Princeton University Press, 1972).

11 Américo Castro's view of this matter in *El pensamiento de Cervantes* (1925) was unnecessarily exaggerated; the suggestion that Cervantes was a 'disguised hypocrite' was sharply contested by Antonio Vilanova in *Erasmo y Cervantes* (Barcelona: Instituto 'Miguel de Cervantes' de Filología Hispánica, 1949), 11–12.

12 *On Copia of Words and Ideas*, trans. Donald B. King and H. David Rix (Milwaukee: Marquette University Press, 1963), I, 5, p. 14.

13 The formal account of indirect discourse goes back at least as far as chapter 3 of Aristotle's *Poetics*, where Aristotle distinguished between two types of 'imitation by narration.' Aristotle explained that a poet-narrator may 'either take another personality as Homer does, or speak in his own person, unchanged.' Trans. S.H. Butcher (New York: Hill and Wang, 1961), 53. This distinction may represent one way of quelling Plato's fear about the divine madness associated with poetry – if not entirely eliminating anxieties about what may happen when poets speak as if possessed by other voices, and then reducing those fears by identifying indirect discourse as one mimetic possibility among a number of others. This is not ultimately the type of imitation that concerns Aristotle, for what the tragedian does is to represent his characters without any mediating narrator at all.

14 Plato, *Gorgias*, 481; trans. Walter Hamilton (Harmondsworth: Penguin, 1971), 75.

15 This is at *Republic*, 487b. Commenting on what amounts to speech-forcing by Socrates, Adeimantus also says that Socrates makes dialogue a sort of game, in which the other players feel 'hemmed in and left without anything to say, though they are not in the least convinced by the conclusion reached in the moves you have made' (487c). Trans. Desmond Lee (London: Penguin Books, 2003).

16 Bakhtin, *Rabelais and His World*, trans. Hélène Iswolsky (Bloomington: Indiana University Press, 1984), 168–9.

17 See, for example, Walter Kaiser, *Praisers of Folly* (Cambridge, MA: Harvard University Press, 1963) as well as the chapter 'El erasmismo de Cervantes' in Marcel Bataillon, *Erasmo y España*, 2nd ed., trans. Antonio Alatorre (Mexico: Fondo de Cultura Económica, 1966), 777–801.

18 This heads up the 'Quarta Excelencia' of his *Libro de las cinco excelencias del Español* (Pamplona, 1629), 7.

19 McKeon, *Origins of the English Novel, 1600–1740* (Baltimore: Johns Hopkins University Press, 1987).

20 For further exploration of this question, see Anthony J. Cascardi, 'History and Modernity in the Spanish Golden Age: Secularization and Literary Self-Assertion in *Don Quixote*,' in *Cultural Authority in Early Modern Spain: Continuation and Its Alternatives*, ed. Marina Brownlee and Hans Gumbrecht (Baltimore: Johns Hopkins University Press, 1995), 209–33.

21 See Aaron Fogel, *Coercion to Speak: Conrad's Poetics of Dialogue* (Cambridge, MA: Harvard University Press, 1985).

22 Needless to insist, perhaps, that the avoidance of ideology implicit in Machiavelli's going to the heart of things – *dietro alla verità effetuale della cosa* – is ideological in its own way.

23 'Larvatae nunc scientiae sunt: quae, larvis sublatis, pulcherrimae apparerent.' Descartes, *Oeuvres complètes*, ed. Charles Adam and Paul Tannery (Paris: Léopold Cerf, 1908), 10:213.

24 Paul Hazard, *Don Quichotte de Cervantes: Etude et analyse* (Paris: Librairie Mellottée, 1931), 213; my translation. For a recent discussion of related issues in Plato, see Daniel Boyarin, *Socrates and the Fat Rabbis* (Chicago: University of Chicago Press, 2009).

25 See *Republic*, 396c–e.

26 'Coloquio de los Perros,' in *Novelas ejemplares*, ed. Juan Bautista Aalle-Arce (Madrid: Castalia, 1987), 3:264; 'The Dialogue of the Dogs,' trans. David Kipen (Brooklyn, NY: Melville House, 2008), 45.

27 See Maurice Molho's introduction to his translation, *Le Mariage trompeur et Colloque des chiens* (Paris: Aubier-Flammarion, 1970), 32–9. Molho decribes this as an instance of *ilusio*, a trope of irony by Quintilian's standards; see also Thomas Hart, 'Cervantes' Sententious Dogs,' *MLN* 94 (1979), 377–86.

28 'Yo por bien tengo que cosas tan señaladas, y por ventura nunca oídas ni vistas, vengan a noticia de muchos y no se entierrrren en la sepultura del olvido.' *La vida de Lazarillo de Tormes* (Madrid: Mestas, 1999), 11; my translation.

29 'Y pues Vuestra Merced escribe se le escriba y relate el caso muy por extenso, parescióme no tomalle por el medio, sino del principio, porque se tenga entera noticia de mi persona, y también porque consideren los que heredaron nobles estados cuán poco se les debe, pues Fortuna fue con ellos parcial, y cuánto más hicieron los que, siéndoles contraria, con fuerza y maña remando salieron a buen puerto' (*La vida de Lazarillo de Tormes*, 12).

30 In the prefatory letter to the *Praise of Folly*, Erasmus employs a similar topos, speaking of not having the time to perfect his work, mentioning incorrect and pirated editions, and claiming that the text was written while in the country, to mitigate the tedium of a journey ('instead of wasting all the time I had to spend on horseback in idle chatter and empty gossip'). *Praise of Folly*, trans. Robert M. Adams (New York: Norton, 1989), 3.

31 Prologue to the *Novelas ejemplares*, 1:63.
32 In *Pro Sestio*, ii.4, Cicero speaks of his ability to discourse 'freely' ('aut acrius egero aut liberius.' *Pro Sestio in Vatinium*, trans. R. Gardner (Cambridge, MA: Harvard University Press, 1984), 38.
33 Cave, *The Cornucopian Text* (Oxford: Oxford University Press, 1979), 5.
34 Herrera writes with reference to Petrarch, Ariosto, and the Italians generally: 'Yo, si deseara nombre en estos estudios, por no ver envejecida y muerta en pocos días la gloria, que piensan alcanzar eterna los nuestros, no pusiera el cuidado en ser imitador suyo, sino enderezara el camino en seguimiento de los mejores antiguos, y juntando en una mezcla a éstos con los italianos, hiciera mi lengua *copiosa y rica* de aquellos admirables despojos.' *Garcilaso de le Vega y sus comentaristas*, ed. Antonio Gallego Morell, 2nd ed. (Madrid: Gredos, 1972), 311; my emphasis.
35 'Desiderius Erasmus of Rotterdam to John Colet,' in *Collected Works of Erasmus*, vol. 24, *Literary and Educational Writings*, ed. Craig R. Thompson, trans. Betty I. Knott (Toronto and London: University of Toronto Press, 1978), 2:284–98.
36 Consider the claims to brevity in the 'Apologia' responding to Edward Lee: 'I shall explain the matter as it stands, in plain speech and attic style, without passion, so that he cannot complain of being overwhelmed by my eloquence … I shall, moreover, explain matters selectively and in a few words, so as not to keep you too long from your studies with this nonsense, and I shall be brief in arguing against his annotations – if only he had been content to do the same!' In *Controversies, Collected Works of Erasmus*, vol. 72, ed. Jane E. Phillips, trans. Erika Rummel (Toronto and London: University of Toronto Press, 2005), 4.
37 'What does Demosthenian mean, Señor Don Quijote?' asked the duchess. 'That is a word I have never heard before in all my days.' '*Demosthenian* rhetoric,' responded Don Quijote, 'is the same as saying rhetoric of Demosthenes, as *Ciceronian* means of Cicero, and they were the two greatest rhetoricians in the world.' 'That is true,' said the duke, 'and you must have been confused when you asked the question' (670–1) ('¿Qué quiere decir *demostina*, señor don Quijote' preguntó la duquesa, 'que es vocablo que no le he oído en todos los días de mi vida?'*Retórica demostina*' respondió don Quijote 'es lo mismo que decir *retórica de Demóstenes*, como *ciceroniana*, de Cicerón …' 'Así es' dijo el duque, 'y habéis andado deslumbrada en la tal pregunta'; II, 32, p. 289). Cicero and Demosthenes were linked and contrasted over the course of a long tradition going back at least to Quintilian's *Institutio Oratoria*. Erasmus speaks of them together in his *Ecclesiastes* and juxtaposes them in the *Apophthegmata*.

38 Plutarch writes that Cicero was 'often carried away by his love of jesting into scurrility, and when, to gain his ends in his cases he treated matters worthy of serious attention with ironical mirth and pleasantry, he was careless of propriety.' 'Demosthenes and Cicero,' *Lives*, VII, 1.4, trans. Bernadotte Perrin (Cambridge, MA: Harvard University Press, 1971), 211–13.

39 On the question of length in general and this passage in particular, see E.C. Riley, *Cervantes's Theory of the Novel* (Oxford: Clarendon Press, 1964).

40 The form occurs in the *Disciplina Clericalis* and the *Libro de los exemplos* among other places. Don Quijote says to Sancho: 'You have told one of the strangest tales, stories, or histories that anyone in the world ever thought of, and this manner of telling it and then stopping it is something I never shall see, and have never seen, in my life, although I expected nothing else from your intellect' (147) (Dígote de verdad … que tú has contado una de las más nuevas consejas, cuento or historia, que nadie pudo pensar en el mundo, y que tal modo de contarla ni dejarla, jamás se podrá ver ni habrá visto en toda la vida, aunque no esperaba yo otra cosa de tu buen discurso; I, 20, p. 244).

41 The 'Coloquio de los perros' is said to be presented in dialogue form for brevity's sake, as Campuzano explains at the close of 'El casamiento engañoso,' 'I've written it out as a dialogue, to avoid the unwieldy repetition of *said Scipio*, or *replied Berganza*, which tends to make things long' (my translation) (Púselo en forma de coloquio por ahorrar de *dijo Cipión, respondió Berganza*, que suele alargar la escritura; *Novelas ejemplares*, 3:238).

42 This is brought out clearly by Alban Forcione in *Cervantes and the Mystery of Lawlessness* (Princeton: Princeton University Press, 1984).

43 To this the retort was that wisdom without eloquence was impotent. When Sancho rules on Barataria, his eloquence is cited as evidence of the seriousness of purpose he brings to weighty matters: 'All who knew Sancho were amazed to hear him speak so elegantly, and they did not know how to account for it except for the fact that serious offices and responsibilities either strengthen the mind or make it torpid' (773) (Todos los que conocían a Sancho Panza se admiraban oyéndole hablar tan elegantemente, y no sabían a qué atribuirlo, sino a que los oficios y cargos graves, o adoban, o entorpecen los entendimientos; II, 49, p. 404).

44 Montano's *Tractatus de Figuris Rhetoricis* (ca. 1585) featured sacred examples; see the discussion in José María Maestre Maestre, 'Bárbaros contra humanistas,' *Estudios de historia y de arqueología medievales* 7–8 (1987–8), 142.

45 On *copia* of *verba* and *res*, see Quintilian, *Institutio Oratoria*, X, 1. 61

46 Cave, *Cornucopian Text*, 19, n. 22.

47 See Cave, *Cornucopian Text*, p. 21. *De Ratione Studii* was published in Spain by the important printer Miguel de Eguía, who also published *De Copia* in

Alcalá in 1525. For the bibliographical details, see Bataillon, *Erasmo y España*, LIV.

48 Bakhtin, *Rabelais and His World*, 22–3.

49 For recent work on this topic in Plato, see Ramona Naddaff, *Exiling the Poets: The Production of Censorship in Plato's Republic* (Chicago: University of Chicago Press, 2003).

50 Alberto Blecua takes a very different view in relation to the *Persiles* in 'Cervantes y la retórica,' in Aurora Egido, ed. *Lecciones Cervantinas* (Zaragoza: Caja de Ahorros de Zaragoza, Aragón y Rioja, 1985), 137.

51 Hobbes, writing the 'third set' of objections to Descartes, as published in *The Philosophical Writings of Descartes*, trans. John Cottingham, Robert Stoothoff, and Dugald Murdoch (Cambridge: Cambridge University Press, 1984), 2:125–6.

52 Bakhtin, *Rabelais and His World*, 22–3.

53 Torquato Tasso, *Discourses on the Heroic Poem*, trans. Maria Cavalchini and Irene Samuel (Oxford: Clarendon Press, 1973), 28–30. '[Mazzone] chiama icastica quella ch'imita le cose si trovano o si sono trovate, fantastica l'altra specie, ch'è imitatrice de le cose che non sono; e questa vuol che sia la perfetta poesia, la qual ripone sotto la facoltà sofistica, di cui è soggetto il falso e quel che non è.' *Discorsi dell'Arte Poetica e del Poema Eroico* (Bari: G. Laterza, 1964), 86.

54 'Dio e suoi ministri e i demoni e i magi, permettendolo Lui,' *Discorsi*, 97.

55 *Discourses*, 39; 'Può esser dunque una medesima azione e meravigliosa e verisimile: meravigliosa riguardandola in se stessa e circonscritta dentro a i termini, nella sua cagione, la quale è una virtù sopranaturale, possente e usata a far simili meraviglie' (*Discorsi*, 97).

56 For an expansive treatment of these issues, see Wesley Trimpi, *Muses of One Mind* (Princeton: Princeton University Press, 1983).

57 Tasso, *Discourses*, 38–9. 'Io non posso concedere né che la poesia si metta sotto l'arte de' sofisti, né che la perfettissima specie di poesia sia la fantastica. Quantunque io le concedessi che la poesia fosse facitrice degli idoli, come la sofistica, e non solamente degli idoli, ma degli iddii ... non gli concederei nondimeno che fosse la medesima l'arte de' sofisti e quella de'poeti. Dico adunque che senza dubbio la poesia è collocata in ordine sotto la dialettica insieme con la retorica, la qual, come dice Aristotele, è l'altro rampollo de la dialettica facultà' (*Discorsi*, 87).

58 He goes on with his aesthetic 'solution' to the problem: 'Fictional tales must engage the minds of those who read them, and by restraining exaggeration and moderating impossibility, they enthrall the spirit and thereby astonish, captivate, delight, and entertain, allowing wonder and joy to move together

at the same pace; none of these things can be accomplished by fleeing verisimilitude and mimesis, which together constitute perfection in writing' (412) (Hanse de casar las fábulas mentirosas con el entendimiento de los que las leyeren, escribiéndose de suerte que, facilitando los imposibles, allanando las grandezas, suspendiendo los ánimos, admiren, suspendan, alborocen y entretengan, de modo que anden a un mismo paso la admiración y la alegría juntas; y todas estas cosas no podrá hacer el que huyere de la verisimilitud y de la imitación, en quien consiste la perfeción de lo que se escribe; I, 47, p. 565).

59 Trimpi, *Muses of One Mind*, 368.

60 Trimpi articulates a similar issue by appeal to the cognitive, judicative, and formal intentions. Literary theory at its best articulates the ways to achieve and maintain 'the delicate balance between the cognitive, the judicative, and the formal intentions of literature' (*Muses of One Mind*, xi).

Index

TORONTO IBERIC

Anthony J. Cascardi, *Cervantes, Literature, and the Discourse of Politics*